# Dynamics of Racism
# in Social Work
# Practice

# Dynamics of Racism in Social Work Practice

edited by JAMES A. GOODMAN

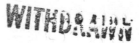

 NATIONAL ASSOCIATION OF SOCIAL WORKERS
1425 H Street NW
Washington, D.C. 20005

Cover and text design by Lenni Schur

Copyright © 1973 by the

National Association of Social Workers, Inc.

International Standard Book No.: 0–87101–068–2

Library of Congress Catalog Card No.: 73–88446

NASW Publication No.: CBA–068–C

Printed in U.S.A.

# Contents

v

*Part Two*
**TREATMENT**

## Part Three
## COMMUNITY ORGANIZATION

## Part Four
## EDUCATION

## Part Five
## RESEARCH

# Preface

SUCH A VAST AMOUNT of literature about black Americans has been produced in recent years that the choice of readings offered in any collection must necessarily be selective by purpose and context as well as content. This group of articles represents an attempt to offer a perspective on the therapeutic encounters between blacks and whites in the client-worker relationship, in which the problems in black-white interaction must be seen in the context of the societal forces that give rise to dysfunctional behavior at all levels of the community.

The individual articles were selected after a review of a wide range of literature in the behavioral sciences. They are not intended to be definitive, nor to offer a single perspective, but are representative of those most directly related to transracial treatment. Yet taken as a whole, the collection seems to make an important statement about current problems and future prospects in the black-white equation. Some of the basic elements in that equation are known and fixed, but the factors that determine their behavior in relationship are still unknown.

In the larger sense, one might say that the authors deal with psychosocial, professional, and institutional issues that are conditioned by sociopolitical arrangements. But the specific message is that in the area of therapeutic intervention, institutional racism proves to be of singular and overriding significance. Black people—clients as well as professionals —are questioning the underlying assumptions of therapeutic approaches whose values mirror the oppressive quality of the social structure that has either denied the humanness of black people or forced them to believe that they have primitive motivational systems.

It is not surprising, therefore, that Part One of this book should deal with the setting, and that parts on treatment (individual and group), community, education, and research, should come afterward. I have chosen to group the articles this way because I believe that the organization of social work into various practice modalities affords it a unique opportunity to deal with individual pathology at the same time that it deals with the sociopolitical context in which that pathology is expressed.

The articles selected for Part One, "The Setting," put the problem of black oppression in perspective. They suggest that the effects of institutional racism expressed through societal barriers on the economic and social status of minority group members have been immense, and they describe with chilling precision some of the cumulative psychological effects of racism on the black person. For not only must the black acquire the usual coping strategies of any member of this complex society; in addition he must also deal with attitudes and behavior on the part of the majority that disparage his very existence.

For this reason, the section on treatment, Part Two, attempts to look at the problems and the hopes blacks and whites experience when they work together in helping ways. It also provides a basis for evaluating the unique ways in which sociocultural and ethnic considerations impinge on the capacity of the client and therapist to reach each other in order to confront the problem at hand. It is my view that the concerns expressed about the influence of racial characteristics on the outcome of treatment are a reflection of a larger issue: Who can perform certain societal roles? I have stated this elsewhere:

> Although the data concerning changing patterns of black identity are not fully available, it appears that blacks have begun to reject imposed definitions of self. Individual black identity thereby becomes a potent force in black group consciousness. Individuals begin to relate their selfhood to the blackness variable as a statement of group unity and cohesiveness.[1]

To me this means that professionals who seek to provide therapeutic

---

[1] James A. Goodman, "Institutional Racism: The Crucible of Black Identity," in James A. Banks and Jean D. Grambs, eds., *Black Self-Concept* (New York: McGraw-Hill Book Co., 1972), p. 126.

opportunities for blacks must recognize that the surge of self-awareness on the part of blacks is a search for a larger sense of community. In this search black people have become keenly aware that they can determine what their lives can become as a function of their own—not others'—definition of self.

> Since the Negro self-concept problem cannot be solved through token integration, it is important that black men turn to the development of their own communities as an alternative and supplementary approach for the building of the Afro-American's self-image and -esteem. Unfortunately, the white man cannot give Negroes "black consciousness," Negro-Americans must give it to each other.[2]

One of the results of this process of self-definition is that blacks and whites are going to be uncomfortable with each other because of the new conception of self achieved by blacks. To many the response of blacks to whites in the role of therapist will appear to be capricious. The roles that they will permit whites to assume will be apt to be highly variable and generally transitory. The claim of many blacks that "black" is an exclusive quality of the black community poses a paradox for professional helpers because it argues for psychological separatism. And if blacks want this separatism, how can they at the same time insist on being included in the larger developmental view of man?

If we view the value of black self-help as a basis for creating egalitarian contacts in treatment situations, perhaps for the first time, we may eventually achieve culture-free treatment approaches in the future, however idealistic this may sound. But the evidence is clear that the processes of socializing black people in this society have produced patterns of identity and modes of behavior that are substantially different from those associated with whites. So it seems logical to argue that at this particular stage blacks would require treatment approaches whose underlying values incorporate the specifics of black development. As Thomas points out:

> The core values of our society are such that they are able to maintain themselves against most new situations that might bring about changes. For this reason, racial groups in America have tended to be captives of their historical, social roles, especially in terms of attitudinal formations and defined structures of behavior.[3]

---

[2] Alvin F. Poussaint, quoted in a paper presented by Robert Williams at the annual meeting of the American Psychological Association, Washington, D.C., 1969.

[3] Charles W. Thomas, *Boys No More: A Black Psychologist's View of Community* (Beverly Hills, Calif.: Glencoe Press, 1971), p. 19.

A number of the articles suggest that the institutionalized advantages of being white—when translated into black-white helping relationships— serve as one might expect, to reinforce the societal values influencing the therapeutic relationship. But if the white therapist can understand the need of black people to have a different value system as an essential part of their healthy development, it should relieve his guilt about the privileged status he enjoys as a consequence of historical racism in American society. Is this not what social workers call "self-determination"?

Although the articles on community organization—Part Three—are more descriptive than analytic, most of them stress the need for knowledge and skill. Other selections provide additional insights. They tell us that this method is critical for changing the structured arrangements of our society. Part Four, on professional education, analyzes current educational practice, but also offers proposals to be tested in future educational endeavors.

These selections bring out clearly that nonblack minority groups are also questioning the adequacy and quality of therapeutic services delivered to their people. There is clear awareness that findings about reciprocal attitudes of whites and nonblack minority groups are of concern. Yet most of the theory and much of the research has been related to black-white issues.

What then do we learn from this group of articles? I think they tell us that black people are challenging the process of therapeutic intervention—which is designed to enable one human being with special skills and understanding to establish a set of conditions whereby another human being can more effectively resolve psychosocial problems—in the same way that other institutional practices of American society have been challenged by various groups of people at other times in history.

But we have to realize that the problem of psychosocial treatment transcends race. As we know, agreement does not exist on which treatment approaches are indicated for given problems. Although the variable of race complicates the picture, it becomes even more complicated when the various helping professions respond in various ways and to different degrees to demands by blacks and other minorities for change in helping approaches. Furthermore, we know that even if new approaches and techniques are introduced, there is no guarantee that we will know how to select the correct treatment technique. Unfortunately, the problem does not suggest the treatment. What is essential is a climate in which multiple treatment models can be evaluated under controlled conditions in a number of settings, and this is difficult in a climate of racial myopia.

Apart from the day-to-day problems associated with black-white therapeutic encounters, a larger question comes to the fore: Can blacks and whites treat each other in the confines of psychotherapy when the conditions that produce their differential perceptions of the possible outcomes require social therapy rather than psychotherapy? Lerner makes a cogent comment when she says:

> War against the uglier features of the status quo with regard to poverty and racism is certainly in order, but even in a war, it is usually a good idea to try to treat the wounded, if for no other reason than that if you don't, you may run short of soldiers, just as Blacks are and must be primary soldiers in the war against racism. Outsiders do not and cannot fight a war for insiders without transforming the fight into a battle over something else which, whatever its own intrinsic merits, is inevitably more-or-less irrelevant to the original group's cause . . .[4]

All of which merely underlines the dilemma—how do we help the individual who needs treatment in a society that reinforces his pathology? The profession of social work cannot afford to sustain practices that would diminish the humanity of any group. It must deny that only blacks can treat blacks, or only whites can treat blacks, or only people of the same culture can understand each other well enough to provide help.

Social work must teach that different is not "better," nor is it "worse." It is *different*. And its technology must be developed, in every sense, to propagate a multiracial set of identities that will continue and extend the search for a common basis in humanity.

JAMES A. GOODMAN, PH.D.

*Institute of Medicine*
*National Academy of Sciences*
*Washington, D.C.*
*August 1973*

---

4 Barbara Lerner, *Therapy in the Ghetto: Political Impotence and Personal Disintegration* (Baltimore: Johns Hopkins University Press, 1972), p. 162.

# Part One

# THE SETTING: SOME PERSPECTIVES

# 1

# Some Observations on the Negro Culture in the United States

## LOIS PETTIT

THE PLIGHT OF the Negro in the United States received world-wide attention on May 17, 1954, when the U.S. Supreme Court declared an end to
the practice of segregation in the public schools. Social workers, long
cognizant of the wide variety of inequities borne by the Negro people,
welcomed this decision.

Problems faced by Negroes are well known to social workers, whose
professional functions are said to include the following: "Restoration of
impaired capacity, provision of individual and social resources, and pre-
vention of social dysfunction. . . . The focus on social relationships . . .
is suggested as the *distinguishing characteristic* of the social work profession." [1] Since the great majority of Negroes formerly lived in southern
rural sections where social work rarely if ever touched their daily lives,
the concern of social workers about the problems of Negroes was at first

Reprinted from *Social Work*, 5 (July 1960), pp. 104–109. LOIS PETTIT, MA, was, at the
time of writing, assistant professor in the Department of Sociology and Social Work
at the University of Detroit, Detroit, Michigan.

largely academic. "Negroes were initially brought to the Southern states and had remained there. After the importation of slaves had ceased, the immigration of Negroes was almost negligible. Changes in distribution were primarily consequences of internal movements." [2] However, the population picture of the 1800's, when over 90 percent of the Negro population was living in the South, changed very drastically, and the exodus of Negroes constituted a one-way migration directed from the South to all other regions of the country. The pre-Civil War distribution of Negro population shifted from 92 percent in the South, 4 percent in the Northeast, not quite 4 percent in the North Central states, and none in the West to a distribution in 1950—a century later—of only 68 percent in the South, over 13 percent in the Northeast, nearly 15 percent in the North Central area, and almost 4 percent in the West. Whereas by 1900 less than 3 percent had shifted away from the South, by 1930 another 11 percent had gone, while the next 11 percent or so required only 20 years to move away.[3]

The most characteristic feature of Negro migration has been his con-

**NEGRO POPULATION AS PERCENT OF TOTAL POPULATION FOR LARGEST URBANIZED AREAS IN THE UNITED STATES: 1950**

(Urbanized Areas by Rank Order According to Percent of Negro Population)

| | | | NEGRO POPULATION | |
| RANK | URBANIZED AREAS | TOTAL POPULATION | TOTAL NEGRO POPULATION | PERCENT |
|---|---|---|---|---|
| | Total, all areas | 40,444,956 | 3,897,027 | |
| 1 | Washington, D.C. | 1,287,333 | 307,224 | 23.9 |
| 2 | Baltimore | 1,161,852 | 239,267 | 20.6 |
| 3 | Philadelphia | 2,922,470 | 433,199 | 14.8 |
| 4 | St. Louis | 1,400,058 | 205,216 | 14.6 |
| 5 | Detroit | 2,659,398 | 346,174 | 13.0 |
| 6 | Chicago | 4,920,816 | 572,180 | 11.6 |
| 7 | Cincinnati | 813,292 | 93,111 | 11.4 |
| 8 | Cleveland | 1,383,599 | 150,163 | 10.9 |
| 9 | New York–Northeastern New Jersey | 12,296,117 | 990,143 | 8.0 |
| 10 | Pittsburgh | 1,532,953 | 117,406 | 7.6 |
| 11 | San Francisco–Oakland | 2,022,078 | 141,865 | 7.0 |
| 12 | Los Angeles | 3,996,946 | 215,697 | 5.4 |
| 13 | Milwaukee | 829,495 | 21,893 | 2.6 |
| 14 | Boston | 2,233,448 | 50,928 | 2.3 |
| 15 | Minneapolis–St. Paul | 985,101 | 12,561 | 1.3 |

Source: U.S. Bureau of the Census, 1950 Census of Population.

version to city dwelling. "During the last half-century, when the proportion of the population living in urban areas increased from 40 percent to 64 percent, the proportion of Negroes living in urban areas increased even more rapidly. . . . Outside the South, nearly all the Negro population is urban." [4] The fact that the Negro population has- become increasingly urban makes available to him more social work services. The extent of Negro population by the 1950 census in the largest urbanized areas of the United States may be seen from the accompanying table.

## ATTITUDES OF SOCIAL WORKERS

Attitudes of individual social workers in recent years have served as a deterrent to increased cultural knowledge regarding the Negro group. A number of them, seeking to make allowance for the effects of discriminatory practices, have attempted to obliterate any differences between Negroes and whites. Because of a belief that to identify a Negro as Negro would imply discrimination, some unsound practices have taken place. For instance, in one agency the workers were no longer indicating the race of the client on the face sheet of the case record. In one large city, the designation of race was dropped from the school census; later it was realized that valuable information regarding population movement had been permanently lost.

Sometimes the denial of specific Negro characteristics is based upon the social worker's belief that the same factors could be found among whites. Such an attitude overlooks the fact that although similarities may exist among individuals of several groups this does not negate the more basic fact of significant biological or cultural differences between those groups. Another attitude common among social workers is what Frazier terms "tender condescension." He claims that this is shown especially in "the exaggerated evaluation of the Negro's intellectual and artistic achievements. In fact, it is difficult to obtain an objective appraisal of the work of Negro students and artists." [5] It may be that these attitudes of social workers seemed to help them adopt an objective viewpoint in professional undertakings,[6] but it is time for the social work profession to become more knowledgeable about real and existing differences.

## REAL DIFFERENCES

The major distinguishing physical feature of the Negro is skin color, although other characteristics such as facial features and hair texture might also be included. However, the social definition determining whether a person is classified as Negro exists in this country on a basis very different from that of physical appearance alone. It does not matter whether the percentage of Negro blood is one-eighth, one-sixteenth, or too minute to be discernible; if a person has any known Negro ancestry he is considered to be a Negro.[7] This social definition is so firmly established in the United States that even the census figures are obtained upon this basis. In the Latin American countries, on the contrary, a person may possess many Negroid features and have known Negro ancestry but he may still be regarded as belonging to the white group. As a result of the prevalence of the social definition prevailing in the United States, persons of Negro ancestry who want to be considered white are forced to use the utmost secrecy in crossing the color line.[8] It has been estimated that 2,000 to 30,000 such persons cross the color line annually. This practice is termed "passing."

Because of his identifiable physical characteristics and the rigid social definition, the Negro in the United States has been consigned to an unalterable status. Allowing for class differences that have evolved, as well as the complex and changing nature of the position of the Negro group, nevertheless some cultural factors can be elucidated.

The first Negroes to set foot in the United States were a group of twenty purchased from a Dutch man-of-war in 1619 by the Virginia settlers. At that time there was no provision in English law for slavery, but the treatment of Negro servants was different from that of white servants. Gradually Virginia incorporated into its laws various references to the Negro as a slave, until the slave status was fixed by law in 1670.[9] In the South the system of Negro slavery developed on the plantations. In the North the picture was quite different, northern slaves being ordinarily domestics and personal servants. During and after the Revolutionary War a number of the northern states put an end to slavery through legislation and other such means, including manumission (formal liberation of a slave); thus a growing number of Negroes achieved free status.

## THE MATRIARCHAL PATTERN

Two and a half centuries of slavery in the United States changed the Negro family structure. The matriarchal system of the Negro family is well known. Under slavery, since the father was more subject to the instability and vicissitudes of the system, the mother was the most constant and dependable member of the family. The Reconstruction Period following the Emancipation Proclamation of 1863 added to the social disorganization of the Negro family unit when refugees swarmed to the army camps and cities in search of employment and housing.

Even today, particularly in lower-class families, the position of the mother is very strong. Her relationship to the children assumes more significance than does that of the father with his more ephemeral presence. She is the mainstay psychologically and economically. Analysis of the census figures reflect the more stable presence of the mother in the family. The Taeubers give the following summary:

> The distinguishing characteristics of the marital status of the Negroes lay more in the dissolution and re-formation of marriages and the prevalence of informal marriages than in such formal facts as age at marriage or prevalence of marriage. Marital instability and high mortality reenforced each other in reducing the proportion of Negro women married and living with husbands and increasing the proportion of the widowed. In 1910 and 1940 the percentages of women who were or had been married was higher for Negroes than for native whites. In both years, however, relatively low percentages of Negro women were living in first marriages with husbands present, while relatively high percentages reported absent husbands. The proportions of widowed and divorced women were also high among the Negroes.[10]

The manifestations of the Oedipal conflict in the Negro family in which the position of the mother is dominant differ from those found in the patriarchal family because the girl as well as the boy is strongly attached to the mother. Even when the children are grown, they consider that their mother has first claim upon their loyalties and earnings and they take pride in coming to her rescue in emergencies. When loyalty to the mother takes precedence over the son's or daughter's newly established family, marital discord can result. As one man expressed it to his caseworker, "I can always get another wife but a man has only one mother." Such an attitude might be considered a neurotic symptom in a white male client, but in a Negro client the cultural factor may be cogent.

The dominant woman in the Negro family is frequently the grandmother, with the mother operating in a sort of second-in-command egoideal of the grandmother. The grandmother, regardless of her physical vigor, occupies such a strong position that she often determines the moral, economic, and emotional structure of the family. She has tremendous power and sets the emotional tone of the household in supervising the adolescent grandchildren, determining the disposition of children born out of wedlock, and so on.

## PROBLEM OF ADOPTIONS

Do social workers take into account the peculiar distinguishing characteristics of the Negro family, particularly in the lower class? They do not appear to do so in adoption work, which may explain why the problem of Negro adoptions has become such a pressing one. Different methods may be required to keep pace with the need. The usual adoption process places upon the applicants much of the responsibility for initiating and carrying through each step of the application. The purposefulness, the energy and forthright attitude, and the unity of husband and wife are tested by this process. These diagnostic procedures work well in the case of white applicants but not in the case of Negro applicants, who are all too few in number anyway.

Essentially the difference between the Negro and white applicant is that the latter carries some reasonable expectation of acceptance of his application, while the Negro applicant consciously or unconsciously expects to be rejected. In general, a Negro's experience with the law has been unfortunate, and he will protect himself from running the risk of rejection unless he has some guarantee of a good chance of acceptance. When the usual adoption procedures, intended to measure motivation as well as to facilitate the agency's work, are applied, the average Negro couple is turned down.

What then, instead? First of all, many of the usual criteria established in adoption practice may need to be reassessed in the light of cultural differences of the Negro group. Even the expressed interest of the husband may be different, for it is common for the Negro husband to want to wait in the automobile while his wife makes arrangements with the social worker in the agency office. The agency may need to reach out through informal contacts to locate and encourage these childless couples. The social worker can be prepared (1) to extend warm friendliness to guarantee acceptance of them as individuals; (2) to arrive at an early diagnostic decision regarding them as applicants; and (3) to follow up the decision of acceptance by aiding them in every way possible to establish their eligibility for an adoptive child.

Other agencies also, to assure better service to the Negro group, may need to review their reception, intake, and continued service procedures and philosophy. Differences of locality as well as social class can be taken into account.

## ATTITUDES OF NEGROES

The Negro's concern about possible rejection for reasons solely of race is always with him whether he lives in the North or South. He may be discriminated against in housing, in employment, in health services, in restaurants, and in theaters. Consequently he has armed himself, and his armor may serve to make him a hypersensitive and suspicious person. For example, a Negro social worker entered a drugstore for a light lunch and was ushered to a rear booth. She immediately protested, whereupon the amazed clerk explained that there was a fine breeze in the rear of the store even on that sweltering day. This trifling incident serves to illustrate the constant expectation of rejection which the Negro may incorporate into his attitudes and ways of thinking. His bitterness may emerge even when he is receiving commendation; some white friends of a Negro educator in admiring the latter's new home happened to mention favorably the luxuriant growth of grass on the lawn. The educator's response was that white people always say that Negroes cannot grow grass because of the bare yards of the Negro hovels in the South.

Other manifestations of the Negro's reaction to his depressed status are manifold. His self-image is very much affected by the extent to which he has Negroid characteristics. Some Negro mothers are outspoken in their preference for the lighter-skinned child with "good" hair (not frizzy or woolly).[11] The Negro in his desire for emancipation often wants to leave behind him activities associated with southern rural living. Disdain may be expressed for everyday tasks of household management on the grounds of not wanting to be a "kitchen girl" or "yard boy." Sometimes habits of indolence are embraced in what Rose terms "traditions of inefficiency." [12]

Relations between Negroes and whites have been difficult to maintain because of the heritage of stress and strain. The specter of the stereotype is ever present. When Negroes are friendly toward whites, they risk censure from other Negroes. One such instance occurred when a social group worker had a chance encounter outdoors with the mother of one of her young clients. The group worker, who happened to be white, considered that she had established a good relationship with the Negro mother after several home visits. Much to the group worker's surprise, the mother, who was standing on the sidewalk with some of her friends in her own racial group, was not at all cordial. It was only later that the worker realized that the mother, in the presence of other Negroes, could not feel free openly to acknowledge their relationship. Another example occurred in a social situation when a Negro couple had invited some white friends to a private seaside resort. The Negro hotel owner refused admittance to the whites on the grounds that they had many recreational resources of their own and had no need of utilizing the few belonging to Negroes. Sometimes, it is true, association with whites is highly valued as a means of gaining status, but many Negroes believe that they could never overcome an ingrained antipathy for a white person with a Southern accent.

Segregation has resulted in many Negroes practicing their own form of Jim Crow isolation in order to be by themselves and relax from the constant strain of the various forms of accommodation. Their purpose may be simply to gain temporary respite or it may be more far-reaching in terms of setting up separate Negro institutions. Frazier has commented as follows: "Some Negro social workers have favored separate agencies to handle the problems of colored people. The Negro's professional interest in segregated schools, hospitals, and welfare agencies is generally accompanied by rationalizations about the peculiar needs of the race; or the exclusion, real or potential, of trained Negroes from employment in non-segregated institutions." [13]

## COST OF EQUALITY

Whites and Negroes alike look to the day when segregation will end and this country will no longer have a well-deserved international reputation for poor race relations. The Supreme Court decision has committed all citizens irrevocably. Segregation has had certain by-products, certain special privileges which some Negroes may find it difficult to relinquish. "It is the Negro professional, the business man, and to a lesser extent, the white collar worker who profit from segregation. These groups in the Negro population enjoy certain advantages because they do not have to compete with whites." [14] The children, too, will be affected. Mildred Faris has observed: "Having won the right to attend school with children of other races, the Negro child must now cope with individual insecurities and individual acceptance or rejection. What was formerly racial rejection has to be dealt with now as rejection of a particular individual or family." [15] Alexander King has phrased his personal belief as follows:

> I suppose this is about as opportune a time as any for me to make clear my attitude on race prejudice. I'm sure I'm completely free from it. I want Negroes and others to get all possible rights of equality because only then will I be able to esteem them, or to loathe them, *individually,* as I do white people. But at this time I'm still compelled to stand a lot of rudeness, boredom and nonsense from some of my darker brothers, simply because some of these specifically offensive individuals happen to belong to an abused and injured minority toward whom I have an unavoidable sense of guilt. I must personally lick up the memory of all the insults, all the humiliations and all the lynchings that their race has suffered, and so I shall never be able to treat them as true equals until all this color iniquity stops, once and for all. You understand? [16]

Social workers, trained in correcting inequities and experienced in overcoming social disequilibrium, do understand the enormity of the task ahead. "As the walls of segregation 'come tumbling down,' the Negro will lose all these petty advantages. If this results in the social and psychological deflation of some, it will nevertheless cause Negroes generally to acquire a saner conception of themselves and of their role in American society. Through the same process, white people will come to regard Negroes as human beings like themselves and to make a more realistic appraisal of their personalities and of their work." [17]

## NOTES AND REFERENCES

1. Werner W. Boehm, *Objectives of the Social Work Curriculum of the Future* (New York: Council on Social Work Education, 1959), p. 54.

2. Conrad Taeuber and Irene B. Taeuber, *The Changing Population of the United States* (New York: John Wiley and Sons, 1958), pp. 109–110.

3. From Table 17, *ibid.*, p. 72.

4. *Ibid.*, p. 124.

5. E. Franklin Frazier, "Human, All Too Human: The Negro's Vested Interest in Segregation," *Survey Graphic*, Vol. 36, No. 1 (January 1947), p. 75.

6. *See* Inabel Burns Lindsay, "Race as a Factor in the Caseworker's Role," *Social Casework*, Vol. 27, No. 3 (March 1947), pp. 101–107.

7. *See* Brewton Berry, *Race and Ethnic Relations* (rev. ed.; Boston: Houghton Mifflin Company, 1958), pp. 30–31.

8. A novel vividly portraying this social phenomenon is *I Passed for White* by Reba Lee as told to Mary Hastings Bradley (New York: Longmans, Green and Co., 1955).

9. *See* E. Franklin Frazier, *The Negro in the United States* (rev. ed.; New York: The Macmillan Company, 1957), pp. 22–26.

10. Taeuber and Taeuber, *op. cit.*, p. 157.

11. Case illustrations are included in Rose Cooper Thomas, *Mother-Daughter Relationships and Social Behavior,* Social Work Series Number 21 (Washington, D.C.: The Catholic University of America Press, 1955).

12. Arnold Rose, *The Negro's Morale: Group Identification and Protest* (Minneapolis, Minn.: University of Minnesota Press, 1949), p. 77.

13. Frazier, "Human, All Too Human," *op. cit.*, p. 75.

14. *Ibid.*, p. 75.

15. Mildred Faris, "Health and Illness: The Dynamics of Family Interaction." Unpublished paper presented at the National Conference of Social Work, San Francisco, 1955.

16. Alexander King, *Mine Enemy Grows Older* (New York: Simon and Schuster, 1958), p. 190.

17. Frazier, "Human, All Too Human," *op. cit.*, p. 100.

# 2

# Dialogue on Racism: A Prologue to Action?

## PAULINE D. LIDE

IN THE *Social Casework* editorial of March 1964, the following observation was made:

> The relative dearth of literature on the racial factor in casework treatment . . . and the conspicuous absence of research on the subject suggest that repressive psychological mechanisms may be at work. Perhaps it is difficult for a profession committed to humanistic tenets to engage in honest appraisal of possible disparities between its ideals and its accomplishments.[1]

This article recounts the efforts of one social agency to examine and loosen these "repressive psychological mechanisms" by means of an honest appraisal that took the form of staff dialogue for a period of approximately five months.[2] The dialogue followed an abortive effort to study the mechanisms as they appeared to operate in casework practice. A descrip-

Reprinted, with permission, from *Social Casework*, 52 (July 1971), pp. 432–437. PAULINE D. LIDE was at the time of writing professor, School of Social Work, University of Georgia, Athens, Georgia.

tion of the content and process of this experience may be useful for social workers who are willing to face the implications of the now clearly observable disparities between social work's ideals and its accomplishments.

Facing the fact and the implications of racism is a herculean task that can threaten the ego immeasurably.[3] Social workers—experienced caseworkers in particular—are generally knowledgeable about the process of loosening repressive psychological mechanisms that are developed to protect the ego. In their struggle for self-awareness they work assiduously to loosen the mechanisms that limit them in many areas of functioning. They have been slow, however, to face the fact of racism and the painful process of dealing with its implications. The recent appearance of several significant articles devoted to various aspects of individual and institutional racism suggests that the social work profession is beginning to become involved in this process.[4]

## A PRACTICE RESEARCH APPROACH TO RACISM

Late in 1967, the writer and a small group of administrative and supervisory staff of the Family Counseling Center of Metropolitan Atlanta began to examine possible ways to improve casework service for black clients.[5] Gradually it was decided to study the influence on the treatment relationship of racial differences between workers and clients. The problems inherent in such a study are obvious; although reality factors prevented its completion, there is little doubt that the complexity of the task may have doomed the study to failure. The experience, however, lay the foundation for staff dialogue on racism, and a description of this abortive effort may be of general interest.

It was postulated that (1) workers and clients of different races experience unique transference and countertransference complications as they engage in treatment, and (2) it is necessary to understand and deal with these complications if treatment is to be successful on more than a superficial level. The study group consisted of four experienced social workers—two blacks and two whites.[6] The writer, then a part-time staff member, served as coordinator. At the close of each case in which the worker and client were of different races, the workers were asked to complete a schedule that was designed to elicit manifestations of transference and countertransference as detected by the workers. The study was terminated in its beginning stages when two of the workers left the agency for professional reasons. At that time the participants were convinced that the approach could prove fruitful.

A retrospective analysis of the experience leads to the conclusion that this approach to racism through practice research was premature. Although it held promise of gain on one level, it was sadly limited in other more significant respects. Designed to approach the problem on an emotional level, its methods were primarily intellectual. The sharing within the study group of insights into transference and countertransference in biracial situations did serve a useful purpose, however, for it increased the participants' awareness of the need to cope with subtle forms of racism that affect services to clients.

The termination of this study effort without the achievement of any real degree of closure was disturbing to the participants, who were left with feelings of hopelessness.[7] Its more useful by-products were overlooked until a renewed effort to gain even minimal closure resulted in the development of a more productive approach to the problem.[8]

## STAFF DIALOGUE

In the fall of 1970, the two remaining study participants agreed to join with the writer in an effort to distill something meaningful from the aborted study in order to share it with the staff. It was fortunate that many other current demands led to a decision to undertake this distillation without formal planning by the participants. In retrospect it is believed that this condition resulted in a spontaneous shift from the intellectual to the feeling level and thus laid a meaningful foundation for the staff dialogue that ensued.

During this period, the agency was engaging in major changes in its administrative patterns, and regular staff meetings were devoted to these changes. The presentation of the aborted research was therefore scheduled as an extra session during a lunch hour, and an invitation was issued to those who were interested in hearing the "report." The response appears to indicate the "felt needs" of the staff. More than forty of the fifty-three staff members attended the first session. The interest level was high, and the session ended with a decision to have a second meeting in two weeks.

From the opening reporting session on October 14, 1970, until the planned termination on February 23, 1971, several significant phases in the process may be identified. The first stage, a period that included three biweekly sessions, was characterized by intellectualization on the part of both black and white staff members. There was a strong tendency to adhere to the use of repressive mechanisms as a means of avoiding both the individual and institutional racism represented in the group. In some ways, the group process could be said to recapitulate the history of black-white relationships in society.

A second phase was entered when the group saw the need to decide whether to pursue the issue on a more meaningful level or to discontinue the meetings. During the fourth and fifth sessions there was controlled confrontation between white and black workers, and many aspects of racism were brought to the fore. The group agreed that the dialogue had existed primarily on an intellectual level. The general tenor of the early sessions is reflected in the following instance:

> There had been a staff party at which square dancing was the featured activity. Although the occasion was not well attended in general, few black staff members were present. In the session immediately following this event, which took place between the first and second meetings, some white workers expressed concern that black staff had participated only minimally in this social occasion. Their remarks led to a minor confrontation.
>
> Black workers accused the white workers of asking inappropriate questions about what they did on their own time and noted that the white staff did not ask whites why they had not attended. The hostile interchange that took place was quickly smoothed over by the group in an effort to recreate a semblance of harmony and good will.

Following this interchange, black workers expressed their disillusionment with the effort and indicated that the sessions, as they were, were not worth an investment of time. What was generally overlooked was that some participants were experiencing this kind of interchange for the first time and that, for a number of black and white people, an intellectual approach was a necessary preamble.

The third phase began during the fifth session, December 16, 1970, when the group decided to have a series of eight sessions to be held at weekly rather than biweekly intervals, scheduled at "prime" agency time rather than during lunch hours.[9] It was later decided to issue an invitation to the total social work staff, thus not limiting the series to those who had attended the first five sessions. At the same time it was decided that those who chose to be present for the opening session on January 4, 1971, were entering into a general agreement to involve themselves for the series of eight sessions. If the desired goals were to be reached, it seemed advisable to eliminate the possibility of people dropping in and interfering with the group process.

These decisions resulted in some dropouts, several of whom were part-time staff members who questioned the desirability of their involvement because of the time that would have to be expended. As a result thirty-three persons, all of whom had been involved in the first phases, became the participants in the eight-session series.

## CONTENT AND PROCESS

The group agreed immediately that these sessions would be productive only if there were a successful departure from intellectualization to communication on a feeling level. A first attempt was made when the participants began to recollect early experiences with persons of the opposite race. They had apparently gained sufficient comfort during the first two phases of group development to share some of the pain, bitterness, anguish, and frustration of early life encounters. Much of the content was highly emotional, and at times both individual and group equilibrium seemed threatened by the impact.[10] Examples of some of the recollections follow.

> A young black woman described her parents' reactions and the closeness that developed within the family and within the community following the "accidental" killing of a black neighbor by a white man. A young black man spoke of his mother's experience as a day worker in white homes and of how he felt about wearing secondhand clothing from those homes. A black case aide shared her personal experiences as a maid in the home of a middle-class white family.
>
> A young white man pointed out that, in the environment in which he had grown up, manhood was considered not fully achieved until the white male had cohabited with a black woman. Another young man told how a generally accepted outlet for restlessness or frustration in white youth in his small town was riding with a group of boys through the black community and throwing rocks. A young white woman described a moment in her childhood when, following a spontaneous expression of affection for a black maid, she was told by her mother that she must never kiss a black person.

The first two sessions of the series, in which such emotionally charged experiences were shared, were followed by a partial retreat to the intellectual level. An air of hopelessness and discouragment permeated the group as this development occurred, and several persons directly expressed their feelings of depression. When individual and group anxiety was handled either by emotional withdrawal or intellectualization, some of the black staff members stated in various ways that they should have known better than to expect anything else. Their disappointment and anger bewildered many white workers who believed that they were making a genuine effort to deal with their own racism, which, by this time, they were no longer denying.

It seems safe to say that by the midpoint in the series the first major objective—loosening the repressive psychological mechanisms—had been accomplished. At this time the participants were understandably concerned about how to handle the rampant anxiety that had been unleashed. The brief retreat to intellectualization as a means of coping with this anxiety was not on an abstract level as it had been previously but entailed a need for action. Confrontation became more direct and more honest. Anger and frustration were identified as common emotions held by both black and white staff. Although at times it was hard to locate, a thread of hope still appeared to run through the sessions, and threats to give up were not carried out.

In the last few sessions the theme of separatism began to emerge, and at times this theme threatened to overwhelm those participants who tended to view separatism as another form of racism or as white racism in reverse. White staff began to confront blacks with accusations of reverse racism. This stage of the dialogue was short-lived. To their credit, most of the white workers had the courage to face the overwhelming impact of the reality that the distribution of power in society spawns the development of white but not black racism. Although it was not specifically stated in group discussions, the participants' understanding of racism appeared to shift from the dictionary definition to a more relevant interpretation:

> . . . the predication of decisions and policies on considerations of race for the purpose of *subordinating* a racial group and maintaining control over that group. . . . It takes two . . . forms . . . individual racism and institutional racism.[11]

Group awakening to the implications of this interpretation produced heightened anxiety. A subtle shift from the more manageable struggle with individual racism to the overwhelming aspects of institutional racism had taken place. The writer, carrying the leadership role, undertook to redirect the group to cope more fully with individual racism as the foundation of institutional racism. The working premise here is well stated by Barbara Shannon in her significant article on the implications of racism for social work.

> The importance of economics and education must not be minimized, but it is only through the individual that racism can be eradicated. Given a pyramidal hierarchy of societal organization, the individual is at the bottom, with the second and third levels being groups (including the family) and institutions respectively. Institutional racism will not disappear until individuals change, because no pyramid has ever been razed by destroying its tip.[12]

Dialogue on individual racism reached a level of honesty that had not been attained in earlier sessions. Some black workers who recognized that they had handled black-white relationships by general acceptance of the white world's approach to integration shifted to a clearer alignment with black staff members who had no faith in this approach. Their courage in taking this step and in sharing their feelings with the group left no individual participant untouched. Grief became a common denomi-

nator. Dialogue, because it requires language and is dependent on cognitive processes, diminished in usefulness.

Group participants—both black and white and in varying degrees
and for varying reasons—struggled with the ambivalence that accompanied the termination of the scheduled sessions. The relative safety of
biracial group dialogue had to be given up, and the uncertainty about
what would replace it stimulated additional anxiety. Would it be informal dialogue, individual to individual without regard to race, or
should there be planned dialogue on a separatist level, with whites
talking with whites and blacks with blacks? [13]

Movement toward planning future steps was curtailed by the group
itself. The experience of "gut-level" sharing appeared to support the
participants in warding off the natural tendency to settle once again
for superficial harmony. By common agreement individual and group
anxiety were left at a level that held promise of being a mobilizing
rather than an impeding force in the eradication of the residuals of
racism in the participants. The general drift of thought and feeling
was reflected in the closing session.

> A young black man who had openly shared his personal experiences with
> racism indicated that he had reached the point of no longer being willing
> to engage in this kind of sharing. He expressed his opinion that continuation
> of the biracial dialogue placed an inordinate demand on him as a black
> person and that not only should he not be expected to pay the price but
> he questioned whether any further purpose could be served through such
> sharing. He thought the time had come for whites to "deal with the mess
> they had created."
>
> This position, which he expressed in various ways throughout the session,
> was supported by other blacks. The young man had emerged as a leader
> among the others, and his softly spoken comments became serious pronounce-
> ments that penetrated intellectual defenses and affected the participants on
> a feeling level. The interchange, which was highly emotional in quality,
> reached a new level of honesty. Group members, both black and white,
> were able to support each other, even across racial lines, in terminating
> at this time. The dialogue closed as the young man quietly observed, "I
> think it's time to go."

## EVALUATION

Planned staff dialogue appears to be a useful approach to racism when
the participants, although at various stages in their own resolution of
black-white issues, share a common concern about the implications of
racism for the profession. The approach, as it was developed by this
particular staff, served to loosen the repressive psychological mechanisms

that are at work in some form in most individuals and that have been institutionalized in the social work profession. The major objective of the dialogue, that of loosening the mechanisms and gaining fuller access to the problem on a feeling level, was reached. Its achievement disclosed other objectives that were beyond the scope of this endeavor.

It has been noted that the group participants—probably without exception—experienced intense pain and had to cope with anguish, frustration, anger, and depression. Some persons who began the dialogue feeling free of racism discovered troubling residuals within themselves. It is noteworthy, in this regard, that no one acted as if he were superior to anyone else and that each individual appeared to cope with the problem as it existed for him. The honesty of the participants was impressive. The sharing of painful insights in so large a group requires courage and a climate of common concern.[14]

## PROLOGUE TO ACTION?

A prologue is a "preliminary act or course of action foreshadowing greater events."[15] Was the described dialogue a prologue to greater events? Implicit in stating that it was a prologue is the recognition that the dialogue was a form of action and not simply an engrossing conversation. When the writer figuratively "took the pulse" of the group, the "reading" suggested that the individuals were experiencing the gratification that comes primarily from a sense of doing something about a problem. During the earlier stages, when the involvement was primarily intellectual, the "reading" showed the frustration that is the usual by-product of "just talking." A final "reading," during the last session, indicated that there was at least a blending of gratification—the result of having engaged in a form of action—frustration, and disappointment in the action's being so limited.

The final session was highly charged emotionally because of the frustration and disappointment. The natural inclination to settle disturbed and conflicting feelings was successfully avoided in favor of ending the dialogue where the participants as human beings really were, that is, hurt, frightened, depressed but, at the same time, clearer about the need for this experience to be truly a prologue to greater events.[16]

## NOTES AND REFERENCES

1.  Editorial Notes, SOCIAL CASEWORK, 45:155 (March 1964).
2.  Child Service and Family Counseling Center, Atlanta, Georgia.
3.  Racism is defined as racialism, "a doctrine or feeling of racial differences or

antagonisms, especially with reference to supposed racial superiority, inferiority, or purity; racial prejudice, hatred, or discrimination"; see *Webster's New Twentieth Century Dictionary,* s.v. "racism."

4. The following articles are of interest: Julia B. Bloch, The White Worker and the Negro Client in Psychotherapy, *Social Work,* 13:36–42 (April 1968); Jerome Cohen, Race as a Factor in Social Work Practice, in *Race, Research, and Reason: Social Work Perspectives,* ed. Roger R. Miller (New York: National Association of Social Workers, 1969), pp. 99–113; Andrew E. Curry, The Negro Worker and the White Client: A Commentary on the Treatment Relationship, SOCIAL CASEWORK, 45:131–36 (March 1964); Esther Fibush, The White Worker and the Negro Client, SOCIAL CASEWORK, 46:271–77 (May 1965); Esther Fibush and BeAlva Turnquest, A Black and White Approach to the Problem of Racism, SOCIAL CASEWORK, 51:459–66 (October 1970); Jean S. Gochros, Recognition and Use of Anger in Negro Clients, *Social Work,* 11:28–34 (January 1966); Seaton W. Manning, Cultural and Value Factors Affecting the Negro's Use of Agency Services, *Social Work,* 5:3–13 (October 1960); Donald E. Meeks, The White Ego Ideal: Implications for the Bi-Racial Treatment Relationship, *Smith College Studies in Social Work,* 37:93–105 (February 1967); Barbara E. Shannon, Implications of White Racism for Social Work Practice, SOCIAL CASEWORK, 51:270–76 (May 1970); Leonard C. Simmons, "Crow Jim": Implications for Social Work, *Social Work,* 8:24–30 (July 1963); and Margaret Weiner, Gentlemen's Agreement Revisited, SOCIAL CASEWORK, 51:395–98 (July 1970).

5. The Family Counseling Center of Metropolitan Atlanta and the Children's Center of Metropolitan Atlanta merged to form the present Child Service and Family Counseling Center in 1969.

6. The social workers were Diane Abernathy, Genevieve Hill, Millie Kagan, and Victoria Scott.

7. Toward the end of the time period in which this study was taking place, the agency became a participant in the National Experiment in Staff Development (NESD) II, a two and one-half year program funded by the National Institute of Mental Health, in which five member agencies of Family Service Association of America participated. The ten staff members involved in this project selected as their focus the impact of urbanization on the black family and the agency's responsibility for becoming "relevant" in its services to the black urban poor. From this specific concern there was a natural drift toward consideration of the effects of individual and institutional racism on the provision of services. This stage in the NESD II group coincided with a period of disquietude that was being experienced by the participants in the study group. The influence of the NESD II effort on subsequent developments is difficult to assess. Whereas the NESD group's work on racism was a planned, organized effort, the staff dialogue was "grass roots" in character.

8. Mary Margaret Carr, director of the agency, is responsible for keeping the issue open. Without persistence on her part it seems likely that inappropriate closure may have been reached.

9. This change presented a scheduling problem. The most feasible time for the dialogue was the period scheduled for biweekly consultations on group treatment with Dr. Sidney Isenberg. The group suggested that he be invited to join as a participant. Thereafter, beginning with the second of the eight-session series, Dr. Isenberg was present and was of invaluable assistance. The writer is a teacher by preparation and experience, and the difficult role shift to group leader and enabler was made less problematic by Dr. Isenberg's involvement.

10. It should be noted that neither the majority of the participants, nor the leader,

wanted this experience to become that of an encounter or sensitivity group. The size of the group provided a natural safeguard against such a development.

11.   Stokely Carmichael and Charles V. Hamilton, *Black Power: The Politics of Liberation in America* (New York: Random House, Vintage Books, 1967), pp. 3–4.

12.   Shannon, Implications of White Racism, p. 272.

13.   For a useful discussion of the sharing of feelings about black-white relationships on a one-to-one basis, see Fibush and Turnquest, Approach to the Problems of Racism.

14.   Although the size of the group undoubtedly inhibited some participants, it also served to protect them. Everyone became a participant, whether verbally or non-verbally, and those who preferred to work on their concerns in silence were allowed the appropriate privacy.

15.   *Webster's New Twentieth Century Dictionary*, s.v. "prologue."

16.   Following the preparation of this article for publication—in essence the re-counting of staff involvement in working on individual racism—the NESD II group planned and sponsored a two-day "live-in" workshop on individual racism in which approximately one hundred staff and board members were involved. Prior to the workshop, May 6 and 7, 1971, there was a four-session series of dialogue for staff who had not attended the eight-session series described in this article. These sessions were primarily preparatory for the workshop on racism.

# 3

# Race, the Polity, and the Professionals

## HYLAN LEWIS

My CENTRAL PURPOSE in this paper is to examine some of the effects of
current facts and tendencies in race relations on the customary and legal
ways public affairs and social services are organized and managed. My
concern is with racial tension and its effects on the difficult arts and
sciences of living together—and living well—today and tomorrow.

Earl Raab, in "The Black Revolution and the Jewish Question," states
a familiar diagnosis and popular lament:

> . . . The American political structure and its traditional coalitions are in
> naked transition. The common democratic commitment trembles within
> both the white and black populations. New kinds of political configurations
> are in the making. The past quarter century turns out not to have been,

Reprinted, with permission, from *Journal of Education for Social Work*, 5 (Fall 1969),
pp. 19–30. HYLAN LEWIS was at the time of writing professor of sociology at Brooklyn
College, City University of New York, and a fellow of the Metropolitan Applied Research Center, Inc. This paper was originally presented at the Seventeenth Annual
Program Meeting of the Council on Social Work Education, Cleveland, Ohio, January
21–24, 1969.

as some envisioned, the passageway to some terminal American dream. It
has been the staging ground for some as yet indistinct future American
design.[1]

I hope to provide some useful cues and clues to those of us who must
make our particular sightings on the as yet indistinct future design of
human service professions. The general question is how will current race
relation facts and tendencies affect the structuring, governing, content,
and quality of professional services in the fields of health, education,
and welfare.

There are many specific questions that derive from this general concern; some are old questions that are surfacing anew. An important
consideration is: Are these questions being taken any more seriously this
time? Some of these questions are: What do Negroes/blacks really want?
What are the essential bases of accommodations between whites and
blacks? Which way for America—separatism or integration? Can Negroes
be viable in pluralistic American society? Can pluralistic American society be viable without changing black and white equities in it? Is
there or will there be a black revolution?

One question—what is the role of blacks in American institutions?—
breaks down into three paired questions. In turn, these questions reflect
the fact that we have a biracial society in many essentials; they also
reflect various assumptions people have about whether it is permanent
or temporary, partial or total, desirable or regrettable, avoidable or
inevitable. The paired questions are:

1.   What is the role of the black institution?
     What is the role of the white institution?

2.   What is the role of the black in the white institution?
     What is the role of the white in the black institution?

3.   What is the role of the black in the black institution?
     What is the role of the white in the white institution?

Even though some of these are familiar questions and many have a
bit of *déjà vu* about them, they are now being asked in a different context. And to an important extent, straight, no-nonsense answers are
being demanded by different people—especially by youths, both black
and white, who fiercely and gallantly demand to be taken seriously. It
must be remembered that their challenge is not so much to the method
and organization of our institutions, but to the aims and meaning of
these institutions. As Peter Marin says: "Their specific grievances are
incidental; their real purpose is to make God show his face, to have

whatever pervasive and oppressive force makes us perpetual children, reveal itself, declare itself, commit itself at last." [2]

In very specific terms, and with direct meaning for those with responsibility for the organization and governing of our institutions, the three key questions are: What is to be done about the participation or representation of Negroes in health, education and welfare institutions? What is to be done about self-conscious black people and health, education, and welfare institutions and services? What is to be done about what is now being called institutional racism—the discriminatory and thwarting effect of practices and policies embedded in institutional structures that no longer appear to have anything to do with race or color? Although related to each other in critical ways, these are entirely different questions. It is important that distinctions be made among them, and that assessments be made of their different implications for organization and institutional action.

One of the specific aims of this paper is to suggest some of the factors that affect the search for answers to the above questions, and the answers, too—those factors that affect the complex interplay between ideas and beliefs about race relations and race and class status. Among these factors are the speed of change in racial perceptions and roles, and the relations among interests, race relations perspectives, and the agendas for change.

A second aim is to sort out (a) some of the alternative goals and scripts for racial change, and (b) some of the key actors and groups who are now variously rehearsing new race relations routines—to look both at those who are adding brand-new roles, and at those who are taking over old roles and giving them new, fresh, and sometimes frightening interpretations. There is concern about the human complexity behind race relations issues that are too simplistically posed as integration vs. segregation, and working within the system vs. revolution. There is also special interest in the changing status and roles of the middle class and of youths, with a special emphasis on the Negro/black middle and lower-middle classes and youths.

Race relations are changing at phenomenal speed; they are both results of and causes of rapid changes in what Brzezinski calls our developing "technetronic" society—"a society that is shaped culturally, psychologically, socially and economically by the impact of technology and electronics, particularly computers and communications." [3] The tensions we know today and their disturbing impact in public and private affairs are in part the result of the fact that changes are taking place in mere fractions of the time necessary to assess the situation. Rapid change in the perceptions of Negroes and whites is one crucial factor in racial tensions. Complicating matters further is the fact that the perceptions Negroes and whites have of each other and of themselves, of their self and group interest—or their individual and social responsibility—and of the public interest are in some instances changing in different directions and at different rates.

In times of racial crisis the cliché cry for more communication between racial, ethnic, and religious groups increases in frequency, but the cry for communication loses all meaning and force if it is not looked at critically. John Wilkinson reminds us that:

> Special pleadings, dogmatic statements, and the lies of politicians and publicists are not dialogue, whatever other useful qualities they might possess. At the most, their propositions enter negatively into dialogue [between groups that are acutely race-conscious] only insofar as dialogue mercilessly exposes them by testing their pretensions against evidence.
>
> Dialogue becomes impossible when it is overlaid with some concept of orthodox dogma, secular or religious. Every man has the natural right, even the duty, to contrive for himself a habitation in the difficult and different times, places and circumstances of this world and to make it meaningful by an appropriate ideology. When he refuses in principle or in practice to engage in colloquy with those who think differently from him, however, he is guilty of dogmatism. Consensus, as Martin Buber emphasized, never means the suppression of individual and cultural differences; it means, rather, that dialogue has succeeded in elaborating a spectrum of alternative available beliefs and strategies.[4]

Communication and consensus are matters of the agenda; the agenda reflects interests as well as ideology. For such reasons, the primary differences between whites and blacks in the urban centers, where the crunch is most severe, stem less from differences in ethnic or racial culture—or from differences in their affirmations of American culture—than they do from the competition for physical space, bread and butter, jobs and income to get these, the political power to affect these, and the social reputations they support.

Making it and being really American actually mean being able to have your ethnic cake and eat it, too. Glazer and Moynihan, in their influential *Beyond the Melting Pot*, point out: "The ethnic group in American society became not a survival from the age of mass immigration but a new social form." And they add and italicize, "The ethnic groups in New York are also *interest groups*. This is perhaps the single most important fact about ethnic groups in New York City." [5]

The important point is that members of white ethnic groups are perceived primarily as members of a dominant white racial category, and secondarily as members of any of the myriad old and new ethnic minority groups who have taken for granted the political machinery and its uses. What is new to the city—and at a time when the city itself seems most impossible as a viable form—is that now the Negroes as blacks—and old Americans—are becoming a self-conscious interest group, politically oriented. But as an explicitly contrasted racial group, they are organized to fight for what others took for granted—the availability of the political system. The blacks are being forced to do this in a more self-conscious and defensive way than any other American group. Blacks are not doing this for exactly the reasons spokesmen for various American ethnics now say that they used ethnic political power. If it is really to count, political power exercised by Negroes and for Negroes now must be related as much or more to redressing old inequities as it is to sharing in the allocations of social rewards made available by public support and subsidy.

This is a sociopolitical matter. And what happens in this context is all the more critical now because the big and critical gap between blacks and whites, the poor and the middle class, is more nearly with reference to social consumption income. We are belatedly beginning to understand the consequences of the fact that the poor, and therefore a significant proportion of the black population, "are not simply poor in individual consumption income . . . but in social consumption income as well." The improvement of consumption income is not essentially a matter of culture, class, or ethnicity, nor is it related directly to granted virtues such as family structure or the willingness to work.

Kenneth Boulding makes the point about how social consumption income is allocated with appropriate bluntness:

> In the task of reducing inequalities and eliminating injustices we have fallen down badly. A large proportion of our grants economy . . . consists of redistributions to the rich and middle class, rather than to the poor. . . . We make one-way transfers only to people with whom we have a sense of community. Because the sense of community is not unlimited . . . the grants economy is subject to scarcity.[6]

To understand, and to know what to do about, happenings on the current race relations scene is difficult and fraught with fateful risks because it is very hard to tell the difference between what James Reston calls "the facts for the moment" and "the tendencies of history." The lack of ability to make this important distinction adds to the Kafkaesque quality of much of our current existence.

This difficulty of making distinctions between facts of the moment and tendencies of history is one reason why race relations discussions, negotiations, and some of the adjustments made and proposed have fitful, *ad hoc,* and contingent qualities about them. Of course, the more important reason for the state of provisional and jerry-built decisions may be the compelling harshness, the implicit and explicit violence, and the unpredictability that mark much of present race relations reality. The practices and policies of many organizations and institutions in race relations matters are likely today to be the result of cumulative small decisions, improvisations, and of half-hearted concessions, rather than of any design, grand or otherwise. This is not bad in itself; however, it often has the effect of extending or prolonging tension, because the fitful, *ad hoc* response does not convince people that they are being taken seriously. The response is often made on assumptions they can't accept. It does not answer questions about aims and relevance. Difficulty comes when the definitions of the situation, and therefore the agendas, are vastly different. The fact that there are different goals and agendas is demonstrated in the confrontations between students and colleges and universities, involving black and white, in the United States and in countries all over the world. The aims of many young activists are, in Vincent Harding's words, to "blow the mind" of business-as-usual institutions here and abroad.[7] One reason is that they see these institutions, as Peter Marin puts it, "breeding a kind of gentle violence, usually turned against oneself." [8] The institutions of learning are strategic staging areas and testing grounds for projected assaults on all key institutions. As Harding says: "The challenge of the Negro to higher education has implications for the society, at large, if America is truly serious about wanting an integrated society—whatever that is." [9]

In a recent discussion of "black consciousness and higher education," Harding interprets the groping of students for an educational or philosophical background for a black curriculum. He first draws distinction between what is meant by "the Negro in higher education" and "the blacks and higher education." Questions about the Negro *in* higher education, he suggests, have to do with "what the people in the dominant group are trying to decide they will do about including black students in otherwise white institutions." And he agrees that "to inquire about blacks *and* higher education is to raise questions beyond who its clients should be; it is to project the notion of what higher education would be from the black consciousness point of view." He offers his "pet idea" about youth, black consciousness, and institutional change.

The idea began with the formation of the Afro-American student groups a couple of years ago and it has grown as these groups have enlarged their numbers—and their bargaining position. Colleges seems to be saying, we've got a microcosm of American society here on the campus and since America is a society with Negroes, let's get some of them onto our campuses and let's show them how wonderful it is to be in America; and then we shall go on, with our Negroes and our society, with business as usual. Well, some black students have come in, but as their numbers have increased they have said you can't go on with business as usual.

My pet idea is that the black student insistence on change is an intimation to America as a whole of what it can expect. If this country is to begin to talk seriously about bringing black people into American society, if there is to be a major input of black people into the mainstream, it will blow the mind of the whole thing. America can't continue with business as usual. It's obvious that students are now testing the mind of the university. They are saying, 'Much that you have here and that you consider good and valuable, we are not interested in.' And I suspect that black America might have a similar commentary to make about lots of institutions in the larger society.[10]

The clarity and force of what black America has to say is affected by the fact that there is a great competition and considerable confusion among the race relations issues and slogans that get public and private circulation and attention. One problem is the classic one that requires telling the difference between what means to group goals are and what the goals are in themselves. A commentary on race relations, and how they get defined and generated, is that black power, separatism, black capitalism, and local control at the start were proposed mainly as means to ends—racial equality, justice, eventual integration, for example. Increasingly, some of these, such as separatism, have come to be seen and accepted by many as ultimate goals in themselves. What are thought of as temporary stages become matters of permanent good; they are rationalized variously on pragmatic, philosophical, natural, mystical, and racist grounds.

The mass media have greatly shortened the time and vastly enlarged the terrain over which attitudes, values, images, and tactics which have significance for race relations are spread. They have a strong and some-times decisive influence on the ways in which race relations issues are phrased and given priorities. Many publicized issues tend to be short-lived, while some of the real issues tend to be obscured and buried. Even though protagonists may protest the phrasing of the issues, their tactics, and their goals by the media, the pressures are such that they eventually accept the pop versions. They respond in terms of them, and tend to fall back on restatements of their views of issues and priorities intermittently, especially when balked, overpowered, or out-maneuvered. For example, in New York City, what began as and remains basically an issue having to do with the quality of education received by black and Puerto Rican students in public schools was defined and transformed into the grossly defined issue of local (sometimes read as black) community control of schools long before it was explicitly recognized as such by the interested parties.

The media have contributed heavily to current tendencies to try to define the key problem of Negroes and the personal and group alternatives of members of the Negro community. Much effort has been expended toward simplifying the problem of the Negro community now as an acute cleavage between those who advocate integration and those who advocate separatism. This is being done without evidence that significant numbers of Negroes perceive the alternatives confronting them as American citizens in this categorical fashion, and before there has been adequate opportunity for any consensus to develop through discussion.

The media's phrasing, and its seeking to impose the issue for American Negro individuals, no matter what their political or ideological leanings, has the effect of setting up forced, if not false, choices; and it diverts attention from the underlying issues and values. These underlying issues and values in the self-conscious black community have to do with ways of maximizing sharing in the rewards of this society. They reflect preoccupation with freedom and flexibility, if anything.

Several points might be made here. One has to do with the fact that black power in its many guises derives from and takes its essential forms and meanings from the American experience. Other points have to do with the existence of many different, shifting clusters of black power adherents and many changing configurations of black power behavior and sentiments; also considered are the important differences between those who are true believers and those who are adherents to selected and competing black power ideas and sentiments.

Whatever the reasons might be, and no matter the stance or color of those who try it, attempts to place Negro people and their behavior along a militant-non-militant axis or in relation to the ideal or literary types of Nat Turner and Sambo, for example, are at best risky. They ignore the complex quality of the varied human responses of the Negro to circumstances and crises. American Negroes have always shown a wide range of response to the perceived racial facts of life and every Negro has a reasonably large repertory of responses rather than a single, all-purpose one. Categorical placement of moderates and militants diverts from the fact that there are millions who identify selectively with some of the many old and new sentiments and themes that are subsumed under black power. There is general identification with those themes stressing powerlessness and affirming the dignity of Negroes denied power as Americans.

Proper perspective demands that what is grossly called the black power movement today be seen as reflecting important continuities as well as significant changes in the experiences, circumstances, and responses of American Negroes. It is a mistake to think of black power phenomena as primarily a dramatic, acute indication of the absence of pride and self-identity. Those who assume that the Negro was without pride before recent developments make a mistake. Distinctions need to be made between morale, power, a sense of the future, confidence, and pride. Even though difficult to sustain, people may have pride in self even when morale is low, the sense of the future dim. Self-esteem among the poor and Negroes is not so rare as much of popular thinking and social science writing asserts. Further, pride is a multifaceted thing. It has a collective dimension and a personal dimension. These latter are separable in practice and in theory, although related. Opting out, bitterness, and resentment are not characteristically prideless acts.

Those who think the prime byproduct, or the goal, of the new thrusts of Negroes/blacks will be simply—or primarily—increased pride are simplistic in their views of people. Pride is not an independent variable, nor is it self-generating over a sustained period. The point is that many who hasten to say a good word about black power, under the impression that the Negro's problem has been essentially a lack of pride, and that with pride through black power or any variation of it he will be less a threat, either proudly integrated or proudly separate, are naïve, to say the least.

Ralph Ellison has stressed that the "affirmation of life [and self] beyond all question of our difficulties as Negroes" is an historical constant.[11] The American experience is filled with indications of refusals by Negroes both to abdicate self-respect and to stifle criticism of the system before black power. The persistence of acts and traditions of pride and protest were due in no small measure to the efforts and will of a variety of proud, anonymous, ubiquitous poor Negroes and "bad niggers," as well as to sung and unsung Negro intellectuals, middle-class persons, and frustrated would-be middle-class persons.

Among the things that are different about current race relations are the new roles for the black middle classes—especially the lower middle class—and for black youths, many of whom are recruits from established black middle classes or are candidates for the new black middle classes. If there are significant discontinuities, they have to do with the stances and outlooks of the successive generations of high school and college youth since 1959. Some of these early sit-in protesters are now young middle-class adults—graduates, likely with a slight difference from their successors, but still identified with them.

Those among black power advocates who seek to discredit the black middle class categorically or to split it off do a disservice to their movement; to the extent that they are successful, they might help cripple the building and governance of future institutions of any order—segregated, integrated, or revolutionary. The current protest movement benefits not only from the large amounts of direction and support that come from many middle-class Negroes, it benefits immeasurably from the partial identification of the many middle-class aspirants who are adherents to some features, if not total converts to all, of the black power precepts.

The importance of the role and position of the lower-middle-class Negro in the present ferment has not been differentiated adequately from the clinically poor black, and from an older or more established black middle class. Along with his white counterpart, the lower-middle-class Negro makes up the critical category for discontent and disenchantment. The lower-middle-class Negro is a prime candidate for radicalizing. The lower-middle-class white worker is the new bastion of conservatism, and, translated into practical terms, this means that he tends to be against any change that will change or improve the position of the black vis-à-vis himself. He is the man who had taken it for granted that he had made it, but who, in the face of demands of lower-middle-class and poor Negroes, begins to have fears and doubts about his position.

The reasons why the Negro middle class is frequently condemned categorically both by politically conscious young whites and Negroes are, of course, complex. One reason is the uncritical acceptance of a simplistic version of E. Franklin Frazier's concept of the black bourgeoisie embracing the symbols of American middle-class status but not sharing its substance and power. The outdated popular view of a homogeneous, apolitical, and sterile black middle class that lacks group sentiments and resentments needs revision. Frazier himself actually saw his black bourgeoisie type acting out a classic human drama that was incidentally, and not essentially, racial in its meaning and lessons.

The label Negro/black middle class is undoubtedly a much grosser stereotype than the label white middle class. In an over-simplified way, it seems that it is all right for any American to be or to strive to be middle class in tastes and behavior (especially in consumption behavior) except the Negro. And the caricaturizing of the Negro middle class is a part of a larger crisis of respect that underlies racial tension. Race relations are in large part a serious, ruthless, sometimes subtle, and often dirty battle of social reputations. In this battle, the Negro middle class is an important target as well as protagonist. The important point is that the view that the Negro middle class is inherently powerless and that black concern about the essential rewards of middle-class status —power, options, social consumption income—should be ignored, needs close examination.

The great practical and symbolic importance of the professional, white-collar, and paraprofessional jobs in health, welfare, and education services—the middle-class and middle-class-making jobs—means that some, but not all, of the ambivalence about associating middle-class status, symbols, and behavior with American Negroes is both strange and dysfunctional for almost any design for movement and black power.

The caricaturizing of the minority middle-class aspirant and the invidiousness with respect to him tend to becloud the stakes the poor and minorities have in the manning and organization of public agencies. These basic stakes have to do with decision-making and with the responsiveness and accountability of dispensers of public services. Whether both the middle-class representatives, as well as the poor in the ghetto, share in decision-making has direct bearing on whether services are available and on the quality of the services for ghetto residents.

In this connection, it is useful to cite what Dr. Robert R. Cadmus, president of the New Jersey College of Medicine and Dentistry, learned in the resolution of the dispute in Newark over the location of the New Jersey College of Medicine and Dentistry—especially with reference to the roles of the educated and the uneducated, and with reference to their competence, relevance, and respect for the professional role. He gave answers to a number of questions about the relationship of the health facility to the community. Among them: How can minority representatives contribute to planning for health services? What have they to offer in the light of the experience in Newark? What groups were involved and what kinds of interests did they represent? How do you identify community leaders?

With reference to community participation and planning for health services, Dr. Cadmus said:

> Community groups have contributed a great deal. Many of the black leaders are well educated, with master's degrees and doctorates. In fact, the amount of talent within these people which is going unused is tragic.
>
> The uneducated contribute in a different way. They understand the needs of their people and frequently are very articulate. Moreover, I have never seen them try to intervene in areas in which they have no competence, such as medical school curriculums, or how to treat illness. They're interested in opportunities to become professionals, to get jobs, to get health services. They only want to enter the mainstream of American life.
>
> It boils down to participation. Most people not only want to participate but want to do so fully, without subterfuge. For example, at a recent meeting, the black representatives wanted to make certain that the building contractors would not merely hire a few black faces for our particular project, but that the unions supplying labor be truly integrated so that the gain would be permanent on all future jobs. Token participation in any form is only camouflage, a thing of the past.
>
> It is logical and just that the consumer be involved in health affairs. One

does not need to be a professional to have a valid opinion about the delivery of health services. Only physicians can practice medicine. But the doctor has no exclusive rights in determining the economics of health services, the location of facilities, or the percentage of the gross national product that is to be allocated for the delivery of care. The professional has a voice, but he has much to learn from the consumer outside of his profession.[12]

With reference to groups involved, he said:

The most vocal groups were the 'disadvantaged,' 'underprivileged,' 'minority,' or whatever you want to call them, but particularly those to be affected by the project. They represented churches, the poor, planning groups, ethnic groups, government, economic and business interests, children's causes, almost any concern you can name. Each had sprung up and found meaning as a result of vast social changes occurring at many levels in our society.

As a result, we were confronted not only with the problems of setting up a medical and dental college, but with such problems as job discrimination, poor housing, and inadequate education, and all the social difficulties that go hand in hand with these. The convergence of these problems caused the explosion. We were only the catalyst, the focal point around which constructive action would take place. In some communities the university bears the brunt of this social revolution. But I believe in most communities the hospital will become the most likely focal point—because of its public nature, because it represents a middle ground between the sanctity of the church and the might of the government. The hospital has tremendous community visibility. Everyone knows where it is and considers it proper to voice his opinion about it. I predict that it will, in many cases, be the tool by which community groups will seek participation.[13]

With reference to identification of community leaders, Dr. Cadmus said:

This is an extremely difficult question, whether one speaks about a white or a black community. The groups themselves will not always agree on who their leaders are. There are frictions in every group, and leadership shifts as the power politics play out. New faces appear as individuals drop from sight, or familiar faces will suddenly change roles, assuming greater or less responsibility in negotiation.

Particularly in the black community there is a tendency for the participants to caucus whenever there appears to be a breach in their solidarity. Dissidents within the group are dealt with in private, never during negotiation, and frequently this process brings about changes in leadership.

With continual and wise liaison in the community, however, leadership can be identified, fluid as it may be. It is first necessary, however, to establish communications on a daily basis—and, above all, to listen. Such liaison is far from simple, and an astute observer is necessary.

In any case, leadership identification is useful only in the direct interests of better communication. To use it otherwise could only deepen a distrust that is already one of our greatest social obstacles.[14]

Dr. Cadmus's experience indicates that superficial political considerations aside, one way to achieve relevance and effectiveness in the organization and distribution of services locally is to insure that minority members take part in the design, execution, and evaluation of social programs and policy. It also justifies Sumner Rosen's judgments that:

> The ghetto's resources are its people and their problems. The ghetto is a living laboratory to observe and deal with these critical problems. The ghetto is rich in experience, negative but immensely instructive, with the nature and impact of the failure of our major systems of social service, primarily health, education, and social services or welfare. Large concentrations of capital and of professional talent in the existing health, education, and welfare system demonstrate that these are the critical elements in an effective solution. What is missing is the innovative and experimental spirit and freedom to effect it.[15]

The innovative and experimental freedom and spirit to get the most out of the already large concentrations of professional talent are largely dependent upon the extent to which there is effective circulation of the elite. This means "movement into positions of political control of persons and social types not heretofore eligible . . . and the outflow of incumbents of the same positions." [16] The entrance of Negroes, Puerto Ricans, Mexican-Americans into policy and administrative apparatuses is a necessary part of this process.

The ways in which this entrance into old and new institutional structures is made by newcomers from different class, racial, and ethnic categories are many. The entrance of the newcomer is frequently disputed and often deplored by some of the incumbents and by some members of the old elite categories with whom incumbents have been used to identifying and recognizing as the prime source of the qualified and deserving—which very frequently means "like me."

The community is made up of competing elites, and some of these groups are beneficiaries more than others of "clientalism," which has been described as "sustained discretionary administrative behavior favorable to the interests of a private person or group." The prime antidotes to clientalism are a political base, a constituency, and jobs in the administration apparatus.

Efforts to achieve circulation—or better, a redefinition—of the elite might or might not involve the creation of new administrative labels and units. And changes in designations and recruitment might result in positions that carry real power and responsibility or they might result in positions that carry just nominal power and responsibility. The real test of effectiveness of the turnover does not lie in whether more middle-class or bread-and-butter jobs are created and shared or in whether minority representatives figure in a changed calculus of power. The critical test is whether the services rendered by the more representative or integrated system are actually more efficient, better, and democratized.

The pressure to change not only the structure, but the control and accountability of service institutions are clearly related to the new public consciousness of black and to the related emergence of the fact and concept of acute black consciousness.

The rapid adoption and circulation of black represents one of the most dramatic inversions of group symbols that has occurred in any society. This managed change of designations for a category of American citizens, the reasons for it, and the speed with which it has happened are without precedent. There is significance in the fact that the change to thinking black and the quest for a black identity and consciousness have come first and most easily among the younger Negroes. And there is significance, too, in the fact that the questions are being asked by some persons in the light of the emergence of black consciousness as an entity or mystique whether it is possible for a white man to be a Negro; and whether there is a basic need for whites to want to be blacks, to desire a black consciousness.

Actually, the very rapid acceptance (or was it acquiescence?) by many whites of the designation black until recently was generally not a matter that called for much examination or sacrifice. It did not matter in any serious way, at first. The point is that the acceptance and the acquiescence of many whites in the matter of what some Negroes firmly and successfully insisted Negroes should be called, as in other matters when the issues are drawn along racial or color lines, tended to be highly selective. The real tests of changes by whites in their basic perceptions of Negroes and of their serious acceptance of the new black image and its implications are just being fully shaped and their implications faced, particularly by those who man the public service institutions.

There is a question as to how really consequential it is to some whites that any significant Negro group insist (1) that Negroes be called something different; (2) that Negroes as self-conscious blacks reject integration, temporarily or permanently; (3) that Negroes wish to do it, that is, achieve their equivalent of the American dream, by themselves. It appears that these kinds of apparently non-gut requests have been readily conceded, sometimes in unseemly haste and with little questioning of self and others. This has been done for a variety of reasons, not necessarily indifference or hostility. However, the evidence is firm that when there is insistence by groups of blacks, and by their spokesmen, that they want either larger shares in controlling, or complete control of, the local institutions affecting their lives, no matter the reasons, the acceptance and acquiescence in these requests by whites have not been as easy, as quick, and as pervasive. This is the reluctance to which black youths are sensitive. This is one of the bases for the many calls for revolution, for radical change, for attacks on the system itself.

Student demands for control of parts of the system for their benefit, for a kind of autonomy, are, in the view of Peter Marin, biblical and Freudian; they represent a need "to unmask the gods and assume their power, to become an equal—and to find in that the manhood one has been denied." [17]

Separatism or withdrawal on a basis of race, even temporarily—legal, ethical, ideological, and biblical and Freudian considerations aside for the moment—is at best a delicate stratagem for all. It may be a Utopian projection or revolutionary goal foredoomed to fail or to be blunted in its specific objectives. Further, there is the fact—and theorists of black power may make a case for the necessity of ignoring this fact—that Negroes in withdrawing and in assuming a false burden of proof about their worth and claims to equity are conceding too much for little or nothing in return.

Outside of sects and cults, no ethnic group or racial category in American society has ever voluntarily tried to become a genuine do-it-yourself or go-it-alone group. Every conventional category that has made it has used and benefited by the public apparatus and by effectively sharing in exercise of power and influence over the political process.

Some, but not all of the calls and preparations for literal urban revolution of blacks are grave matters, and all need serious examination and weighing by all.

One difficulty lies in the confusion among the respective strategies and goals of cultural revolution, economic revolution, and political revolution, and of any viable packaging of all three, as in the black nation concept, on the one hand, and the various types of community development projects designed to decrease powerlessness through participation, training, and varieties of self-help, on the other. These are related ideas or concepts, but separable. The first approach is ostensibly radical, if not revolutionary; the second is reformist. For example, Harold Cruse, author of *Crisis of the Negro Intellectual* and *Rebellion or Revolution?*, advocates a cultural revolution, and is dubious about the other two. Roy Innis's and Floyd McKissick's CORE models of black capitalism and economic development, although backed by separatist slogans, are, in fact, more conservative than radical; more reformist than revolutionary; more eclectic and pragmatic than doctrinaire and inflexible. Actually, there is little or no basic difference between the CORE/Nixon black capitalism approach and the Urban League or the Bedford-Stuyvesant Development approach in terms of their placement on any reformist-revolutionary scale.

In my own view, the prognoses for sustained black revolution, in the sense of dramatic, violent change in the distribution of power, and for real black separatism, in the sense of a full complement of independent, autonomous black institutions either encapsulated in or set off from American society, are not good. This does not mean in any sense that the tactics and strategies of racial protest that contribute to present pressures, tensions, and conflict have been or are counterproductive. It means, rather, that the lessons of history are that "urban movements that start off with the aim of revolutionary change [sooner or later] either turn into reformist movements or succumb in competition with reformism." [18] I suggest that there are no convincing reasons why this axiom does not apply to present facts and trends; further, the blunting and the incorporation of many so-called revolutionary efforts are already happening.

The future chances and the course of a specific black urban revolution are affected also by three other telling considerations. One is the predictable mobilization of massive forces by unified dominant whites, once a black revolution really threatens, to throttle or squash it. The second consideration is whether and how our society uses an incomparable productivity to grant substantial social income benefits to the working classes—to black and white, and to the lower middle class even more than to the very poor—thereby facilitating their full social and legal incorporation into the larger society. The indications are that more of this is going to be done, albeit begrudgingly, and in agonizingly too-small amounts. One answer to revolution is to change the prevailing formulas and definitions of eligibility for the allocation of social benefits. One of Alvin Schorr's computations in this context is pertinent: The federal contribution to low-cost housing in 1962 for the bottom fifth of the population was $820 million, while the subsidy to the top fifth in the form of tax deductions was $1.7 billion.[19]

A third consideration affecting the chances of black revolution is that the chances are extremely high that most Negroes/blacks, like whites in this society, and without regard to their ideological leanings and without regard to whether or not they display now a revolutionary solidarity, basically do now—or eventually will—prefer an order that provides the flexibility and means for them to "search for . . . private and more familiar everyday solution(s) to their problems." [20]

The imperatives to change the organization, policies, and practices of our helping professions have to do with their failures to deal with people and problems marked by the intersection of blackness and poverty. If, in changing, our institutions still do not make it possible for people to search for private and familiar everyday solutions to most of their problems regardless of, not because of, race and income, the reformation of professional services will have still failed.

## REFERENCES

1. Earl Raab, "The Black Revolution and the Jewish Question," *Commentary* (January, 1969), p. 33.

2. Peter Marin, "The Open Truth and Fiery Vehemence of Youth: A Sort of Soliloquy," *The Center Magazine* (January, 1969), p. 73.

3. Zbigniew Brzezinski, "The Search for Meaning Amid Change," *New York Times*, National Economic Review (January 6, 1969), p. 141.

4. John Wilkinson, *The Civilization of the Dialogue: An Introduction*, an occasional paper, Center for the Study of Democratic Institutions (December, 1968), p. 4.

5. Nathan Glazer and Daniel Moynihan, *Beyond the Melting Pot* (Cambridge, Mass.: The M.I.T. Press, 1964), pp. 16–17.

6. Kenneth Boulding, "The American Economy: The Many Failures of Success," *Saturday Review* (January 2, 1968), p. 30.

7. Vincent Harding "Black Consciousness and Higher Education," an occasional paper, The Church Society for College Work (Winter, 1968), p. 6.

8. Marin, *op. cit.*

9. Harding, *op. cit.*

10. *Ibid.*

11. Ralph Ellison, *Shadow & Act* (New York: A Signet Book, The New American Library, Inc., 1966), p. xiv.

12. "Interaction with the Inner-City: An Interview with Robert R. Cadmus, M.D." Interview by Michael Lesparre, *Hospitals* (September 1, 1968).

13. *Ibid.*

14. *Ibid.*

15. Sumner M. Rosen, "Better Mousetraps: Reflections on Economic Development in the Ghetto," *Social Policy Papers* (New York: New Careers Development Center), pp. 14, 15.

16. Scott Greer and Peter Orleans, "Political Sociology," in R. E. L. Faris (ed.), *Handbook of Modern Sociology* (Chicago: Rand McNally and Company, 1964), p. 832.

17. Marin, *op cit.*

18. Barrington Moore, Jr., "Revolution in America," *New York Review of Books* (January 30, 1969), p. 8.

19. Alvin Schorr, *Explorations in Social Policy* (New York: Basic Books, 1968).

20. Moore, *op. cit.*

# 4

# Ethnic Cleavages in the United States: An Historical Reminder to Social Workers

## RALPH L. KOLODNY

THE SOCIAL WORK literature and the professional thinking of most social workers generally deal with two kinds of reality—intrapsychic and interpersonal. In discussing the interplay between these, much attention has been given to the social arrangements and patterns among collections of people that in some way regulate their actions toward one another, individually and in groups. Currently, the social patternings that engage the greatest interest of social workers and others in the helping professions are those subsumed under the idea of "class." The social worker who is concerned with social as distinguished from psychological factors is likely, when he uses the word "social," to be thinking of "class," and when he uses the word "class," to be thinking mainly, if not solely, in terms of economic variables, hence the burgeoning number of studies

Reprinted from *Social Work*, 14 (January 1969), pp. 13–23. RALPH L. KOLODNY was at the time of writing associate professor, Boston University School of Social Work, Boston, Massachusetts.

on the relationship between income and mental illness, lower-class use of agency services, and the common use of phrases such as working-class attitudes, middle-class values, and the like.[1] Today, a social work client's position in the class structure is perhaps the major variable besides primary family experience that is used to explain his behavior.

## ETHNIC TIES

The student of society can surely have no quarrel with the notion that there are attitudinal and behavioral as well as economic differences in clients from different classes, although the formulations concerning the existence and causes of these differences may be cruder than we care to admit. It is important, however, to recognize that in the American experience there has always been another aspect of social reality related to "class"—that is, to the pattern of distribution of wealth and the life-styles of aggregates of people possessing various forms and amounts of wealth—but distinguishable from it. In 1924, for example, Kallen, in discussing immigrant groups in the United States, wrote: ". . . the poor of two different peoples tend to be less like-minded than the poor and the rich of the same people. . . ."[2] Ethnic ties, sometimes in addition to but at other times distinct from or even in opposition to those of class, have historically influenced the behavior and views of individuals in this country toward others and how they feel about themselves. These ties would still appear to have serious meaning for many persons today who in many respects have become "assimilated." Hansen, an historian, hypothesizes that the third generation in the United States manifests "an inevitable tendency to identify once again with the cultural tradition . . . of their immigrant forebears."[3] His viewpoint is echoed by Messer, a psychiatrist, on the basis of clinical practice.[4]

Social work thinking for many years has been committed to the notion of cultural pluralism. There are few social workers today who would quarrel with the idea that people of various national backgrounds in this society have a right to differ from one another in their customs and ceremonies, value orientations and priorities, food habits, language usage, and so forth. Yet many have little knowledge of what these differences have meant and continue to mean to clients and group members. A decade ago, Stein and Cloward were suggesting that the general lack of a systematic appraisal of ethnic factors in their more subtle forms impairs the fullest use of the social worker's understanding of psychology and philosophic orientations.[5] More recently, Spiegel has argued that the client's cultural value orientations are a form of "behavior without awareness" and thus influence the therapeutic relationship profoundly. Consequently, he notes, all mental health practitioners will in the future have to give as much consideration to problems of cultural dynamics as has been given in the past to purely psychological processes.[6]

An examination of the social work literature of the past two decades, however, reveals little professional concern with or interest in ethnic phenomena.[7] This is interesting when one realizes that although this paper will approach the problem from an historical standpoint, the ethnic cleavages it will describe tend in some significant respects to persist today. Sherif and Sherif, for example, noted in 1961:

> With some variations from region to region and from class to class, . . . the rank order of various groups is remarkably similar throughout the country and has been substantially the same through decades that have witnessed both rapid change and earth-shaking events. At the top are "native" white Americans followed by the Canadians, the British and the various north European groups. Next in rough order, come the Slavic peoples, south Europeans, Jews and American Indians. At the bottom of the ladder are Oriental peoples, Mexicans, Near Eastern groups, and Negroes. . . . Groups at the low end of the scale are characterized in terms alien to dominant American values.[8]

It is possible that interest in ethnic matters among social workers will be rekindled as a result of the Black Power movement. Ethnic references abound in the pronouncements and theories of social work and social science supporters of the movement. Arguing for Negro separation, for example, two social work educators have recently emphasized how the approaches developed by ethnic groups in the past offer a model of action for the present-day Negro community. The communal organizations these groups created, they believe, provided a base from which to convert ethnic solidarity into the political force required to overcome various forms of class inequality.[9] Ethnic separatism, they argue, is a precondition for eventual penetration of the ruling circles.[10] They suggest that if any lesson is to be learned from the experience of other minorities in the United States, it is that the strength to resist majority prejudices, to advance in spite of them, and ultimately to overcome them must be found within a countervailing ethnic community.[11] Proponents of this point of view regard ethnic separation as a continuing fact of life in this country and emphasize that most Americans are living in two worlds at once, one of them largely integrated and the other primarily separated.[12]

The emotional significance of ethnicity in client behavior is matched by its importance as a contemporary social phenomenon. Ethnic factors thus deserve serious consideration by social workers, both as clinicians and as social planners. The material that follows is designed to further the social worker's understanding of ethnic phenomena by providing him with an historical perspective on relations between ethnic groups in the United States. For these purposes the writer has drawn principally on accounts of ethnic encounters within the American working class between 1870 and 1945.

## ETHNIC VERSUS CLASS SOLIDARITY

The extensive violence that has recently accompanied one minority group's quest for justice and identity does not have many precedents in American history. It should be remembered, however, that it was only some twenty years ago that intergroup relations involving various ethnic groups were being described in cold-water terms. At that time, one prominent observer of the national scene wrote the following about his area of residence:

> The "old Americans" are now an outnumbered clan, grimly holding on to financial and social power where they can, yielding only to death and superior taxes. The social cleavage they have thus created is, of course, the New England tragedy. . . . Finding they are not wanted, the "immigrants" have struck back by two characteristically American attacks: they have conquered at the polls and they are trying to conquer in the counting house. New England is therefore a house divided against itself.[13]

This was the same period when Anderson said of Burlington, Vermont:

> Such . . . is the map of social life in Burlington. Economic barriers running horizontally and religious and ethnic barriers running vertically divide the community into small patches and set the pattern of its social life.[14]

When she asked some 450 Burlington residents the question: "Of what nationality are your close friends?" Anderson found the French-Canadian and Jewish respondents highly conscious of group loyalty. But even more "ethnic group conscious" were the "old American" interviewees, 87 percent of whom stated they had intimate friends only among their own people.

The ethnic patterns of the 1930's and '40's described in the foregoing comments had been preceded by many years of tension. An examination of relationships among laborers of different national origins beginning with the second half of the nineteenth century indicates the forms this tension took within the working class. As the nineteenth century drew to a close the major clash was between members of what may be termed "native and old immigrant" groups and those of the "new" immigration. In 1870, for example, English-speaking groups made up over 90 percent of the foreign-born people in the mining regions of Pennsylvania. By 1910, 178,000 Slavs and Italians inhabited the region, making up 66 percent of the foreign-born, and Warne wrote of a struggle for industrial supremacy in the hard coal industry between old and new immigrants whom he saw as "two distinctly marked groups." [15]

The industrial supremacy of which Warne wrote was not supremacy in the sense of one group controlling the ownership or management of the industry, but one group's supremacy in obtaining the bulk of the jobs. It was a situation in which industrial employers continually substituted or attempted to substitute more tractable immigrant workers for their current labor force when the latter presumably became more interested in unionization and less willing to put up with poor working conditions. Under these circumstances the cry of "scab" and "strikebreaker" was often leveled at the Slavic and Mediterranean newcomers. Actually, native, old immigrant, and new immigrant workers at various times took these roles, as will be seen. The important fact, however, is that, whatever the justice of the accusations they leveled at one another, each of the groups saw or came to see the others as profoundly antagonistic.

Events such as those that occurred in the Lowell, Massachusetts, strike of 1903 were likely to produce sharp ethnic conflicts. In the Lowell textile plants there were only one thousand union members out of nineteen thousand workers. All the workers, however, followed the unionists' lead and walked out of the mills. Strike sentiment spread to the largely unskilled foreign-born workers. Members of the separate workers' organizations, which included Greeks, Poles, and Portuguese, showed definite enthusiasm for the strike and, together with the native-born workers, took their places on the picket lines. At just this time, however, the price of raw cotton rose and the manufacturers were able to sell their stocks of it at a considerable profit. Since the strike now could not really hurt them financially, they could afford to wait the strikers out. Enthusiasm for the strike lagged. The mills reopened and offered jobs at the old wages. A small body of original native-born unionists held out after most of the other strikers went back to work, but the textile council was forced to call off the strike. What is important to note is that

The Portuguese, Poles and Greeks, who had been listed as unskilled help only, had meanwhile advanced to better positions when they went back to

work while the more skilled workers stayed out, and when the unions
terminated the strike, many of the positions of their members had been
filled and the union members displaced.[16]

The feeling against immigrant workers this engendered can well be
imagined.

The American worker, if one is to believe some of his defenders
earlier in this century, was faced by two enemies—the employer and
cheap immigrant labor. Unionism was his protection. Warne wrote:

> The employer also knows that if the union is destroyed or weakened, the
> control of the latter over the price of the immigrant's labor will be prevented,
> unrestricted competition of labor with labor will be secured, control of the
> supply of cheap immigrant labor will permit. him to introduce a still
> greater number, and thus wages can always be kept at the minimum.[17]

It is not the author's purpose to question this argument. Warne's
statement actually describes what took place in some American industrial
areas. What is to be emphasized is that under these circumstances the
new immigrant worker was not simply an impersonal force with which
the native worker had to contend. He was of flesh and blood, speaking
a certain language, having specific customs, and eating certain foods.
He and the rest of his group were identifiable. They became objects of
resentment and a stereotype of the group was created. Its members,
according to the stereotype, were not only different, they were physically
and morally dirty; they were ignorant, their food habits were unsanitary.
The economic enemy became an ethnic enemy and social intercourse
between the two groups was kept at a minimum. It is not strange that,
apart from the obvious barrier of language, the new immigrant's chances
of fraternization with other workers, if he desired it, were limited.

One might ask why more stress was not put on organizing the immigrant workers during the period in which they were arriving in great
numbers from eastern and southern Europe. The United Mine Workers,
of course, came to emphasize such a program. But others, such as the
United Textile Workers, who had no real desire to organize the Greek,
Syrian, Portuguese, and Polish mill hands of New England, did not
adopt it.[18] In view of their fear of unorganized immigrant labor being
used as a weapon by the employers against organized American labor,
one would imagine they would have been at haste to organize these
recently arrived workers.

The fact is, the craft unions, such as the United Textile Workers,
sought above all to limit the number of competitors. They tended to

exclude rather than include new immigrants. The members of various national groups found themselves excluded from workers' organizations to which, on the basis of their occupational position in society, they would have been expected to have had access. Economic gain and ethnic antagonism were interwoven in this situation. As Young, writing in 1932, pointed out:

> Temporary and individual gain, however, may still result from holding tight the reins of race and nationality. For example, labor as a whole suffers from the exclusion of Negroes and other minorities from the benefits of union organization, but individual workers may for a time ride along in an impermanent security from minority competition. It is this ever-present possibility of immediate gain which helps keep alive a belief in the value of racial solidarity even where economic forces may be shown to make it a detriment rather than an advantage in mass competition.[19]

The United Textile Workers could go so far as to bait workers from minority groups. In 1919 it attacked an organization that represented largely new immigrant labor—the Amalgamated Textile Workers—as "un-American, Bolshevik and Jewish." [20]

There were times when eastern and southern European immigrant workers had ample reason to complain of "treason" by their native fellow workers. In some cases it was the Slavic immigrant, for example, who provided the strongest support for a strike, only to be let down by the American or old immigrant worker. Davis pointed out that when the Pennsylvania steel strike of 1919 was lost, the Russian immigrant participants felt the union was useless and called the American workers traitors for going back before the strike was ended. One of the Russian workmen said to Davis:

> Americans are at the head of it. They told us we would be traitors to our fellow workmen if we did not support it. Now we have done it and the newspapers call us Reds, I.W.W.'s and Bolsheviks. Us, they refuse to take back but the Americans get back their jobs.[21]

Eleven years later, speaking of the McKeesport (Pennsylvania) strike, Feldman noted that even several foreign-born persons who were interviewed stated they had not participated because it was only a strike of "foreigners"—Italians and Slavs.[22]

Whether the new immigrant or the native and old immigrant workers were most responsible for the failure of strikes or the keeping down of wages, however, it was the former who were believed to be most responsible. Whatever differences of opinion there were among experts on

the question of the negative effects of foreign labor on wages, most were
agreed that

> . . . no matter what the economist may think to the contrary, the American
> workman believes that such is the case and it is his belief, rather than the
> actual facts, which determines his attitude and conduct toward the foreign-
> born.[23]

## STEREOTYPES OF NEW IMMIGRANTS

As a matter of fact, what the American workman was willing to believe
about foreign workmen, especially those from southern and eastern
Europe, suggests that there was more to his antagonism than dislike of
economic competitors. His antipathy may in many cases have first been
aroused or reinforced by economic competition with the southern and
eastern European, but there is an element that cannot be explained only
in these terms. The official reports of the United States Immigration
Commission early in this century make this point strongly. The commission noted that in all industries and industrial communities a certain
reproach was attached to native American or old immigrant employees
who were engaged in the same occupation as southern and eastern
Europeans. This feeling on the part of the older employees, the investigators felt, while mainly owing to habits of life and conduct and to
the ready acceptance of undesirable working conditions by recent immigrants, was also attributable to a ". . . conscious or unconscious antipathy,
often arising from ignorance or prejudice toward races of alien customs,
institutions and manners of thought." [24] It was "racial" antipathy toward
the new immigrants and dislike of the stigma attached to working with
them that sometimes prompted native American workers to turn their
backs on economic gain and even to accept lower wages. The commission
reported that when native workers remained in an industry that new
immigrants entered, they sometimes relinquished their former occupations and segregated themselves in others, rather than work with the
new immigrants. In the bituminous coal industry this even led to the
segregation of the older class of employees in occupations that, from
the standpoint of compensation, were less desirable than those occupied
by the immigrants.[25]

A glance at the writings of some of the middle- and upper-class supporters of American labor indicates that prejudice against the new
immigrant was not considered at all unrespectable during the first
part of the twentieth century. In a number of articles the native and
Anglo-Saxon workers were described as clearly superior to the new

immigrant laborers. Racial differences were assumed in some cases. "Consciousness of kind" among all industrial workers in this situation could be thought of, in a sense, as morally wrong. The native American workers and their Anglo-Saxon immigrant comrades would be corrupting themselves by identifying with the new immigrant groups. Shaler, for example, was quoted by Commons in 1907 as saying that the European peasant knew himself to be by birthright a member of an inferior class from which it was unlikely he would escape. This being the case, he could have no large sense of citizenly motives. His qualities were far different from those of the archetypal American citizen whose forefathers created the American democracy. By his "inherent nature" the typical American citizen looks forward and aspires to the highest positions.

> But the peasants of Europe, especially of southern and eastern Europe, have been reduced to the qualities similar to those of an inferior race that favor despotism rather than democracy.[26]

Warne, one of the greatest supporters of the American labor movement, wrote:

> The situation confronting us today has been complicated a thousand-fold by the tremendous differences between the qualities of the peasant immigrant of southern and eastern Europe and the American whose forefather erected our edifice of representative democracy. These peasants have become almost a distinct race—drained of those superior qualities which are the foundation of democratic institutions.[27]

These were some of the points of view taken toward the Slavic worker by some of the educated spokesmen for and supporters of the American labor movement. It is not strange that some of the native workers themselves viewed many of the southern and eastern European immigrant workers as a race apart. A cursory survey of the literature shows Slavs being distinguished from "white" men by their fellow laborers in Iowa in 1885 [28] and in Pennsylvania in 1904 [29] and Italians denied "whiteness" over a long period in many other places.[30] Feldman, as late as 1930, cited one typical factory foreman who, in speaking of his section's accident record, referred to those hurt as "five men and twelve hunkies." [31]

## ETHNIC SEGREGATION

Social segregation, however, was never simply a result of exclusion by native workers or those of Anglo-Saxon extraction. The new immigrants were scattered in clusters throughout the various areas of a strange country. Under these circumstances, of course, consciousness of kind with fellow countrymen came to take on a special significance for them. For some eastern or southern European workers the idea of nationality first became real only after they left their native shores. The most important social division for them in their new home came to be that between those who spoke their language and those who did not. The most tangible expression of this solidarity was the number of fraternal organizations formed by these immigrants. Indeed, the profusion of societies that sprang up among Slavs, for example, was surprising to investigators since nothing in their previous history would have led one to expect such a high degree of organization among Slavic peasants and workers. In reading various writers of the 1920's and '30's it is interesting to note how each suggests that the specific immigrant group with which he is concerned is the most highly organized.[32]

The leaders of these ethnic societies and organs of information tended to focus most of their attention on the problems their followers faced as ethnic group members rather than as industrial workers. The social status of the individual immigrant was to be raised by improving the status of his entire "national group" as it competed with other "national groups." In 1907, the Italian immigrant, who in most cases was an unskilled laborer, was being told by the newspaper *Bolletino della Sera:* "We must organize our forces as the Jews do, persist in exhausting that which constitutes gain for our race over the Anglo-Saxon race." [33]

Thirty years later one finds the same notion of ethnic competition as a driving force in the work of Polish societies in Chicago. Again it should be noted that the members of these societies were primarily low-income persons.[34] The centennial of Chicago's Polish community, for instance, describes the purpose of one of its affiliates in the following terms:

The Polish-American Democratic Organization was formed chiefly through the efforts of the Honorable M. S. Szymczak (now governor of the Federal Reserve Board in Washington) who, together with a few other prominent Americans of Polish extraction, foresaw the necessity of a united political body in order to obtain proper political recognition in proportion to their voting power. . . . Through the concentrated and energetic efforts of this organization the citizens of Polish extraction in Chicago and Cook County gained the majority of the present public offices and positions, elective and appointive. . . . The organization has proved that the Poles can obtain proper political representation and recognition if they remain solidly united. It has proved the old saying, "In unity there is strength." [35]

## CONFLICT AMONG NEW IMMIGRANTS

It should be added that a united front against the dominant Anglo-Saxon group was never a goal of the various southern and eastern European groups. There is little evidence that they acted in concert. On the contrary, many new immigrant workers who were the butts of ridicule and abuse by native American laborers fought among themselves with no small degree of ferocity. In 1906, Steiner, a defender of the new immigrants, was bemoaning the intragroup strife among the Slavs. He complained:

> Unfortunately they have imported into this country their racial prejudices which are keenest towards their closest kin, and each mining camp becomes the battleground on which ancient wrongs are made new issues by repeated quarrels and fights which become bloody at times. . . . In a large number of these cases these unfortunate divisions are intermingled with religious differences, although the Slovak and the Pole do not speak well of one another even if they belong to the same church.[36]

Another investigator had earlier centered his attention even more directly on the conflicts among immigrants from different southern and eastern European countries. Ripley had found the Poles were industrious but were hated by their neighbors in industrial districts because they seemed to have little sense of working-class solidarity. It was their priests, he felt, who were partly responsible for this attitude of hostility toward labor organizations. It was believed that through these priests the Chicago strike of 1896 was broken.[37]

Clothing contractors who discovered that the Poles would refuse to go out on strike with Jews and Bohemians encouraged "Polish" shops as a consequence. The only nationalities more disliked by other new immigrants, Ripley reported, were the Armenians, Greeks, and Syrians. They were all sometimes lumped together as strikebreakers, in a class by themselves, and where employed in large establishments, as in one Philadelphia house of the time, they were so disliked that it was necessary to segregate them in departments by themselves.[38]

In 1914, Jews, Italians, and Poles who felt they were being treated unfairly by the older immigrant groups in the United Garment Workers Union left to form the Amalgamated Clothing Workers of America. On the other hand, Jews and Poles split apart in the Chicago needle trades strikes of 1920 and in the strikes in Passaic, New Jersey, later in the decade.[39]

In the coal fields of Pennsylvania, Polish-Lithuanian strife was constant in mining communities. The Pole, according to Claghorn, would assert his right to a higher social status because of his country's glorious record in European history. The Lithuanian would "die of shame" at being mistaken for a Pole.[40] The national conflicts of Europe, especially at a time when such regions as Poland, Bohemia, and Slovakia were but parts of greater empires and the struggle for independence in Europe was growing more and more violent, were transferred in many cases to the United States. These transferred conflicts naturally took place quite often in workingmen's communities, since the Slavic immigrants were mainly unskilled laborers. Under these conditions, the Ukrainian and Pole simply continued their ancient feuds, although they might work in the same mine at the same kind of job and, together, were abused by their fellow workers. After World War I, Bercovici was still writing of how the Poles, for example, did not "neighbor" well. They sneered at the Jews, detested the Russians, and considered the Czechoslovaks traitors.[41]

Thus not only were industrial workers in the United States often split up into "hunkies" and "white" men, but also among the former there were definite divisions based on national differences. Any movement, therefore, that aimed at developing class consciousness and solidarity in the ranks of American labor was constantly retarded in its progress, not only by the conflict between the new immigrant and the native and old immigrant workers, but by intragroup strife among the new immigrants themselves. Indeed, in 1932, Young was convinced that it would be many years ". . . before cultural differences will have so far disappeared that all minorities . . . will be able to identify themselves with labor." [42]

Whatever one's estimate of the accuracy of Young's prediction in the light of the subsequent history of unionization in this country, the tensions he and the other authors described make it clear that ethnic loyalty rather than loyalty to an economic class remained a referent point for many people for a considerable period. As Anderson noted in Burlington in 1938, the French-Canadian did not like the Italian, the Italian distrusted the Greek, and the Greek was suspicious of the Jew. "All of these emotions cut through the common concerns of the working class itself." [43]

## RETENTION OF ETHNIC TIES

As the children of immigrants grew up and sometimes moved into the higher income groups during the 1930's and '40's, many retained their ethnic ties. Studies of marriage trends during this period indicated clearly how strong these ties were. Wessel, in her survey of Woonsocket,

Rhode Island, in 1931, found that only 8.4 percent of the second-generation Italians and 7.2 percent of the Slavs had married outside their own groups. With reference to the latter, she also pointed out that these intermarriages were almost all with other Slavic groups. For the Italians this figure represented only a slight increase (1.3 percent) over intermarriage by first-generation Italians. The Slavic figure was the same for both generations.[44]

In 1940 in Derby, Connecticut, Barron noted that the Italians intermarried at a higher rate than in 1929–30, but they continued to have the highest in-marriage rate of all the four large groups in 1940.[45] The percentage of intermarriages for Poles actually declined from forty-four per one hundred in 1929–30 to thirty-six per one hundred in 1940.[46] As for the Czechs and Slovaks:

> The overall record for both groups is an equal distribution between in- and intermarriage, remarkable for its reflection of the relatively strong in-marriage tendencies of a group handicapped by small size.[47]

Bossard, in his 1939 study of 68,000 marriages in New York State (exclusive of New York City), found that as a whole, second-generation Americans tended toward in-marriages about as much as the first generation. This was more pronounced among Italians, Poles, and Russians. Three-quarters of the second-generation Italians, for example, picked mates from their own nationality group.[48] Of 885 marriages representing ten ethnic groups in Wright County, Minnesota, over two-thirds of the husbands and wives were of the same nationality group.[49] Of all the marriages in which Italians participated in New Haven, Connecticut, in 1940, 85.5 percent were in-marriages. Kennedy, on the basis of her studies here, came to believe in the possibility of the development of segregated communities based on ethnic, racial, and religious characteristics throughout the country.[50] It should be added that of the persons studied in New York State in 1939, native-born whites of native parents were the most endogamous of all (72 percent for men and 70 percent for women), which means that those of foreign stock had few chances to marry native-born persons of native parentage. There was a block from outside as well as a pull from within the group in the case of ethnic endogamy.

Brown and Roucek, as late as 1946, in discussing the three phases of assimilation—(1) the economic or technological, (2) the cultural, i.e., the discarding of old cultural traits and the acquisition of new ones, and (3) intermarriage—wrote: "While there is occurring among children of immigrants a shift from parental to native occupations, assimilation has a long way to go in the other two phases."[51]

## CONCLUSION

The general tendency is to consider the phenomena described in this paper only casually or to suggest they have meaning in only a few special areas of American life. Many of us would concede, for example, that there is still frequently block voting by "nationality" in urban areas. Ethnicity, however, is expressed and reflected in much more than block voting by nationality groups. As Danzig pointed out:

> The truth is, . . . that the economic structure of the nation has been no less strongly influenced by ethnic factors than political ones. Wherever we look—whether at heavy industry or dairy farming, public utilities or banking, the building or the garment trades, organized crime or law enforcement— we find clearly marked ethnic patterns of occupational opportunities. Though these patterns have been breaking down in recent decades, in many of the older industries and vocations it still makes a difference whether one's fore- bears came from Ireland or Italy or whether one's first name or last name is Milton.[52]

The Negro-white situation aside, ethnic tensions persist in America and ethnic awareness continues to play a prominent part in the self-perception of those who grow up in our country. As the Sherifs point out:

> When the child goes to school he sees the lines of cleavage forming in his age-mate groups. By the time he reaches high school, he finds that by and large the members of ethnic groups high on the scale are clustered in social groupings which [may] exclude him. . . . It comes as no surprise to find that his identification as a member of a particular ethnic or religious group becomes such a central and sensitive part of his self-conception.[53]

It is not amiss, incidentally, to remember that the hierarchy of ethnic groups the Sherifs describe until recently found a kind of legal expression in the archaic National Origins Act under which immigrants entered the United States. The psychological impact of this on Americans whose fellow ethnic group members were variously treated by this act and who themselves were tacitly branded as inferior by its provisions is little discussed. Buried though this impact may have been, however, it forms an important part of the social reality to which all Americans have to relate.

Ethnic origins and divisions in our society strongly affect the views persons hold toward themselves and others and condition many of the behavioral choices they make as family members, producers, citizens, clients, and patients. The interest of social workers in these origins and divisions has tended to lag. This paper has sought to reawaken such interest by presenting a segment of the history of interethnic relations in the United States. In putting the "social" back into social work, attention is now being given to class structure and class tensions. No less important to this enterprise is an understanding of the ethnic patterns and conflicts outlined in this paper. Hopefully, the perceptive social worker will give them more than passing notice.

## NOTES AND REFERENCES

1. For an extensive discussion of the concept of class, which covers conflicting sociological theories about how it is to be defined and understood as well as an attempt to distinguish social class from economic class, see R. M. MacIver and Charles H. Page, Society (New York: Holt, Rinehart & Winston, 1949), chap. 9.

2. Horace Kallen, Culture and Democracy in the United States (New York: Boni and Liverwright, 1924), p. 96.

3. Marcus Hansen, "Family Structure and Ethnic Patterns," Introduction, in Herman D. Stein and Richard A. Cloward, eds., Social Perspectives on Behavior (Glencoe, Ill.: Free Press, 1958), p. 4.

4. Alfred A. Messer, MD, "Ethnocultural Identity and Mental Health," Social Work Practice, 1963 (New York: Columbia University Press, 1963), p. 142.

5. Stein and Cloward, op. cit., p. 5.

6. John Spiegel, "Some Cultural Aspects of Transference and Countertransference," in M. N. Zald, ed., Social Welfare Institutions (New York: John Wiley & Sons, 1965), pp. 576, 593.

7. Among the few articles that are exceptions to this statement are Peter Sandi, "The Psychocultural Approach in Social Casework," Journal of Social Casework, Vol. 28, No. 10 (December 1947), pp. 377–381; Otto Pollak, "Cultural Dynamics in Casework," and William V. Gioseffi, "Culture as an Aspect of the Total Personality," Social Casework, Vol. 34, No. 7 (July 1953), pp. 279–284, and Vol. 40, No. 3 (March 1959), pp. 115–118, respectively; and Henry Maas, "Culture and Psychopathology," Mental Hygiene, Vol. 41, No. 3 (July 1957), pp. 408–414.

8. Muzafer Sherif and Carolyn Sherif, "Psychological Harmony and Conflict in Minority Group Ties," American Catholic Sociological Review, Vol. 22, No. 3 (Fall 1961), pp. 213–214.

9. Frances Fox Piven and Richard A. Cloward, "The Case Against Urban Desegregation," Social Work, Vol. 12, No. 1 (January 1967), p. 20.

10. Ibid., p. 21.

11. Frances Fox Piven and Richard A. Cloward, "Separatism Versus Integration: A Rejoinder," Points and Viewpoints, Social Work, Vol. 12, No. 3 (July 1967), p. 111.

12. David Danzig, "In Defense of 'Black Power,'" Commentary, Vol. 42, No. 3 (September 1966), p. 46.

13. Howard M. Jones, Ideas in America (Cambridge, Mass.: Harvard University Press, 1944), pp. 214–215.

14. E. L. Anderson, We Americans (Cambridge, Mass.: Harvard University Press, 1938), p. 182.

15.  Frank J. Warne, *The Immigrant Invasion* (New York: Dodd, Meade & Co., 1913), p. 150.

16.  Herbert Lahne, *The Cotton Mill Worker* (New York: Farrar & Rinehart, 1944), p. 74.

17.  Warne, *op. cit.*, p. 184.

18.  *Ibid.*, p. 246.

19.  Donald R. Young, *American Minority Peoples* (New York: Harper & Bros., 1932), p. 417.

20.  Lahne, *op. cit.*, p. 248.

21.  Jerome Davis, *The Russian Immigrant* (New York: Macmillan Co., 1922), p. 39.

22.  Herman Feldman, *Racial Factors in American Industry* (New York: Harper & Bros., 1930), p. 221.

23.  *Ibid.*, p. 142.

24.  *Abstracts of the Reports of the Immigration Commission*, Vol. 1 (Washington, D.C.: U.S. Government Printing Office, 1911), p. 501.

25.  *Ibid.*, p. 502.

26.  J. R. Commons, *Races and Immigrants in America* (New York: Macmillan Co., 1907), pp. 10–11.

27.  Warne, *op. cit.*, pp. 138–139.

28.  Isaac Hourwich, *Immigration and Labor* (New York: G. P. Putnam's Sons, 1912), p. 43, *n.* 1.

29.  Peter Roberts, "The Slavs in the Anthracite Coal Mines," *Charities*, Vol. 13, No. 10 (1904–05), p. 216.

30.  Feldman, *op. cit.*, p. 156.

31.  *Ibid.*, p. 148. "Hunkies" was an epithet that referred to all people of Slavic or Magyar extraction.

32.  *See*, for example, K. D. Miller, *The Czechoslovaks in America* (New York: G. H. Doran Co., 1922), p. 73; Joseph S. Roucek, *Poles in the U.S.A.* (Gdynia, Poland: Baltic Institute, 1937), p. 11; Konrad Bercovici, *On New Shores* (New York: Century Co., 1925), p. 396.

33.  As quoted in Robert Park, *Old World Traits Transplanted* (New York: Harper & Bros., 1921), p. 240.

34.  In 1922, for example, 6 percent of Polish-Americans were in trades, 4 percent in domestic service, and the remainder in unskilled labor. *See* Paul Fox, *The Poles in America* (New York: G. H. Doran Co., 1922), p. 69.

35.  Centennial Committee, *Poles of Chicago* (Chicago: Polish Pageant Committee, 1937, pp. 166–167.

36.  Edward Steiner, *On the Trail of the Immigrant* (New York: Fleming H. Revelle Co., 1906), p. 204. The following description by Shannon of Irish-French-Canadian relations is also noted here to keep the religious variable in perspective. He notes that just as a common allegiance to Catholicism was no guarantee of amity between the Poles and Lithuanians, it proved no bond between the French-Canadians and Irish. The latter were ". . . notoriously unsuccessful, for example, in coming to terms with French-Canadians in the New England mill towns. The French-Canadians regularly favored the Republicans largely because the Irish were Democrats (until the coming of the depression and the New Deal revolutionized politics in the 1930's)." William V. Shannon, *The American Irish* (New York: Macmillan Co., 1963), p. 137.

37.  W. Z. Ripley, "Race Factors in Labor Unions," *Atlantic Monthly*, Vol. 94, No. 57 (March 1904), p. 301.

38.  *Ibid.*

39.  William Leiserson, *Adjusting Immigrants to Industry* (New York: Harper & Bros., 1924), p. 92.

40.  Kate H. Claghorn, "Slavs, Magyars, and Some Others in the New Immigration," *Charities*, Vol. 13, No. 10 (1904–05), p. 205.

41.  Konrad Bercovici, *Around the World in New York* (New York: Century Co., 1922), p. 396.

42.  Young, *op. cit.*, p. 138.

43.  Anderson, *op. cit.*, p. 63.

44.  B. B. Wessel, *An Ethnic Survey of Woonsocket, R.I.* (Chicago: University of Chicago Press, 1931), p. 108.

45.  M. L. Barron, *People Who Intermarry* (Syracuse, N.Y.: Syracuse University Press, 1946), p. 129.

46.  *Ibid.*, p. 140.

47.  *Ibid.*, p. 149.

48.  J. H. Bossard, "Nationality and Nativity as Factors in Intermarriage," *American Sociological Review*, Vol. 4, No. 6 (December 1939), p. 792.

49.  Lowry Nelson, "Intermarriage Among Nationality Groups in a Rural Area in Minnesota," *American Journal of Sociology*, Vol. 38, No. 4 (March 1943), p. 588.

50.  R. J. R. Kennedy, "Premarital Residential Propinquity and Ethnic Endogamy," *American Journal of Sociology*, Vol. 38, No. 4 (March 1943), p. 584.

51.  Francis J. Brown and Joseph S. Roucek, *One America* (Englewood Cliffs, N.J.: Prentice-Hall, 1946), p. 481.

52.  David Danzig, "The Meaning of Negro Strategy," *Commentary*, Vol. 37, No. 2 (February 1964), p. 43.

53.  Sherif and Sherif, *op. cit.*, p. 222.

# 5

# The Native-Settler Concept: Implications for Community Organization

## PAUL A. KURZMAN

THOSE COMMUNITY ORGANIZATION practitioners who have worked with low-income Negroes in the Deep South or with recent southern immigrants to the large urban ghettos of the North have begun to recognize an organizational problem and to search for a solution. The problem, especially acute in the South, is that the brand of militant confrontation that has been so successful for whites and northern Negroes does not seem to be as comfortable a pattern of response for Negroes today in the South. It was not by chance that Martin Luther King chose the technique of passive resistance, just as Gandhi deliberately used it in India's confrontation with the British. Yet with all of the apparent gains that King wrought in Birmingham and Atlanta, for example, one does not have to be in these cities long to see that in everyday life the essential plight of the southern Negro has not been improved substantially. While, for example, there is nominal integration of the police

Reprinted from *Social Work*, 14 (July 1969), pp. 58–64. PAUL A. KURZMAN, formerly staff associate, Two Bridges Neighborhood Council, and senior community organizer, Lower Eastside Neighborhood Association, New York, New York, was a doctoral student at the time of writing.

and fire departments in a city as relatively liberal as Atlanta, this is mere tokenism and does not represent equality throughout these departments even by northern standards.

The statistics are there to be read. By June 1968 only 14 percent of Negro students in the eleven Deep South states were attending integrated classes. This means that fourteen years after the 1954 Supreme Court decision, approximately 86 percent of Negro pupils in the South were still in segregated schools.[1] Although they represent almost 12 percent of the national population, Negroes have been unable to elect even one person to the hundred-member U.S. Senate (Senator Edward Brooke of Massachusetts was elected from a state with a 97.5 percent white population, and he made it clear that he would not be representing the Negro cause.) Since Reconstruction not one member of the national legislature from the eleven Deep South states has been Negro. In 1967 the legislative body stripped Adam Clayton Powell (the only Negro legislator ever to achieve a committee chairmanship) of a post it had taken his ghettoed constituents twenty years to acquire. A bitter black community watched as a white congressman, guilty of far more serious charges, was reluctantly chided after an "investigation" in which much damaging evidence was withheld.[2] Well-meaning Americans habitually apply an irrational double standard when they ponder Negroes or racial problems. Says Negro psychiatrist Alvin F. Poussaint:

> This is not surprising, since Americans come from a heritage in which signers of the Declaration of Independence that avowed "all men are created equal" were in fact slave owners, and few white citizens saw the contradiction.[3]

## NATIVE-SETTLER RELATIONSHIP

What has happened, then, is that conditions today in the segregated urban ghettos and in most of the Deep South resemble *apartheid*. As in the Union of South Africa, the relationships between blacks and whites are carefully governed, if not by law, by long-standing sets of informally maintained traditions. In the absence of strong federal laws and firm enforcement, the weight of tradition is frequently as strong as the weight of the law.

There are basically two types of people, the ins and the outs, or, in the words of Negro psychoanalyst Frantz Fanon, the settler and the native.[4] Fanon, in a study of the revolution in North Africa that won independence for Algeria a few years ago, emphasizes the native-settler relationship as a key to understanding the perpetuation of colonialism in Algerian society.[5] He goes on to indicate why he feels it was the native's ability to break the bonds of this relationship that permitted him to revolt successfully and establish self-government and independence.

If we are willing for a moment to admit that there are some parallels between the condition of the Negro in the Deep South today and the slave-master relationship of colonial Africa (and indeed of America before the Emancipation Proclamation), we may find Fanon's ideas relevant to an understanding of the difficulty southern Negroes experience in trying to break free. In light of the conditions in the South today that have just been outlined and the Negro's long history of slavery and quasi-servitude prior to the civil rights movement of this decade, there would seem to be reason to explore the parallel further. Even in 1969, for the majority of whites and blacks in the South a double standard exists, and the native-settler relationship continues to dominate the informal structure known as the "southern way of life."

In brief, Fanon says that there are certain bonds that tie the ins and the outs, the settler and the native: First, is a symbiotic need for each other. While it is easy to see why the native is dependent on the settler, it must not be forgotten that dependency works both ways.[6] A second relationship is charity: the settlers' desire to keep the natives "off the streets," to make them the "invisible poor." [7] The third and most important link between the two is that of force—of violence, if you will. As Gunnar Myrdal perceptively notes, the principal point of contact between the two is the police, who through violence or—equally effective—the threat of violence maintain the status quo and keep the relationship stable and intact.[8]


## THE NEGEYA BOND

From years of living this way the native learns to adapt in order to minimize punishment and maximize pleasure. He comes to see himself as he is seen by others.[9] He is bound by what the Vietnamese term the *"Negeya* [neg-ee'ya] bond." Briefly, this means that in order to explain his own condition, the native sees the settler as "having the will of God." The will of God is preordained and therefore is not to be disturbed. In a primitive society that is tradition bound, such conclusions are common.

Even a brief visitor to the Deep South will be struck by the parallel. Today, as in the past, tradition plays a strong part in the Negro's (the native's) way of life. Superstitions are rampant and religion plays a dominant role in explaining phenomena from poor health to poor roads. Every meeting, no matter how small, opens with a long series of emotional prayers. If the settler (the white) has given the native something extra for his bale of cotton, that he chose to do so is attributed to "the will of God."

Traditional patterns are strong. All whites, even civil rights workers who have worked side by side with Negroes for more than a year, are "Mr. Ted" or "Miss Barbara." If the white worker makes a suggestion, it is right; for most Negroes no further effort to explore the idea more deeply seems necessary. In politics, while Negro candidates are being elected in northern cities (where the "traditional" orientation and *Negeya* bond do not prevail), Negro candidates in most southern counties—even with black voting majorities—are defeated. For example, in November 1967 a well-qualified Negro candidate, Lofton Mason, ran for the office of beat supervisor in Beat 2 of Jackson, Mississippi—an area in which Negroes represented 80 percent of the population and 70 percent of the registered voters—and lost.[10] (Long before the election an experienced local observer predicted privately to the author that Mason would lose.[11]) The opposing white candidate, although poorly qualified, had "the will of God." As one life-long Negro resident of Beat 2 said, "Running a beat—that's white man's work."

Yet on that same Election Day Negroes Richard Hatcher and Carl Stokes won the mayoralties of Gary, Indiana, and Cleveland, Ohio. In Gary, Negro precincts supported Hatcher with 76 percent of their votes; in Cleveland, Stokes received an estimated 94.5 percent of the Negro votes cast.[12] In the nominally integrated northern city, where the native-settler relationship no longer prevails, the *Negeya* bond has long since been broken, and somehow the white candidates no longer have the will of God.

## BREAKING THE BOND

The important question for community organization is how the bond between native and settler in the Deep South can be broken. How can southern Negroes achieve the personal freedom from traditional bonds and superstitions that can make democracy work for them today in the South? As a starting point, let us look to Frantz Fanon, and see what his thinking has been.

At the risk of oversimplification, Fanon feels that the crippling relationship of native and settler can only be destroyed by violence, because this has been the principal point of contact between the two. Fanon feels that the catharsis of absolute violence by the natives against their colonial oppressors will liberate the former from the bond of the *Negeya:*

The native cures himself of colonial neurosis by thrusting out the settler through force of arms. . . . When the peasant takes a gun in his hands, the old myths grow dim and the prohibitions are one by one forgotten. . . . To shoot down a European is to kill two birds with one stone, to destroy an oppressor and the man he oppresses at the same time: there remains a dead man, and a free man; the survivor, for the first time, feels a national soil under his foot.[13]

Fanon tells the story of the native rebel preparing to overthrow his oppressive master, against cautions from his mother, who is bound by centuries of tradition. In a verse from the French poet Aimé Cèsaire, the rebel approaches the house where the master is smoking a pipe in the library, surrounded by his trappings. The rebel is mesmerized by tradition for moments, then enters and, to the settler's surprise, plunges the knife decisively:

It was I, even I, and I told him so, the good slave, the faithful slave, the slave of slaves, . . . and I struck, and the blood spurted; that is the only baptism that I can remember today.[14]

"That's when I was born," he cries, "that's when I became a man." [15]

## NONVIOLENT CONFRONTATION

Fanon, Styron, and the poet Cèsaire all comment on the same general phenomenon, which in psychiatric terms might be referred to as identification with the oppressor or turning against the self.[16] The natives have indeed been brainwashed or programmed into a way of life that assures their subservience to the settler, whom they see as somehow possesing the will of God. The relationship that traditionally binds native and settler to one another perpetuates the subservience of the native until, through a supreme act of confrontation and violence, he breaks this *Negeya* bond and emerges as a man.

In so doing, the native is released from his traditional position or is, in effect, liberated and "deprogrammed." Blacks then no longer tone down their own aspirations or accept the inferiority attributed to them by the settler.

As Preston R. Wilcox has observed, Martin Luther King moved the natives toward freedom bestowed by the settler, but Malcolm X moved them toward liberation from a reliance on white sanctions. One can be technically "free" but not liberated; a liberated man is de facto free. Liberation is self-defined, self-bestowed, and self-earned.[17] Malcolm X, Stokely Carmichael, and Ron Karenga are all "deprogrammers," who stress the need for the natives to confront the settlers and to win their freedom—in all probability through an act of violence.[18]

The first requisite for the community organization worker among natives and settlers, then, is to recognize the existence of the *Negeya* bond and to see how it might be broken. The most pressing question is whether these bonds can truly be severed without the violence Fanon describes—and some contemporary civil rights organizers recommend.

Since we are not willing to advocate riots and violence, yet recognize the seriousness of the *Negeya* phenomenon, it is suggested that an attempt be made to recreate the native-settler encounter through non-violent acts of confrontation. There appear to be three possible stages of confrontation: (1) At the earliest level, the role of the professional community organization practitioner would be as actor-teacher, actually carrying out the symbolic confrontation in the presence of the native and on his behalf. (2) At the second level, the native himself would enact the confrontation, with the presence and active support of the worker, functioning as catalyst-team member. (3) Finally, the participating native, having begun to achieve a psychological breakthrough, would confront the settler directly, with the community organization worker in the background role of advocate-observer.[19] Although there would have to be a gradual process involved in progression from the first to the third stage, the writer believes that *the* Negeya *bond would not effectively be broken until the final stage had been reached and the act had been repeated by various natives with different settlers in a variety of settings.*

The confrontations, furthermore, must be personal, subjectively meaningful, symbolic acts of defiance. They must take place in a small group, and the native must get a sense of individual involvement. The leader must feel that he, with his fellow natives, is symbolically "plunging the knife." Further, for positive reinforcement, the confrontation must be perceived as successful and catch the settler on his own grounds.

## THE MISSISSIPPI EXPERIENCE

Staff and volunteers with the Michael Schwerner Memorial Fund experimented with this on all levels in the summer of 1967, with some noteworthy results.[20] On the earliest level, a professional organizer from the Schwerner Fund confronted an untrained racist welfare worker at a local social agency *in the presence and on behalf of a client.* The worker was so upset that she visibly shook, spoke openly like a racist, and was shattered when made to look foolish and incompetent by the organizer. The client looked on with silent satisfaction as the knife was effectively plunged and the worker squirmed in helpless exposure. Later the client could speak of nothing else for hours, and said, "I can take care of her next time—she's nothing but a nasty old woman."

Other examples of Stage 1 activity include the project co-ordinator's confrontations with welfare department supervisors at fair hearings. In the presence of the client and on her behalf, Schwerner Fund staff have made local welfare workers appear as foolish, inept, and arbitrary as so many of them are. Despite the quasi-judicial setting, the staff worker in almost every hearing has been able to create a cathartic confrontation, leaving the punitive hearing officers feeling helpless and breaking down the effectiveness of the *Negeya* bond. Some clients later took the staff worker's role in fair hearings on behalf of their fellow clients, thereby moving on to a Stage 2 confrontation.

In Stage 2 the natives act, but in the presence of and with the support of the organizer. One example in the 1967 summer experience was the integration of the bathrooms in a rural county courthouse. The clients, all Negro, resented having to use segregated toilets; they wanted to use the staff facilities, which were for whites only. With some trepidation, *but in the presence of and with the support of the organizer,* they went one by one to the staff bathroom, sustaining stares of disbelief from the whites present.

Examples of Stage 3 activities are much rarer in the Deep South, for this is why the *Negeya* bond has not yet been broken. There are a few new leaders emerging who have experienced or are ready to experience such symbolic confrontations. Most are young and frequently veterans of the civil rights activity of 1963–64; a few are products of the training and community development process that has been encouraged by such groups in Mississippi as the Freedom Democratic Party, Child Development Group of Mississippi, Michael Schwerner Memorial Fund, and the Delta Ministry.

## SIGNIFICANCE FOR THEORY AND PRACTICE

The process of placing the theory into a conceptual framework, which must effectively precede its systematic practice, has only begun. The experiences of Fanon in the Algerian revolution of the 1950's, of the slave rebellions in the South in the 1800's, and of black militants in the civil rights struggle in the 1960's now must be woven together and distilled for their significance to community organization theory and practice.

Several values would appear to accrue from achieving an understanding of the concept of the native and settler, apart from a much-needed refinement of its broader applicability.

1. It may provide an increased understanding of riots and other forms of ghetto violence. It is not hard to understand why Black Power advocates encourage the use of the "knife-plunging" technique on a mass scale: they are not only eager to gain attention for their demands; they also recognize the cathartic value of the experience of confrontation. In the long run, the value of the catharsis outweighs the wrath of the press, public officials, or the Congress—who represent settlers in the overall scheme.

2. It is equally easy to explain why riots and similar acts of violence are more common in northern ghettos than in the Deep South. Where the *Negeya* bond is strongest, the native-settler relationship will be most firmly established, and the tradition of *apartheid* and segregation in the Deep South effectively perpetuates the myth that the white man has the will of God.

3. Most workers among low-income Negroes who are first-generation migrants from the South will find the *Negeya* bond still present, albeit in a subtler form. The bond is not easily broken, even by moving north, except through confrontation. Most practitioners in the black ghetto can cite numerous examples of their struggle with this elusive phenomenon; the subtlety of its appearance in a more liberal northern setting can make it in many ways more difficult to handle there.

4. Most important of all is the possibility of using the cathartic confrontation on all three stages as a deliberate community organization strategy. As a first step, it would be well to recognize that in all-black areas, especially those closest to southern patterns of segregation and bondage, there are special and discrete phenomena to which the trained worker must be sensitized. There are special community organization tools to be added to his generic equipment. While one could argue that the use of a black organizer might speed the progress from Stage 1 to Stage 3 involvement, this has not as yet been proved. One can say, however, that the situation provides a special challenge for any worker, who must also have the willingness and ability to work within the limits of the native-settler model.

It is possible that further practice refinement of the concept may add to the growing literature of community organization theory. Hoffman's theory of the "single-purpose leader," Minnis's power structure research, Whitaker's "divide-and-conquer" concept, Wilcox's "deprogramming tool" and theory of "functional anger," and Seaver's "professional Mau

Mau" are recent steps in the direction of building a new community organization theory out of practice experience.[21] It is hoped that the native-settler concept will provide still another contribution to the charting of social work theory.

## NOTES AND REFERENCES

1.  Marjorie Hunter, "A Lag in Schools of South Decried," *New York Times*, October 16, 1968, p. 19. These figures were compiled by the U.S. Department of Health, Education, and Welfare.

2.  Ernest Dunbar, "Memo from the Ghetto: The Dispirit of '67," *Look*, September 19, 1967, p. 92.

3.  "The White Press Distorts Race News," *New York Times*, November 12, 1967, sect. IV.

4.  Fanon uses the terms settler and native to connote the oppressor and the oppressed. Rather than adhering to a historical definition, Fanon is concerned (as the writer is) with the psychological dynamics that seem to govern the relationship between settlers and natives—i.e., master and servant, oppressor and oppressed.

5.  Frantz Fanon, *The Wretched of the Earth* (New York: Grove Press, 1966).

6.  Douglas Turner Ward's powerful play, *A Day of Absence*, told of the dependence of the settler on the native in a way few had the courage to recognize before. Ward portrayed the helplessness of southern whites on a day when all local Negroes left town, including a poignant satire of a white woman who suddenly realized she did not know how to cook or to care for her children, because she had never before had to do these things.

7.  Michael Harrington, *The Other America* (New York: Macmillan Co., 1962).

8.  *An American Dilemma: The Negro Problem and Modern Democracy* (New York: Harper & Row, 1962), p. 535.

9.  *See* "the self-fulfilling prophecy" in Robert K. Merton, *Social Theory and Social Structure* (Glencoe, Ill.: Free Press, 1957); and a more specific application in Thomas F. Pettigrew, *A Profile of the Negro American* (Princeton, N.J.: D. Van Nostrand Co., 1964).

10.  In Mississippi, counties are run essentially by a series of supervisors, each elected from a "beat," or district, of which they will be in charge. They have a great deal of power: They set the county taxes, hear appeals from the county tax assessor, decide on the boundaries of the voting districts in county elections, hire the county police, and control expenditure of public moneys for everything from building roads to welfare. *See A Political Handbook for the Black People of Jackson County* (Tougaloo, Miss.: Freedom Information Service, 1967), p. 5.

11.  Ted Seaver, former co-ordinator of the Schwerner Fund operation in Mississippi, made this observation, which proved on Election Day to be perfectly correct. The author is indebted to Mr. Seaver for his many valuable observations on this paper and for his analysis of the significance of Fanon's concept and its nonviolent application through the symbolic act.

12.  Anthony Ripley and Donald Janson, "Stokes Picks White Aides; Hatcher Victory Certified," *New York Times*, November 9, 1967, p. 33.

13.  *Op. cit.*, pp. 18–19.

14.  Aimé Cèsaire, "*Les Armes Miraculeuses*," in Fanon, *op. cit.*, pp. 67–69.

15. Fanon is not the only writer to tell of this "plunge-the-knife" phenomenon. William C. Styron, in his controversial *Confessions of Nat Turner* (New York: Random House, 1967), refers to the reaction of the formerly docile servant Hark after slaying his master: "A servant of servants was Hark no more; he had tasted blood."

While Styron's fictional account varies liberally from the text of Turner's *Confessions,* even Styron's critics do not appear to question the cathartic quality of these violent confrontations. *See* John H. Clarke, ed., *William Styron's Nat Turner: Ten Black Writers Respond* (Boston: Beacon Press, 1968).

16. *See* Charles Brenner, *An Elementary Textbook of Psychoanalysis* (Garden City, N.Y.: Doubleday & Co., 1955), p. 103; and Sigmund Freud, *Civilization and Its Discontents* (Garden City, N.Y.: Doubleday & Co., 1958), chap. VII. *See also* the application of this psychiatric concept to the Negro question in Robert W. Friedrichs, "Interpretation of Black Aggression," *Yale Review,* Vol. 57, No. 3 (Spring 1968), pp. 358–374.

17. "So You Want To Be Black," *Black Caucus,* journal of the Association of Black Social Workers, Vol. 1, No. 1 (Fall 1968), p. 34. The author is grateful to Mr. Wilcox for his thoughtful and perceptive suggestions on this paper.

18. *See* Malcolm X and Alex Haley, *The Autobiography of Malcolm X* (New York: Grove Press, 1966); Stokely Carmichael and C. V. Hamilton, *Black Power* (New York: Random House, 1967): and Ron Karenga, *The Quotable Karenga* (Los Angeles: US Organization, 1967).

19. In moving through the three stages of confrontation, the ultimate goal would be to free the client of any need for or dependence on the worker. It should be understood, however, that this process probably would be gradual and require an ongoing social work assessment. In this regard, the new roles of actor-teacher, catalyst-team member, and advocate-observer may prove quite demanding on both the professional and adaptational skills of the worker.

20. The Michael Schwerner Memorial Fund was established shortly after the death of Schwerner in 1964. A social worker, Schwerner was one of three young men who lost their lives in the fulfillment of their duties as civil rights workers in the summer voter registration project in Mississippi. One purpose of the fund is to provide social work services on behalf of civil rights in southern communities.

21. *See* Nicholas von Hoffman, *Finding and Making Leaders* (Nashville: Southern Student Organizing Committee, 1968)· Jack Minnis, "The Care and Feeding of Power Structures," *New University Thought,* Vol. 4, No. 1 (Summer 1964), pp. 73–79. William Whitaker, *In the Lions' Den* (Columbus, Ohio: Welfare Rights Organization, 1967); Wilcox, *op. cit.,* pp. 32–36; Wilcox, "Is Integration Relevant?" *Renewal* (August 1966), pp. 3–4; Ted Seaver, *The Care and Feeding of Southern Welfare Departments* (Washington, D.C.: Poverty/Rights Action Center, 1966).

# 6

# The Sane Slave

## An Historical Note on the Use of Medical Diagnosis as Justificatory Rhetoric

## THOMAS S. SZASZ

I

THE PASSION TO DEHUMANIZE and diminish man, as well as to super-humanize and glorify him, appears to be a characteristic of human nature. For millennia, the dialectic of vilification and deification and, more generally, of invalidation and validation—excluding the individual from the group as an evil outsider or including him in it as a member in good standing—was cast in the imagery and rhetoric of magic and religion. Thus, at the height of Christianity in Europe, only the faithful were considered human: the faithless—heretics, witches, and Jews—were considered subhuman or nonhuman and were so treated. At the same time, the popes were thought to be infallible and kings ruled by divine decree.

With the decline of the religious world view, and the ascendancy of

Reprinted, with permission, from *American Journal of Psychotherapy*, 25 (April 1971), pp. 228–239. THOMAS S. SZASZ was at the time of writing professor of psychiatry, State University of New York, Upstate Medical Center, Syracuse, New York.

the scientific, during the Renaissance and the Enlightenment, the religious rhetoric of validation and invalidation was gradually replaced by the scientific. I have described and documented this transformation in *The Manufacture of Madness*,[1] showing, in particular, the birth, development, and flowering of the lexicon of medical diagnosis as a rhetoric of rejection.

In this essay, my aim is to offer an additional illustration of the foregoing thesis. In May, 1851, an essay entitled "Report on the Diseases and Physical Peculiarities of the Negro Race," written by Samuel A. Cartwright, M.D., was published in the then prestigious *New Orleans Medical and Surgical Journal*.[2] In this remarkable document, Dr. Cartwright asserted—not only in his own name but also in his capacity as chairman of a committee appointment by the Medical Association of Louisiana to report on the "diseases and peculiarities of the Negro race"—that Negroes are biologically inferior to whites, and sought to justify their enslavement as a therapeutic necessity for the slaves and a medical responsibility for the masters. In support of this thesis, Dr. Cartwright claimed to identify two new diseases peculiar to Negroes: one, which he called "drapetomania," was manifested by the escape of the Negro slave from his white master; the other, which he called "dysaesthesia Aethiopis," was manifested by the Negro's neglecting his work or refusing to work altogether.

## II

I consider Cartwright's "Report," and especially the two diseases afflicting the Negro that he discovered, of special interest and importance to us today for the following reasons: first, because Cartwright invoked the authority and vocabulary of medical science to dehumanize the Negro and justify his enslavement by the white man; second, because the language and reasoning he used to justify the coercive control of the Negro are identical to those used today by mental health propagandists to justify the coercive control of the madman (that is, the so-called "psychotic," "addict," "sexual psychopath," and so forth); and third, because Cartwright's "Report" is the sort of medical document that has, for obvious reasons, been systematically ignored or suppressed in standard texts on medical and psychiatric history.

One such omission, discussed in detail in *The Manufacture of Madness*, is Benjamin Rush's theory of Negritude, according to which the black skin and other physical "peculiarities" of the Negro are due to his suffering from congenital leprosy (1, pp. 153–159). This grotesquely self-serving explanation—which postulated white as the only "healthy" human skin color, and defined the normal physiologic state of the Negro as a dreadful disease, justifying his segregation for reasons of alleged ill health rather than imputed racial inferiority—was, moreover, merely a part of Rush's medical world-view in which all types of undesired human characteristics and conduct were considered diseases—usually of the mind. Thus by the time the "Report on the Diseases and Physical Peculiarities of the Negro Race" appeared, the habit, especially among medical men, of passionately degrading their adversaries as sick, while pretending to be impartially "diagnosing" them, was well established. It is against this general background, and the steadily increasing influence of the abolitionist forces in the United States at that time, that we must consider the Cartwright "Report."

I shall reproduce below excerpts from the "Report" describing drapetomania and dysaesthesia Aethiopis, and shall then offer some comments on them.

### Drapetomania, or the Disease Causing Slaves to Run Away

Drapetomania is from *"drapetes,"* a runaway slave, and *"mania,"* mad or crazy. It is unknown to our medical authorities, although its diagnostic symptom, the absconding from service, is well known to our planters and overseers, as it was to the ancient Greeks, who expressed by the single word *"drapetes"* the fact of the absconding, and the relation that the fugitive held to the person he fled from. I have added to the word meaning runaway slave, another Greek term, to express the disease of the mind causing him to abscond. In noticing a disease not heretofore classed among the long list of maladies that man is subject to, it was necessary to have a new term to express it. The cause, in the most of cases, that induces the negro to run away from service, is as much a disease of the mind as any other species of mental alienation, and much more curable, as a general rule. With the advantages of proper medical advice, strictly followed, this troublesome practice that many negroes have of running away, can be almost entirely prevented, although the slaves be located on the borders of a free State, within a stone's throw of the abolitionists. . . .

To ascertain the true method of governing negroes, so as to cure and prevent the disease under consideration, we must go back to the Pentateuch, and learn the true meaning of the untranslated term that represents the negro race. In the name there given to that race, is locked up the true art of governing negroes in such a manner that they cannot run away. The correct translation of that term declares the Creator's will in regard to the negro; it declares him to be the submissive knee-bender. In the anatomical conformation of his knees, we see *"genu flexit"* written in the physical structure of his knees, being more flexed or bent, than any other kind of man. If the white man attempts to oppose the Deity's will, by trying to make the negro anything else than *"the submissive knee-bender,"* (which the Almighty declared he should be) by trying to raise him to a level with himself, or by putting himself on an equality with the negro; or if he abuses the power which God has given him over his fellow man, by being cruel to him or punishing him in anger, or by neglecting to protect him from the wanton abuses of his fellow-servants and all others, or by denying him the usual comforts and necessities of life, the negro will run away, but if he keeps him in the position that we learn from the Scriptures he was intended to occupy, that is, the position of submission, and if his master or overseer be kind and gracious in his bearing towards him, without condescension, and at the same time ministers to his physical wants and protects him from abuses, the negro is spell-bound, and cannot run away. . . .

Before negroes run away, unless they are frightened or panic-struck, they become sulky and dissatisfied. The cause of this sulkiness and dissatisfaction should be inquired into and removed, or they are apt to run away or fall into the negro consumption. When sulky and dissatisfied without cause, the experience of those on the line and elsewhere was decidedly in favor of whipping them out of it, as a preventive measure against absconding or other bad conduct. It was called whipping the devil out of them.

If treated kindly, well fed and clothed, with fuel enough to keep a small fire burning all night, separated into families, each family having its own house—not permitted to run about at night, or to visit their neighbors, or to receive visits, or to use intoxicating liquors, and not overworked or exposed too much to the weather, they are very easily governed—more so than any other people in the world. When all this is done, if any one or more of them, at any time, are inclined to raise their heads to a level with their master or overseer, humanity and their own good require that they should be punished until they fall into that submissive state which it was intended for them to occupy in all after time, when their progenitor received the name of Canaan, or "submissive knee-bender." They have only to be kept in that state, and treated like children with care, kindness, attention and humanity, to prevent and cure them from running away.

### Dysaesthesia Aethiopis, or Hebetude of Mind and Obtuse Sensibility of Body—A Disease Peculiar to Negroes— Called by Overseers, "Rascality"

Dyaesthesia Aethiopis is a disease peculiar to negroes, affecting both mind and body, in a manner as well expressed by dysaesthesia, the name I have given it, as could be by a single term. There is both mind and sensibility, but both seem to be difficult to reach by impressions from without. There is partial insensibility of the skin, and so great a hebetude of the intellectual faculties as to be like a person half asleep, that is with difficulty aroused and kept awake. It differs from every other species of mental disease, as it is accompanied with physical signs or lesions of the body, discoverable to the medical observer, which are always present and sufficient to account for the symptoms. It is much more prevalent among free negroes living in clusters by themselves, than among slaves on our plantations, and attacks only such slaves as live like free negroes in regard to diet, drinks, exercise, etc. It is not my purpose to treat of the complaint as it prevails among free negroes, nearly all of whom are more or less afflicted with it, that have not got some white person to direct and to take care of them. To narrate its symptoms and effects among them would be to write a history of the ruins and dilapidation of Hayti and every spot of earth they have ever had uncontrolled possession over for any length of time. I propose only to describe its symptoms among slaves.

From the careless movements of the individuals affected with the complaint, they are apt to do much mischief, which appears as if intentional, but is mostly owing to the stupidness of mind and insensibility of the nerves induced by the disease. Thus, they break, waste and destroy everything they handle— abuse horses and cattle—tear, burn or rend their own clothing, and paying no attention to the rights of property, they steal other's to replace what they have destroyed. They wander about at night, and keep in a half-nodding sleep during the day. They slight their work—cut up corn, cane, cotton or tobacco when hoeing it, as if for pure mischief. They raise disturbances with their overseers and fellow servants without cause or motive, and seem to be insensible to pain when subjected to punishment.

The fact of the existence of such a complaint, making man like an auto- maton or senseless machine, having the above or similar symptoms, can be clearly established by the most direct and positive testimony. That it should have escaped the attention of the medical profession, can only be accounted for because its attention has not been sufficiently directed to the maladies of the negro race. Otherwise, a complaint of so common occurrence on badly-governed plantations, and so universal among free negroes, or those who are not governed at all—a disease radicated in physical lesions and having its peculiar and well-marked symptoms, and its curative indications, would not have escaped the notice of the profession. The northern physicians and people have noticed the symptoms, but not the disease from which they spring. They ignorantly attribute the symptoms to the debasing influence of slavery on the mind, without considering that those who have never been in slavery, or their fathers before them, are the most afflicted and the latest from the slave-holding South the least. The disease is the natural offspring of negro liberty—the liberty to be idle, to wallow in filth, and to indulge in improper food and drinks.

In treating of the anatomy and physiology of the negro, I showed that his respiratory system was under the same physiological laws as that of an infant child of the white race; that a warm atmosphere, loaded with carbonic acid and aqueous vapor, was the most congenial to his lungs during sleep, as it is to the infant; that, to insure the respiration of such an atmosphere, he invariably, as if moved by instinct, shrouds his head and face in a blanket or some other covering, when disposing himself to sleep; that if sleeping by the fire in cold weather, he turns his head to it, instead of his feet, evidently to inhale warm air; that when not in active exercise, he always hovers over a fire in comparatively warm weather, as if he took a positive pleasure in inhaling hot air and smoke when his body is quiescent. The natural effect of this practice, it was shown, caused imperfect atmospherization or vitalization of the blood in the lungs, as occurs in infancy, and a hebetude or torpor of intellect—from blood not sufficiently vitalized being distributed to the brain; also, a slothfulness, torpor and disinclination to exercise, from the same cause—the want of blood sufficiently areated or vitalized in the circulating system.

When left to himself, the negro indulges in his natural disposition to idleness and sloth, and does not take exercise enough to expand his lungs and to vitalize his blood, but dozes out a miserable existence in the midst of filth and uncleanliness, being too indolent and having too little energy of mind to provide for himself proper food and comfortable lodging and clothing. The consequence is, that the blood becomes so highly carbonized and deprived of oxygen, that it not only becomes unfit to stimulate the brain to energy, but unfit to stimulate the nerves of sensation distributed to the body. A torpor and insensibility pervades the system; the sentient nerves distributed to the skin lose their feeling to so great a degree, that he often burns his skin by the fire he hovers over, without knowing it, and frequently has large holes in his clothes, and the shoes on his feet burnt to a crisp, without having been conscious of when it was done. This is the disease called dyaesthesia—a Greek term expressing the dull or obtuse sensation that always attends the complaint.

When aroused from his sloth by the stimulus of hunger, he takes anything he can lay his hands on, and tramples on the rights, as well as on the property of others, with perfect indifference as to consequences. When driven to labor by the compulsive power of the white man, he performs the task assigned him in a headlong, careless manner, treading down with his feet, or cutting with his hoe the plants he is put to cultivate—breaking the tools he works with, and spoiling everything he touches that can be injured by careless handling. Hence the overseers call it "rascality," supposing that the mischief is intentionally done. But there is no premeditated mischief in the case—the mind is too torpid to meditate mischief, or even to be aroused by the angry passions to deeds of daring. Dysaethesia, or hebetude of sensation of both mind and body, prevails to so great an extent, that when the unfortunate individual is subjected to punishment, he neither feels pain of any consequence, or shows any unusual resentment, more than by a stupid sulkiness. In some cases, anaesthesiae would be a more suitable name for it, as there appears to be an almost total loss of feeling. The term "rascality," given to this disease by overseers, is founded on an erroneous hypothesis and leads to an incorrect empirical treatment, which seldom or ever cures it.

The complaint is easily curable, if treated on sound physiological principles. The skin is dry, thick and harsh to the touch, and the liver inactive. The liver, skin and kidneys should be stimulated to activity, and be made to assist in decarbonising the blood. The best means to stimulate the skin is, first, to have the patient well washed with warm water and soap; then to anoint it all over with oil, and to slap the oil in with a broad leather strap; then to put the patient to some hard kind of work in the open air and sunshine, that will compel him to expand his lungs, as chopping wood, splitting rails or sawing with the cross-cut or whip saw. Any kind of labor will do that will cause full and free respiration in its performance, as lifting or carrying heavy weights, or brisk walking; the object being to expand the lungs by full and deep inspirations and expirations, thereby to vitalize the impure circulating blood by introducing oxygen and expelling carbon. . . .

Such treatment will, in a short time, effect a cure in all cases which are complicated with chronic visceral derangements. The effect of this or a like course of treatment is often like enchantment. No sooner does the blood feel the vivifying influences derived from its full and perfect atmospherization by exercise in the open air and in the sun, than the negro seems to be awakened to a new existence, and to look grateful and thankful to the white man whose compulsory power, by making him inhale vital air, has restored his sensation and dispelled the mist that clouded his intellect. His intelligence restored and his sensations awakened, he is no longer the *bipedum nequissimus,* or arrant rascal, he was supposed to be, but a good negro that can hoe or plow, and handle things with as much care as his other fellow-servants. . . .

Although idleness is the most prolific cause of dysaethesia, yet there are other ways that the blood gets deteriorated. I said before that negroes are like children, requiring government in everything. . . .

According to unalterable physiological laws, negroes, as a general rule, to which there are but few exceptions, can only have their intellectual faculties awakened in a sufficient degree to receive moral culture, and to profit by religious or other instruction, when under the compulsatory authority of the white man; because, as a general rule, to which there are but few exceptions, they will not take sufficient exercise, when removed from the white man's authority, to vitalize and decarbonize their blood by the process of full and free respiration, that active exercise of some kind alone can effect. A northern climate remedies, in a considerable degree, their naturally indolent disposition; but the dense atmosphere of Boston or Canada can scarcely produce sufficient hematosis and vigor of mind to induce them to labor. From their natural indolence, unless under the stimulus of compulsion, they doze away their lives with the capacity of their lungs for atmospheric air only half expanded, from the want of exercise to superinduce full and deep respiration. The inevitable effect is, to prevent a sufficient atmospherization or vitalization of the blood, so essential to the expansion and the freedom of action of the intellectual faculties. The black blood distributed to the brain chains the mind to ignorance, superstition and barbarism, and bolts the door against civilization, moral culture and religious truth. The compulsory power of the white man, by making the slothful negro take active exercise, puts into active play the lungs, through whose agency the vitalized blood is sent to the brain to give liberty to the mind, and to open the door to intellectual improvement. The very exercise, so beneficial to the negro, is expended in cultivating those burning fields in cotton, sugar, rice and tobacco, which, but for his labor, would, from the heat of the climate, go uncultivated, and their products lost to the world. Both parties are benefitted—the negro as well as his master—even more. But there is a third party benefitted—the world at large. The three millions of bales of cotton, made by negro labor, afford a cheap clothing for the civilized world. The laboring classes of all mankind, having less to pay for clothing, have more money to spend in educating their children, and in intellectual, moral and religious progress.

The wisdom, mercy and justice of the decree, that Canaan shall serve Japheth, is proved by the disease we have been considering, because it proves that his physical organization, and the laws of his nature, are in perfect unison with slavery, and in entire discordance with liberty—a discordance so great as to produce the loathsome disease that we have been considering, as one of its inevitable effects—a disease that locks up the understanding, blunts the sensations and chains the mind to superstition, ignorance and barbarism. Slaves are not subject to this disease, unless they are permitted to live like free negroes, in idleness and filth—to eat improper food, or to indulge in spirituous liquors. . . .

Our Declaration of Independence, which was drawn up at a time when negroes were scarcely considered as human beings, *"That all men are by nature free and equal,"* and only intended to apply to white men, is often quoted in support of the false dogma that all mankind possess the same mental, physiological and anatomical organization, and that the liberty, free institutions, and whatever else would be a blessing to one portion, would, under the same external circumstances, be to all, without regard to any original or internal differences inherent in the organization. . . .

The dysaethesia Aethiopis adds another to the many ten thousand evidences of the fallacy of the dogma that abolitionism is built on; for here, in a country where two races of men dwell together, both born on the same soil, breathing the same air, and surrounded by the same external agents—liberty, which is elevating the one race of people above all other nations, sinks the other into beastly sloth and torpidity; and the slavery, which the one would prefer death rather than endure, improves the other in body, mind and morals; thus proving the dogma false, and establishing the truth that there is a radical, internal, or physical difference between the two races, so great in kind, as to make what is wholesome and beneficial for the white man, as liberty, republican or free institutions, etc., not only unsuitable to the negro race, but actually poisonous to its happiness.

## III

The content of the Cartwright "Report" hardly requires comment. Its form however, which closely resembles contemporary forms of psychiatric denigration, deserves further attention. I shall list my observations in the order in which the statements to which they refer occur in the text—first on "drapetomania," then on "dysaesthesia Aethiopis."

1.   Although "running away," or escaping from captivity, is ordinarily thought of as a human act, a deliberate or willed performance, Cartwright refers to it as an occurrence or happening, an event "caused" by certain antecedent events: thus drapetomania "causes" slaves to run away.

2.   The "cause . . . that induces the negro to run away from service" is, moreover, identified as a "disease of the mind."

3.   Premonitory symptoms of drapetomania are said to be "sulkiness" and "dissatisfaction." When displayed by whites, such emotions were then viewed as the normal expressions of unhappiness with one's lot in life; but when displayed by Negro slaves, they signaled the onset of a dread mental disease.

4.   To prevent the full-blown development of drapetomania, exhibited by the actual running away of the slave, whipping is recommended as medical therapy. This treatment, in a revealing allusion to its historical origins, is called "whipping the devil out of them."

5.   Finally, the cure of drapetomania, and the restoration of the slave to sanity, is said to require the submission of the Negro slave to his white master. "They have only to be kept in that [submissive] state," concludes Cartwright, "and treated like children, with care, kindness, attention and humanity [sic], to prevent and cure them from running away."

Since Cartwright's foregoing observations, Lincoln has emancipated the Negro slaves and the medical profession has negritized the free whites. Thus, what had been drapetomania became depression. The Negro slave ran away from slavery. Modern man runs away from a life that seems to him a kind of slavery. In trying to escape, he may abandon his family, his job, his very life. Since such behavior is socially disruptive, and in the case of suicidal propensities is life-threatening, it is now generally regarded as a medical problem justifying the involuntary hospitalization and treatment of the alleged patient.

In short, the sane slave is the Negro who accepts his role as the natural and proper order of things. The Negro who rejects this role is defined as insane. In this view, formed more than a century ago,

we recognize the current criteria of mental health and mental illness—
that is, the acceptance of the social roles imposed upon us by birth,
fate, law, or our superiors in life, or their rejection.[3, 4]

6. "Dysaesthesia Aethiopis" is an illness which Cartwright identifies as "a disease peculiar to negroes—called by overseers 'rascality.'"
It is thus clearly a product of relabeling, pure and simple.[4]

7. As with drapetomania, Cartwright further identifies dysaesthesia
Aethiopis specifically as a "mental disease . . . accompanied with
physical signs or lesions of the body, discoverable to the medical
observer. . . ."

8. Although Cartwright mentions not a single free Negro who
has consulted him as a patient, for this or any other illness, he refers
to "the complaint [sic] as it prevails among free negroes. . . ." Actually, dysaesthesia Aethiopis points to certain types of behavior on the
part of Negroes deemed offensive to whites—by the whites, not the
blacks. It is Cartwright who "complains," not his alleged "patients."
This linguistic form—the oppressor labeling the undesired behavior
of his victim a "complaint" or a "symptom"—continues to remain
basic to, and indispensable for, the theory and practice of institutional
psychiatry.[1]

9. "Nearly all" free Negroes "that have not got some white person
to direct and to take care of them" are said to be afflicted with dysaesthesia Aethiopis. This alleged finding re-affirms the equation between sanity and subjection for the black—and sanity and domination
for the white. Today, we equate sanity with psychiatric subjection
for the patient—and sanity with psychiatric domination for the physician. Since nowadays everyone is considered more or less mentally
ill, the measure of mental health is "insight" into, and acceptance of,
the role of mental patient by the layman—and the role of mental
healer by the physician. The drama of mental illness is thus merely
a new version of the drama of Negritude: the cast is new, but the
play is the same.

10. The chief symptoms—"complaints," as Cartwright calls them—
of dysaesthesia Aethiopis are the doing of "much mischief": the individuals afflicted with the malady "break, waste, and destroy everything
they handle . . . slight their work—cut up corn, cane, cotton or
tobacco when hoeing it, as if for pure mischief." These acts speak
for themselves. Their meaning, and the human dignity of those whose
protest they express and signify, are medically redefined as the mean-
ingless manifestations of a mental disorder. And so it is today—except
that we now dehumanize black and white equally. From insane
"rascalities" in Louisiana to insane murders in Dallas and Los Angeles,
it is only a short step.

11.   Cartwright not only describes the signs and symptoms of the disease he calls "dysaesthesia Aethiopis," he also identifies its etiology and prescribes its cure. "The disease," he asserts, "is the natural off-spring of negro liberty. . . ."

12.   "The complaint [sic] is easily curable." To cure the "patient," the doctor is exhorted "to anoint it [the skin] all over with oil, and to slap the oil in with a broad leather strap; then to put the patient [sic] to some hard kind of work in the open air and sunshine, that will compel him to expand his lungs, as chopping wood, splitting rails or sawing with the cross-cut or whip saw." This posture is indistinguishable from the "therapeutic attitude" of our "liberal" psychiatric criminologists.[5, 6] The basic formula is here in its entirety: call the victim "patient" and the punishment "treatment," and he will surely be "cured" of his "affliction"—provided, of course, that the physician is left in full charge not only of the patient and his treatment but of the evaluation of the therapeutic results as well.

13.   Although Cartwright attributes the destructive behavior of Negroes to dysaesthesia Aethiopis and claims that the disease is curable, even complete recovery from this affliction fails to restore the blacks to a physiologic state comparable to that of the whites. "Although idleness is the most prolific cause of dysaesthesia, yet there are other ways that the blood gets deteriorated. I said before that the negroes are like children, requiring government in everything."

14.   Lastly, Cartwright provides us with an exceptionally clear and unqualified statement regarding the subhuman character of Negroes which, though rarely put so badly nowadays, applies equally to the modern view of all men—black *and* white—stigmatized as mentally ill. "Our Declaration of Independence," Cartwright writes, "which was drawn up at a time when negroes were scarcely considered as human beings, 'That all men are by nature free and equal,' and only intended to apply to white men, is often quoted in support of the false dogma that all mankind possesses the same mental, physiological, and anatomical organization. . . . The dysaesthesia Aethiopis adds another to the many ten thousand [sic] evidences of the fallacy of the dogma that abolitionism is built on. . . ." Liberty, Cartwright concludes, is beneficial for the white man, but is "actually poisonous to the happiness" of his black brother. No more fitting epitaph could be written for involuntary mental hospitalization, a practice that enshrines the identical proposition: Liberty, beneficial for the sane (psychiatrist), is actually poisonous to the happiness of the insane (patient).

**IV**

It would be misleading to leave off here, implying that our forebears accepted Cartwright's claims without the skepticism that is as characteristic of man as is his gullibility. In the September, 1851 issue of the *New Orleans Medical and Surgical Journal,* there appeared a devastating criticism of Cartwright's paper. Written by James T. Smith, Surgeon, Louisiana, it is titled: "Review of Dr. Cartwright's Report on the Diseases and Physical Peculiarities of the Negro Race." [7] I shall quote from it only those passages that are relevant to our contemporary infatuation with the rhetoric of mental health and mental illness.

Commenting on "drapetomania," Smith writes: "This may well be called a new disease, discovered by Dr. Cartwright. . . . It is calculated to marshal the way to the pathology of a very numerous class of diseases hitherto never dreamed of as being anything but vices; for if a strong desire to do what is wrong be a disease, the violation of any one of the ten commandments will furnish us with a new one so that with a long Greek word for the commencement, and the addition of the magic 'mania,' we shall have a disease for coveting your neighbor's money (a disease common to both the white and black races), or a disease of bearing false witness, or a disease for cutting your neighbor's throat, commonly called 'murder'; all of which shall no longer be treated by the penitentiary, but by calomel, capsicum, etc. This we consider as the greatest step in the progress of philanthropy made in modern times." [7]

Smith was no less astute in his remarks on Cartwright's treatment of dysaesthesia Aethiopis. For this disease, he writes, Cartwright "suggests a species of remedy which, with some modifications, the Greek master applied to his drapetes and the Roman to his fugitivus—it is, the 'strapping-in' recommended by the doctor. 'The best means,' says he, 'of stimulating the skin is to have the patient well washed with warm water and soap, then to anoint it all over with oil, and to slap it in with a broad leather strap.' Now they, the Romans and the Greeks, used the strapping in without the anointment, and with a much narrower strap than the one recommended." [7]

And one final comment on drapetomania: It may be of some interest to note that standard medical dictionaries (such as *Gould's* and *Stedman's*) continue to list this term, defining it as "a morbid desire to wander or run away."

## V

It would be misleading still, to stop here, implying that Cartwright's vicious paternalism toward the Negro is safely behind us. In 1851, Samuel A. Cartwright, M.D., asserted that the Negro was a child who must be governed by the white man. In 1969, Graham B. Blaine, Jr., M.D., chief of Psychiatric Service of the Harvard University Health Service, asserts that the Negro is an adolescent whose "symptoms" must be borne with "patience" and "tolerance" by the white man.[8] From the "drapetomania" and "dysaesthesia Aethiopis" of the black slave, to the "adolescence of the black race" and its "identity conflict," the road is direct and the passage swift: The way is through the land of medicine and is marked clearly, all the way, by diagnostic labels.

As to the Negro's present medical condition—couched in the vocabulary of the most up-to-date and "humanistic" terms of psychiatry—I shall let Blaine speak about it for himself. "In addition to helping black students cope with the problems of their individual adolescence," he writes, "they must also be helped to deal with the conflicts that arise from the adolescence of the black race. It is in this country, at this time, a group which is struggling to define its identity. After such definition occurs, the race can take its place harmoniously within the larger culture. Rebellion and group distinctiveness are symptoms of this identity conflict. The rest of society must be patient and tolerant about these symptoms much as parents must deal with the paradoxical, provocative behavior of their adolescent children." [8]

## VI

I have tried to call attention, by means of an article published in the *New Orleans Medical and Surgical Journal* for 1851, to some of the historical origins of the modern psychiatric rhetoric. In the article cited, conduct on the part of the Negro slave displeasing or offensive to his white master is defined as the manifestation of mental disease, and subjection and punishments are prescribed as treatments. By substituting involuntary mental patients for Negro slaves, institutional psychiatrists for white slave owners, and the rhetoric of mental health for that of white supremacy, we may learn a fresh lesson about the changing verbal patterns man uses to justify exploiting and oppressing his fellow man, in the name of helping him.

Perhaps Shaw—and Hegel whom he was paraphrasing—were right: "We learn from history, that we learn nothing from history."

## REFERENCES

1. Szasz, T. S. *The Manufacture of Madness: A Comparative Study of the Inquisition and the Mental Health Movement.* Harper & Row, New York, 1970.
2. Cartwright, S. A. Report on the diseases and physical peculiarities of the negro race. *New Orleans Medical and Surgical Journal,* 7:691–715, 1851.
3. Szasz, T. S. *The Myth of Mental Illness.* Hoeber-Harper, New York, 1961.
4. ———. *Ideology and Insanity.* Doubleday-Anchor, Garden City, N.Y., 1970.
5. Halleck, S. L. *Psychiatry and the Dilemmas of Crime.* Hoeber-Harper, New York, 1967.
6. Menninger, K. *The Crime of Punishment.* Viking Press, New York, 1968.
7. Smith, J. T. Review of Dr. Cartwright's Report on the diseases and physical peculiarities of the negro race. *New Orleans Medical and Surgical Journal,* 8:228–237, 1851.
8. Blaine, G. B., Jr. What's Behind the Youth Rebellion? *Sunday Herald Traveler* (Boston) November 16, 1969, pp. 22–23.

# 7

# Racial Differences: Impediments to Rapport

## CLEMMONT E. VONTRESS

COUNSELING, as a relationship between two or more individuals, suggests ipso facto the establishment of a mutual bond between the interactants. The emotional bridge between the counselor and counselee is referred to as rapport, a concept which pervades the therapeutic literature. Simply defined, it connotes the comfortable and unconstrained relationship of mutual trust and confidence between two or more individuals (Buchheimer & Balogh, 1961, p. 4). In a counseling dyad, it implies positive feelings combined with a spirit of cooperativeness (Harrison & Carek, 1966, p. 73). In therapeutic groups, rapport is the existence of a mutual responsiveness which encourages each member to react immediately, spontaneously, and sympathetically to the sentiments and attitudes of every other member (Hinsie & Campbell, 1960).

Reprinted, with permission, from *Journal of Counseling Psychology*, 18 (1971), pp. 7–13. CLEMMONT E. VONTRESS was at the time of writing affiliated with George Washington University, Washington, D.C. This article was originally presented at the American Personnel and Guidance Convention, New Orleans, Louisiana, March 1970.

Counselors frequently misconstrue rapport to mean initial "small talk" designed to put the counselee at ease. Such a simplistic conception may be dangerous, especially if the counselor does not know what small talk is appropriate. Although this may be an extreme example, consider the white counselor who started an interview with a black client thus: "Say, John, you don't happen to be from Mississippi, do you?" Receiving a negative nod and an inquisitive look from the client, the smiling counselor continued, "I swear, if you ain't a spittin' image of a boy who used to work for my momma when we lived down in Pascagoula." Obviously, trite conversation often results in a more strained relationship than would exist if the counselee were allowed to state his business immediately (Brammer & Shostrom, 1968, pp. 192–193). If a counselee is motivated to seek assistance, the counselor's "small talk" may be interpreted as disrespect for him and the urgency of his problem. Also the counselor's verbal trivia may be falsely understood as an attempt to delay the unpleasant.

Harrison and Carek (1966, p. 73) indicate that rapport is an emotional bridge or line of communication. As such, it must be maintained throughout the interview. During the relationship, the interactants are assessing each other. They take note of what is said and how it is said. The nature of the content can cause the counselee to alternate from mutual trust to tacit reserve. Exploring content that is threatening to the ego generally requires a more positive relationship bridge than is otherwise needed.

## RACIAL IMPEDIMENTS

White counselors find it difficult to establish and maintain adequate rapport with black clients. In this country the color of an individual's skin defines an aspect of his subculture, not so much because of the manifest physical difference which singles him out, but because of social reactions to it (Crites, 1969, p. 224). That is to say, color differences have resulted in racial separatism, which in turn contributes to cultural differences. People who are separated one from the other for whatever reason develop over a period of time unique ways of perceiving and relating to their environments. Although blacks are products of the larger American culture, their subculture has telling and lasting effects on their behavior, on their attitudes toward themselves, and on their attitudes toward whites.

Although the problem of strained rapport between the white counselor and the black counselee can be analyzed in several ways, an understanding of transference and countertransference should throw some light on the problem.

*Transference* Essentially, transference refers to an individual's reacting to a person in the present in a manner similar to the way he reacted to someone in his past. Transference is a repetition, a new edition of an old relationship (Greenson, 1964, pp. 151–152). Transference feelings may be positive or negative. When the counselor is white, they are almost always negative. However, negative transference does not lead to obvious expressions. Often, it manifests itself in sullen reserve, loquaciousness, obsequious overaffability, and even frequent smiles (Rosen & Frank, 1962). Although usually these reactions are unconscious, they constitute a form of resistance to the goals of counseling and sometimes to the counselor himself (Harrison & Carek, 1966, p. 182). Transference is especially knotty in the white-black dyad, because the black client brings to the relationship intense emotions derived from his experiences with and feelings toward whites in general, as Greenson (1964, p. 352) points out. The Negro's membership in an ostracized subcultural group tends to lead to certain habitual ways of relating initially to a member of the majority group (Rosen & Frank, 1962). This is particularly true today, not only because blacks still experience discrimination, insult, segregation, and the threat of violence, but also because they have become more sensitive and less "adjusted" to these affronts to human dignity. To them, the current problems and conflicts have much more significance than those in the past. Schooled in the American creed, they no longer talk about Freedom in '63; they talk about Freedom Now (Rose, 1965). When their demands are not met, they are angry at anyone perceived as somehow being responsible for The American Lie.

*Countertransference* Whites and blacks are probably more separated today, physically and psychologically, than ever before in the history of this country. Whites have fanned out across the countryside surrounding major cities; about 70% of all blacks are bunched in overcrowded inner-cities. The white and black worlds never meet except in a superficial way on the job, in school, and sometimes on Brotherhood Sundays. Each group develops its own values, attitudes, and approaches to coming to grips with its environment. Although whites and blacks are a part of the same umbrella culture, they are uniquely different at the subcultural level, and since the total culture tends to hide effectively more than it reveals, especially from its own participants (Hall, 1966, p. 39), few people, white or black, are willing to accept the fact that whites and blacks in this country are worlds apart. One might add that these worlds are drifting further away from each other with the passing of each day.

The counselor expects himself to be objective, detached, and scientific on the one hand, and warm, empathic, and congruent on the other

(Harrison & Carek, 1966, p. 192). Although he recognizes the importance of personal feelings, he pretends that he, himself, is devoid of them in his work. It is important for the white counselor to acknowledge racial feelings and attitudes he brings to any counseling interview he conducts with blacks. As a product of a racist society, he perforce brings to that relationship certain preconceived ideas and attitudes toward Negroes. The counselor must be aware of his countertransference reactions toward blacks. Simply put, countertransference refers to the counselor's reacting to the counselee as he has reacted to someone else in his past (Greenson, 1964, p. 348); in this case, it means that the white counselor unconsciously perceives the black counselee as he always has perceived other blacks.

Several countertransference reactions intrude in the white-black counseling relationship. The Negro, still perceived by many whites, especially white women, as a phobogenic object (Fanon, 1967, p. 151), causes great anxiety in many white female counselors, especially if he happens to be between the ages of 16 and 30. This period is understood tacitly as the sexually dangerous age for black males, but not for white males, especially if the female counselor is about the same age as her client and, one must add, especially if the door is closed.

Countertransference also may be evidenced by the counselor's overzealousness to help; that is, his going beyond the call of duty (Harrison & Carek, 1966, p. 200). Often such behavior can be understood as the counselor's attempt to atone for the sins of his race or an effort to assuage his own guilt feelings about the residual traces of racism gnawing at him, racism he feels should not be there but is.

Closely related to overzealousness is the "great white father syndrome." The counselor must communicate to the black client that he is not only somewhat omnipotent (probably because he is white) but that he means him nothing but good as well. In other words, he literally guarantees the black counselee that he can "deliver," if he will only put himself in his hands. Simultaneously, he communicates, albeit unconsciously, the implication that if the black client does not depend on him, he will be doomed to catastrophe. The great white father syndrome may be interpreted as countertransference, because it suggests that the counselor is extremely ambitious to prove to the counselee that he is not like all the other whites he has known (Hinsie & Campbell, 1960). The counselor protests too much.

Finally, the counselor not only may be excessively sympathetic and indulgent with black clients, but what is worse, he may be patronizing. Often, he tends to oversimplify the concerns of his clients. A great danger is his tendency to ascribe all problems Negroes bring to him as difficulties growing out of cultural and racial conflicts (Adams, 1950).

He may fail to realize that black people are human beings first and black second, that they become tired, grow old, and finally die, like all other human beings.


## SELF-DISCLOSURE

Self-disclosure, or the willingness to let another person know what you think, feel, or want, is basic to the counseling process. It is especially crucial in the rapport-establishing phase of the relationship because self-disclosure is the most direct means by which an individual can make himself known to another person (Jourard, 1959), and this is prerequisite to achieving the goals of counseling.

In this country, white people consistently disclose more of themselves than do blacks (Jourard & Lasakow, 1958). Also, women tend to reveal themselves more readily than do men (Jourard, 1962). Thus, the white female discloses most readily, the white male next, the black female next, and the black male least. The black male, the most disenfranchised person in the American society, is also the individual who is most alienated from his fellows and consequently from himself, because of the link between the way he feels about himself and the way he feels about others. The alienated man is not known by his fellows; he doesn't know himself, and he doesn't know his fellows (Jourard, 1964, pp. 15–16).

If the counselor is white, the black client is apt to be hesitant to disclose himself, for a person will permit himself to be known only when he believes that his audience is a man of good will. Self-disclosure occurs most readily in a context of trust (Jourard, 1964, p. 4). Moreover, counselees tend to disclose themselves to the degree to which the other person resembles them in various ways. Self-disclosure is a by-product of the perception or belief that the other person, the person to whom one is disclosing himself, is similar to oneself (Jourard, 1964, p. 15). People disclose themselves when they are fairly sure that the target-person (the person to whom they are disclosing) will evaluate their disclosures and react to them as they, themselves, do. It is easy to see why racial differences become crucial barriers to self-disclosure, especially when the client is a black male.

To a great extent reserve in self-disclosure among black males is not only linked to the black man's disenfranchisement in the American society, but it is also a result of the much talked about black matriarchy. The black boy, so often without a male adult with whom to identify and from whom he can incorporate the various aspects of the masculine role, aims to project a unidimensional masculine image. In order to prove to himself and the world that he is not succumbing to feminizing influences of the matriarchy, he develops a super-masculine facade (Vontress, 1967).

This helps to explain the "cool-it syndrome" so prevalent among black male adolescents. One must be careful not to let the other person know what you think, feel, or want, for to do so is to render yourself vulnerable. You must keep your "dukes up," psychologically speaking; otherwise somebody will "do you in" or take advantage of you. Thus, the black male, especially the younger one, builds around himself an iron-clad facade, designed to protect an insecure, fragile ego. Although the counselor can penetrate the facade, he should be gentle in the process, for to chip away at the psychological armament without replacing it with something equally as durable is to leave a human being naked to what he perceives as a hostile world.

## INTRAGROUP DIFFERENCES

Although one may characterize a cultural or subcultural group in general terms, individual variations within a given group of people must be recognized. Simultaneously, one must keep in mind that the life history of an individual is first and foremost an accommodation of the patterns and standards traditionally handed down in his community, as Ruth Benedict (1934, p. 2) points out. From birth, customs into which he is born shape his experiences and behavior. By the time he can talk, he is a little creature of his culture or subculture, and by the time he is grown and able to take part in its activities, its habits are his habits, its beliefs his beliefs, and its impossibilities his impossibilities. For this reason it seems logical to think of the black experience and the black subculture in America; it also seems logical to think of the Black Personality in this country.

If one concedes this point, one still must recognize that from time to time, in a given society, great social upheavals cause a group of people formerly held together by a history of experiences to perceive themselves, their environment, and others in that environment differently. Although persons of African descent in this country share a common heritage, today this group apparently is being segmented, and the segmentation has occurred as a result of diverse perceptions held by subgroups of what used to be referred to as Negro Americans. These subgroups may be labeled black, Negro, and colored Americans, because each group perceives itself differently and thus reacts differently to disenfranchisement. Each group reacts differently to whites in the society. That is why a consideration of the groups is basic to the question of rapport in counseling.

*Blacks* Although the concept *black* is still in the evolutionary stage, as currently used it refers to a state of mind, an attitude toward self, and ipso facto an attitude toward others. The individual who designates himself black suggests that he is no longer ashamed of his skin color, his kinky hair, or his slave heritage. He ceases to deny traits that hereto-fore caused him great anxiety. Simultaneously, new perceptions of him-self mean that he has developed new understandings about the sufferings inflicted upon him and his forebears, and he is more acutely aware and intolerant of present affronts to his human dignity.

Although depicting an age differential among blacks, Negroes, and coloreds may be untenable, blacks appear more prevalent among young people of African descent, those who live in urban areas, those who are educated, especially the males, and those who live in the North. Blacks are intolerant of, and hostile toward, whites who approach them with the usual racist stance, in terms of language, attitudes, and be-havior. They, therefore, are apt to cause whites, particularly those who harbor residuals of racism, a great deal of anxiety. Their new self-perception puts many whites on the defensive. The white counselor who is unable or unwilling to acknowledge the new self-concept of this group is apt to be ineffectual in relating to its members.

*Negroes* Negroes constitute the large silent majority of Americans of African descent. They are still "on the fence" about the way they feel about themselves, about white people in general, and about their plight in this country. The term Negro aptly describes, at least psychologically, a group of people with shifting values and attitudes, a group still willing to give whites a chance to prove their goodwill. In this group are integrationists, most of whom are middle-class people, who have found a comfortable niche for themselves in a predominately segregated society.

A preponderance of females, especially those who are moderately well-educated, are among this group. This is probably so because females of African descent have received more favorable acceptance in the American society than their male counterparts. For this reason they generally have a more positive self-concept than do males. They manifest greater ac-ceptance of themselves and of others than do males. This may help to explain why Negro women have not been as militant as men, even though they, because of their greater freedom in this country, undoubt-edly could have brought about certain changes that have been more difficult for the men.

Negroes are the people whites have usually known. They do not use language that creates anxiety in the listener or wear extreme styles that perplex the observer. Blacks frequently refer to members of this group as "Uncle Toms." Even so, white counselors, except the most blatant racists, should be able to relate to individuals in this category with little difficulty. Especially is this true of middle-class Negroes who still are devoted to the concept of integration.

Whether Negroes remain the silent majority depends on how the white establishment reacts to and treats blacks, especially the so-called militant blacks. Oppressive measures used against such groups as the Black Panthers undoubtedly will cause Negroes to abandon their efforts to integrate with people who appear basically opposed to integration.

*Coloreds* Among people of African descent in this country is a large segment of individuals who continue to perceive themselves as whites perceive them, who continue to evaluate themselves as whites evaluate them, and who still call themselves "colored," the designation used by many whites who refuse to acknowledge the dignity of the race by referring to it as black. In general, colored people have of necessity maintained a symbiotic relationship with whites, who tell them not only what to call themselves but who go a long way in determining their behavior as well.

These honest, hard-working, God-fearing people often find it difficult to understand what the Civil Rights struggle is all about, since it has meant so little to them. Their white employers often use them to validate their own feelings and attitudes about "all those trouble makers." They often go through life living and acting a lie, especially those who are completely dependent on whites. They dare not expose, even to themselves, the agony and frustration they have to endure. A religious group, colored people sometimes quickly assume a "God will provide" attitude toward life.

The white counselor should find it easy to establish what appears to be a workable rapport with such people. However, he may be duped by their willingness to do whatever he says. Respecting as they do the judgment of whites, they find it inconceivable that a white person would want them to think for themselves, even in a counseling interview. This undoubtedly helps to explain why in an employment interview a colored person often will consent to go on a job suggested to him by the counselor and never show up at the work destination. He cannot bring himself to disagree with a white person. Thus, he leaves the interview making the counselor believe that, indeed, he is going to apply for the job discussed.

The purpose of this tedious and protracted excursion in semantics is to indicate that not all people who look alike are indeed alike. Today, persons of African descent experience and view their environment and those in it differently. Obviously, one might go on to characterize segments within each group delineated. For example, one could talk about the differences inherent in establishing and maintaining rapport with blacks who live in the North as opposed to those in the South. Further, one could discuss the differences in counseling young people and their seniors.


## CONCLUSIONS

Racial differences constitute impediments to establishing and maintaining rapport in counseling, especially when the counselor is white and the counselee a person of African descent. The difficulties stem not so much from race, per se, but from the implications of being black in a society that assigns secondary status to American Negroes. The separate status, in turn, causes blacks and whites to develop unique perceptions of and approaches to coming to grips with their environments. In sum, separatism causes members of the black and white races to meet and greet each other with perceptual distortions, anxiety, and hostility, all of which constitute barriers in the counseling relationship.

Inherent in this discussion are several implications for preservice and in-service training of counselors. Most obvious is the need for a careful look at approaches to training therapeutic professionals. Presently, counselors are not being trained to work effectively with counselees of African descent. Basic to such training should be a curriculum designed to help would-be counselors understand the implications—psychological, physical, and economic—of being black in a white society.

Although some observers might think it most crucial to change the attitude of blacks toward whites, it seems more realistic to modify the manner and approaches of white counselors who counsel blacks. The counselor has responsibility for learning to relate to black people. One of the requirements of effective counseling is the counselor's understanding of himself (Johnson, 1953). Productive counseling depends on the ability of the counsel to permit himself to become a part of the total counseling situation and this involves countertransference. The counselor must know what he is doing and why, and this is not possible unless he understands to some degree his own psychodynamics and his cultural conditioning. That is why a part of the counselor's training should consist of what might be called sensitivity training.

However, sensitivity training in the usual manner is not recommended. Instead, the counselor should live and work in black communities in order to approximate what it is like to be black in an alien society. Counselors-in-training must experience at first hand the agony and frustration of being black in a white society.

Counselors already in service must be retrained if they are to work successfully with blacks, Negroes, and coloreds in a society that has "fractured the minds" of people who were uprooted from their native Africa over 300 years ago. The training should include readings in the nature and needs of the counselees, but what is more important, it should also include direct exposure to the environment of the clientele. This means that counselors in service should live and learn on location in the ghetto if they are to learn to relate effectively with angry, hostile, and suspicious Africans who are now citizens in but not a part of America.

## REFERENCES

Adams, W. A. The Negro patient in psychiatric treatment. *American Journal of Orthopsychiatry*, 1950, 20, 305–310.

Benedict, R. *Patterns of culture*. New York: New American Library, 1934.

Brammre, L. M., & Shostrom, E. *Therapeutic psychology* (2nd ed.) Englewood Cliffs, N.J.: Prentice-Hall, 1968.

Buchheimer, A., & Balogh, S. C. *The counseling relationship*. Chicago: Science Research Associates, 1961.

Crites, J. O. *Vocational psychology*. New York: Mc-Graw-Hill, 1969.

Fanon, F. *Black skin, white masks*. New York: Grove Press, 1967.

Greenson, R. R. *The technique and practice of psychoanalysis* Vol. I. New York: International Universities Press, 1964.

Hall, E. T. *The silent language*. Greenwich, Conn.: Fawcett Publications, 1966.

Harrison, S. I., & Carek, D. J. *A guide to psychotherapy*. Boston: Little, Brown, 1966.

Hinsie, L. E., & Campbell, R. J. *Psychiatric dictionary* (3rd ed.) New York: Oxford Press, 1960.

Johnson, D. The understanding and use of the self in counseling. *Bulletin of the Menninger Clinic*, 1953, 17, 29–35.

Jourard, S. M. Healthy personality and self-disclosure. *Mental Hygiene*, 1959, 43, 499–507.

Jourard, S. M. Some lethal aspects of the male role. *Journal of Existential Psychiatry*, 1962, 7, 333–344.

Jourard, S. M. *The transparent self*. Princeton, N.J.: D. Van Nostrand Co., 1964.

Jourard, S. M., & Lasakow, P. Some factors in self-disclosure. *Journal of Abnormal and Social Psychology*, 1958, 56, 91–98.

Rose, A. M. American Negro problem in the context of social change. *Annals of the American Academy*, 1965, 357, 1–17.

Rosen, H., & Frank, J. D. Negroes in psychotherapy. *American Journal of Psychiatry*, 1962, 119, 456–460.

Vontress, C. E. Counseling Negro adolescents. *The School Counselor*, 1967, 15, 86–91.

# 8

# Race as a Factor in Social Work Practice

JEROME COHEN

RACE EXERTS a pervasive and powerful influence on the delivery of professional services. In complex ways, race or the effects of race are visible in the answers that have been developed to some basic questions: Who needs help? What help is needed? Who can extend the help? For in current social work practice, which constitutes the profession's collective answer to these questions, race is a mediating factor.

The barriers to effective integration of the Negro into social service efforts probably run the gamut from overt, active, and deliberate expressions of discrimination to subtle, passive, inadvertent, or unwished-for arrangements that tend to exclude the Negro. If overt discrimination is rare, a quiet, unintentional dissuasion commonly may operate against the Negro. No social service efforts are entirely free from distortion by the variable of race.

Examined here are some of the inadvertent general forces that reduce

Reprinted from *Race, Research, and Reason: Social Work Perspectives*, Roger R. Miller, ed. (New York: National Association of Social Workers, 1969), pp. 99–113. JEROME COHEN was at the time of writing associate professor, School of Social Welfare, University of California at Los Angeles, Los Angeles, California.

the likelihood that accommodation will be found between the needs of the Negro and the operation of the service network. Considered are some of the restrictive effects of American culture on the Negro's orientation toward service and the congruence of practice arrangements with these orientations. The material suggests that the Negro encounters numerous obstacles in the path to service that conspire against his seeking help, against finding it offered under acceptable conditions, and, perhaps most tragically, against his utilizing it fully.

## THE 'REALITY PRINCIPLE'

Malcolm X described in his autobiography the advice a school counselor gave him concerning his ambition to be a lawyer. The counselor attempted to persuade him that this was an unrealistic goal for a Negro, and counseled him to be something he *could* be:

> You're good with your hands—making things. Everybody admires your carpentry shopwork. Why don't you plan on carpentry? People like you as a person—you'd get all kinds of work.[1]

Such efforts by people to be of "help" are duplicated innumerable times in the life of the average Negro youngster. They serve eventually to grind ambitions down to a level of reality imposed by the structure of limited opportunity rather than by the limitations of individual capacity.

Perhaps the counselor was attempting to help him avoid the shame of failure and rejection he might encounter in seeking a status that the counselor thought unattainable for a Negro in our society at that time. He urged substitution of a goal that was perhaps less desirable, but more likely to result in success. In other words, he helped Malcolm X adjust to the "reality of his social situation." This is a common orientation expressed in the methodology of the various helping professions. It derives from the goal of promoting adjustment to existing conditions that appear beyond change and is generally viewed as appropriate to social realities. It is this unintended and passive element of discrimination that is frequently revealed by an examination of social work practice.

## STRUCTURE OF DISCRIMINATION

Discrimination that is an action of differential treatment of individuals belonging to a specific human group may be present with or without a prejudicial attitude. The relationship between prejudiced attitudes and discriminatory behavior is a complex one with innumerable patterns. Yinger has developed a field theory of prejudice and discrimination.[2] He suggests that it is only by virtue of combining individual levels of prejudice and situational influences that we can gain a more accurate understanding and prediction of discriminatory behavior. He developed a paradigm that combines individual tendencies and structural supports that lead to active discrimination. It suggests the possibility that a social worker who possesses a low individual tendency toward prejudice but works in a situation with strong institutional supports for discriminatory behavior may engage in such behavior himself. Such analysis enables one to understand the nature of social work practice and its relationship to factors of race in a manner that reflects more accurately the profession's person-in-situation model of behavior.

## THE POWER OF SYMBOLS

Along with the strong emotional basis of prejudiced attitudes is found an important cognitive dimension. Belief, perception, and symbolic language tend to mold attitudes as well as behavior. Allport has described the power of linguistic factors in the nature of prejudice.[3] Words enable us to form categories, generalize, reflect, and recall. Racial and ethnic labels are often powerful stimuli of this type. The symbols frequently tune out the finer discriminations that could otherwise be perceived. A category once formed with the aid of a symbol of high potency tends to be tenacious and to attract an increasing number of attributes for which it becomes a referent. The label then may become an indiscriminate referent of the original attribute, probable attributes, and highly imaginative and nonexistent attributes.

The Whorfian hypothesis suggests that language not only serves as a means of communicating the various aspects that make up a culture but also serves as a critical component of socialization that directs its members to the reality of their cultural perspective.[4] The language of social work practice then becomes a critical issue not only in the description of the reality but also in the shaping of the reality the practitioners—and especially students—will see and believe. This is, of course, a condition common to all professional education. It is recognized here as a reflection of the way in which a limited view of a problem may be maintained and thus increase the possibility of stereotyping both the client and the social condition that underlies his problem.

It is ironical that while language enables man to describe and generalize the complexity of reality, it also enables him to distort it. Psy-

chiatric labels attached to certain behavioral disorders continue to call
for inappropriate responses from both the public and the professional
practitioner. The same eccentric aunt who lived with reasonable comfort
in her family surroundings is no longer accepted after being labeled
schizophrenic.[5] Likewise in social work, when social differences are
labeled in pathological terms, a new formula for action is required. How
frequently do these professional terms lead to a self-fulfilling prophecy?

## ORIENTATION TO SERVICE

In the variously global or microscopic analyses of the plight of the Negro,
at least one common consequence is discernible: His life experiences fail
to provide a foundation conducive to the unfettered use of social resources, including social work services. Instead, orientations are induced
that impede or complicate the use of social resources.

### Consequences of Discrimination

Duncan has succinctly characterized some of the consequences of discrimination against Negroes:

> Negroes, in disproportionate numbers, (1) experience unstable family situa-
> tions and depend on meager family resources; (2) attain less than average
> amounts of education; (3) are employed in lower level jobs; (4) secure low
> incomes; (5) have an inefficient pattern of expenditures; (6) in consequence,
> are characterized by inferior life chances, low levels of living and welfare,
> and impaired satisfactions. Each of these handicaps operate to set up the
> handicaps at later stages; schooling is terminated early partly because
> family support is inadequate; job opportunities are inferior partly because
> educational preparation is not good; low income is partly due to poor job
> opportunities; expenditures are inefficient and insufficient partly because of
> low income; Negroes get less out of life partly because of cumulative inade-
> quacies at each stage of the life cycle.[6]

Locked into such circumstances of life for generations, a large segment
of the Negro population has come to be justifiably suspicious of contacts
with members of the majority who represent the forces that have brought
about the dilemma.

A more detailed analysis of the impact of these abrasive social forces
on the development of the Negro was presented by Kenneth B. Clark.
He concluded that as minority group children learn the inferior status
to which they are assigned and observe the fact of segregation, they often
react with feelings of inferiority and a sense of personal humiliation.
Many become confused about their own personal worth. Under these

conditions, they are thrown into conflict with respect to their feelings about themselves and their group. This conflict and confusion frequently lead to self-hatred and rejection of their own social group.

Various patterns of coping with this conflict develop, depending on a number of interrelated factors, e.g., stability and quality of family relations, social and economic class, cultural and educational background of parents, personal characteristics, intelligence, and the like. Some children, usually those of lower socioeconomic status, react with overt aggression and hostility directed toward their own group as well as toward the majority group. Middle-class minority group children are more likely to react to frustrations and conflicts by withdrawal and submissive behavior or by compensatory and rigid conformity to prevailing middle-class values and standards. Many develop a determination to succeed in spite of the handicap of minority status. However, many minority group children react with generally defeatist attitudes and lowering of personal ambitions. They tend to be hypersensitive and anxious about their relations with the larger society. There is a heightened tendency to see hostility and rejection even in those areas where it might not actually exist.[7]

This cross-sectional look at the variety of feelings about self and others and of the disposition of aggression elaborates the conception of mistrust as a barrier to service. The overdetermined pursuit of success or renunciation of aspiration and the pull toward conflict or overconformity define stances that influence the decision about seeking help and that are carried to that situation.

The attempts to describe the Negro have been extended in a number of different directions. For example, the Negro child's rejection of his own color and group, cited in innumerable studies, appears to be changing with the development of a new pride in self and group consequent to the civil rights movement and the various nationalistic sentiments that surround it.[8] A study by Grossack reports an increasing amount of positive feelings associated with being Negro.[9] More than 90 percent of his 183 Negro respondents were able to find some good things in being Negro. Pride was evidenced in the progress Negroes have made and are making in all fields. Personal characteristics such as tolerance of frustration, remaining a loyal citizen despite inequality of treatment, and capacity to maintain ability to learn despite serious deprivation were cited frequently. The negative responses were not of the self-hatred type but rather reflected the conditions under which Negroes must still live. Perhaps it is this new ability to direct aggression outwardly that has reduced the amount of inward aggression that in the past led to self-hate.

## Significant Social Worlds

A recent study by Thompson suggests that Negro identity can best be understood in relation to a distinct social segment of their social world.[10] He found that the individual responds to a much smaller psychological reality than social class or color caste. Among the New Orleans Negro community he located the following significant social worlds: (1) the middle class, (2) the matriarchy, (3) the gang, (4) the nuclear family, and (5) the marginal.

Among the *middle class* he cited the value placed on respectability and the need for success as an indicator of self-validation. There was ambivalence about skin color and evidence of deep feelings of self-hate.

In the *matriarchy* category he discovered a high degree of inner solidarity among the females, men being regarded as enemies. While he found some persons of this type in all social levels, the majority were among the lower class. There was a high degree of mutual dependency between mother and daughter and girls early regarded themselves primarily as women, all other roles being secondary. The outside world is of little concern and there is not much evidence of self-hate. Marked ambition or striving to succeed are limited. The high degree of dissatisfaction with segregation is connected to economic and sexual exploitation. Males in the family must conform to female patterns or renounce the home. Under these conditions they are forced to identify with the gang and become "men."

The *gang* is the place that articulates the male principle in society. Matriarchy and gang are natural enemies in this respect. Each owes allegiance to mutually exclusive ideologies. Manhood is defined in terms of independence, secretiveness, progressiveness, and sexual prowess. There appear to be a high degree of fear of women, scorn for middle-class standards, and hatred of outside authority. There is little in the value scheme of this group that provides a basis for the establishment of a stable family life. Ties are necessarily temporary and loose. Members have almost no interest in community affairs unless these threaten their way of life. There is considerable sensitivity about race and great bitterness about discrimination.

The *nuclear family group* is most characteristic among lower middle-class Negroes. For this subgroup the family roles are regarded as central in members' lives, all others being secondary. Strong "we" feelings tend to limit concern for outside persons or institutions unless these contribute something to the family welfare, e.g., church or union. Most tend to value the skin color characteristic of their families. Attitudes toward discrimination varied considerably' but all thought of it as a personal, individual phenomenon, the result of evil people's actions. There was high occupational ambition.

Finally, those who lived in conditions of *marginality* shared no satisfactory self-identity. Some attempted to develop an organized "bohemian" philosophy of life, but this was inconsistent and fell short of a meaningful choice.

Research that uncovers the conditions that mediate the broad category of race reveals the complex network of constraints that impinge on the utilization of services and programs. Whether social work is providing opportunities and resources or helping individuals to use the resources that are available, it is necessary to understand the way in which the client views himself and these services, and it is necessary to organize the delivery of services to articulate this view.

## STRUCTURE OF SOCIAL WORK PRACTICE

The structure of social service delivery systems is critical to the understanding of race and social work practice. The slogan "You can't eat civil rights" is heard increasingly in lower-class Negro communities. It may be equally true that one cannot resolve some of the complex problems of service effectiveness by good will alone. Skill, understanding, and positive intention may be thwarted by the conditions under which service is given.

A pervasive problem exists in the assumptions about Negro problems and the action following these assumptions. Herzog cites the issue of unmarried parents as a reflection of this condition:

> If he is a member of the middle-class . . . he is likely to be viewed as one who is troubled . . . and needs help . . . the help is likely to be offered under the auspices of a voluntary agency staffed by professional caseworkers. Efforts will be made to understand the individual's background and circumstances, and to work out the problems involved in a situation viewed as a unique constellation of factors. On the other hand, if the unmarried father comes from a deprived background, characterized by low income and poor education, the paramount question is not how the pregnancy came about and how he can be helped but how he can be made to shoulder his share of the financial burden.[11]

A differential approach to out-of-wedlock children can be documented adequately. In low-income families, especially Negro families, the problem is viewed as a cultural phenomenon and the parties are seen as public charges. Little can be found in the literature describing the complex emotional entanglements that prevail in the case of Negro parents of out-of-wedlock children.

An intensive case study of one family agency in southern California over a ten-year period offers further evidence of these perceptual distortions.[12] The Negro population in the geographic area served by this agency is not characterized by the extreme poverty found in the urban ghetto. Although the agency had always been underused by the Negro population, the ten years between 1950 and 1960 showed a further decline. Case records revealed that psychological problems presented by Negroes were frequently ignored, with attention focused mainly on concrete service. This can be as inappropriate as the opposite approach. For example, premature judgment about the treatability of marital problems occurred frequently, referrals were made for public assistance with little attempt to deal with other concrete or emotional problems, arrangements were made by the agency for child care placement with little attention paid to such matters as one parent's comment that her son had "bitten a neighbor child's penis." In general, the authors give evidence of a mechanical and superficial approach to service for Negroes rather than the more fully developed treatment given to others.[13]

### Service Use in South-Central Los Angeles

The existence of social services does not in itself insure their meaningful use by the population requiring assistance. Various factors such as the style of delivery, accessibility to the client's residence, agency policies, and staff attitudes are known to influence the effective and appropriate use of services. An opportunity to inquire into these matters was found in conjunction with a large interdisciplinary study developed in the aftermath of the 1967 Los Angeles riots.[14] The availability and usability of social services in the south-central area of Los Angeles revealed in this research suggest the kinds of impediments to service that may be general.

Interviews of two to three hours' duration were conducted in order to collect data from agency executives and line workers in a stratified random sample of all agencies in the area providing direct social services to clients. These included (1) primary agencies such as public assistance and family agencies, (2) social service departments or branches of host settings such as schools, hospitals, and courts, and (3) other agencies providing a variety of general welfare services. Excluded from the study were organized committees not giving direct service and agencies serving the area but based outside it. Forty-two agencies offering both public and private health, education, or welfare services were examined. The interviews were carried out by second-year graduate social work students.[15]

To be available, an agency must not only be located within reasonable distance of the population using its services, but must also be recognized as a resource for its potential users. On the whole, agencies were not engaged in a concerted effort to make their services known or to reach out with case-finding techniques to the population located within their service boundaries.[16] It was on word of mouth, unproductive referrals from other agencies, and the client's ingenuity that the agencies relied. These are not methods that bring people in need to agencies in large numbers. The area covers forty square miles and the cost of transportation was often prohibitive to a family living at a subsistence level or below the poverty line.

Approximately half the agencies had provisions for emergency service. A number of the other agencies reported emergency services, but the social workers had to provide them on their own time without compensation. It should not be surprising that these agencies were rarely open after hours. In the public income maintenance programs social workers had to use their own time if they were to meet the emergency needs of their clients. The most serious gap in emergency service was found in the social service component of hospitals or in outpatient physical and mental health clinics. Finally, a large number of youth-serving agencies seemed to be without resources to help youngsters in times of emergent distress outside the usual agency hours.

Eligibility requirements for income and residence were not a barrier to the use of most agency services. However, among the eight agencies that did have such requirements were found the most basic services being offered—income maintenance and medical care. Other kinds of eligibility requirements proved to be more restrictive. These were the requirements of specialized agencies governing the conditions under which service can be offered. A number of highly specialized agencies required client stability in areas other than those covered by their specific service and would not accept persons with multiple problems.

Immediacy of service is an important factor in working with low-income clients. Most of the agencies had no waiting period and staff would see clients immediately, even when they came without an appointment. The new poverty program agencies did not, in fact, use an appointment system. The agencies with waiting lists were those offering a highly skilled professional service in health, mental health, and family service programs.

The advantages of client participation in the planning of agency services have been stressed in the literature. Only four of the forty-two agencies included representatives of the client population on their policy-making boards. However, a much larger number reported indirect methods of client contribution to the determination of agency policy. It should be said that some were very indirect indeed.

Knowledge of the local community and sufficient autonomy to respond to the needs of the community's population are considered important factors in the effectiveness of agency services. Fewer than one-third of the agencies reported that the majority of the workers lived in the south-central Los Angeles area. Eighteen agencies, primarily poverty program agencies, reported the use of indigenous workers. Professional practitioners are not generally expected to live in the locale in which they practice. However, when the population served is locked in a community by virtue of the existence of a ghetto, the impression of the social worker is of a "visiting professional." In other than poverty program agencies, only one sectarian family agency took an official position on some aspect of the civil rights movement. Apparently the accusations of aloofness of the social caretakers are not always ill founded.

To avoid dividing the client, co-ordination of services is essential. To avoid gaps in service, planning is necessary. Most of the agencies reported maintaining contact with other agencies serving the same client. Nearly all agencies also reported that they plan jointly with other agencies in the community. It is unclear whether the rhetoric of planning is followed by integrated social services. It appeared that the major condition of meaningful co-operation in planning was absent in this community of agencies—the willingness to relinquish a small degree of autonomy for the advantage of over-all planning.

In general, the study found that the majority of agencies did not seem to block access to their services with excessive intake demands and long waiting lists. However, there was limited case-finding or reaching out for clients who could not connect without some additional help. Little effort was made to bring back those who failed to keep appointments or dropped out of treatment. As with most agencies, if the client does not have the strength to get there and stay there, he goes unserved. Some agencies located in the same geographic area are frankly not serving the population. These agencies—several with widespread reputations in their respective fields—were doing work of exceptional excellence, and their services would be a valuable asset to members of the local community. The study replicated the findings of many other investigators that the highest level of expertise is frequently not available to the low-income family. This may lead to an increased sense of relative deprivation, which is the seed of violence.

## STIGMA OF WELFARE SERVICES

Coser, building on Simmel's work, characterizes the process of granting public assistance as an act of degradation. "To receive public assistance means to be stigmatized and to be removed from the ordinary run of men." [17] In order to be eligible for public assistance, a person is obligated to open his private life to public inspection. Such an invasion of privacy is often experienced as humiliating and degrading. Further, when moneys are allocated, the disposition of their use is limited. In essence, the poor are treated like children who have to account to parents for the wise use of their money. Through such procedures, the public assistance recipient is infantilized and dependency is insured rather than resolved. The point is made that the process of being helped assigns the recipient to a career that impairs previous identity and becomes a stigma marking his intercourse with others. The good will of the social worker, the administrator, or the volunteer does not eliminate degradation. There is no way of eliminating the power that the social worker has over the client under conditions of service in the current public welfare situation. Clark recognizes a similar estrangement between client and agency:

> Agencies that encourage their clients to accept dependency or to accept transparent "make-work" contribute to the perpetuation of the pathology of ghetto communities. It is reasonable to assume that people who have not already been severely damaged want wholesome work. When the client cannot find such work, the professional cannot have wholesome work of his own either. This necessarily leads to a mutually protective estrangement of the client and worker; to the "flight from the client" illustrated by the exodus of most of the family service agencies out of Harlem.[18]

Negroes of the urban ghetto are so frequently involved in such transactions that these become a critical part of their self-definition.

## RACE AND RELATIONSHIP

Relatively little has been written about the factor of race as it influences the relationship between client and social worker in the common pursuit of problem-solving. What has been written involves descriptions of practice experience with little attempt to collect and analyze these data systematically. Periodically an attempt is made to describe empirically the nature of these relationships. The only experimental work in this area pertains to the effect of race on examiner bias in various diagnostic testing and research situations. Nearly thirty years ago, in a paper describing the socialization patterns of Negro children and adolescents, Allison Davis suggested:

> If we then wish to do anything to change this group's behavior, (1) we must make it possible for a much larger proportion of Negroes to obtain the kinds of occupations, income, education, and legal protection necessary for middle-class training, which means that the caste-system must be gradually changed, and (2) we must learn to do a new kind of remedial work with individuals, in which we direct them toward new goals and show them the techniques for reaching these goals. . . . It is not to be expected that lower-class children will be especially hopeful about social mobility, or be especially responsive to efforts of remedial workers along this line. The first step in the retraining of children, by teachers or social workers, therefore, is to stop punishing lower-class children by contempt or condescension. The second step is to make them understand that the social rewards of higher status are satisfying enough to justify hard work. . . .[19]

This theme is to be found time and time again in the current literature of class, race, and social work practice.

A growing literature is addressed to understanding the social and cultural factors that underlie behavior of the client group in question, in an attempt to reduce the strangeness between helper and client.[20] There has also been a concern with the attitudes of both Negro and white professionals as these affect the relationship with both Negro and white clients in various combinations. In the mental health field, a series of articles and investigations have been cast in the form of transference and countertransference mechanisms and their distortions when client and professional are of different races.[21] Some suggest that race prejudice may be used as an unconscious defense to conceal more basic conflicts in the life of the individual. They warn against allowing racial differences to blind the clinician to the more central problem.[22] Others warn against interpreting as transference the reality of the therapist's behavior toward the client owing to their racial difference. In these cases, the behavior of the client is seen as a reality reaction to the attitudes or behavior of the professional rather than as a reflection of the client's experience with earlier significant figures.[23]

### Negro Client, White Worker

Similar concerns have been voiced directly in relation to social work practice. In 1938 DuVinage reported a study of responses of Negro clients to the casework relationship when the caseworker was white. She noted a considerable amount of accommodative behavior under these conditions and suggested that such behavior interfered with the effectiveness of the casework intervention.[24] Submissiveness based on fear and distrust of white persons, along with circuitously expressed aggressions, blocked treatment. She reported that the clients able to make good use of the casework relationship had caseworkers whose feelings toward Negroes were both comfortable and positive.

The following year Hart replicated the DuVinage study but used Negro caseworkers and Negro clients.[25] She found some of the same accommodative and secretive behavior on the part of the clients, but to a lesser extent. This early study was predictive of later ones indicating that all problems are not solved by the use of a professional of the same race as the client. The Negro social workers were warned not to be too demanding of their Negro clients or to foster dependency in them by taking for granted that discrimination is their problem.[26]

Frequently mentioned is the white social worker's paternalistic and dependency-supporting behavior toward the Negro client.[27] Special treatment arising from guilt and discomfort does not enhance the developmental potentials of the client.[28] A lack of knowledge and understanding of the Negro client's subcultural patterns and general life circumstances is universally seen as a barrier to an effective helping relationship. Some are concerned that superficial understanding will lead to stereotyped behavior by the white social worker, confusing interaction and limiting the possibility of developing a meaningful plan of action.[29]

### Integrated Groups

As part of a large natural experiment in two children's summer camps that were shifting from a policy of segregation to one of integration, the effects of a racial mixing of campers and counselors were observed with particular clarity.[30] Both camps served low-income children. The counselors were all positively motivated toward desegregation, although nearly all the Negro counselors showed some anxiety about their acceptance by the white children, and all of the counselors felt unsure of themselves in working out the new social relationships among the children in the newly integrated groups.

Decisions made on the basis of race dominated the initial operation, but lessened later. Control techniques tended to take a more extreme form in the integrated groups. Ambiguous situations quickly led to counselor intervention. The counselors verbalized feelings of greater social distance between themselves and the children in integrated groups. They found it more difficult to appraise objectively their successes and failures with the children. Not unexpectedly, the counselors tended to rank the children who were racially different from themselves more favorably than those of their own race, which was especially true of

Negro counselors' evaluations of white children. This tendency also increased among white counselors as time went on. Yet it was reported that the counselors performed consistently well despite these difficulties. Their success illustrates the time-honored professional dictum that self-knowledge is one key to overcoming behavior that interferes with the helping process.

### White Client, Negro Worker

It is interesting that most of the literature concerns the Negro client and the white social worker despite the fact that there is an increasingly large number of Negro social workers. It is likely that the Negro is most often thought of in terms of being a client and that this preconception therefore establishes this priority. Relatively little has been written about the problems of a Negro social worker with a white client. Some observers report that the Negro social worker's sense of adequacy is challenged by the white client's attitudes.[31] Others, while recognizing that white clients may feel prejudice and hostility toward Negro social workers, report that these do not necessarily serve as a deterrent to the treatment relationship.[32] It has also been noted that a Negro social worker may be unsympathetic or punitive toward a white client or may overidentify with the client's whiteness and be too permissive to be of help to him.[33]

Recognizing that the casework relationship is a product of mutual perceptions and expectations based on the life experience, Curry documented the variety of possibilities in such a relationship.[34] Frequently the white client has difficulty recognizing and accepting the Negro social worker's authority and professional ability. Curry noted that some clients, while able to accept the social worker as giving service, found it necessary to screen out the authoritarian aspect of the role. He stressed the fact that emotional distance as well as social distance between worker and client are powerful forces that must be recognized. In some instances the white client's reactions are influenced by the countertransference of the Negro worker as well as by his conscious reactions to a white client. If the Negro social worker is uncertain about his own identity, considerable anxiety is stimulated in the relationship. The author warned against using the white client as an audience before whom the Negro social worker plays out his own needs.

### Hostility

It is interesting to note that while hostility is not generally considered a barrier to treatment, it is thought of in these terms when the hostility reflects interracial antagonisms.[35] Indeed, hostility is one of the expected responses to deprivation, especially when the deprivation is associated with discrimination. What would be grist for the casework mill in other circumstances here becomes a barrier to effective service.

Gochros has recognized and attempted to use anger in working with Negro clients, from experience indicating that it is essential to explore racial attitudes quickly and directly as a general rule rather than as an exception.[36] White social workers were seen as either blind to the suspicions and hostility of Negroes or fearful of bringing them out into the open.

> Rather than encouraging expressions of anger, social workers' total efforts have been perhaps unconsciously directed toward clamping down lids, irrationally forgetting their usual convictions about expressing hostility.[37]

Noted also is a double-bind communication in which the social worker may first encourage expressions of hostility and then point out that the client is overgeneralizing unfairly to whites. At times even honest discussion is inhibited, let alone attempts to resolve underlying psychosocial problems.

### Empirical Studies

Special mention needs to be made of the Luna Brown study, inasmuch as it is one of the few empirical efforts to describe the effects of race as a factor in establishing a casework relationship.[38] Questionnaires were sent to forty agencies in thirteen states to inquire about the difficulties encountered in mixed racial client-worker relationships. Of the twenty-five agencies returning the questionnaires, twenty reported few difficulties, while five reported a number of problems. Only one agency thought that the difficulties were serious enough to contraindicate undifferentiated case loads for Negro workers (e.g., resistance of white clients to home visits by Negro workers). Difficulties stemming from racial differences alone were infrequent and transfer of cases on this basis was not generally necessary. Nevertheless, a number of interesting observations were reported in the questionnaires. A number of agencies reported a lack of understanding of cultural forces that served to make the white social worker seem either naïve or offensive to the Negro client. In terms of client attitudes it was noted that

> some special problems were observed in Negro clients who had a great deal of feeling about their race. While some Negro clients express appreciation when a Negro caseworker is assigned, feeling this constitutes recognition of

professional ability found in their own race, others feel insecure with a Negro worker or think of the Negro worker in the same inferior position as the themselves and thus too enfeebled to be of help. . . . Another Negro client, who could not accept herself as a Negro, completely rejected a Negro worker . . . also, . . . a stereotyped dependent relationship with a white worker was mentioned as an adverse factor. . . . A feeling of white superiority on the part of white clients might account for difficulty in assigning Negro workers to them. . . . A white client might feel that a Negro worker would be more attentive to his material needs, presuming the worker's pleasure at serving him. . . . A white client may show resistance to a Negro worker based upon the client's belief that the Negro worker is inadequate or that he is vulnerable to intimidation.[39]

It was observed that social workers, like clients, may project onto racial factors the difficulty they are having in a casework relationship. The key word used by agencies in describing the basis for the Negro social worker's difficulties was "insecurity." It was suggested that these feelings may lead to aggressiveness, hostility, and a domineering manner with white clients. A number of agencies made the observation that Negro social workers were more likely to be punitive toward Negro clients. Deviations from accepted standards would be seen as a reflection on the race itself. Feelings of superiority on the part of white social workers as well as denial of any feelings about race hampered effectiveness in interracial contacts. With denial or guilt frequently came the granting of material requests.[40] In concluding, Brown suggested:

The assumption that racial differences form an invisible barrier interfering with the development of a constructive casework relationship is not proved by the data submitted by the twenty-five agencies based on an analysis of actual experience. . . . The most important conclusion of the study was that much of the difficulty attributed to the factor of racial difference appeared to be based upon various difficulties in the client-worker relationship of a kind that may be found in any casework relationship and, as a rule, can be overcome through the experience, skill, and professional security of the worker. Racial differences may be used by a client as one of the many rationalizations of his resistance. The participating agencies were in general agreement that the personal adjustment and professional skill of the worker were more important than race.[41]

One recent experimental study has produced some evidence about the expectations with which a relationship across social lines may be approached. Meeks found that the aspirations of Negro and white boys were differentially responsive to the race of an examiner. Specifically, the lower-class Negro and white boys set significantly lower aspirations for themselves when dealt with by a Negro rather than a white adult.

And while the performance of white middle-class boys was uninfluenced by the race of the examiner, Negro middle-class boys tended to overaspire in their encounter with a white adult.[42] These data describe divergent predisposing orientations toward a Negro-white relationship. Only for the middle-class white subject was the issue of race irrelevant; for other class and race combinations, race influenced behavior.

## DIRECTIONS FOR FURTHER RESEARCH

Race as a social category is not only difficult to study because of the uncertain "race" concept, but because a great many other characteristics mediate identity and behavior. The Negro has been used as a case in point. It is clear that income, education, religion, and location affect the meaning of the referent for the label Negro. It is somewhat like the American Indian, who found himself an *Indian* only after he was so defined by the European adventurer who discovered the Americas. Before that he was a Crow, Onondaga, Cherokee, or any of dozens of other tribal groups. It is within these subgroups that similar behavior is found. The differences among the subgroups are considerable. Pan-Indianism prevails only as a result of mutual concerns in the face of prejudice and discrimination, not as a condition of basic identity affiliation. Social workers talk mostly about the Negro poor, but even among this group it is necessary to differentiate with other subclassifications. It will be increasingly important to understand the nature of those subclassifications as they mediate behavior. While it is true that a disproportionate number of Negroes in our society share the status of "poor," there are increasing numbers of stable working-class and middle-class Negroes. It will be necessary to learn more than is now known about their responses to prejudice and discrimination.

Twenty years ago Frazier discussed the issue of vested interest on the part of some Negroes in maintaining segregation.[43] These attitudes are increasing today for many reasons. In addition to the Black Nationalist movement, which views the possibility of temporary, self-inflicted segregation (as opposed to outside-imposed segregation), there are those in the ghetto who have reaped considerable profit for their services and are reluctant to relinquish it.[44] Research is needed to understand the conditions under which progressive social programs can be fielded successfully in the communities having the greatest need.

Central to our purpose should be an increase in research devoted to understanding the conditions under which social distance between client and social worker can be reduced. What combination of characteristics, what structural conditions of agency service, what educational efforts and training programs can be established to reduce the strangeness between helper and client? [45] The variation among professional social workers and the conditions under which they engage in their work offer a wealth of possibilities in studying the combinations that affect social distance. Further, experimental studies are becoming increasingly possible as research is built into many government-funded demonstration projects and development programs.

There are several major ways to reduce prejudice toward a specific social category. One way is to destroy the category. Another is to make an equivalent value of that social category. The latter condition is more likely to prevail in our society. Additional research is needed to discover the conditions under which subcultural identity can be promoted and enhanced. The melting pot mythology served a purpose under conditions of extensive immigration that existed earlier in our history. We may now look toward a unity-in-diversity theme in society. Can we experiment with strengthening secondary ethnic and racial identities without the evils of invidious comparison and discriminatory consequences? Can a strong secondary identity be developed without the necessity of hating the outgroup? These are concerns directly related to the purposes of the social work community.

Continued attention must also be directed toward the conditions under which "passive discrimination" exists. What are the conditions of service set by social service agencies? Are these related to the needs of the client, to the technical methodology, or to the conditions of service defined by social workers? These are questions about which we do not have clear answers. Yet accusations are hurled back and forth, both within and outside the social work profession, as if the answers were self-evident and conclusive.

Research in this highly charged area needs to find a balance between color blindness and meaningful awareness of cultural and social differences. Only as we articulate a set of values about our common goals in the race relations area will we be able comfortably to engage in the necessary research that such a commitment demands. Only then will we be able to devote ourselves to the task of joining one another in shedding some light on the dark problem of our time.

## NOTES AND REFERENCES

1. Malcolm X with Alex Haley, *The Autobiography of Malcolm X* (New York: Grove Press, 1965), p. 37.

2. J. Milton Yinger, *Toward a Field Theory of Behavior* (New York: McGraw-Hill Book Co., 1965).

3. Gordon W. Allport, *The Nature of Prejudice* (New York: Doubleday & Co., 1958).

4. Benjamin L. Whorf, *Language, Thought and Reality* (New York: John Wiley & Sons, 1956).

5. Elaine Cumming and John Cumming, *Closed Ranks* (Cambridge, Mass.: Harvard University Press, 1957).

6. Otis D. Duncan, "Discrimination against Negroes," *The Annals,* Vol. 371 (May 1967), p. 88.

7. Kenneth B. Clark, "Social Scientist's Brief to Supreme Court," in *Prejudice and Your Child* (2d ed.; Boston: Beacon Press, 1963), Appendix III, pp. 166–184.

8. *See* Melvin Seeman, "Skin Color Values in All Negro School Classes," *American Sociological Review,* Vol. 11, No. 3 (June 1946), pp. 315–321; and Bingham Dai, "Some Problems of Personality Development Among Negro Children," in Clyde Kluckhohn et al., eds., *Personality in Nature, Society and Culture* (New York: Alfred A. Knopf, 1962), pp. 545–566.

9. Martin M. Grossack, "Group Belongingness Among Negroes," in Grossack, ed., *Mental Health and Segregation* (New York: Springer Publishing Co., 1963), pp. 18–29.

10. Daniel C. Thompson, "Development of Attitudes in Respect to Discrimination: Formation of Social Attitudes," *American Journal of Orthopsychiatry,* Vol. 32, No. 1 (January 1962), pp. 74–85.

11. Elizabeth Herzog, "Some Notes About Unmarried Fathers," *Child Welfare,* Vol. 45, No. 4 (April 1966), p. 195.

12. Ruth Anderson and Rosalee Shaw, "Utilization of a Casework Agency by Its Negro Community." Unpublished master's thesis, School of Social Welfare, University of California, Los Angeles, 1963.

13. *Ibid.,* p. 39.

14. Jerome Cohen, "A Descriptive Study of the Availability and Usability of Social Services in the South Central Area of Los Angeles," in "Los Angeles Riot Study" (Los Angeles: Institute of Government and Public Affairs, University of California, June 1967).

15. The following UCLA graduate social work students participated in the research project: Diana Bechler, Dorothy Ferri, Sylvia Gressit, Audrey Gunther, Constance Haskell, Valarie Hastings, Jean Mack, and Sonia Zipperman.

16. It should be noted that the absence of outreach efforts was due, at least in part, to the common circumstance that service resources were taxed by clients who did find their way to the agency. Whether these are the most appropriate claimants of scarce resources is unclear. That a population is underserved by agencies relying on substantial client initiative is, however, perfectly clear.

17. Lewis A. Coser, "The Sociology of Poverty," *Social Problems,* Vol. 13, No. 2 (Fall 1965), p. 144.

18. Kenneth B. Clark, *Dark Ghetto* (New York: Harper & Row, 1965), p. 49.

19. Allison Davis, "The Socialization of the American Negro Child and Adolescent," *Journal of Negro Education,* Vol. 8, No. 3 (July 1939), pp. 264–274.

20. *See* Fred R. Crawford, Glen W. Rollins, and Robert L. Sutherland, "Variations Between Negroes and Whites in Concepts of Mental Illness and Its Treatment," *Annals of the New York Academy of Science,* Vol. 84, No. 17 (December 8, 1960), pp. 918–937; Hugh McIsaac and Harold Wilkenson, "Clients Talk About Their Caseworkers," *Public Welfare,* Vol. 23, No. 3 (July 1965), pp. 147–154; Seaton W. Manning, "Cultural and Value Factors Affecting the Negro's Use of Agency Services," *Social Work,* Vol. 5, No. 4 (October 1960), pp. 3–13; Elizabeth Meir, "Social and Cultural Factors in Casework Diagnosis," *Social Work,* Vol. 4, No. 3 (July 1959), pp. 15–26; Lois Pettit,

"Some Observations on the Negro Culture in the United States," *Social Work*, Vol. 5, No. 3 (July 1960), pp. 104–109.

21. *See* Andrew E. Curry, "Some Comments on Transference When the Group Therapist Is a Negro," *International Journal of Group Psychotherapy*, Vol. 13, No. 3 (July 1963), pp. 363–365; Curry, "The Negro Worker and the White Client," *Social Casework*, Vol. 45, No. 3 (March 1964), pp. 131–136; Janet Kennedy, "Problems Posed in the Analysis of Negro Patients," in Martin Grossack, ed., *Mental Health and Segregation* (New York: Springer Publishing Co., 1963), pp. 199–221; and John P. Speigel, "Some Cultural Aspects of Transference and Countertransference," in J. H. Masserman, ed., *Individual and Familial Dynamics* (New York: Grune & Stratton, 1959), pp. 160–182. Maas developed a short review of the treatment variations between Negroes and Caucasians in cases of mental illness, highlighting the major findings of some recent studies and commenting on the difficulties in comparing data. *See* J. P. Maas, "Incidence and Treatment Variations Between Negroes and Caucasians in Mental Illness," *Community Mental Health Journal*, Vol. 3, No. 1 (Spring 1967), pp. 61–65.

22. Walter A. Adams, "The Negro Patient in Psychotherapy," *American Journal of Orthopsychiatry*, Vol. 20, No. 2 (March 1950), pp. 305–310.

23. Alexander Thomas, "Pseudo-Transference Reactions Due to Cultural Stereotyping," *American Journal of Orthopsychiatry*, Vol. 32, No. 5 (October 1962), pp. 894–900.

24. Thelma DuVinage, "Casework with Negro Clients," *Smith College Studies in Social Work*, Vol. 9, No. 2 (February 1938), pp. 181–182.

25. Z. C. Hart, "Accommodation Attitudes of Negro Clients to Negro Caseworkers and Their Influences on Casework," *Smith College Studies in Social Work*, Vol. 10, No. 2 (February 1939), pp. 154–155.

26. *See* Inabel B. Lindsay, "Race as a Factor in the Caseworker's Role," *Journal of Social Casework*, Vol. 28, No. 3 (March 1947), pp. 101–147; and Sol W. Ginsburg, "The Impact of the Social Worker's Cultural Structure on Social Therapy," *Journal of Social Casework*, Vol. 32, No. 8 (October 1951), pp. 319–325.

27. Esther Fibush, "The White Worker and the Negro Client," *Journal of Social Casework*, Vol. 46, No. 5 (May 1965), pp. 271–277.

28. Jean S. Gochros, "Recognition and Use of Anger in Negro Clients," *Social Work*, Vol. 11, No. 1 (January 1966), p. 33.

29. *See* Ginsburg, *op. cit.;* Fibush, *op. cit.;* and Manning, *op. cit.*

30. Leon J. Yarrow and Marion R. Yarrow, "Leadership and Interpersonal Change," *Journal of Social Issues*, Vol. 14, No. 1 (Winter 1958), pp. 47–59.

31. Luna B. Brown, "Race as a Factor in Establishing a Casework Relationship," *Journal of Social Casework*, Vol. 31, No. 3 (March 1950), pp. 91–97.

32. Eric Layne, "Experience of a Negro Psychiatric Social Worker in a Veterans Administration Mental Hygiene Clinic," *Journal of Psychiatric Social Work*, Vol. 19, No. 2 (Autumn 1949), p. 69.

33. Leonard C. Simmons, " 'Crow Jim': Implications for Social Work," *Social Work*, Vol. 8, No. 3 (July 1963), p. 26.

34. Andrew E. Curry, "The Negro Worker and the White Client," *Social Casework*, Vol. 45, No. 3 (March 1964), pp. 131–136.

35. Olga Verin, "Manifestations of Racial Conflict in Negro Clients of a Child Guidance Clinic," *Smith College Studies in Social Work*, Vol. 16, No. 1 (October 1945), pp. 1–25.

36. Gochros, *op. cit.*, pp. 28–34.

37. *Ibid.*, p. 31.

38. *Op. cit.*

39. *Ibid.*, p. 93.

40. *Ibid.*

41. *Ibid.*, p. 97.

42. Donald E. Meeks, "The White Ego Ideal: Implications for the Bi-Racial Treatment Relationship," *Smith College Studies in Social Work*, Vol. 37, No. 2 (February 1967), pp. 1–93.

43. E. Franklin Frazier, "Human, All Too Human: The Negro's Vested Interest in Segregation," *Survey Graphic*, Vol. 36, No. 1 (January 1947), pp. 74–75.

44. For example, a new comprehensive community health service in the Watts area of Los Angeles was bitterly fought by Negro members of the medical profession practicing in that area.

45. *See* Jona M. Rosenfeld, "Strangeness Between Helper and Client: A Possible Explanation of Non-Use of Available Professional Help," *Social Service Review*, Vol. 38, No. 1 (March 1964), pp. 17–25; and Charles Kadushin, "Social Distance Between Client and Professional," *American Journal of Sociology*, Vol. 67, No. 5 (March 1962), pp. 517–531.

# Part Two

# TREATMENT

# 9

# The Black Client's
# View of Himself

## OLIVE PETRO AND BETTY FRENCH

RACISM HAS ALWAYS BEEN an ugly and destructive feature of the nation's experience, although it was only in 1968 that it was given official recognition as the most urgent problem facing the country.[1] Over the course of lifetimes and generations of lifetimes, black individuals and black families have coped with the impact of racism on their daily lives. Black individuals and black families have also faced the range of problems that are generally part of day-to-day living in our society; it is difficulties coping with these problems that bring some blacks to social agencies. Although the life experiences of blacks are different from those of other minorities and whites in relation to the effects of racism, there is relatively little in social work literature that considers the impact of this difference on developmental issues such as self-esteem and on social-role functioning. Social casework has largely been "color blind." Andrew

Reprinted, with permission, from *Social Casework*, 53 (October 1972), pp. 466–474. OLIVE PETRO was at the time of writing assistant district director, Stockyards District Office, United Charities of Chicago, Chicago, Illinois; BETTY FRENCH was district director, Midway Center, Family Service Bureau, United Charities of Chicago, Chicago, Illinois.

Billingsley has identified the myth prevalent in social work that "people are people" and "race does not matter" as a barrier to the level of understanding needed to make the social work profession a useful instrument in the liberation of black people.[2]

The principles of psychological and social functioning, by definition universal to the human experience, are incomplete in work with black clients without attention to the unique aspects of the black experience.[3] This article reports on the effort of one family agency staff to develop a framework for understanding the impact upon clients of being black, with respect to self-perception, life experiences, and current problems. A related issue involved the impact of race and racism on the treatment relationship. This aspect took on special importance in a setting where the client population was 90 percent black and the casework staff was 50 percent black and 50 percent white. The area of staff development was a crucial one as the staff worked to develop a common frame of reference about racism; they sought to take hold of the complex emotions involved for all persons around race and racism, whether in the treatment relationship or in interpersonal and staff relations.

The Midway Center of Family Service Bureau of United Charities of Chicago is located in Woodlawn, a black community subject to all the problems of a northern black urban community. The center serves a larger area of Chicago's South Side which is predominantly populated by blacks, including a large black middle class as well as the poverty-stricken. Staff development efforts in the two-year period from September 1969 through June 1971 focused on the issue of race and racism as a dimension in the casework process. This report concentrates on efforts in the second year when a research study was undertaken.

## STUDY CONCERNS

The staff was concerned about how to particularize general knowledge about the effects of racism in a way that not only refined diagnostic understanding of the individual but also increased therapeutic value of casework for the family. For the group of practitioners—half of whom were black and half of whom were white—the overriding concern was that the study be geared to practice issues.[4] It was to yield a greater sensitivity to what is involved for clients in being black in predominantly white America, a deeper diagnostic understanding of the impact of racial experiences as well as coping capacities, and greater ease with, and more effective intervention around, racial content. When the opportunity arose for research consultation with Dr. William Reid of the School of Social Service Administration, University of Chicago, it was expected that this research would provide a systematic means of examining the issues and testing practice hunches.

## STUDY PLAN

Because the study interest was broadly defined—the effect of racism on self-image, self-esteem, and role performance—an exploratory design was used to refine the questions, focus, and approach. A semistructured interview schedule was employed with focused exploration or probes occurring within the context of a service end. The instrument was developed with some trial and error, and analysis of the material occurred in staff meetings held every two weeks. The three question areas were as follows:

1. *How would you describe yourself as a person?* Probe for client's conception of strengths and weaknesses and for other major ways in which he characterizes himself.

2. *What kinds of experiences have contributed to the picture of yourself that you have just given me?* Probe for kinds of experiences perceived by client to be influential, including his early relationships with parents and siblings and his experiences in adolescence. If client spontaneously refers to being black as a source of influence, probe for client's view of his ethnic experience and identity as a source of influence on his self-concept. Probes might include how client first learned he was black, his parents' attitude about being black, his early relationships with the white community, and his encounters with and reactions to racist attitudes and behavior. If client does not refer to racial influences on his own, ask "How do you think being black has influenced the picture you have of yourself?" and probe as above.

3. *How do you think these experiences have affected the way you relate to ——?* If family problem, name role partner with whom client is having the greatest difficulty—spouse, child, and so on. If other kind of problem, revise wording accordingly. Probe for connections between racially connected experiences, attitudes, self-percepts, and client's behavior relating to current problems.

Self-concept was defined as "how the client views himself." It was assumed that clients could give a meaningful answer to how being black can affect self-concept and would do so in the context of the interview. The questions were worked into interviews with clients at various points in their course of contact with the agency. The focus of the questions was to be through the client's perception of himself rather than through his relationship to the outside world. It was suggested that workers use what information and feeling they had about and for the client in forming follow-up questions. It was assumed that the worker would set the stage for this approach with some introduction to the questions. Workers selected clients for participation in the study on a variety of bases including accessibility and assessment of client's receptivity to the idea. Workers' ease with a given client is also assumed to have been a factor. In the early phase of use of the interview schedule, some clients were included on workers' judgment that posing the study questions would not "hurt" the client or the service.

## THE CLIENT SAMPLE

The twenty-one clients in the study came to the agency from December 1970 through April 1971 for help with marital, parent-child, or individual adjustment problems. All were black, and fifteen were women. On the average they were in their early thirties, with ages ranging from twenty-four to fifty-four. They were evenly divided in marital status between single (never married, separated, or divorced) and married. Most (86 percent) had spent their adult life (since age twenty) in Chicago. Sixteen clients were born in the urban North, and five were born in the South.

Fourteen of the study clients were employed at the time of the study interview. The annual income was known for twelve clients. The lowest income was $4,380, and the highest was $16,000, reflecting a considerable range in earnings. One-half made less than $7,000.[5] Five families had more than one wage earner at the time of the interview; this fact resulted in a greater spread for family income from the lowest at $4,380 to the highest at $20,500. The midpoint of the incomes shifted to $15,120 for such families. Of the seven unemployed clients, five were receiving Aid to Dependent Children (ADC) payments.[6] One-half of the employed clients were engaged in work which might be regarded as professional or quasi-professional, that is, teacher, administrator, insurance salesman, or secretary. One-half of the clients had partial or complete high school education; the remainder had education beyond high school, business training or some college; one man had completed college.

The study clients represented twenty families, for one marital pair was included in the study sample. The number of children in each family ranged from none to seven. One-child families were represented most often, followed by two-child and four-child families.

The client sample thus included a range of socioeconomic statuses and means, from unemployed mothers receiving ADC payments to families with two incomes and comfortable financial situations. Their education ranged from high school drop-outs to college educated.


## STUDY FINDINGS

Study findings were looked at along four dimensions—what clients said about themselves, about racial experiences, and about coping with racism, and, finally, what clients did not say about these three areas.

### What Clients Said about Themselves

Asked for a description of themselves, most clients described themselves in predominantly negative terms. Only one person described himself positively, and eight persons gave a mixed description. There was no spontaneous mention of being black in clients' descriptions, although some made reference to race in the interview. Although it is possible that white clients would also describe themselves in negative terms and not mention being white, the contradictory set of circumstances—that color was not mentioned but had been the important determinant of where clients lived, where they went to school, and the nature of education and job opportunities—dramatized the dilemmas that pervade the black experience. The parallel between clients' predominantly negative self-description and their predominantly negative racial experiences is a striking one, as is the fact that clients did not draw a connection between the two.

The dilemma of evaluating one's self-worth apart from situational stresses is illustrated by Mrs. C. She started to present her "strong points" but then seemed bogged down in how much struggle it was to maintain a sense of positive self-regard in oppressive circumstances.

> I carry burdens. . . . It is terribly hard to be the only parent for four children. We have always been so poor. . . . I try to be a good mother. Maybe I'm not the best, but I try. I want them to have a better life. I need to understand my kids better. I don't always know what to do. I don't really know what is best for them.


### What Clients Said about Racial Experiences

Clients did not spontaneously include mention of being black in their descriptions. When workers asked specifically about how it had been for them, being black in predominantly white America, eighteen of the twenty-one responded with accounts of negative racial experiences, and the other three recounted some negative and some positive experiences. The overwhelming preponderance of negative experiences is all the more striking when it is noted that the question was open-ended and not a probe for painful or hurtful experiences. Often after an initial reaction that "it didn't make a difference" being black, clients went on to share, vividly and richly, their encounters with racism and how they had coped with them.

The incidents clients reported were examined in relation to what had been the message about themselves as a black person, whether it was a negative message or a positive one. There were two types of messages—explicit and implicit. Of whichever type, the negative message added up to: "To be black is to be inferior." The source of the reported incidents was also examined to learn whether the message had come from whites, the family, or other blacks. Although there is therapeutic advantage in the positive messages from both black and white sources, the reporting concentrated on the most difficult and likely, that is, the negative messages.

Overall, clients reported four times as many negative incidents as positive ones. The largest category of negative messages came from white sources, evenly divided between explicit negative messages and implicit negative ones. The second largest category of negative messages was implicit negative messages from other blacks (outside the extended family), and the next largest category was implicit negative messages from the family.

To illustrate explicit negative messages received from whites, the following excerpt is taken from an interview with Mr. G as he recalled one experience which was particularly painful to him.

> A skilled artist, he worked for his homeroom teacher and for the school art magazine. This work gave him certain mobility in the halls. One day, he had a note to admit him late to class. He met a white boy in the hall who was late and who asked him to add his name to the note. Mr. G explained that he had done it, but without knowing why; he did not like the boy, and he thought the boy was generally prejudiced against blacks. The forgery was discovered, and it hurt Mr. G very badly when the teacher came up to him and said, "That just shows you can never trust Negroes."

The following are examples of implicit negative messages from whites:

> Mrs. O had wanted to be a secretary, but white high school counselors gave her no encouragement to take secretarial courses. It was subtly discouraged, and another course was encouraged instead. She could not re-

member what she had actually taken, but she dropped out of high school shortly after. The thing that annoyed her was that they were not honest about it. "It would have been so much easier if they had said, 'Look, there aren't office jobs here for blacks.' Then you could understand that if you went into that program, you could make a choice and know that if you wanted to do office work it would mean not in this city."

Miss A's white employer expected her to work a night shift but he considered that shift too dangerous for the white girl.

An example of explicit negative messages from the family is taken from Miss K's interview:

People would always be harping on skin differences in the family, especially those who were lighter-skinned, saying "You black so and so."

Examples of implicit negative messages about being black from family and other blacks follow.

Mrs. O was pushed by her family to exert unusual effort just to be "qualified," with no recognition of the reality of racial barriers to opportunity and achievement.

Miss I remembered that lighter-skinned girls were more popular in school.

### What Clients Said about Coping with Racism

A constant in the negative messages about being black is the conviction that to be black is to be inferior. What was not constant was how clients coped with this message. Indeed, coping mechanisms were rich and varied. There was variety within the range each individual used, and there was variety across the range used by individuals in the study.

The frame of reference of the following material emphasizes coping activities—mental, verbal, and behavioral—which enable the individual to handle himself in the face of a variety of attacks from a hostile environment. These coping processes have a defensive aspect insofar as they function to manage the internal responses of anxiety, fear, and anger stimulated by the external world. However, the defensive function serves to support continued coping and survival.

Five predominant mechanisms were seen in clients' coping with racism. They were denial, reasonableness, compensation, manipulation of the system, and identification with the aggressor.

*Denial* as a coping mechanism is a complex configuration which is used in a variety of ways, frequently in combination with other coping mechanisms. In some cases, clients seemed to be saying that they had not let hurtful encounters with racism defeat them and that they had found ways to survive, despite the onslaughts to their self-esteem and sense of integrity. Some clients found it necessary to suppress the aggressive negative intent, and often their own aggressive reaction, in order to focus on coping with such survival issues as keeping a job. The price paid is often high in regard to depression. In some cases, the individual seems to maintain the value of individual responsibility whatever the societal circumstances. He is then left to deal with the difference between his considerable coping efforts and the paltry pay-off and his feeling of not having a sense of direction in life. Some clients seem to reject the application of prevailing negative stereotypes to themselves in order to avoid its interference with their broader coping efforts. Where use of denial was on a selective basis, current functioning was better than where it was used pervasively.

*Reasonableness* as a coping mechanism is akin to denial but takes the form of a philosophical rationalization, expressed in statements such as, "There are good and bad in all races." Often there is a feeling of being too reasonable, which results in the person's being taken advantage of by others. As described by some clients, efforts to be reasonable seem to be efforts to sidestep feeling angry; often, however, this attempt broke down when they still ended up being treated unfairly. The acceptance of reasonableness in our society can make it an adaptive mechanism in dealing with one's self and with others. However, when it significantly interferes with being reasonable with one's self or with being essentially honest about one's feelings, then it becomes maladaptive to positive ego-functioning.

The mechanism of *compensation* represents an attempt to overcome disadvantages in being black by which the person pushes himself to try harder and rise to the challenge of impossible odds. When it is experienced as an overcompensatory effort to counter all the stereotypes about being black, the result can be that the individual is as bound by the stereotypes as any holder of racial prejudice. However, compensation often yields considerable achievement as well as pride in achievement where efforts have paid off. In that event the person is more apt to be a doer in mastering life's tasks and accomplishing goals. All in all, it seems to be a successful coping strategy if there is accompanying flexibility within the system and a directed use of this adaptive mechanism by the individual.

*Manipulation of the system* is an aggressive, active coping mechanism. It can have a defensive quality—as in, "I'll fight for what is coming to me"—with the ring of certain knowledge that there are few fair breaks in life if you are black. The individual is clear about the disadvantages, but seeks to find or make his own advantage in the situation. This mechanism, like others, is used both adaptively and maladaptively. In its positive context, it created and capitalized on the recent expansion in the job market for blacks. It also interfered with and changed discriminatory practices in civil rights, education, and use of service facilities. It becomes more negative when the individual has to use huge amounts of energy to struggle with feelings of anger, bitterness, and despair when results are meager.

*Identification with the aggressor* as a coping strategy is a stance taken by some persons that racist stereotypes may be true of many blacks but not of themselves. This mechanism protects against the hurts of racism to which the individual is always exposed and a sense of shame about qualities implicitly believed to be true and typical of blacks. It also muffles hostility toward whites which might be overpowering. By displacement of self-hatred, usually along class lines, the individual invokes the rule of the exception to deny that the negative stereotypes that he holds in common with the majority culture apply to himself.[7] In some instances, it takes the form of insistence that racial handicaps do not affect the course of an individual's life and that he himself is to blame when things go wrong. In the material from this study, expression of this attitude is seen in the extent of negative messages about being black that came from black sources. It is not surprising that, having encountered negative racial stereotypes from so many directions throughout life, some individuals accept that they hold validity. However, negotiating with the system for acceptance on one's own merits along this dimension involves paying an excessive price in terms of positive identification and basic self-esteem.

### What Clients Did Not Say

What clients did not say about themselves, about racial experiences, and about coping with racism is an important component of the findings. Clients themselves made no obvious connection between the negative description they gave of themselves and their negative racial experiences, nor between how they were coping with racism and how they were coping with the presenting problem. There seemed to be a tendency to isolate problems related to being black. Clients also seemed to minimize connections between how parents were able to provide for and to protect their families and the influence of racism on opportunities that had been available to parents. Some parents were judged harshly for not having good jobs and not providing the necessities, much less the extras; the conclusion was drawn that parents did not try hard enough. In contrast, clients spoke with pride about how parents had taken direct action in individual encounters with racism.

But, again, it is as if there were no connection between the specific incidents of racism and the broader pervasiveness of racism in terms of social opportunities for jobs, housing, education, and the like. The values of the majority culture may be seen to influence the perception of minority persons, in which blacks apply negative stereotypes about blacks and discount the fact of racism and its real limitations on individual choices.[8] This fact is of concern to practitioners because it underestimates the very real obstacles which racism presents and the struggle involved in coping with it. This viewpoint fails, often, to appreciate the achievements blacks have made in surviving in order to have a base for further achievements. The same individual is often very hard on himself, with self-criticism and self-depreciation in proportion to how he has underestimated his parents' struggle with an oppressive environment.

## *DISCUSSION*

The study was undertaken as a staff development project with goals of raising the level of sensitivity to and understanding of clients' experiences as black persons. The approach was an exploratory one which sought clients' own view of themselves, their reports of their experiences as black individuals, and the influence of life experiences on the problem for which they were seeking help at the agency. Although there are limitations as to the size of the sample and the selection of the twenty-one individuals it included, some inferences can be drawn which may apply to the broader population, to casework practice, and to staff development efforts in this area.

In contrast to the relative silence in social work literature about the experience of black clients with racism, a wealth of vivid and eloquent material was found which documents the pervasiveness of racism. There was no support for the idea that black clients would withhold racial material from workers, white or black.[9] Instead, clients were willing, almost as if they wanted to talk about their experiences of being black.[10] For many, it was an opportunity to talk about some ways in which they had coped successfully.

Societal and institutional racism is shown in the preponderance of negative messages. The racism underlying such messages directly influences blacks as a racial group with regard to such crucial life areas as employment, housing, and education, as well as the nature of health and welfare services. Racism also impinges upon the social status and self-esteem of blacks as individuals. Explicit negative messages abound. Their blatancy makes them more amenable to recognition, hence to correction and to coping efforts by individuals and by groups toward institutional change. Implicit negative messages, on the other hand, are especially insidious in their impact because the content and form of the transmission are veiled. Thus, the messages defy ready recognition as racist in character, yet the racist attitudes and actions are nonetheless experienced in their damaging intent.

The clearly higher proportion of all negative messages, whether explicit or implicit, comes from whites. Beyond being the majority in terms of numbers of people in this country, whites also express the desire to reserve advantages for their majority group and to present obstacles to the achievement of the black minority. Defensiveness of whites arises out of their participation on some level with the system of racism, either directly or implicitly, as recipients of its benefits.

The large number of negative messages about being black which came from black sources deserves some comment. The finding that the family participates in transmitting or at least tolerating the message that to be black is to be inferior is a seriously disturbing one. The insidiousness of racism is seen in black parents' passing on to their children the negative stereotypes which they had received from the white community. This occurrence highlights again the lack of protection against the impact of racism. A preferred model would be the family as a stronger buffer against experiences with racism. It is too early to see the effects of recent black pride movements on the current generation, but the strength of black families seen in the resilience of coping mechanisms holds promise for intervention in the transmission of such stereotypes.[11]

A theme that occurred repeatedly in various forms concerned the lack of protection and lack of privileges that were implicitly part of the experience of being black. A related aspect to being black is having to be more careful about behavior than whites, since the chances of unfair treatment are so much higher.[12]

## IMPLICATIONS FOR PRACTICE

The demonstrated willingness of clients to share racial experiences opens an important area in the casework process that has been neglected too long. The extent of implicit negative messages that assault the self-esteem of blacks suggests the need to clarify the misperceptions and ambiguities inherent in the messages that an individual encounters. Alertness to the need to identify how negative stereotypes about being black are transmitted by white individuals and institutions may sensitize workers to consider ways to engage the client in the challenge of the assumptions involved in racist attitudes and actions. Similarly, clarification can be appropriate when the person underestimates the reality of racism or judges the efforts of self and others with excessive harshness.

Black parents have had to help their children learn to combat racism and will continue to have this task for some time. Supporting coping mechanisms that do not exact an excessive emotional price hold the potential of freeing energy for growth-producing achievements and satisfactions. A richer understanding of the development of successful coping mechanisms can aid a fuller sharing from one family to the next. Agencies might develop opportunities for parent discussion groups in which the focus could be an exchange of ideas on how to help their children deal with encounters with racism in ways that are most ego-syntonic.

## IMPLICATIONS FOR STAFF DEVELOPMENT

A primary objective of this project concerned staff development. Given the social context with its bombardment of racially disturbing events on both clients and staff, there was need for staff to develop a common frame of reference about racism to be able to help clients with this aspect of their lives. The most sensitive area for all staff was counter-transference feelings. There was need for both black and white workers to develop greater sensitivity and greater practice skills in dealing with the impact of racism. Although black workers initially may have an easier entry with black clients, there are pitfalls involved in management of reactions to clients' experiences. These include overidentifying with the clients' experiences, understanding on an intuitive level which may foreclose exploration and individuation, or reacting to the hurt and outrage to an extent that temporarily renders the worker helpless to relate to the client's feelings. The pitfalls for the white worker are many; they include defensiveness, which limits efforts to explore and listen, and hasty acceptance of the client's message that racism has no bearing in the relationship, that the worker is an exception to the rule of hurtful experiences with whites. The white worker's counter-transference may also take the form of an overreaction to prove to himself, as well as to the client, that he is not guilty of participation in the system of racism, in spite of benefiting from it in either important or incidental ways. A common pitfall for both black and white workers is that of underidentification with the human hurts the client has experienced owing to differences in class and life-style; this problem may occur when the worker and client hold different social statuses.

The structure of the study kept the focus on the client and limited the self-conscious defensiveness which tends to develop for even the best-intentioned individuals when race and racism are discussed. Staff meetings, with all staff members presenting interview material, provided an opportunity to share perspectives and reactions at both emotional and intellectual levels. The mutuality of struggles and the support experienced in these meetings stimulated renewed efforts when they were getting bogged down. The clinical material yielded a deeper understanding of clients' individual racial experiences, and the perspective across a group of cases highlighted the pervasiveness of racism. The combined perspectives brought about a greater sensitivity to the odds clients were struggling against and a richer respect for their coping strengths.

There was evidence that with successive use of the interview guide, workers were increasingly comfortable in exploring racial material; this ease encouraged in turn a fuller response from clients in the next interview situation. The racially mixed staff ranged in experience from new graduates to workers with extensive experience, but no apparent differences in quantity or quality of response from clients was revealed along these dimensions. The extent of racially related material appeared to relate to workers' experience in exploring for such material, rather than to race, age, or years of social work practice. This possibility is one of the most significant and encouraging results of the study; it is within the practitioner's scope to expand such experience, with confidence based on the study findings that his efforts will result in greater sensitivity, a stronger treatment relationship, and enriched practice skills.

## CONCLUSION

Racist attitudes and actions are so deeply imbedded in American society that the extent of their impact on individuals, both black and white, can easily be underestimated. Particularly in the urban North, blacks are subjected to negative stereotypes of both explicit and implicit kinds from multiple sources. Implicit negative messages are more insidious, hence more devastating and difficult to deal with; mixed in with other messages, they affect every life sphere. Social caseworkers in a family agency have a unique opportunity to intervene in the transmission of racism. Staff development efforts, such as the study reported here, can be instrumental in sensitizing staff to the many forms of racism and in developing strategies to halt its transmission.

## NOTES AND REFERENCES

1. *Report of the National Advisory Commission on Civil Disorders* (New York: Bantam Books, 1968).

2. Andrew Billingsley, Conference Summary, in *Black Agenda for Social Work in the Seventies* (Atlanta: Atlanta University School of Social Work, 1971), p. 33.

3. William H. Grier and Price M. Cobbs, *Black Rage* (New York: Basic Books, 1968), p. 155.

4. Participants in addition to the authors were Joy Burns, Nancy Kyte, Lucille Levitan, Alice Moss, Yolanda Schuenneman, Joan Small, and Marcia Treffman.

5. According to the Bureau of the Census, in 1970 most black families earned less than $8,000 (62 percent) compared to 54 percent of white families. The black median income was $6,270; the white median was $10,236. The families in our study, with a median income of $7,000, appear to be slightly better off than black families in the nation as a whole, with a median income of $6,270. However, the Bureau of the Census figure includes the lower rural incomes, which bring the national average down. Thus, the study families appear comparable to the national average for urban blacks.

6. Within the study period, one client became employed and another entered a study program to obtain a General Education Development diploma and secretarial training.

7. Gordon W. Allport, *The Nature of Prejudice* (Garden City, N.Y.: Doubleday Anchor Books, 1958), pp. 147–49; E. Franklin Frazier, *Black Bourgeoise* (New York: Collier Books, 1967), pp. 184–88; and Anna Freud, *The Ego and the Mechanisms of Defense* (New York: International Universities Press, 1946), p. 128.

8. Andrew Billingsley, *Black Families in White America* (Englewood Cliffs, N.J.: Prentice-Hall, 1968), p. 164.

9. The findings are consistent with those reported by Donald Brieland, Black Identity and the Helping Person, *Children*, 16:170–76 (September–October 1969); and Franklin T. Barrett and Felice Perlmutter, Black Clients and White Workers: A Report from the Field, *Child Welfare*, 51:19–24 (January 1972).

10. We do not wish to minimize the initial denial of most clients that race had made a difference in their life experience. It was a baffling phenomenon, particularly in light of the content that followed which illustrated how much difference race had made. Once the worker made clear her intention and proceeded to explore and enable clients to share their experiences, they did so richly.

11. Billingsley, *Black Families in White America*, p. 38.

12. Grier and Cobbs, *Black Rage*, p. 61.

# 10

# A Look at the Effect of Racism on Clinical Work

## SHIRLEY COOPER

We are all heirs to the legacy of racism. Deeply pervasive, touching almost all aspects of our lives, racism corrupts all human relationships. Mordecai Richler, the novelist, gives us a glimpse of this in his description of a friendly Sunday baseball game:

> Gordie came in to pitch with the go-ahead run on third and Tom Hunt stepping up to the plate for the first time. Big black Tom Hunt, who had once played semi-pro ball in Florida, was a militant. If he homered, Hunt felt he would be put down for another buck nigger, good at games, but if he struck out, which called for rather more acting skill than was required of him on the set of "Othello X," what then? He would enable a bunch of fat, foxy, sexually worried Jews to feel big, goysy. . . .

Reprinted, with permission, from *Social Casework*, 54 (February 1973), pp. 76–84. SHIRLEY COOPER was at the time of writing chief psychiatric social worker, Mount Zion Hospital and Medical Center, San Francisco, California, and professor, Department of Counseling, California State University at San Francisco. This article was adapted from a paper presented at a workshop of the American Association of Psychiatric Services for Children, Beverly Hills, California, November 20, 1971.

Meanwhile the pitcher is thinking:
I must bear down on Hunt . . . because if he touches me for even a scratch single, I'll come off a patronizing ofay. If he homers, God forbid, I'm a s. . . liberal. . . .[1]

Clearly racism bites deeply into the psyche. It marks all its victims—blacks and whites—with deep hurt, anger, fear, confusion, and guilt. Precisely for this reason, clinicians must examine their own thinking with special care, since their efforts to acknowledge and deal with racial and ethnic factors are affected by highly emotional attitudes. White therapists influenced by a culture rampant with racism and unfamiliar with the intricacies and nuances of the lives of ethnic people may, even with the best intentions, fail to recognize when social and cultural forces predominate in clinical work. Ethnic therapists are vulnerable to the opposite sort of clinical error. Because they are so centrally involved, they may exaggerate the importance or impact of ethnic factors, thus replacing ethnicity with ethnocentricity. In both color blindness and ethnocentricity, patients tend to lose their individual richness and complexity; there is the danger of no longer treating people—only culture carriers.

Sensitive white clinicians struggling with their own unavoidable guilt about living in a privileged and segregated society are apt to defend against this feeling through unrealistic rescue fantasies and activities—a form of paternalism. When white guilt remains unconscious it can lead to overcompensation, denial, reaction formation, an intense drive to identify with the oppressed, and a need to offer to the victim special privileges and relaxed standards of behavior no more acceptable to minorities than to the general population.

Ethnic oppression also produces its own personality and clinical distortion in the oppressed. It may lead, among other things, to overstriving and overachievement at the expense of more normal development. It may create concerns about utilizing one's ethnic position to gain special favor while simultaneously introducing anxiety that one's achievement is not, in fact, a consequence of adequate performance, but based upon special considerations now appropriately, but still inadequately, offered minority people. The sense of competence and certainty in one's own productivity is thus in doubt, leaving anxieties about self-worth and providing no reasonable measures for judging one's own behavior.

It is with these issues that this article is concerned; the exploration and examination of the impact of racism on our clinical behavior is essential if we are to minimize its distorting effects. More specifically, this article will deal with the importance of correctly appraising political considerations in clinical work in order to evaluate where they have a proper place and where they may, in fact, lead to clinical problems; and with the problem of white guilt as a countertransference phenomenon which serves to impede clinical excellence.

Until recently, a color-blind attitude in clinical work was valued as representing a true regard for the individual. We know now that such an attitude is not totally possible, realistic, or useful. Ethnic origins, experiences, and specific life-styles are proper concerns in clinical work and therapeutic programming. Much has been written recently to this point. For example, Alvin Poussaint, recognizing the relationship between oppression and psychological functioning in blacks, has commented in a recent article on this subject:

> The inability of Negroes to be self assertive has fostered a dependency which has devastating consequences for the social behavior and psychic responses of Negroes . . . [this creates] self hatred that comes from feelings of helplessness and powerlessness in the face of overwhelming oppression. . . . The old passivity is fading and being replaced by a drive to undo centuries of powerlessness, helplessness and dependency under American racism.[2]

## POLITICAL CONSIDERATIONS

During the 1950s and 1960s we observed blacks trying to arouse the conscience of America through integration. Failing in this attempt, many turned toward separatism to develop power to wrest that equality which was their birthright. Separatism stresses ethnic difference from the majority in order to develop a firm and proud identity—one that no longer tolerates asking and being "given to." Florence Halpern writes compellingly of the struggles of blacks in building a sense of identity. She comments that an identification with black liberation can be a source of strength, "providing an outlet for feelings of rage, while at the same time affording . . . a sense of 'belonging.' " [3]

Stressing the psychological value of political separatism, Poussaint asserted:

> Now we have seen emerge in segments of the civil rights movement a disenchantment with the social and psychological consequences of American "integration." . . . The Negro has found himself in the demeaning and uncomfortable position of asking and demanding that the White man let him into *his* schools, *his* restaurants, *his* theaters, even though he knows that the White man does not want him. In both the South and the North, many Afro-Americans have resented the indignity of constantly begging for acceptance into the White man's institutions. Such a posture placed Blacks in the same old dependent relationship to the White man.[4]

In seeking acceptance among Whites, many Afro-Americans expend a great deal of internal energy trying to prove that they are all right, but this effort is vain and fruitless because personal acceptability must be repeatedly proven to each new group of Whites. . . . Hence there can be no individual freedom for any Negro until there is group freedom for all.[5]

Groups urging ethnic identity do a service to all Americans. The capacity to value difference is a positive phenomenon; it mitigates against human suspicion of others unlike ourselves and against the need to measure everyone by a single standard of behavior. The ability to feel comfortable with differences is consonant with mature psychological states. Thus the assertion of difference by ethnic groups serves their own needs by fashioning a unified self-conscious struggle for equal rights; it serves all America, helping to harmonize our dreams with our behavior.

The enunciation of intergroup differences makes it necessary to bring intragroup commonalities into awareness. Blacks correctly insist that they must take the lead in this process. Several black writers comment variously on such matters: John H. Clarke, quoting from a 1926 book by Vandercook, states that "a race is like a man. Until it uses its own talents, takes pride in its own history and loves its own memories, it can never fulfill itself completely." [6] James P. Comer comments:

Many researchers make the explicit or implicit assumption that Blacks and Whites have had the same experience in America. The experiences are vastly different, and it is not responsible science to make assumptions about the meaning of Black and White differences when the "scientist" does not know the Black experience or fully understand or take into account the implications of the experiential differences . . . even Blacks with the same occupation and income as Whites have not had a comparable life experience, and the groups cannot be measured or compared without qualification.[7]

These are, of course, not altogether new sentiments, although they are now beginning to win wider credence. It was thirty years ago that A. Philip Randolph commented:

The Negro and other darker races must look to themselves for freedom. Salvation for a race, nation, or a class must come from within. Freedom is never granted; it is won. Justice is never given, it is exacted.[8]

If political separatism makes important psychological as well as political contributions, what, if any, are its clinical problems? No understanding of the commonalities within groups is enough to guide us totally in understanding individual human function or individual difference:

> Individuals are always idiosyncratically different in terms of unique developmental histories; they differ radically in what they demand, what they desire and what they fear with respect to aspiration and position. . . . Social institutions mold role behavior that is processed through the individual participants, each reacting in ways congruent with his own developmental history, his abiding character dispositions, as well as his fluctuating expectations, aspirations and apprehensions. Conversely, every individual uniquely constituted out of his own history lives out his personality within an impinging and determining social context.[9]

In short, in clinical work with minority patients an overbalanced stress on difference, on ethnicity, and on its concomitant psychological meaning can distort the helping process. It may lead a therapist to focus so centrally on ethnic factors that individual problems and individual solutions become obscured. Thus, racism can become the screen upon which the minority patient and the therapist may project a number of other difficulties.

## CASE ILLUSTRATION

> A young Chinese student arrives at a crisis service to ask help with feelings of alienation and fear of making friends within his own ethnic group. He is seen by a Chinese therapist who explores the patient's hesitance in reaching toward Chinese friends, perceiving that such a request may be a function of the student's heightened sense of his own ethnic identity. Tentatively, the student describes his abortive attempts to meet Chinese girls, commenting that he has never had much exposure to Chinese culture and thus might be less acceptable to Chinese parents who value it. He describes an incident in which a white woman attempted to seduce him; until then he thought he was more at home in the white world. The therapist encourages him to "try his wings" in his own ethnic community, recommending several social and interest groups there. Not until several hours pass and the interview is drawing to a close does the student comment that perhaps he should abandon his struggle and simply yield to becoming a homosexual. Although this patient's sense of alienation may be deeply troublesome, his concerns about homosexuality are clearly central to his seeking help at this time. The Chinese therapist, preoccupied by what appeared to be efforts to develop a firmer ethnic identity, failed to attend to his patient's masked and frightening fears of homosexuality—a far different identity issue.

In the above instance, the diagnostic issues were obscured by the ethnic ones. Resistance and projection are hardly new to clinicians, nor is the problem of misdiagnosis. However, the point this case illustrates— and this example is not an isolated case—is that ethnocentricity has become a newer form of resistance and must be observed, understood, and dealt with if we are to be clinically effective.

Closely related to this point is the one made by black psychiatrists, Poussaint and Comer, who state:

> It is possible that drilling Black pride into a child's head in a stereotyped and isolated manner may actually have the reverse effect. Those who teach by rote the slogans of Black dignity, "I am Afro-American," "Black is Beautiful"—may be too extreme in their approach. Our job is to help children develop that delicate balance between appropriate control and appropriate display of anger and aggression, love and hate.[10]

Poussaint and Comer are discussing the dangers of an overbalanced and rote view of ethnic matters in child-rearing. It is just as likely that stereotypical and rote drilling will occur in clinical encounters, working at cross-purposes to the patient's needs. There have been many articles recently in professional journals discussing the treatment of minority patients. Many of these articles make productive and useful suggestions. In some, however, recommendations are made about invariable and early-raising of the issue of race, regardless of the individuality of the patients, their needs, and their unique styles of pacing and defending. For example, in an article discussing countertransference problems between black therapists and black clients, the author asserts that delay in identifying racial issues is always an oversight. He adds:

> There are also those therapists who refuse to mention racial issues for therapeutic reasons. They feel that the immediate therapeutic situation takes precedence over the existing Black therapist/Black client relationship. This seemingly honest attempt to control counter-transference actually covers up the therapist's almost unconscious pretense that he and his client are White and that racial problems are of little consequence.[11]

Another related issue, one also hinted at by Poussaint and Comer, concerns the current imperative to be attentive to different life-styles. Again, this is a matter in which balance is central. There has been until now too little concern with the cultural impact upon personality and differences in adaptive styles. Nevertheless, when political rather than clinical considerations dictate our judgment in treating patients, we become less helpful. Consider, for example, the following:

The purpose of this paper is to study the disruptive behavior of American Black male children, so frequently described under the categorization of hyperactivity and poor impulse-control. Such behavior could conceivably be the result of ego defects, perhaps in combination with neurotic symptoms, but can we not also view this as an attempt to express the aggression in a more adaptive way? A normal reaction to a society whose laws, when carried out, do not respect him. Can it be viewed as constructive masculine behavior? [12]

Perhaps so, but must we view such disruptive behavior as either a deep expression of pathology without adaptive elements or a normal reaction to an oppressive society? Certainly, aggressive disruptive behavior is often defensive against powerful feelings of helplessness and injustice. Such defenses have highly adaptive components. But what of the costs to the child? Confusing normal assertion with disabling aggression, stubbornness with independence, or active motoric styles with hyperactivity does not help child patients. Anna Freud has suggested that childhood disturbance cannot be assessed alone by damage to one or another ego function or activity. Instead, and more properly, she says that behavior and defenses can be more fully and accurately understood in terms of how such behavior impedes a child's further development.

Clearly none of us work in value-free surroundings. Our prior attitudes, hardly overcome, have not been healthy ones, and we certainly should not return to color-blind, middle-class, monolithic standards for patient behavior. However, today we face a different jeopardy, dealing with clinical racism while overreacting ineffectively in our efforts to combat it.

This writer is inclined to agree with Bayard Rustin who sees clearly that:

It is essential that we make an important distinction between issues of politics and problems in psychology. We should see this as a distinction between what we do in order to influence the political and economic relations in the society and what, in a more personal way, we do to achieve self-knowledge and identity. Now I do not think that these are hard and fast categories that totally exclude one another. A just society certainly encourages a healthy psychology, and individuals can find personal fulfillment through political involvement. But I think we must make this distinction, because in periods of great social upheaval—and we are living through such a period—there is a tendency to politicize all things, including scholarship, art, friendship, and love. The most extreme form of this total politicization is totalitarianism, a state we have not yet reached.[13]

## WHITE GUILT

White guilt, now a common psychological phenomenon, was largely dormant before the mid-1960s, at which time it was engendered by a radical change in the political relationships between majority and minority groups. Prior to the mid-1960s, liberal whites were engaged with minorities in a common enterprise to effect social justice. At about that time, the civil rights movement, a united front of white liberals (often Jews), blacks, and a sprinkling of other ethnic people split apart. Blacks, convinced of the necessity to build their own centers of power, took the lead in organizing themselves. Other ethnic groups later followed this pattern.

Whites were excluded; they felt abandoned, bewildered, and betrayed. Having considered themselves friends of social justice, they were now told they were the enemy. The tactic of confrontation, alien to middle-class styles, was a further affront, provoking anxiety and rage as well as guilt. Whites closest to the fight for equality were the very groups against whom blacks fashioned confrontation skills, tactics to wrest practical and concrete gains that persuasion had failed to achieve.

White mental health workers, forced by conscience, necessity, or both, began to engage in activities designed to reach out to previously un-served or underserved groups. No longer leaders, they set out to learn more about the specifics of black and other minority cultures. The effects of the struggle for black identity began to appear in clinics and patients in ways not previously observed. For example, passive-aggressive modes shifted toward more overtly aggressive behavior or feeling.

Blacks began to ask for black therapists rather than accepting any therapist assigned to them. It was repeatedly heard that whites could not understand or know what it felt like to be black, and in fact were themselves consumed with the sickness of racism. Often political under-tones could be sensed in clinical material that was still new to blacks and, therefore, expressed in extremes. "Black is beautiful" was avowed with vigor, but latent attitudes of shame about being black could still be discerned. The darker black claimed superiority esthetically; yet in clinical encounters there still remained confusion about rapid shifts in political standards not yet thoroughly incorporated in psychological attitudes. Politics and rhetoric were, however, not without their effect, though rhetoric was often far ahead of action or attitude. Things for-merly spoken only among blacks were now directed more openly to whites, yet at the same time separatism broke relationships between blacks and whites. Shifts and changes were everywhere challenging belief systems. Belief systems are the stuff of which convictions are made, helping to guide, advise, and direct. In holding to our beliefs we are safe; we know who we are, where we stand, and where we are headed. To give up our beliefs leaves us anchorless and without direction.

To complicate further the revolution in thinking about minorities, clinics began to see larger numbers of people from classes other than those from which the clinicians had come. We were not only confronted by people different in color and culture from us, we were also confronted by people whose life-styles, modes of behavior, cognitive functions, and needs were as influenced by being poor as by other factors.

Tolerance for ambiguity is a valued ego asset, but there is a limit to this tolerance; many of us seek closure and certainty in order to retain sanity. In any case, it is against this constantly shifting and ambiguous backdrop that white guilt emerged as a significant counter-transference phenomenon in work with minority patients. Clinically, white guilt serves to bind political and clinical considerations inappropriately, interfering with useful patient service.

It is a truism that any sensitive American who has some compassion for the deprivation of minority groups experiences a sense of guilt that he, as a member of the majority culture, has participated either by omission or commission in keeping minority members oppressed. Although this feeling is close to the stuff of which empathy and the willingness to act to correct inequities is made, white guilt, when operative in a clinical situation, can create distortions. In effect, it works to deprive minority patients of full growth and full understanding.

Human beings cope with guilt in various ways. For some, guilt must be isolated and warded off, an attitude which leads to a turning away from situations which evoke such feelings. This behavior is seen among white groups who have decided that an accommodation between minority and majority citizens is too difficult. Such whites often retreat to scenes where minority confrontations do not occur.

Other whites who have felt insulted by black demands and confrontations resort to the backlash—a political stance supported by psychological reaction formations. Feelings of helplessness and anger screen the ability to use empathic corrective understanding. A sense of bewilderment and confusion support the view that minority people "have gone too far" and have encroached on one's own domain and interest—and hence the backlash.

Another way of dealing with white guilt is to become one with the group which calls forth this feeling. All of us have observed whites who have, in their behavior and life-styles, emulated blacks. Through imitation and identification such whites become one with the oppressed, sharing in the feeling of being victimized and oppressed. This behavior serves the dual purpose of doing penance while simultaneously extruding the feeling of guilt itself.

Other whites alternate between compassion and resistance, shifting back and forth between these poles, a difficult resolution, if it is a resolution at all. But this solution does have the virtue of recognizing a central reality, namely the shifting position of minority groups vis-à-vis the majority and among the minority groups themselves. Moreover, this position recognizes that in fact minorities do, in the short haul, threaten majority privilege; it also has the advantage of resisting closure about highly complicated issues in rapidly changing times. Feelings of guilt, compassion, anger, and resistance, often provoked by minority groups who—sometimes rationally, sometimes irrationally—activate guilt in the interest of compelling us to act to alter racist states of affairs, are painful to tolerate. Yet if these are experienced consciously, they permit individuals to struggle to clarify positions they must take about specific racial and ethnic issues—be these clinical or political.

An example of white guilt in clinical action can be seen in each of the following cases.

## CASE ILLUSTRATIONS

A twenty-four-year old black man recently released from a mental hospital attends an outing arranged by his day treatment center. He only occasionally joins in the group's activities, but he does engage in a conversation initiated by one of the counselors, a young, bright, white woman, deeply conscious of injustice to blacks. She has read about such experiences and is in no small way eager to even the score. As the conversation proceeds, the black patient talks of his visions, filled with aggression and violence. He is certain he can predict the future. As the group returns to the center the patient elects to sit beside the counselor commenting, as they pass through an affluent neighborhood, that the people who live there "sure have it good," and adding, "What would be so bad about blowing it up? Everybody would sure call me a bad boy then." It is white guilt that keeps the counselor from a helpful response. Instead she reports that neither she nor any white has the right or the capacity to intervene, only a black therapist can be of help. Yet this black man's controls are tenuous, his impulses overwhelming. He is not just putting the counselor on, although there may be some of that; he desperately needs the strength to control impulses as he takes his first faltering steps back into the community. White guilt denied him the help he needed.

An intensely sensitive, bright, and talented black man seeks help for not being as productive as he would like. As the treatment proceeds, other problems become evident: a fear of closeness, the wish to compete and fear of competing, a constant struggle between submission and rebellion. Many of his problems are in fact deeply colored by his blackness. The patient makes significant gains over a year's time with his white female therapist. There has been a sharp reduction of anxiety, depression, and fear of intimacy; his real life reflects these in new and closer friendships. His intense ambivalence toward his parents yields to a more benign view, as his need to alternately submit to and rebel against them is understood. He can be more available and comforting toward his wife. Yet his productivity is not greatly altered and he reports constant striving compounded by unremitting self-doubts. As he starts to work more focally and more deeply on his competitive struggles, he reports that he cannot remember a time when he was not forced to strive. He recalls his father's admonishment: "You have to be better to be as good as the whites." He is sure this attitude was stressed as he entered school and that it has had a decisively important influence on all his activity, particularly with respect to learning and achieving. His therapist listens receptively and responsively to the struggles of a black man in an alien and unyielding white world, no doubt experienced vividly and frighteningly by a small child just entering school.

Although this information is certainly important to an understanding of this man's precocious independence achieved by turning inward, nothing much alters now in the treatment. It is not until the patient has returned to these issues again and again that the therapist is struck by a now rather atypical lack of affect. She comments on it. The patient mentally shrugs and acknowledges that it is to be expected; after all, he "was already one of six kids." The therapist reflects on this seemingly unconnected comment and is met with the further comment that he had "gotten used to being kicked about." The therapist responds that he had not always been one of six; once he had been the second of two, then one of three. Slowly and painfully he recaptures the memory of his brother's arrival. He can describe his mother's homecoming, how he had been afraid of his grandmother who cared for him during his mother's confinement, and how his brother was given his crib. (Later he can correct his memory to recall further that this crib was not immediately given over to his brother; his brother must have been at least six months or one year old before he "was displaced.") It is of importance that this brother not only became the favored son, but died in adolescence. The patient's subsequent working through of intense and frightening sibling rivalry heralds a reduction of his self-doubts, an increase in productivity, and, perhaps most importantly, pleasure in achievements.

There is no question that this man's blackness continues to influence his competitive strivings, his self-doubts, and his fear of, as well as his wish for, success; but it is equally true that his personal history and personal experience were just as inhibiting of actual performance. How else can we account for his progression when this material was captured, recovered, and worked through? Could we not properly ask why this therapist took longer than necessary to catch on? It is of no use to this black patient to confuse personal historical binds with cultural interferences.

Five-year-old Bernard, a black child, lived with his maternal grandmother. In the first interviews the grandmother spoke of her fear of the ghetto in which she and Bernard lived and the unreliability of black men which led, she felt, to the placement of Bernard with her when her daughter's common-law husband left her. She spoke of blacks in denegrating terms of violence and hypersexuality.

Bernard was seen in the local child guidance clinic because of temper outbursts, bedwetting, and general defiance.[14] The therapist, a young white woman, observed Bernard's play with great perceptiveness. She noted initially that he seemed to use all the toys indiscriminately while moving rapidly from one to the other. After several months of treatment, Bernard's capacity to stay with a toy and to interact with the young worker increased. In playing house, however, he repeatedly failed to differentiate between black and white dolls. After a further period of testing in treatment which exposed concerns about object constancy, Bernard began to sort the toys into distinct piles. He began to notice the difference between black and white dolls, though making many slips in describing them. He interchanged the words *right* and *white* in describing the dolls. The worker commented that he seemed to be confused about white and right. This comment elicited all sorts of reality experiences as well as Bernard's fantasies. "White boys go first in line," he reported. "White-right boys are nice."

The white therapist used this opportunity to point out to Bernard that he seemed to think white and right were the same. Then followed a lecture about people being different but not better than one another, that neither white or black were right and that white boys did not always have to be first in line.

It appears to this writer that this young worker's well-intentioned effort to help Bernard evolve a better sense of himself was not particularly helpful. To cut off emerging fantasies about his view of blackness by offering a too-quick corrective version about differences denies the right each of us has to his feelings and the need to explore them in the light of our own fantasies, life histories, and experiences. The early skillful treatment becomes a lecture in race relations, in much the same way that we have in the past tried to give children good factual sexual information to no avail.

Selma Fraiberg in an article written some twenty years ago discusses the side-by-sideness of sexual fantasies that grow out of developmental and pathological concerns and good sexual information given by therapists in an effort to correct fantasy misinformation.[15] She concludes, after presenting many case illustrations, that the only time to provide the needed corrected sexual data is after full exploration of the child's own versions of sexual life and the individual conflicts surrounding these. Only then can valid and age-appropriate information be given. Simply to tell someone that he should feel better than he feels does not seem useful. This therapist's feelings of white guilt forced premature comfort before Bernard was ready.

> A thirty-year-old black man, the only child of a large family who escaped from a grinding culture of rural poverty, is referred to a department of vocational rehabilitation for help with securing a more comfortable prosthetic device. His leg had been amputated below the knee after he had been shot during a fight with a white store owner while traveling with a friend through the Southwest. The patient's initial request shifts from help with the prosthesis to help with finding "meaningful work."
>
> His history reveals that his father, whom he describes as a drifter, left the home when the patient was nine, that he alone of his siblings managed to complete high school and some college work. He was successfully employed as a newspaper artist in the North and was married until "one day [he] left . . . wife and the newspaper game" and that he obtained several other jobs which he also precipitously left. The white counselor, in bringing this case for consultation, reported that her client was a controlled, bright, and dignified man, but that he left her confused and puzzled about the help he required. She repeatedly affirmed that she was white, female, and older than her client, clearly implying that it was impossible for her to work with him productively.

In reviewing this material, a black student perceptively commented:

> In directing herself toward the client's blackness in this society, I feel the counselor is avoiding the real issues. Even more, we can't find out what the real issues are. The statements this counselor makes about her difference from the client makes me feel that she is not looking at and seeing the client as a person with a real problem, a person with his own personal trauma, but as another black person with much the same hangups as every other one. I believe the counselor has to deal with her hangups; she sees this client in much the same way as you view the saying "All black people got rhythm"—as if he has no individuality of his own—just a racial identity.

In this and in other instances, white guilt entraps us in what a black colleague of this writer calls "cripple psychology." In an effort to relate compassionately to the very real oppression of minorities, many therapists lose clinical objectivity. They view all minority patients as victims, unwittingly reinforcing personal pathology.

Ernest Gaines, the black novelist, delineated this problem well:

> The point is, we're never written about strictly as human beings. Whites write about us as victims. We write about ourselves as victims. I'm not saying we haven't been victims. But there are other things going on in Black lives, bigger things.[16]

Ralph Ellison put it another way when he wrote of his "struggle to stare down the deadly and hypnotic temptation to interpret the world and all its devices in terms of race." [17]

It is tempting to review the above cases in terms of general clinical ineptitude, and there is much to that. But there are styles to our clinical errors, and the times and white guilt promote particular kinds of clinical error.

In Rustin's terms, can we resist the temptation to "politicize all things" while we struggle to help individual patients to find personal fulfillment, simultaneously working to eradicate racism in our institutions and in our own perception? It is, after all, a matter of balance.


## NOTES AND REFERENCES

1. Mordecai Richler, *St. Urbain's Horseman* (New York: Bantam Edition, 1972), p. 228.

2. Alvin Poussaint, Minority Group Psychology: Implications for Social Action in Thinking About Cities, in *New Perspectives on Problems*, ed. Anthony H. Pascal (Belmont, California: Dickerson Publishing Co., 1969), pp. 21, 23.

3. Florence Halpern, Self-Perception of Black Children and The Civil Rights Movement, *American Journal of Orthopsychiatry*, 40:520–26 (April 1970).

4. Poussaint, Minority Group Psychology, p. 24.

5. *Ibid.*, p. 26.

6. John H. Clarke, *Reclaiming the Lost African Heritage in Black Fire* (New York: William Morrow, 1968).

7. James P. Comer, Research and the Black Backlash, *American Journal of Orthopsychiatry*, 40:8–13 (January 1970).

8. Quoted by Bayard Rustin in A Letter to Black Youth, *Dissent*, 17:496 (November-December 1970).

9. R. S. Wallerstein and Neil J. Smelzer, Psychoanalysis and Sociology: Articulations and Applications, *International Journal of Psychoanalysis*, 50:693–710 (1969).

10. Reported in the *San Francisco Chronicle*, February 21, 1971.

11. Maynard Calnek, Black Therapist and Black Client, *American Journal of Orthopsychiatry*, 40:39–45 (January 1970).

12. Joan O. Hoffman, Joel H. Fields, and Rhea Schwartz, Mental Illness or Maleness in Black Males—Aggressive Behavior in Black Males: A Contemporary Interpretation. Unpublished manuscript presented at American Association of Psychiatric Services for Children Conference, 1970.

13. Rustin, A Letter to Black Youth, p. 583.

14. This case was reported in a symposium on Race and Psychotherapy.

15. Selma Fraiberg, Enlightenment and Confusion, *The Psychoanalytic Study of the Child*, 6:325–35 (1951).

16. *San Francisco Chronicle*, April 25, 1971.

17. Rustin, A Letter to Black Youth, p. 584.

# 11

# Black Patient–
# White Therapist

## CLIFFORD J. SAGER,
## THOMAS L. BRAYBOY,
## AND BARBARA R. WAXENBERG

IN A RECENT EDITORIAL in a campus newspaper, black and Hispanic students called upon their Brothers and Sisters to boycott the white psychologists of the college guidance department and to insist that they be assigned instead to counselors of their own race and ethnicity. This demand can hardly be regarded as unreasonable when considered in the light of the students' previous destructive experiences with the educational system. It is hardly unexpected that blacks would refuse to accept from whites a form of therapy that must be based on a personal relationship and on trust.

It is neither unreasonable nor unexpected; but the demand for an adequate number of black counselors and therapists is unmeetable. At the present time, the pool of black professionals is pitifully small, not

Copyright, the American Orthopsychiatric Association, Inc. Reproduced by permission from *American Journal of Orthopsychiatry*, 42 (April 1972), pp. 415–423. CLIFFORD J. SAGER, THOMAS L. BRAYBOY, and BARBARA R. WAXENBERG were at the time of writing affiliated with Beth Israel Medical Center and the Mount Sinai School of Medicine of the City University of New York, New York. This study was supported in part by USPHS-NIMH grant 02304.

nearly sufficient to meet existing needs. Many of the necessary services must be provided by white personnel.

This new aggressiveness and forthrightness of the black community, this new ability to struggle directly for what they want, and this diminished eagerness to accept the services and benevolence of whites, has forced community psychiatry to reevaluate its therapeutic methods, emphases, and goals. More specifically, this new militancy raises the following questions:

1. Can a white therapist, operating against the background of a three hundred year history of discrimination and deprivation, and within the context of today's tense racial situation, engage a poor black person in therapy?

2. Are there specific techniques of engagement into treatment that are more likely than others to prove successful, and where do traditional approaches fail?

3. What is the role of the therapist who treats individuals or families where prime concerns are subsistence and survival rather than self-exploration and change? Which problem areas are legitimately within the sphere of psychiatry and which lie outside its domain and competence?

4. Are our models of psychopathology still relevant?

One thing is certain: the issue of blackness cannot be ignored. To regard skin color as irrelevant to treatment overrides the central importance that the patient's blackness has for him. At the same time, it avoids the glaring truth that the therapist's whiteness and middle-class station are of the greatest consequence to the patient. Years of humiliating contact with whites have taught the black person not to share his personal feelings with them. Whites do not understand the values of blacks, and many tend to be judgmental and mocking. Moreover, whites have generally felt no need to be candid in return. Black-white relationships have thus been permeated with sham, the blacks sometimes adopting self-protective Uncle Tom servility while privately ridiculing the gullibility of whites; the whites basking in the mythology that superior status derives from inherently superior qualities. Since most forms of psychotherapy are predicated on achieving absolute openness on the patient's part, this fraudulence provides a shaky substructure for the therapeutic process.

*Can a white therapist, operating against the background of a three hundred year history of discrimination and deprivation, and within the context of today's tense racial situation, engage a poor black person in therapy?*

The answer, of course, cannot be absolute but must depend upon the interrelation of patient, therapist, and social climate. It is our contention that most people can be reached if we can find the right road and that the major barrier to finding this meeting ground lies in the attitude of the professional. This statement implies that the indispensable ingredient in the engagement process is the therapist's commitment to it.

It is an axiom of treatment that the therapist needs to know himself as well as his patient. A suppressed hard core of feelings about black people is one corner of self-awareness that eludes even well-intentioned middle-class white professionals. To illustrate: after a recent sit-in at a university, during which black students had forcibly "liberated" several buildings, one white professor of psychology, the head of a large psychotherapy clinic, was stunned to hear himself report to his wife, "Do you know what those *niggers* have pulled now?" Threat to his power and authority had allowed a word long exorcised to slip through, trailing with it memories of gang fights on Brooklyn streets, his father's laments over what "they" were doing to the neighborhood, his mother's grievances and vague suspicions about the Negro maid. These same checked angers, disgusts, anxieties, sexual feelings, and fears are readily awakened in whites who work in ghetto areas with this large, clearly segregated, and alienated segment of our population. Such feelings are apt to emerge at crucial and often unexpected times in therapy, and to cripple the therapeutic process. This latent reserve of racism, this submerged sense that the black man is "different," not governed by the white's warm, human emotions or worthy motivations, is part of our American heritage. The status of mental health professional offers no immunity to the malady.

As in any other therapeutic situation, the source of the therapist's fear, anger, or sense of alienation from the patient warrants careful examination. What stimuli are triggering these emotions, and how are they expressed? In this setting, in addition to the more widely recognized wellsprings of countertransferential reactions, the professional needs to be alert to another spectrum of subjective responses—those based on racist concepts.

But the patient also brings *his* doubts, fears, resistances, and racial stereotypes to the consultation room. It must be borne in mind that the treatment of the black patient and his family is affected not only by the usual resistances that most persons bring to therapy but by the specific ones that relate to the fact that he is black. The years in which black men were constantly reminded of their alleged ignorance, bestiality, inferiority, and irresponsibility have instilled a trigger-readiness to react to any suspected put-down from a white man. As a white person, the therapist may be held responsible and accountable for the condition of black people in this country. The patient's confidence and trust must be painstakingly earned; it is not given automatically.

Although in some instances the patient's perception of the therapist may be distorted, it should be appreciated that often this twisting of reality is adaptive in that it is a manifestation of behavior learned in order to cope and survive in the ghetto. But blacks have as many fixed notions and stereotypes about whites as whites have about blacks, and frequently a patient's distorted perspective may form an insurmountable obstacle to developing and continuing a therapeutic relationship.

It can be disastrous for the therapist either to deny the suspicion and hostility of the black patient or to feel guilty that these negative sentiments exist. The therapist works with these powerful negative feelings as distortion and resistance when they are unfounded, and, conversely, accepts them when they are accurate. If he fails to do this, he interfers seriously with the patient's reality testing.

It is essential that the therapist know and, more important, *want* to know and to understand the living conditions, cultural patterns, and value systems of the people he seeks to help. Without this appreciation, it may be difficult for persons removed from the ghetto to accept the style of life of those who are part of it and to refrain from attempting to impose a Puritan-ethic-tinged morality upon it. Certain areas of sensitivity require an understanding and tact that can come only from intimate knowledge of black people and their culture. A number of the particular areas of difficulty relate to prevailing stereotypes such as those concerning out-of-wedlock pregnancy, male sexuality, drinking, violence, joblessness and aimlessness, matriarchal households, and marital patterns. The accuracy of these assumptions has been questioned by several serious studies.[4] Knowing the concerns of black people lessens the likelihood of offending, but pitfalls will be avoided only when fear and hostility toward black people have been resolved within the white himself.

In summary, the therapist who works in ghetto areas must *want* to treat black people and must be willing to listen to and understand them. Motivation must go hand-in-hand with familiarity with black lower-class family life and the openness to explore one's own feelings about it. We believe that it is possible for white therapists to treat black patients, but the patient's priorities must be dealth with from the start.

*Are there specific techniques of engagement into treatment that are more likely than others to be successful, and where do traditional approaches fail?*

There is little in the treatment of the black person that is not common to all good therapy. Techniques developed in private practice are equally applicable to clinic populations; similarly, those learned in the clinics enrich private work. Practice is the same for all. What is unique relates more to the therapist's understanding and attitude than it does to specific techniques of treatment.

It is not uncommon for the white middle-class professional to approach the ghetto patient with an armload of stereotypes and myths and an outlook clouded by a long-standing perjorative view of lower-class culture. The pages of our scientific literature are dotted with references to the "cultural deprivation" of the poor, to their presumably limited vocabularies and ability to deal only with concrete and immediate problems. Since therapy rests to a large extent on the exchange of words, the nonspectacular results obtained thus far with poverty-stricken, minimally educated persons are attributed in part to the limitations of their language. Yet anyone familiar with the "jiving" and patois of the ghetto, with the prestige and power of the fast talker, must recognize that "nonverbal" translates to "non-verbal-in-white-terms." It would seem that many white middle-class professionals have failed to understand a style of communication that is alien to them.

As to the matter of dealing with concrete problems only, any people struggling for survival necessarily have as their first concerns such "concrete" issues as how to get clothing so the children can go to school, how to survive in rat and roach infested housing, where to place a toddler so a mother can work, and how to stretch a welfare budget. Individuals or patient-families must, therefore, be reached in terms of their priorities. Therapy begins where their concerns are. Once the most pressing environmental aspects of the difficulties have been clarified and dealth with, efforts can then be made to grapple with underlying psychological issues. In contrast, the usual procedure followed by most clinicians is to restructure what the patient or family presents so that it conforms to the therapist's theoretical bias and formula for conducting treatment. The therapy that results may bear little relationship to the problem for which help was originally sought. Professionals have to be encouraged to expand their conception of treatment, and resources have to be developed that will deal with environmental life stresses.

Referral for individual private therapy is only one of many modalities available. Psychiatry has changed rapidly in the past fifteen years. We no longer regard individual psychotherapy as the optimum form of treatment for all psychiatric disorders. Many patients may be done a disservice when some of the newer forms of therapy and combinations of these modalities are not utilized in the overall treatment program. It is not the black patient who is responsible when he fails to respond to our prescribed method of treatment, but the diagnosis or therapy that may be in error.

It would seem that family therapy is particularly relevant to the needs of the ghetto poor. In addition, with many persons, regardless of ethnicity, short-term therapy geared toward dealing with a crisis situation is more appropriate and effective than a long-term approach aimed at more fundamental character change. The therapist attempts to capitalize on immediate motivation in order to expand and deepen the perception of the nature and causes of the patient's difficulties.

Based on these considerations, the authors, with the help of colleagues, developed a short-term treatment program for ghetto families.[2] Families treated in this program were encouraged, after a limited number of sessions (ten to fifteen), to terminate therapy but were informed that if, in time, another crisis should arise or if the members feel dissatisfied with their own or with the family's functioning, they should feel free to return. We found that by structuring treatment in this way we could more readily meet the family on the level of their priorities and were better able to offer them not only what they wanted but what they needed. The sessions were used to help the patient or patient-family set new goals and reach for new horizons, but at *their* pace and in terms of *their* values. As immediate pressures were relieved during the course of treatment, the focus of therapy frequently changed. Often a new series of crises was precipitated as the "patient" attempted to carry out new responsibilities, and the focus shifted again.

Individuals or families who returned to therapy for a second series of sessions often worked toward achieving further changes that might not have even been considered in the first group of visits. Long periods of resistance due to poor motivation were thus avoided, since the returning family now had sufficient motivation to move in treatment.

In general, in work with black patients one need not be primarily concerned with sweeping modifications of technique, but rather with avoiding manifestations of racism and class prejudice.

*What is the role of the therapist who treats individuals or families where prime concerns are subsistence and survival rather than self-exploration and change? Which problem areas are legitimately within the sphere of psychiatry and which lie outside its domain and competence?*

Environmental factors are often more compelling behavioral determinants than are intrapsychic ones. Many of the families we treat are fragmented; many live crowded together, fighting to survive on marginal incomes, their fortunes riding with the vagaries of welfare regulations; many of the children roam the streets unsupervised, falling further and further behind in school, easy prey to pushers, pimps, and petty criminals. Male-female relationships are stormy, marital affairs and bloodspilling common. There is a possibility that the household will consist of a matriarch, her daughter, and her daughter's children, with "uncles" and boarders sporadically joining the menage and then departing. If change is to occur, intervention should be aimed at stresses deriving from the patient's social conditions as well as at manifestations of intrapsychic pathology.

Although the ghetto develops its own subculture with its own distinct patterns for coping with social and economic realities, it is important to recognize that its residents are not oblivious to the more stable and functional family patterns outside. Comparison of the disruption of their lives with the televised image of the comfort and security of suburban middle-class existence is a constant source of frustration and discontent.

It is the responsibility of the professional to recognize the malignant impact of slum life and to deal with its harsh realities, rather than to construct arbitrary dichotomies between psychic and social realms. Assistance with matters related to one's daily life cannot be regarded as merely the sugar frosting that seduces a person into therapy. *It is an essential part of the treatment itself,* one that frequently turns out to be instrumental in producing far reaching psychological change.

When indicated, active intervention into problems with welfare agencies, housing authorities, courts, schools, and employers should be incorporated as part of treatment. Although the therapist shows his recognition of the importance of the patient's request by doing something about it, "doing" is frequently defined as encouraging and supporting the patient's autonomous pursuits. Interest and concern can also be demonstrated by effectively and personally carrying through a referral to another service.

A word of caution is in order here. For a therapist to attempt to appease misguided demands in response to a challenge to win over black patients is paternalistic and condescending, a reinforcement of the patient's sense of helplessness, and is no less offensive than the authoritarian rejection of these demands was in the past.

If a meaningful service is to be offered to deprived persons it cannot be fragmented, with psychotherapy split off from active intervention aimed at ameliorating the dehumanizing conditions under which the patient lives. Clinics and agencies must offer a variety of services, so that the possibility of changing outer as well as inner life exists. This type of involvement is often frustrating to the professional. The network of social agencies that governs the lives of slum-dwelling families is typically unresponsive, unyielding, and bound in mazes of red tape. A sense of helplessness and futility is a frequent companion in one's early contacts with the dead ends of ghetto life. With experience, we are learning how to use more effectively the entire resources of the community, how to contact, cultivate and collaborate with other agencies and institutions, and how to exert pressure. Such extensions into community, political, and social realms are necessary if we are to be effective in behalf of the patients we treat.

*Are our models of psychopathology still relevant?*

This question is central to the problem of building meaningful treatment programs. The most commonly used therapeutic models are rooted either directly or indirectly in psychoanalytic theoretical constructs. Among other factors, these fail to take sufficient account of the patient's family situation and of the cultural milieu in which he was raised, in evaluating whether his behavior is disturbed or adaptive.

Judged in terms of conventional middle-class morality, such patterns as wife beating, hustling, and continuous unemployment become cardinal sins, and the man who indulges in them is clearly out of joint. Viewed against the backdrop of ghetto life, these may become appropriate adaptive measures, consonant with acceptable standards of manhood. The "jiving," the gambling, the unrealistic fantasies are all part of the ethos of the slums and reflect the dream to "strike it rich." Within the ghetto there is little condemnation of these activities. The fancy talker, the splashy dresser, the owner of the Cadillac—these are the men who have made it. Black poet Nikki Giovanni [1] expresses this gulf between black pride and white understanding in her poem, *Nikki-Rosa:*

> . . . and I really hope no white person ever has cause to write about me because they'll never understand Black love is Black wealth and they'll probably talk about my hard childhood and never understand that all the while I was quite happy.

Given the set of circumstances in which he lives, is a young black man's militant stance, his distrust and hatred of white society, a pathological response or an adaptive mechanism that could lead to positive changes in his own life and that of others? It would seem that his militancy gives him hope and strength, whereas otherwise he might be crushed and defeated.

While it cannot be denied that blacks enjoy no monopoly on discrimination and social misery, it is equally non-refutable that no other group in the United States—with the possible exception of the American Indian—can match the degradation they have suffered. Even the staunchest of white supporters cannot fully identify with what it means to be set apart by skin color and isolated from the favored group. When the black man contrasts the unrelenting poverty of the ghetto with the affluence outside it, when he counts the circumscribed possibilities and choices open to him, when he sees his color as a threat to his existence, when he feels that all norms of beauty and goodness are based on whiteness, when he realizes that all cherished historical figures have white skin automatically bestowed upon them—then all these must sum to an accusation of inferior stock. The mark of inferiority and oppression has been branded not only on his forehead but on his body and down into his very guts.

If we view each patient in this light, we are not led off into preoccupation with deep intrapsychic sources of pathology but are more able to remain attuned to immediate concerns. *If inner psychology is to be altered, outer life must change.* When a black man steps out of the pattern of ghetto thinking either by taking on the aspirations of the taste-making middle class or what he considers healthy values of his own race, or by aligning himself with more militant blacks to fight for his place in the sun, a profound change in personality frequently ensues. It is up to the therapist to help his client or patient see and choose for himself among the many alternatives that *are* open to him, rather than just those born of the ghetto's approach to adaptation and limitation.

We are in the midst of a period of concentrated change in black-white relations, and the understanding of that change is crucial to effective therapeutic work. A sense of comradeship between blacks and whites is far more difficult to achieve today than it was in the days of Selma, Alabama, and "We Shall Overcome," when integration was still the dream. In the words of John Steptoe,[3] a seventeen-year-old black artist:

I have never felt I was a citizen of the U.S.A.—this country doesn't speak to me. To be a black man in this society means finding out who I am. So I have got to stay on my own, get out from under induced values and discover who I am at the base. One thing I know: at the base there is blackness. A white man and I can sit together and talk and communicate, but we are different. He is my fellow man, but not my brother. Not many white people can accept that.

The wariness that centuries have bred into North American blacks becomes an integral part of the treatment situation, a part that the white professional often either fails to note or is distressed to unearth. It is not uncommon for a mental health professional who throughout his lifetime has allied himself with liberal and civil rights causes, who feels that he can relate to blacks, who goes to bat for his patients beyond the traditional boundaries of the therapeutic relationship, to find that black patients fail to respond to his efforts with the expected openness and trust. To add to his perplexity and discomfiture, black colleagues attack him for what they interpret as subtle manifestations of underlying racist feelings. When he refers to the discrimination he has suffered as a Catholic or a Jew, or when he describes his struggles against early poverty, he does not comprehend why his black colleagues and patients impatiently brush aside these attempts to erect a common base of experience. He is deeply hurt when, despite sincere efforts, he is not fully accepted by blacks but is made to feel that the gulf that separates him from black acquaintances, colleagues, and patients is impassable.

Moreover, the white therapist finds that his daily efforts to practice in accordance with the tenets of his training are unsuccessful with patients whose first priorities are the pressing and immediate concerns of survival. After a series of unrewarding attempts at treatment, he may conclude, "Who needs it?" and drift back to seeing patients who are more like himself in class, color, and values, and who more readily respond to what he offers. The therapist's need for achievement and for gratification from his daily work is more easily satisfied in this other arena.

The mood of the times has combined with the anachronism and intransigence of some of our traditional methods of treatment to tarnish the promise of the much-vaunted community mental health movement. The modern black, assertive and proud, will no longer docilely accept programs he had no share in developing. As this sense of community tightens and blacks unite on a local level, it becomes impossible for the agencies servicing these neighborhoods to continue to operate with the arbitrariness and aloofness of the past. If professionals are to perform their work effectively, they must respond to the expectations of the larger community. To remain community based, a mental health service must become community responsive. The agencies that continue to function as another tentacle of a hostile establishment, that maintain their refusal to allow representatives of the community a place in the decision-making bodies, may soon find themselves ignored, picketed, or ousted from the arena.

It is clear that our current therapeutic programs for the poor need to be reappraised. Services must be made available in forms that will be appropriate and in places that will be comfortably accessible. Methods of engagement that are more deeply rooted in the patient's world, and that reflect his priorities rather than the therapist's, need to be developed. The mental health professional can no longer rely on the usual tools of his trade, on therapeutic methods that have proved successful with a small percentage of highly selected patients but that may be irrelevant to the population he now treats.

The conditions of life that stem from long-standing political, economic, and educational disfranchisement are well known. What remains unsolved is how to remedy them. It is clear that the alleviation of the mental ills of a population rests first on the remedying of the social ills of the nation. Similarly, the treatment of the psychic pains of an individual or family cannot be divorced from treatment of the conditions in which they live. If we can view the problem in this broad way, we will achieve a sounder perspective on how to use our skills as mental health practitioners.

## REFERENCES

1.  Giovanni, N. 1970. Nikki-Rosa. *In* The Black American Experience, F. Freedman, ed. Bantam Pathfinders Edition, Toronto.

2.  Sager, C. *et al.* 1968. Selection and engagement of patients in family therapy. Amer. J. Orthopsychiat. 38(4):715–723.

3.  Steptoe, J. 1969. Quoted in Life Magazine, August 29.

4.  Ten Houten, W. 1970. The black family: myth or reality. Psychiat. 33:145–173.

# 12

# The White Professional and the Black Client

## ALEX GITTERMAN AND ALICE SCHAEFFER

As WE BECOME increasingly conscious of the depth of racism in our society,[1] and as tensions between blacks and whites continue to surface, it is imperative to examine the impact of these racial pressures on the helping professions—especially upon those encounters that find the white professional trying to serve the black client. It is not an uncommon experience, for both black client and white professional, that the supposedly therapeutic contact is a frustrating and unsatisfying one during which service is neither delivered nor received. Each party may tend to "explain" this result by blaming the other, and at present there is a substantial body of literature—professional and popular—attacking the inadequacies of both white professionals and black clients. The stereotypes are familiar: the middle-class white professional is labeled as distant, unfeeling, uncaring if not actually racist, malicious, and puni-

Reprinted, with permission, from *Social Casework,* 53 (May 1972), pp. 280–291. ALEX GITTERMAN was at the time of writing a lecturer at the Columbia University School of Social Work, New York, New York; ALICE SCHAEFFER was a social worker at the Jewish Child Care Association, New York, New York.

tive; [2] the lower-class black client is stigmatized as unmotivated, resistant, inaccessible, and lacking mature personality development and family organization.[3]

Because of these negative experiences, question has been raised within the professional and lay community as to whether white professionals can, indeed, provide meaningful service for black clients. This question has stimulated vigorous debate and will continue to do so for years to come. It is not the intention of the writers to attempt to answer this question. Rather they choose to view the present situation as given —one in which because of social service manpower conditions and the needs of this country's population, white professionals *do* work with black clients and will continue to do so. Therefore, the crucial issue becomes, *How* will this work be carried out—what can white professionals *bring to* and *do in* the encounter with black clients to make their services most useful? The writers address themselves to this concern by (1) identifying the obstacles emerging from the black-white encounter that impede the development of a helping relationship; (2) offering a professional vision, a frame of reference, that lends itself to a meaningful black-white engagement; and (3) presenting case material to demonstrate one worker's struggle with these obstacles.

## OBSTACLES INHERENT IN THE BLACK-WHITE ENCOUNTER

The problems confronted in the white professional and black client encounter may be perceived as emerging from, and being obstacles to, the joint effort rather than as flaws or faults of one party or the other. Three basic situational factors define the framework and substance of the encounter between middle-class white professional and lower-class black client: institutional racism, social distance, and mutual unknownness. These factors greatly influence what the client and professional bring to the encounter and how they perceive and deal with each other.

The encounter occurs in the context of American society—its culture, norms, and values. This context is essentially a racist one based on a history of black slavery and oppression within a culture of white dominance and supposed superiority.[4] Race is a crucial dimension in American culture and carries with it a host of rigidly institutionalized roles and connotations. Both black client and white worker have experienced this racial dimension in the course of their lives; indeed they have been conditioned to it. They have adapted to it, reacted against it, incorporated it, rejected it, struggled with it—each in his own way—but cer-

tainly they have not been able to avoid a self-consciousness about race
and its significance in America.

One direct consequence of the institutionalized racial positions of
blacks and whites is social distance. This consequence is further accentu-
ated by the differential of available opportunities through which whites
are able to attain greater social mobility than blacks.[5] In many ways,
the specific helping encounter represents a microcosm of these societal
conditions. The white professional is of the middle class, well educated,
and functioning within and according to the rules of the established
system. He has a fair degree of power over his own life as well as
power over his client and the service his client needs. The lower-class
black client tends to be poor, is less well educated, and has fewer tools
and opportunities to help him negotiate the established system on its
own terms. As he perceives it, he has little power over his own destiny,
including the outcome of his encounter with the white professional.
Both parties perceive that the white professional has the upper hand—
both in the larger society and in the specific encounter between them.

As a result of these conditions, there emerge two separate and distinct
experiences, each somewhat unknown and alien to the other. It is this
very quality of mutual strangeness which characterizes the initial black-
white encounter. It may be camouflaged, denied, or rationalized. The
void may be filled by stereotyped "knowledge" and preconceptions, but
the essential unknownness remains. Not only are the two different, but,
not having lived or known each other's differences, they can only
speculate about them. They see each other and the world, and are in
turn viewed and treated by the world, in different ways.

Thus separated by race, money, education, social position, power, and
lack of real knowledge of and feeling for the other's life experience,
the white professional and black client come together. They face each
other and are confronted with the necessity of doing something together.
The reactions they may have to each other and to the situation in which
they find themselves are the dynamics of the encounter with which they
must cope in order to work together. In essence, both professionals and
clients are what they are, based upon their past experiences and the
society in which they live and interact. They do not know each other;
they do not trust each other. Indeed, they most probably have many
feelings about each other, themselves, and their respective positions
which in reality impede the development of trust and concomitant
mutual honesty. First, there is suspiciousness and fear between them.
"What is the other really thinking and feeling? What does he really
want? What does he really mean? How much does he hate me, blame
me, or want to con me? How can he hurt me or take advantage of
me?" The phenomenon of fear and suspicion has been discussed and

documented in many sources as coming from the black client.[6] It is an equally active dynamic for the white worker. It is an inevitable consequence of the three basic factors already identified. This phenomenon is in part a reaction to, and in part a precipitator of, the fear and suspiciousness of the black client. It is both a defense and an offense. Regardless of whether the white professional is aware of it, the black client usually is.

There is also anger between them. Once again, much has been written, especially in recent years, of the rage that is felt by black people.[7] The white worker also feels anger of which he may or may not be aware. He may be angry at the black client for being so troubled, or helpless, or dependent, or hard to reach. He may be angry at himself for his inability to do very much to really help his client; or he may be angry at the client for being angry at him. The anger is there on some level. It is most likely that the client perceives it even if the worker does not.

There is also pain between them. This pain is one of the most complex dynamics because it stems from so many different sources. There is pain and suffering connected with whatever presenting problems caused the client to seek service. There is, of course, the underlying pain of being black in white America. There is also the pain felt by the worker in response to his client's pains and in reaction to them. In addition, there is the pain from the guilt felt by each party—guilt by the client at having problems with which he cannot cope and in being in a subordinate and powerless position—and guilt by the worker at having the feeling that he is somehow responsible for his client's problems or that he cannot really do anything to alleviate them. Most profoundly, there is guilt caused by repressed anger and other negative feelings experienced by both.

Furthermore, there is defensiveness and guardedness between them. Keeping each other at arm's length may decrease the hurt and danger, make them less vulnerable, and somehow ease the struggle. If they blame each other, perhaps they can avoid looking at themselves. If they have ready answers for all accusations, real or imagined, perhaps they need not really listen to each other or touch each other. If they try to relate by masking their feelings, perhaps they will be safer. They may deny, avoid, project, rationalize, internalize, externalize, or just plain lie. The defensiveness and guardedness between worker and client are of the encounter and are not characteristic of either worker or client. Rather, they become a reaction and an obstacle between them, which come out of the situation and must be perceived and dealt with as such. In a real sense, both worker and client are simultaneously victims and perpetuators of these obstacles.[8]

## A PROFESSIONAL VISION

Nevertheless, there is hope. Despite the obstacles between them, worker and client do express a need for each other in the very act of coming together. The client requests some kind of help, and the worker and sponsoring agency indicate a willingness to try to provide it. This force pulling them toward each other even while myriad counter forces are pulling them apart may be seen as a potential underlying symbiotic attachment between worker and client.[9] William Schwartz has postulated a "symbiotic" relationship between the individual and society:

> . . . each needing the other for its own life and growth, and each reaching out to the other with all the strength it can command at a given moment . . . [based on] . . . the person's urge to belong to society as a full and productive member and the society's ability to provide certain specific means for integrating its people and enriching their social contributions.[10]

This formulation suggests that a fully realized and healthy society can develop only through fully realized and healthy people and that to the extent that any segment of the population is diminished, total society suffers. It is therefore in the interest of the whole society to enable every single member to become fulfilled and productive, and it is in the interest of every individual member to have a healthy society in which he can grow. On the other hand, a counter potential also exists—one in which the relationship can become parasitic and mutually destructive. These potentials represent two extremes on a theoretical continuum, neither of which exists completely in a real society. A part of one potential, however, coexists with a part of the other in any given situation. The question to resolve is: Toward which potential do we want to strive?

In the specific encounter between the white worker and black client, occurring in an admittedly imperfect and sometimes destructive society, there is still potential for a symbiotic relationship. It is found in the fact that the worker is employed by an agency that has been charged with the responsibility of serving people who have difficulty obtaining and utilizing society's resources. Concomitantly, lower-class black people in need of assistance are encouraged to look to these agencies to provide the needed services. Thus, there is a direct societal mandate for workers and clients to attain a goal together. This goal may or may not be realized, and the forces impeding it are tremendous. However, because such a symbiotic potential exists—because the racist, master-slave, parasitic microcosm can be countered by a mutual need, mutual aid microcosm—the potential can begin to be uncovered and realized through a professional orientation.

The orientation envisions the helping process as a mutual endeavor between active participants, each trying to reach and touch each other in the giving and using of help. This emphasis on mutuality is crucial because it counters the superiority-inferiority dynamic within the relationship. It says that it takes *both* participants to do the job—that they are equally important, that they must listen to each other, that they must recognize each other's rights and responsibilities, and that they must respect each other.

The notion of active participation directed toward reaching and touching each other emphasizes the emotional engagement deemed necessary for the accomplishment of real work. It sets up a demand for involvement, sharing, and feedback between white worker and black client in opposition to passive or secret observation and analysis. This part of the vision attempts to counter the forces of isolation, alienation, and unknownness. It says, "Get in there and do, open up, make mistakes, express what you are feeling and thinking." It also encourages the worker actively to support the client's desire and efforts to combat the social conditions affecting his life by struggling beside him. It says that the worker cannot be an uninvolved outsider who ignores or minimizes those societal factors that contribute to his client's problems. What is envisioned is an endeavor in which client and worker jointly tackle relevant social problems in contrast to the situation depicted in Kenneth Clark's indictment of unhelpful professionals.

> The pervasive need to turn one's back on any clear evidence of man's inhumanity to man exemplified in the cool objective approach is possibly most clearly seen . . . in the detached professionalism of many social workers. . . . Some members of these helping fields too often define as objectivity, what to the client, feels more like insensitivity. Furthermore, in their preoccupation with the problem of the individuals and their insistence upon reducing him to a manageable system of assumptions, the disturbing and dehumanizing social realities behind his personal agonies may be avoided.[11]

The foundation of this professional orientation is the belief that the black client has the right and capacities to determine what he wants to do and the strength to move himself in that direction. With this perspective, the worker does not set himself up as the omniscient expert trying to direct or control his client. Carl Rogers states that "it is the client who knows what hurts, what directions to go, what problems are crucial, what experiences have been deeply buried."[12] The worker reaches for what lies within the black client—his desires, dreams, aspirations, strengths, creativity. It is the client's life; he must live it in his own way. The worker struggles to become a source of help, a resource

to be used by the client as he grows. If the worker really believes in
the client, he can lend himself in the encounter without having to
impose himself. Thus, the potential conflict between different value
systems—between different judgments of right and wrong, sickness and
health—is mitigated. Such judgments are basically irrelevant. What matters is the client's choices and the development of his ability to recognize
his options and take advantage of them.

The worker can give of himself freely, offering his knowledge, opinions, and feelings. He can also offer a vision of how things might be
different for the client by affirming the client's right and ability to
use what he wants on his own terms. Thus, the vision emphasizes the
client as his own person, making his own way. This vision contrasts
with a view of the black client as powerless, submissive, inferior, or
someone to be led by the expert. The worker strives to stay with the
client as he offers his faith in the client himself.

> Can I meet this other individual as a person who is in process of *becoming*,
> or will I be bound by his past and by my present? If, in my encounter
> with him, I am dealing with him as an immature child, an ignorant student,
> a neurotic personality . . . each of these concepts of mine limits what he
> can be in the relationship. If I accept the other person as something fixed,
> already diagnosed and classified, already shaped by his past, then I am
> doing my part to confirm this limited hypothesis. If I accept him as a
> process of *becoming* then I am doing what I can to confirm or make real
> his potentialities.[13]

Finally, the orientation is essentially a *human* one in which white
worker and black client struggle to gain the freedom to reveal themselves as real human beings. It is based on the belief that growth occurs
primarily through interaction between real people who have weaknesses
and strengths, flaws and attributes, and who can benefit by revealing
them and coming to grips with them and each other.

> Crisis, shock, confrontation, resistance, struggle, rejection, defeat as well
> as joy, silence, the excitement of discovery, the peaceful smile, the gesture
> of affirmation and growth—all these enter into the process of therapy in
> which real persons rather than ghosts engage in the challenging struggle
> of wills and the ennobling pursuit of meaning and value in living.[14]

The orientation challenges the unknownness between worker and
client by demanding that their feelings—including the rage, fear, and
mistrust—be shared and squarely faced. If the pain is avoided, the
humanness is avoided; life is deadened; black client and white worker
remain apart, relating to each other only through masks. The obstacles

between them grow because they are not confronted; they destroy all potential for real help to be given or received. Only when the risks are taken, when the pain is felt and lived through, when there is struggle and confrontation, when black client and white worker open themselves to each other, can they be freed to experience the caring that can be between them.

> The essential ingredient is the capacity of the therapist to love his patient —to say to him that . . . you have a listener and companion who wants you to make it. If you must weep, I'll wipe your tears. If you must hit someone, hit me, I can take it. I will, in fact, do *anything* to help you be what you can be—my love for you is of such an order.[15]

## CASE ILLUSTRATION

The following excerpts illustrate the struggles of one white social worker and one black client to begin to establish a helping relationship based on mutual honesty and trust. The focus on the helping relationship does not imply that the development of this relationship was the primary concern of worker and client. Rather, the central focus was, and had to be, the services desired by the client and the joint efforts of worker and client to meet the client's needs. However, aside from specific concrete assistance which could be offered somewhat impersonally, the major part of their work together involved struggling with intimate and painful problems and necessitated a sharing, honesty, and trust between worker and client. Thus, the helping relationship was the vehicle through which service could be offered. The excerpts selected trace the course of the work between client and worker, highlighting both the obstacles within the encounter and the efforts made to deal with these obstacles.

Mrs. R, a thirty-year-old, black mother of seven children, called the neighborhood social service office to request help in finding summer camps for her older children. The worker receiving the call was a twenty-two-year-old, unmarried white woman. After discussing the request briefly on the telephone, the worker offered to gather information on camps and to meet with the client in her home to discuss the matter further.

### The Struggle for Mutuality

From the beginning, the worker emphasized the need to develop a mutual definition of what was needed, ways to proceed, and expectations

of each other. Her reason was to let Mrs. R know that they would
have to be real partners in the endeavor in order to get anywhere and
that neither one could impose a point of view upon the other. This
beginning was an attempt immediately to challenge the potential obstacles of distance and power differential. These obstacles, although
present in every helping relationship, are heightened in the black-white
encounter because of institutionalized racial attitudes in America. The
worker realized that she would have to demonstrate that she really meant
her words of mutuality by listening for subtle cues, drawing out critical
responses, and guarding against pushing Mrs. R into actions about
which she might be hesitant.

> WORKER: I brought Mrs. R information about camp for the children and
> talked enthusiastically about their going. She seemed pleased but began
> anticipating that things might be wrong with the camp. At first, I tried
> to explain away all her objections; then I realized she might have mixed
> feelings about sending them to camp or might fear I was trying to railroad
> her into just any camp. I tried to draw out this feeling by saying that
> maybe all these questions on her mind made her unsure about wanting
> to send the children away to camp. She said she did want them to go
> but only to a good camp. I added, "And one you can see for yourself
> is good, not just because someone says it." She smiled and said she had
> to make sure. I said that I was glad she checked me before I started
> running away with my enthusiasm and that it certainly was up to her to
> get all the information and make the final decision on which camp was
> best.

The client responded to the worker's efforts to extend herself—
willingness to work in Mrs. R's own home, promptness in gathering
camp information, and responsiveness to Mrs. R's wishes—by beginning
to share some of her other concerns. These concerns included Mrs. R's
despair about her severe obesity and her desire to obtain a homemaker
so that she could enter an inpatient weight reduction program, her
difficulties with her ten-year-old son who had been expelled from school
and was frequently in trouble in the community, her sense of being
overwhelmed by the demands of raising seven children without a consistently available husband and father, and her struggle to survive the
strain of coping with the institutions impinging on her life—welfare,
schools, housing.

The worker made an offer of help with these concerns, trying to
present an intensive, flexible service that Mrs. R could make use of
in her own way. Although no attempt was made to deal with racial
factors explicitly in the early sessions, the worker made every effort to
set a tone of partnership, respect, and getting to know each other

which would challenge the potential obstacles of the black-white encounter.

WORKER: After about an hour (at the third interview) I said, "Listen, I want to ask you about an idea I've been thinking about, and I hope you will be able to let me know what you really think about it." I asked her about the possibility of my using my last few months at social service to get her really started in help for herself and her family, by seeing her three times a week and being available to her for a variety of services: just talking, helping in meetings with such other agencies as housing and management, helping her with physical tasks, or figuring out problems about the children. She smiled and said no one ever had done this for her before. I said I wanted to lend a hand to her efforts and maybe things could be worked out better for her. She then began talking about past workers who had tried to help her and how little they had accomplished. I said that I heard a warning, like the one she had made once before, that we should not get our hopes up because nothing could be done.

She sighed and said no one ever really did anything for her. I said I could understand that it often seemed hopeless and maybe it seemed too much even to try again. She said that maybe this time would be different. I agreed, but hearing her express this hope worried me that she might expect the impossible of me or become angry or frustrated if changes took a long time. She laughed and said sometimes she became angry at her worker. I said she had a right to get angry and could at me, but still we could not accomplish miracles and maybe she would be disappointed again. She said, "I know, just one step at a time." I said I thought it was not much, but it was all we had. She said, "That and more nerves than brains." We both laughed.

The specific course of the work was guided by the nature of the problems being tackled by worker and client. If concrete assistance or material goods were needed, the worker lent her efforts to the client's own attempts to obtain them. If outside systems or institutions needed to be dealt with to obtain better services for the client, worker and client strategized together, with the worker accompanying the client, whenever necessary, to lend support, skills, and influence. If the client was struggling with personal and family problems, the worker offered help with these problems.

Always, the emphasis was on the task at hand and developing the best ways for worker and client to work together to deal with the tasks before them. The obstacles and tensions within the black-white encounter were viewed as potential impediments to a successful service and therefore had to be confronted and challenged in order for the work to proceed.

## Empathizing through Honest Sharing

Having decided, however tentatively, that they wanted to try to work together, black client and white worker had to struggle to begin to close the gap of distance and unknownness that separated them. They had to risk revealing themselves, thereby becoming more vulnerable, but also more human and accessible to each other. In defining themselves for what they were and how they felt, worker and client were confronted by their real differences—not only in race, but in class, education, social position, and outlook on life. This was a painful, halting process. There was no right way to do it. In the struggle, a bond began to develop between them.

WORKER: We talked a while longer and I had to leave. As I stood up she said, "That's a nice dress, you look good today. Are you gonna meet your boyfriend?" I thanked her but must have appeared embarrassed. She said, "Why do you always get embarrassed when I ask about your boyfriend?" I was silent a few seconds, and then said that she was right in sensing that I did get embarrassed. I said I was not sure why, but thought it might be because I did not feel I should share my personal life with her since I was there to help her. She said maybe if she knew I had problems, she wouldn't think about her own so much. I said maybe that was true but it wouldn't help her work on her problems to think about mine. She said, "You have problems? Don't kid me." I asked, "Do you believe I don't have problems as you have?" She agreed. I said that I knew she thought I had a better life than she had and was more fortunate, and in many ways it was true.

I said that sometimes I guess she'd resent me for it because I was in a position to help her, and she might wish that the tables were turned. She smiled a knowing smile and said that such a situation would be nice. Then she asked, "You do have some problems, don't you?" I said that I did and I guessed all people had problems, although they might be of a different nature. She said that she sometimes felt life was bad only for her and that she wished others had their share too. I said it was natural to feel that way, especially when things were going bad for her. I said it was all right even when she wished I would find life a little difficult.

One day she asked me where she could buy inexpensive beds (two of her children needed beds). I suggested a large department store. Mrs. R howled, slapped me on the back, and said, "Girl, you are crazy." Her friend joined in the laughter. Then they informed me about the prices at that store. I admitted I had never shopped for beds and was just guessing. I felt embarrassed by my ignorance and guilty that I had never had to learn to shop with as little money as she had to do. I did not know what to say, yet it seemed all right to say nothing.

## Confronting Anger and Suspiciousness

If there was to be real honesty between them, worker and client had to face the painful areas of negative feelings in the relationship. Especially in a black-white encounter in which anger, tensions, and fears are almost built into the situations, an attempt to deny or avoid them would have implied that the relationship could not withstand them and that honesty had to be limited to "nice" feelings. Moreover, when it really came down to the basic issues, they still had to "play the game" with each other. Making this black-white experience different necessitated squarely acknowledging the negative feelings. This acknowledgment was a difficult task, and at times the worker's own apprehension prevented her from tackling it. Nevertheless, the necessary direction remained clear even when it was not successfully followed.

WORKER: Then she began talking about another social worker, an investigator she had known. She said she liked them mean and rough; then she could hate them and know they were enemies and that there was to be a battle. She said the nice ones were sneakier and they double-crossed one with a smile. I asked, "Do you always have the feeling that you can't trust anyone, that behind the smile they don't like you and will double-cross you?" She said that the worst thing was that the smile cooled off her anger and took her off guard. I said, "That sounds as if it could mean me, at least sometimes. I know you're still afraid to trust me and I have a good idea of the reason, since you have been let down so often."

I said that I also knew that sometimes when she was angry, I cooled her off by being nice. I cited a recent incident when I had not visited when she expected me and then I telephoned to say I was sorry, so that she didn't feel she could scold me after that. She laughed and said, "You are something else, you even remembered that." I said I thought she did too. I asked if she had been very angry at me then. She laughed and asked, "What do you think?" I replied, "But you couldn't show it or tell me?" She said it didn't seem worth the effort, and then I had called to apologize. We both smiled at this "cooling out" piece. I said that maybe now that we have talked, it will be easier for her to tell me next time I upset her or make her angry or make her feel any kind of way. She nodded and said, "Maybe it will."

During the next half hour, the sarcastic exchanges that seemed to mask deep feelings were very frequent. First she said, "I hear you have a maid—like a rich kid." I said I guess sometimes she thought of me as a rich person. She laughed and said she didn't, but she knew I surely was not poor and couldn't know how hard it was for poor people. I said that was true, and sometimes it would bother her, that maybe life was better for me and that was one reason I could help her. She said that I was a "do-gooder."

At this time I should have picked up her anger, but I did not. I said I just wanted to help her and her children if I could. Then she said, "I bet you'll leave here as soon as you can get something easy." I said that I guessed she thought that I wanted to leave as soon as I could. She said, "Sure you do, you're just here to get experience, like the student teachers. I don't blame you." She went on to say that she would do the same thing in my place and go where it was easier.

I asked if it would make any difference if I said it wasn't true for me, that if I could get a job here, I would stay. What I meant was that my words would not change the feelings she had about me. However, she said, "Sure if it's true, say it; I don't think you are a liar." I said, "What I mean is that some part of you does think I'll pick up and run to a nice rich area in the suburbs as soon as I can get out of here, and just my words won't really affect that." She laughed and said, "Well, you will go back to the suburbs, won't you?" I said I could see how angry she was about the possibility that I might leave her. She said that she wasn't angry but that she just knew how it was. I said that I presumed that all people who helped her eventually left her. She could not respond to this statement, but again asked if I was leaving. I said that I had told her before that I would be leaving in May—not because I wanted to, but because my job here was over. I realized that by making excuses I was cooling her out but I could not tolerate her anger and sadness coupled with my own.

## Challenging Racial Obstacles

Although racial position and attitudes were deeply entwined in every experience and feeling between worker and client, it was important in the course of the work to confront the racial dynamic explicitly. Again this area was painful, and the temptation to avoid it and feign "color-blindness" was great. The worker had to demonstrate her own willingness to reveal her racial attitudes before Mrs. R would risk sharing hers. It was crucial that worker and client relate directly to themselves as white and black and not discuss race on a theoretical plane, denying its impact on themselves and their work together. Only by facing their differences and trying to share the meaning of their own black and white experiences could they begin to bridge the gap of racial distance and unknownness.

WORKER: Mrs. R said that the only other person she had ever talked to a long time ago was Miss O, a social worker, and she was different too. I asked if she were black or white. She said she was white, then stopped to think and said, "I'd never have believed I could talk like this to a white person." She said that the way white people treat colored people made her angry. She said it made her angry that she had to call white ladies "Miss" and they called her "girl" or "Frances." She said, "If you're white, you're right, if you're black, stay back."

I said that blacks did have a pretty bad deal in America and I would expect her to be angry and bitter. She said life was difficult for a black person and the whites never let them pick themselves up. She added that mixed marriages made her furious because it was "like the black needed the white to get ahead." She commented that it just infuriated her to see an interracial couple in the street. I asked her why she felt so strongly about it, as if it were a personal insult. Mrs. R replied, "Listen, it is an insult. My mother looked white and I was the black child of the white mother and that was a terrible feeling."

She began talking about herself and how she had never had a break in life. Then she said, "Colored people never get much—no decent jobs, no education, nothing." I said I knew it was very rough to be black in America. She said, "It's rougher than you could know, you just can't imagine." I said, "I guess you're saying I really can't know how it is, how it feels, what it's like to be black because I'm white." She said that was true and that the black people had it worse than any others; they just received a rotten deal from the whites. I said, "I'm one of the whites; does it bother you sometimes that I have more than you, that I can't even begin to know how life is for you?" She said, "No it doesn't bother me, that's life." Then she paused and said, "Yes it does bother me, it bothers me a great deal. The whites can do anything and get away with it, but let a black man or a black child make a slip and they get the works!"

She continued, "And you know the worst part is when the northern whites make like they care, and we know they don't. At least in the South they're honest; they hate us and they say it." I said, "I guess I fit in here too; I am one of the whites who acts as though she cares, and you're not sure whether I do. Maybe you are not even sure if I don't hate you." She shrugged and we were both silent. I said it was hard to get that out and now we felt uncomfortable, but it was good that we had made a start in talking about this subject—her feelings about being black and my being white did matter, and so did my feelings, and we should try to share them.

### Challenging the Sense of Worthlessness and Hopelessness

The intensity of pain and hardship suffered by Mrs. R was sometimes enough to overwhelm both worker and client and caused both to experience despair, defeat, hopelessness, worthlessness, self blame, and guilt—all obstacles to productive work together. While the worker was struggling to deal with these feelings within herself, she also had to show Mrs. R her faith in her and her vision of hope and progress for her. At the same time, she had to guard against making empty declarations of concern or minimizing Mrs. R's tremendous burdens. The worker had to show sincere concern. By letting Mrs. R's pain touch her, by opening herself to the closeness between them, and by staying with Mrs. R through difficult times, the worker showed that she cared, that Mrs. R mattered to her, and that she believed in what Mrs. R could accomplish.

> WORKER: I did not try to talk her out of her sadness. When she seemed to have run dry and looked to me, I said, "For a while I guess you'll just feel totally hopeless and not even have the energy to try to do something but after a time this hopelessness will get less and your stronger part will come out, and then I'll ask you what you want to do." She showed a spark of anger and said, "*Do*, there's nothing that can be done." I said I didn't believe that and knew that some part of her didn't believe it either and would want at least to try. She challenged me and said, "You tell me what to do, how to make all the problems go away." I said, "Now you are challenging me to do the impossible and I cannot. Let us pick one problem and try to work on that." She began discussing her obesity—the embarrassment, physical discomfort, and her resulting iso-lation. As she gave vent to these feelings, she started to think of ways to deal with the problem—specifically, inpatient weight reduction programs. We began to think through the steps needed to get her into one of these programs.
>
> Mrs. R indicated the way she would like all the arrangements to be made and we began developing strategies for proceeding. At one point I said to her, "Listen, I've never fooled you up to now, and I'll try not to as we work together. We both know it will be very difficult for you to lose weight and begin to make things better for yourself and your children; however, something about you makes me believe in you and your ability to do it and get some of that better life you want." She was silent for a while and then said, "No one ever said that to me before."
>
> As I stood up I must have sighed because she said, "You're gonna go crazy, taking my problems so seriously." I asked if she meant I shouldn't take her problems seriously because they weren't my own. She said social workers never really cared about their clients; they just listened and nodded and then forgot. I was silent for a few seconds and then I said, "I have to care, I know you and I have feelings for you." She was stunned and said, "You know, I think you're really telling the truth." I asked, "Did you think no one could really care about you?" She said she didn't think anyone ever really did. She kept marveling, almost talking to herself. She said, "You really did something; I just told you about that money and expected you'd forget about it and then you go and think about it and even tell your supervisor and then you come up and do something. You really did something for me." She repeated, "I think you really care." I could only nod. As I walked through the door she said, "You know, if you don't change; I mean, if you somehow manage not to get hardened

so that you hear so many problems that they don't mean a thing, you're going to be a good social worker."

### Contact as Real Human Beings

Through it all, Mrs. R and her worker were just two people—of different race, class, social position, background and fortune—but still just two people struggling, against tremendous obstacles, to do a job together. They accomplished no miracles, overturned no oppressive structures, proved no major point, and left no lasting mark upon the world. Although they had a great impact upon each other, they were not really changed in dramatic or visible ways. They continued to function in their own worlds, in their own ways, separated by so much, and still scarred by the racism of America. However, because of their step-by-step efforts, they began to make a dent on the terrible problems that had previously overwhelmed Mrs. R and on the feelings of helplessness and powerlessness that had made her believe things could never be any different. They made only a beginning. They struggled and suffered and shared and fought and loved and cried. With every moment of profound and intimate sharing, they reaffirmed the potential of two human beings to reach and touch each other.

WORKER: I winced and Mrs. R noticed it. She said, "I guess you think I'm a bad mother." I said, "I know you saw me react when you yelled at Tony and I won't lie to you. I don't think you're a bad mother, but it bothered me to hear the way you talked to him. It bothers me even more because I know that's not really how you are or how you want to be. When you talk to me you come across so differently. I believe you want to be a good mother and want to give them something good. However, when you let all your anger and hurt come out on them, you're hurting them and going against what you really want." She was silent and I said, "Maybe you're thinking, 'Who is she to tell me these things; she doesn't know how miserable it is and what a poor life I've gotten stuck with.'" She replied, "That's true, you don't know, so it's easy for you to talk, but still I don't always want to yell and be mean to the kids. It's just that sometimes I get so angry that things are like this for us that I'm afraid that if I beat them I'll kill them so I try to yell and let the anger out so I won't hit them so much."

I said that I had some idea what it must feel like, although I couldn't feel it as she could—how just seeing the children reminded her of all she wanted for them and couldn't give them, and also how they prevented her from having freedom and the things she needed in her own life. She shook her head slowly and there was pain in her eyes, "That's some of it; there's so much more; I'll try to let you know how it is."

We talked about her needing help to manage all her problems and her large family. I supported her feeling that it was not her fault that she needed help and that her problems were real and very serious. She told me about the group she had been in at the mental health clinic because her social worker there believed it would be good for her to have something to do and people to talk to other than her children. Then she found it was a group for recently released hospital patients many of whom were still psychotic. They talked to themselves and sometimes lost sight of reality for moments. She said she was very frightened by them and also upset that she was placed in a group with them. She said, "Look, I know I'm nuts, but I'm not that nuts. Maybe someday I will be, but let me get there in my own time. When I have a nervous breakdown, I want it to be my very own and not taught to me by members of my therapy group!"

I literally howled at this speech. She was very pleased that I responded in this way, and we both laughed. I said I knew she wasn't really kidding and had a great deal of serious feelings about this problem, especially about being crazy, but she'd said it in such a great way, seeing the comedy of the situation, that I had to laugh. She said, "Sometimes if you don't laugh at ridiculous but painful situations, you just go nuts." I said, "You know I'm glad you let me see this part of you, the part that can laugh and be warm even in the midst of pain." She said, "You know, I'm glad we can laugh together."

## CONCLUSION

The writers have identified those critical societal conditions of institutional racism, social distance, and mutual unknownness that profoundly influence the white professional-black client encounter. In this encounter, as in society, it is the white professional who has the perceived and defined power, status, and control. This predefined, institutionalized role relationship triggers deep feelings of mistrust, anger, fear, pain, and resentment within both worker and client. These feelings represent potential obstacles to the development of a helping relationship through which desired services can be delivered. Certain kinds of social services, such as assisting in budget preparation or making referrals, may be effectively offered without the establishment of a helping relationship. However, when desired services involve more complex needs and deeply felt and intimate struggles, the helping relationship becomes a crucial vehicle. Moreover, this relationship can be effective only to the extent that it is open, trusting, and real. Thus, those obstacles that impede the development of such a helping relationship must be dealt with by worker and client in order for them to work successfully together.

The writers have attempted to define some of the specific obstacles within the white professional-black client encounter and have offered a way of approaching and dealing with them. The writers do not suggest that the basic social problems involved in institutional racism will be mitigated through the described frame of reference or social work skills. To provide an effective and needed service to the black client does not change the society in which he must continue to live. To the extent that some segment of a black client's life can change and become more satisfactory to himself, however, something significant has been accomplished. The primary proposition is that by challenging the obstacles of the white professional-black client encounter and by working in such a manner that worker and client can build a helping relationship based on trust and honesty, the client can begin to demand and receive more of those services he needs and desires.

The specific case illustration demonstrates how a deepening helping relationship—in which both worker and client struggled against the obstacles keeping them apart to make themselves known, real, and available to each other—freed the client to demand and make use of ever more extensive and intensive services. By developing trust in the worker, the client was able to demand a variety of services. She obtained country camp placement for her older children, secured minimum standards from the Department of Social Services, and developed a more successful working relationship with the Department of Social Services worker. She also improved communication with her housing manager, clarified the fine system and successfully challenged several situations in which fines had been incorrectly levied, gained reinstatement of her son in public school, was admitted into an inpatient weight reduction program, and obtained homemaker service for her children. In addition, she was enabled to open new avenues of understanding and exchange among family members, develop a greater emphasis on dealing with family problems without violence and recriminations, and begin to deal with deep sources of family tension.

In essence, the client's acquisition of entitled services was always the major emphasis, rather than the work on the obstacles in their relationship. However, only to the extent that the worker and client were able to "reach and touch each other as real human beings" was it possible for genuine services to be delivered.

## NOTES AND REFERENCES

1. See, for example, National Advisory Commission on Civil Disorders, *Report of the National Advisory Commission on Civil Disorders* (New York: Bantam Books, 1968).

2. Kenneth Clark, *Dark Ghetto* (New York: Harper & Row, 1965), p. 77.

3. James Farmer, Stereotypes of the Negro and Their Relationship to His Self-

Image, in *Urban Schooling,* ed. H. C. Redman and R. L. Featherstone (New York: Harcourt, Brace & World, 1968), pp. 135–50.

4. See, for example, Stokely Carmichael and Charles V. Hamilton, *Black Power* (New York: Vintage Books, 1967); Eldridge Cleaver, *Soul On Ice* (New York: McGraw-Hill, 1968); Louis L. Knowles and Kenneth Prewitt, *Institutional Racism In America* (Englewood Cliffs, N.J.: Prentice Hall, 1969); August Meier and Elliot Rudwick, *Black Protest in the Sixties* (Chicago: Quadrangle Books, 1970); Malcolm X, *The Autobiography of Malcolm X* (New York: Grove Press, 1964); and Sidney M. Willhelm and Elwin H. Powell, Who Needs the Negro?, *Trans-Action,* 1:3–6 (September–October 1964).

5. For statistical description, see Elizabeth M. Eddy, *Walk the White Line* (New York: Vintage Books, 1964), p. 12; Clark, *Dark Ghetto,* pp. 34–55; Michael Harrington, *The Other America* (Baltimore: Penguin Books, 1965), pp. 65–82; and Arnold M. Rose, Characteristics of Socio-Economic Status Amongst White and Non Whites, in *Urban Schooling,* ed. Redman and Featherstone.

6. Grier and Cobbs identify the fear and suspicion as a defense for survival and refer to it as "cultural paranoia . . . in which every white man is a potential enemy and every social system is set against him unless he personally finds out differently." See William H. Grier and Price M. Cobbs, *Black Rage* (New York: Bantam Books, 1969), p. 149.

7. Grier and Cobbs, *Black Rage,* pp. 1–17, 152–67; and Charles Silberman, *Crisis in Black and White* (New York: Vintage Books, 1964), pp. 58–67.

8. For good discussions on the white professional and black client relationship, see Julia Block, The White Worker and the Negro Client in Psychotherapy, *Social Work,* 13:36–42 (April 1968); Dorcas Bowles, Making Casework Relevant to Black People: Approaches, Techniques, Theoretical Implications, *Child Welfare,* 48:468–75 (October 1969); Esther Fibush, The White Worker and the Negro Client, SOCIAL CASEWORK, 46: 271–78 (May 1965); Esther Fibush and BeAlva Turnquest, A Black and White Approach to the Problem of Racism, SOCIAL CASEWORK, 51:459–66 (October 1970); Jean Gochros, Recognition and Use of Anger in Negro Clients, *Social Work,* 2:28–34 (January 1966); Harold Rosen and Jerome Frank, Negroes in Psychotherapy, *American Journal of Psychiatry,* 119:456–80 (November 1962); and Barbara F. Shannon, Implications of White Racism for Social Work Practice, SOCIAL CASEWORK, 51:270–76 (May 1970).

9. *Webster's New International Dictionary,* 3d ed., s.v. "symbiotic."

10. William Schwartz, The Social Worker in the Group, in *New Perspectives on Services to Groups: Theory, Organization, and Practice* (New York: National Association of Social Workers, 1961), p. 15.

11. Clark, *Dark Ghetto,* p. 77.

12. Carl Rogers, *On Becoming A Person* (Boston: Houghton Mifflin, 1970), pp. 11–12.

13. *Ibid.,* p. 55.

14. Clark Moustakas, *Existential Child Therapy* (New York: Basic Books, 1966), p. 3.

15. Grier and Cobbs, *Black Rage,* p. 180.

# 13

# Race and Its Relevance to Transference

JAMES H. CARTER AND
THOMAS M. HAIZLIP

UNTIL RECENTLY, very few articles were written by black therapists describing their techniques and methods in working with white patients. However, most black psychiatrists have been under white supervision at some point in their training, and, due to the ethnic composition of most residency training programs, black residents frequently must treat white patients. Racial differences can make the handling of the transference phenomenon threatening for both black trainee and white supervisor, particularly in the South. The general feeling has been that prevailing social attitudes would foster resistance that would greatly distort, or even prevent, the development of transference. Kennedy [12] and Bernard [2] were among the first whites to point out the problems that could be created between white therapists and black patients be-

Copyright, the American Orthopsychiatric Association, Inc. Reproduced by permission from the *American Journal of Orthopsychiatry*, 42 (October 1972), pp. 865–871. JAMES H. CARTER was at the time of writing associate assistant professor at the Department of Psychiatry, Duke University Medical Center, Durham, North Carolina; THOMAS M. HAIZLIP was director, Child Psychiatry Training, Dorothea Dix Hospital, Raleigh, North Carolina.

cause of cultural differences. On the other hand, Silverman,[17] another white therapist, wrote that cultural differences between white therapist and black patients have little relevance to the success of therapy. Several black psychiatrists have addressed themselves to the question of working with white patients, but under a less potentially threatening environment than that of the South.

We propose to illustrate the development of transference between a black psychiatric resident and an eleven-year-old white girl in a Southern town, and to support further the idea that an effective transference can develop in spite of cultural differences and many complex social issues. We recognize, of course, that few subjects are capable of arousing deeper feelings and consequent behavior reactions than the social contact between black males and white females, even in a psychiatric encounter. For "transference" we are using the definition of Greenson: [9]

> . . . a distinctive type of object relationship. The main characteristic is the experience of feelings toward a person which do not befit that person, and which actually apply to another. Essentially a person in the present is reacted to as though he were a person in the past.

The black resident and the co-author, who is white, contend that race (or racism) is an issue that should be dealt with as a resistance and that can be used by patient and therapist alike to prevent development of transference. The resident was encouraged to examine his feelings about race and to come to grips with his true feelings regarding racial differences when it was felt appropriate. Myths about racial differences have made many psychiatrists uncomfortable with cross-cultural psychiatry. In brief, some of the more common myths that bear upon this case, and upon black-white psychiatric encounters, are: 1) black males are super-sexual and comparatively uninhibited; 2) blacks are generally intellectually inferior, which of course would prevent a black psychiatrist from comprehending the full impact of his white patient's difficulties; and 3) the seldom-discussed fantasy, which child psychiatrists in general must deal with, of "child-molesting" and of how this is actually dealt with in the South. We feel that these may constitute issues that have kept black psychiatrists out of the South, where the reality of the social scene can be shocking but nevertheless remains a challenging frontier for psychiatrists interested in effecting changes in racial attitudes. This is not intended as black recruitment for the South, but to point out that many "well-recognized" training programs in the South have never trained or actively recruited black residents, probably because of their ambivalence about some of the issues we wish to raise here. We fully agree with Adams *et al*[1] that:

. . . because the net effect of these mutual projections is to prevent both members of the dyad from knowing one another as individuals, mishandling of the initial transference–countertransference situation will grossly affect the prognosis, whether or not adverse racial experiences are at the root of the patient's pathology . . .

and that this factor can, in fact, prevent the development of transference.


## CASE REPORT

The patient, a rather bright, chubby eleven-year-old girl was first seen at the local mental health clinic at the age of six for excessive masturbation. She was an adopted child, and knowledge of her biological parents was limited to the supposition that they were quite immature and that they neglected the child. The patient, referred to as Sonja, had been removed at the age of one year from her parents and placed by the welfare agency in a foster home where she was cared for by an elderly couple. This foster home was in a low income, rural setting. She was adopted into her present home at the age of three years and five months. Once in her new home, she obviously missed her foster parents, as manifested by somnambulism and excessive crying. Overeating was also noted and she has remained chubby.

Within a few months after adoption, Sonja was seen to masturbate by the new parents, but they elected to ignore the problem until she began school. The disruption that her masturbatory habits had upon the class was apparently the key factor that led the parents to bring her to the mental health clinic. She was six years old, and after treatment for one year by a social worker it was felt that she had greatly improved, with marked remission of her masturbation.

However, two years later there was exacerbation of the original complaint, and she was brought again to the clinic; but because the father did not wish to become involved in the case, no treatment took place. With some prompting by the pastor of their church, however, the parents eventually decided to request treatment and the case was re-opened. Sonja was then treated by a white psychiatrist resident, and she remained in therapy for one year.

At the time of transfer to the black resident, she was ten years of age, and the diagnostic appraisal was that she was a neurotic personality and that the primary goal of therapy would be to help her deal with her neurotic feelings about separation, to improve her tremendously lowered self-esteem, and to help her with her marked reversal of affect. The classical casework approach with the parents was employed along with uncovering psychoanalytic psychotherapy with the patient. The patient was assigned to the black psychiatric resident, and the parents to a white resident. These foster parents, middle-class whites, had their own problems. The mother came periodically depressed, and the father had been impotent for the past two or three years. The parents had one older daughter, aged fourteen, who had been adopted at age three months and was apparently doing very well.

These parents had had little contact with blacks and were not aware that their child's therapist was black until the mother and child came for their first appointment. The father had previously offered a great deal of resistance to participation, and had refused to accompany his wife to therapy except on rare occasions. Upon learning that his daughter would be working with a black psychiatric resident, he began to use race as an issue to support his continued uncooperativeness, stating that he thought his daughter would develop racial attitudes that would be in conflict with those held by her community.[4] It could be argued that anger with blacks in general for recent racial disturbances in the neighboring community and in the school was being misplaced onto the therapist, and that the father was consciously fearful of what his neighbors would think if they knew his daughter was being seen by a black therapist. One can also speculate that his resistance was reflective of his impotence, in that his daughter was now being seen by the "virile" black psychiatrist,[10] though he had previously been un-cooperative with her white psychiatrist as well. The child, on the other hand, attended an integrated school and had had contact with blacks on a limited social and academic level.

From the very first interview, her feelings regarding working with a black psychiatrist were explored and she stated that "race made no difference." This was done purposefully to indicate to her that she was free to discuss race or racial issues as she liked. Our experience shows that early confrontation with racial issues tends to encourage the white parent to express his feelings without fear, and to be comfortable in the knowledge that his black therapist shares this freedom. The reader may feel that this approach may be merely reflecting paranoid feelings or defensiveness on the part of the black therapist and that he is, in fact, actually daring the patient to be prejudiced, or even that the approach is "unanalytic."

Initially, treatment was rather stormy and the patient maintained that she no longer needed psychiatric help. Most of the work was done with the patient alluding to her intrapsychic difficulty metaphorically, displaying a great deal of aggression, and, when confronted, reverting to a rather masochistic stance. This can best be seen by the following example. During the third hour, she was asked how she felt about having to terminate with her previous therapist.  She replied that she had managed to keep herself busy playing.  The therapist then commented that separation seemed to be a process that confronts everyone at some point in their life, which remark was immediately followed by the patient making an alligator puppet gnaw at the therapist's arm, but avoiding contact.  The therapist further commented that the alligator seemed angry and that he wondered if his anger had anything to do with the discussion about separation.  Without verbal response, the patient immediately began to make the alligator puppet savagely gnaw at her own arm.

After approximately six months of treatment (on a once-a-week, 45-minute basis) she decided to tell Dicken's Christmas story about Scrooge.  She saw Scrooge as the ghost of the past, present, and future, and she metaphorically compared her life to that of the character Scrooge, who had seen the "error of his ways" and was in need of change.  Ironically enough, it was the Christmas season, and the patient brought the therapist as a present an antique which belonged to her father, with his "permission."  This act was interpreted as an indication of subtle changes in the father's attitudes, and as his way of expressing appreciation for what he saw as improvement in his daughter.  Indeed, at the termination of therapy with the previous white psychiatric resident, she had been doing poorly in school, and now, after months of therapy with this black resident, she was showing some academic improvement.  This had been frequently mentioned to the parents' therapist by the mother.

This "permission" granted by the father had positive effects on the progress of therapy.  Such a permission is most desirable, of course, under any circumstances.  The black therapist had had a similar experience with a white boy, aged five, whom he had seen in diagnostic intake and had diagnosed as a psychoneurotic personality.  This patient had found it extremely difficult to remain in the office with the black therapist for any appreciable period of time without having to run out.  Accidentally, while out of the office one day, this child met his father who escorted him back to the therapist's office.  With this "permission" on the part of the father, the patient began to show progress.  In the case of Sonja, her father continued to refuse to accept therapy, yet signaled a modification in his earlier attitudes in a way that helped his daughter to proceed.


## DEEPENING OF TRANSFERENCE

As the transference deepened, Sonja began to inquire about where the therapist lived and what his marital status was; she imagined he would not be a good husband because he "talked too much."  An example of

her developing feelings toward the therapist can be seen in the following episode. During the eighth month of therapy, immediately following Valentine's Day, she came into the office with a broad smile, sat
down in a rather adult fashion with her legs crossed, and placed an
envelope on the desk in front of the therapist. This envelope was addressed to the therapist, and he inquired if he was to open it. Sonja
said that it was a surprise for him, and that he had her permission to
open it. The envelope contained a Valentine's greeting that showed
an adolescent white boy sitting on a fence and a small black dog with
an envelope in its mouth. Both the dog and the boy seemed quite
happy, and just behind the boy was a large heart, which had inscribed
upon it, "Doggone it, why don't you be my Valentine?" The patient
commented that she had liked the card, but because of lack of finances,
she had "purchased cards for only special friends." She immediately
began to go through the motions of photographing the therapist with
her hands, saying that she would like to photograph him and place
his photograph in her album at home, which she would keep forever.

After approximately ten months of therapy, Sonja began to inquire
about the therapist's racial origin and family. She had assumed that
for a black American it would be difficult to substantiate family lines.
As an adopted child, her family lines and traditions likewise were difficult to establish, and in fact, she had begun to question whether she
was white. Further, she had asked her parents about the origin of her
name, and had concluded that it was Indian. This seems clearly to
be an attempt to establish a common heritage with the therapist. The
discussion of racial similarity was preceded by the patient telling the
therapist of a paper that she had been required to write at school. She
had chosen to describe how the world would appear through the eyes
of a bird. She had imagined that a bird would see the world as free
from wars and "conflict," with everyone living harmoniously together,
both black and white. Then, deviating from the theme which she had
written, she pointed to a white spot in her dress, maintaining that it
was "white" and really quite different from her own skin color. Her
attempt to "deny her racial difference was dealt with by the therapist
having her consider that perhaps respect and admiration for people
could develop in spite of obvious cultural and racial differences.

The question now arises as to why Sonja felt the need to establish
a common heritage with the therapist. There are several answers that
might be suggested. One is that she was relating to the therapist as
a "real love object" and not as a transference object and that this
was a means of coping with the social taboos of such a relationship.
However, we agree with Mattsson [14] that the preadolescent has not
given up her incestuous love objects, and that it is later that bi-sexual

tendencies fully recede with the acceptance of the female role.[3, 8, 11] For the adult, white female patient, our experience supports the idea that, in analysis, black frequently represents the parent of the opposite sex.[7] Searching for a common racial heritage with the therapist, we feel, was Sonja's way of dealing with her unconscious infantile striving with her father and, ultimately, with the feeling that the therapist was her father. The phenomenon of adopted children developing feelings that the therapist is their parent is well known in child psychiatry.

## SUMMARY

The development of an effective transference between a black psychiatric resident and a white child in the South has been described. Freud's definition [6] of "effective transference" as a rapport that must be established before an interpretation should be given to the patient, is intended.

Countertransference, equally as important as transference but not the subject of this paper, can be summed up by saying that the black therapist was by no means free of all prejudices. Early confrontation helped him to look realistically at his own feelings toward the patient and toward himself. Attempts to identify with white culture as a means of substantiating his capabilities as a therapist were a constant threat throughout the therapeutic process. The expression of racial antagonism either by over-agression or over-solicitousness [15] (the "Uncle Tom" behavior seen in blacks) were areas that frequently had to be examined. Conscious and unconscious fears of physical contact and the social taboos of such had been skillfully explored by the supervisor from the beginning of therapy. These are but a few of the dilemmas that every white-trained black psychiatrist must face.[13] Before a black therapist can deal adequately with countertransference, it becomes obvious that a suitable atmosphere of respect for him as a person and as a professional must be created.

The supervisor in this instance was able not only to follow the transference between the black psychiatric resident and Sonja, but also was able to note the similarities between this transference and the relationship Sonja had had with the previous white psychiatric resident, since both residents had been under his supervision. While working with the white psychiatric resident, Sonja had developed ideas that he, too, was her father. Undoubtedly, race can become a serious issue, but race itself does not necessarily preclude the development of an effective transference. Further, it seems preferable to view the race issue as another form of resistance. The transference in this case seems to be supported by others, especially Schachter and Butts,[16] who, in discussing transference-countertransference phenomena in interracial analysis, concluded that they are "apparently no greater than obstacles encountered in analysis in which race is not an issue."

For completeness we can report that Sonja did resolve her transference with this therapist, and that the parents' marriage was strengthened. Ultimately, the father was able to verbalize his appreciation to the black therapist for Sonja's improved self-image. The masturbation was no longer observed and, academically, the patient climbed to the top of her class.

## REFERENCES

1.  Adams, P. et al. 1969. Frontiers of Clinical Psychiatry. Roche Report. Hoffman-LaRoche, Inc., Nutley, N. J.

2.  Bernard, V. 1953. Psychoanalysis and members of minority groups. J. Amer. Psychoanal. Ass. 1:256–269.

3.  Bornstein, B. 1951. On latency. Psychoanal. Stud. Child 6:279–285.

4.  Dollard, D. 1949. Caste and Class in a Southern Town. Doubleday Anchor Books, New York.

5.  Foster, D. 1970. A dilemma for the black psychiatrist. Presented at the American Psychiatric Association meeting, San Francisco.

6.  Freud, S. 1958. On beginning the treatment. In The Standard Edition of the Complete Psychological Works of Sigmund Freud. Hogarth Press, Ltd. London. 12: 121–124.

7.  Gearhart, L. and Schuster, D. 1971. Black is beautiful. Arch. Gen. Psychiat. 24 (5):482.

8.  Geilard, E. 1957. Some aspects of analytic techniques in adolescence. Psychoanal. Stud. Child 12:263–285.

9.  Greenson, R. 1968. The Techniques and Practice of Psychoanalysis. International Universities Press, New York. (pp. 30–31, 151–152)

10.  Grier, W. and Cobbs, D. 1968. Black Rage. Basic Books, New York.

11.  Haworth, M. 1964. Child Psychotherapy. Basic Books, New York. (pp. 206–236)

12.  Kennedy, J. 1952. Problems posed in the analysis of Negro patients. Psychiatry 15:313–327.

13.  Mackay, E. 1971. The psychosocial plight of the black psychiatrist in the black colony. J. Nat. Med. Ass. 63 (Nov.):457.

14.  Mattsson, A. 1970. The male therapist and the female adolescent patient. Sandoz Psychiatric Spectator 6:8–12.

15.  McLean, H. 1949. The emotional health of Negroes. J. Negro Ed. 18:283–290.

16.  Schachter, J. and Butts, H. 1968. Transference and countertransference in interracial analysis. J. Amer. Psychiat. Ass. 16:792–808.

17.  Silverman, D. 1971. The influences on the Negro patient dropping out of psychiatric treatment. Psychiatric Opinion 8(1):29.

# 14

## Hear It Like It Is

### EVELYN STILES, SUSAN DONNER, JEAN GIOVANNONE, ELIZABETH LOCHTE, AND REBECCA REETZ

A YOUNG DEPRESSED BLACK MOTHER, struggling to maintain herself and her small children in a city ghetto, recounted to a white social worker her sadness in not fulfilling her educational potentiality and her recognition of the disastrous effect of racism on her life.

> We lived out in the country, a long way from school. I liked school and did well, but I got tired out from the walk. What I remember most is that bus with white kids that went zooming past us every day to our school. I remember always wondering how come they got to ride, and we didn't. It didn't seem fair. It was always one way for whites and another for blacks. I never could see it.

This woman's racially indoctrinating experiences as a child in Georgia and as an adult in the North will form the warp of her transactions

Reprinted, with permission, from *Social Casework*, 53 (May 1972), pp. 292–299. EVELYN STILES was at the time of writing chief psychiatric social worker, and SUSAN DONNER. ELIZABETH LOCHTE, and REBECCA REETZ were social workers, Boston University Medical Center, Boston, Massachusetts. JEAN GIOVANNONE was a social worker, Erich Lindemann Mental Health Center, Boston, Massachusetts.

with the social worker. Because of the continuous destructive encounters of blacks with discrimination in this country, the barriers between a black person and a white social worker have to be recognized and dealt with early in the relationship. The discussion of race has to become an integral part of the casework treatment.

Understanding the necessity for open communication about race requires an appreciation of the life experience of blacks with whites as well as of the attitudes of many blacks toward social work. As an example of societal patterns, the young mother's story is neither isolated nor extreme. She could have related numerous incidents illustrating the individual and structural aspects of racism. From both the historical and personal experience, these repetitive onslaughts have developed in blacks an "oppression phobia . . . an expectancy of violent mistreatment with a feeling of utter helplessness." [1] The phobia has none of the unconscious and neurotic elements usually inherent in such a condition; it arises directly from everyday reality. The black person has little reason to exempt the white social worker from this expectation.

Indeed, social work has not been free of racism. Products of the culture, social workers and other professionals have often applied negative and prejudicial generalizations to blacks.

> For years the black American has had to face the charges of white racists that he is supposed to be innately lazy, unhealthy, unintelligent, and criminal. White American psychiatry has its equivalent racial stereotypes about the black psychiatric patient: hostile and not motivated for treatment, having primitive character structure, not psychologically minded, and impulse-ridden.[2]

Social work has had its own terminology for such persons: multiproblem, nonverbal, present-oriented, having a different value system.

White social workers have commonly ignored race in their work with black persons. Sometimes the rationale has been that the most appropriate focus should be the psychological aspects of the clients' problems; this thinking implies that dealing with racial issues excludes dealing with unique individual differences. Perhaps social work professionals must deny—for their own comfort—the profound effect of discrimination on the social-psychological functioning of black Americans. For the black person, however, the mutual nonrecognition of race can only substantiate the distance between him and the social worker. In this relationship the black must negate the essence of his identity and question silently the therapist's ability or willingness to see him in his totality. "To pretend that the color difference is not noted is to say,

'I will only like you if we are the same,' rather than, 'I like you in spite of our differences.' " [3]

A crucial factor in the black person's view of social work has been his recent burgeoning sense of pride and positive black identity. Within the black community there is a deep antagonism to social work and a repudiation of it, along with the rest of white society, as an instrument for oppression.

> There is no difference between the ghetto and the old African colonies. The military is the police, the mercantile is the white ghetto storekeeper who exploits the community and takes the money back to the suburbs, and the missionary is the social worker who helps the blacks "to adjust" to their state of oppression.[4]

And it may be true that social work has at times supported accommodation by not comprehending the nature of racism in this country. Recognizing the powerful impact of race on any transaction between a black American and a white social worker, the writers offer the following material to consider the reasons and means for an open discussion, the role of open discussion in treatment, and the reactions of the white social worker in this process.

## ASPECTS OF BEGINNING TREATMENT

A sensitive discussion of race at the beginning of treatment has several consequences. It may enable the black person to continue in treatment, it provides the basis for a trusting relationship, and it gives permission for the discussion of color as it has relevance in the treatment process.

Black clients have been treated successfully by white social workers with minimal comment about race. This course becomes more difficult, however, in our rapidly changing racial climate. There are more frank and deeply controversial debates in the country about black-white relations. There is more intense pressure from the black community to eliminate discrimination. It is becoming more difficult for some blacks to suppress racial feelings in treatment. This fact is particularly true for young blacks with their hard-won sense of black identity. Without an opportunity for free expression, a number of blacks may be unable to continue with a white social worker.

The development of a constructive relationship early in treatment depends on quickly established mutual respect. For the social worker this development rests partly on a correct appraisal of the client's behavior and potentiality. Never an easy task, such an appraisal becomes more complex with a racial factor. Behavior can be misread when its many facets are not considered. For example, when a black person misses appointments at the beginning of treatment, it may be understood dynamically as a lack of interest in personal change. Another possibility may be, however, an assumption by the client that no help is forthcoming anyway or his reluctance to contend with presumed subtle indignities. Another example of misunderstood behavior involves a client who has a bristling quality as he begins treatment. This truculence may be misconstrued as his characteristic approach to all human beings. Another interpretation may be, however, that this attitude is a defensive reaction to a white institution. When a client is pleasant and keeps appointments regularly, it may be understood as indicating his ease with a white person and his readiness for help. Another possibility may be, however, that this behavior is a learned accommodation to white society at a great personal cost.

For the black person entering the casework relationship, there will be little expectation of awareness from a white about his experiences as a black or of an honest discussion about these experiences.

> The whites seemed far away, out there in their parts of the city. The distance between them and me was far more than the miles that physically separated us. It was an area of unknowing. I wondered if it could really be bridged.[5]

The white social worker's perceptiveness and openness early in the contact bring a needed dimension of shared understanding into the relationship, thus providing a real basis for respect and trust.

To establish a constructive relationship, it must be understood that all blacks have intense feelings about race, regardless of their age, social class, or economic background.

> And of the things that need knowing, none is more important than that all Blacks are angry. White Americans seem not to recognize it. They seem to think that all the trouble is caused by only a "few extremists". . . . We have talked to many Negroes under the most intimate of circumstances and we know better.[6]

Yet, in the writers' experience only a few blacks have initiated a direct discussion about color difference.

Early in treatment the social worker must be alert to ways to introduce this subject. He may comment upon client remarks related to it, or he may initiate discussion around appropriate material. The purpose is a recognition of color as a crucial factor in the client's life; this acknowledgment leaves the client free to respond in a way most comfortable for him.

At the onset of treatment Miss B recounted details of her life at college. Although she and her roommate, a cousin, participated in school activities, they never went to parties. Other girls on their dormitory corridor went out a lot. Wondering if a racial factor was a part of the isolation, the social worker asked about the other girls. Miss B said she barely knew them and was not sure she wanted to get acquainted. She stopped talking and fidgeted nervously. When asked if she was feeling uncomfortable, Miss B replied that she did not want to discuss it. Then she blurted out, "You and I are different." With encouragement from the social worker, she went on, "You are white. I am black." She said she was uneasy talking about white people because she was uncertain about the social worker's reaction. The social worker asked if the girls on the corridor were white. Miss B said that they were. With anger and hurt, Miss B added that they never included her and her cousin in social events. The white girls were friendly to Miss B in the dormitory, but on the campus with someone else they acted as though they did not know her.

Mr. D, a young chemist, talked about his job and his strivings to advance in a large company. He spoke with reserve, choosing his words carefully and limiting his comments to specific answers to the social worker's questions. Although seriously depressed in the past, there were no signs of depression aside from his verbal behavior. In connection with his employment, the social worker asked if his fellow employees and supervisor were black or white. Mr. D replied that most of the personnel were white. When the social worker inquired if racial matters were a factor in his daily work, Mr. D's manner changed. Spontaneously, he described in bitter detail the episodes of prejudice he had encountered from whites at his job.

Clients' initial response to the subject of race varies. Some quickly reveal their experiences of dehumanization, some assure the therapist that they have no complaints, and some criticize black activists. The manner of response is related both to personality structure and to prior necessary accommodation as a black. Nowadays, young clients are usually forthright in their reaction. However, persons with internal restrictions about aggression or with a long experience of accommodation may have to deflect their true feelings. Mrs. L is an example of both problems.

Mrs. L, a middle-aged former domestic worker, came to the psychiatric clinic because she had had severe headaches for many years. There was no physical cause for the symptoms, and they seemed related to unexpressed resentment. At her current employment as a clerical worker, for instance, she developed headaches when criticized by her superiors. Although basically she liked her jobs, absenteeism because of the headaches led to frequent work changes.

After a period of psychiatric treatment, Mrs. L was referred to the social work department for help with current life problems. At one point the social worker mentioned race. Mrs. L was unresponsive. As the therapist pursued the topic gently, Mrs. L began to scorn black militants as "a bunch of rabble-rousers." Heatedly, she censured even the more moderate blacks who spoke out against repression by whites. "People are people, and color makes no difference." This attitude on Mrs. L's part persisted for many months. On her job she allied herself with whites and disparaged other black employees. She spoke of being different from blacks; she had trained her lips to stay close to her teeth so that they would be thin like those of whites.

With encouragement from the social worker, Mrs. L slowly began to relate her own experiences as a black. With increasing anger she described the injustices she had encountered as a young black mother raising a family on welfare funds. She began to express sympathy about the indignities suffered by other blacks and to feel a kinship with them. She started to wear an Afro-American hair style and became active in the Panthers' breakfast program for children.

Whatever the initial response, an appropriately handled discussion will lead ultimately to the client's overt anger. It is essential that the social worker hear it out completely with a purpose greater than that of ventilation. The anger has several dimensions, each very important in the interaction of these two persons. First, the expression of anger is the realistic reaction to the injustices in the client's life. Its verbalization has a legitimacy in the special intimacy that personal therapy involves. Second, the anger has an educational function. It instructs the white social worker about the scope and depth of the black experience. Third, it is a test of the therapist. Can he understand? Can he tolerate hearing about his society's pervasive repression and about the rage of blacks against whites?

## COURSE OF TREATMENT

The discussion of race is part of the content as treatment progresses whenever it is pertinent in the problem-solving process. Such discussions assist the client to a fuller realization of his capacities through changes in several areas of his personality—in the ego ideal, in the integrating functioning of the ego, and in the ego defensive structure. For the black person there can be special difficulties in these areas because of his life experiences as a black. The areas of personality and their changes through treatment are described and followed by illustrative material.

## Ego Ideal

The ego ideal plays a decisive role in adult functioning, providing the person's "concept of himself among men." [7] Part of the superego, the ego ideal is the individual's picture of himself, with prescribed and glorified expectations in standards and behavior and with demands on the ego to satisfy these expectations. With precursors in early childhood, the ego ideal is established in latency and becomes more fully defined in adolescence. Its development reflects the values and aspirations of parents, of other admired persons chosen as models for identification, and of the general society. In treatment it involves the values and aspiration of the therapist as perceived by the client.

For the black person the ego ideal has been tied closely to color.

> At an early age Negro youngsters begin to perceive that white skin is exalted. . . . [It occurs] regardless of [geographic] region . . . [and] prior to the establishment of an organized superego. This implies that the glorified white standard exerts a powerful influence in the shaping of the ego ideal. . . . Since black skin is devalued, white identification is cathected as a means of attaining self-realization.[8]

This process is further reinforced in latency and adolescence when a youngster turns to figures outside his family to emulate. The respected models offered to a black youngster historically have been white. In our country black heroes of the past have remained hidden, and contemporary ones have been mainly ignored or defamed. This admiration for white models poses a serious dilemma in ego ideal development for it includes an identification with white values about blacks. The whites' hostility and stereotyped expectations about blacks are lodged in the latter as poor self-image, self-hate, and self-repudiation.

An open discussion in treatment about race provides an opportunity to alter the ego ideal. First, the identification of the client with the therapist will include an identification with new white values, including the white caseworker's explicit respect for the black person and encouragement for him to be strong in his blackness. Second, the client's use of esteemed blacks as models for identification can be encouraged. As the client mentions such persons, his knowledge about and admiration for them can be discussed fully to support their role in the evolution of an ego ideal with more positive black characteristics.

## Integrating Function of the Ego

The ego, as a synthesizing part of the personality, has the task of maintaining a balance among the id, the superego, and the outer world. Striving for harmony among these forces, the ego continually modifies behavior to cope with outside realities without renouncing instinctual feelings or ethical principles.

> Thus, from birth onward, the ego develops methods of dealing with chaotic drives, external danger, and superego prohibitions. . . . [It] thinks of consequences, . . . anticipates things that haven't happened, and . . . works out solutions. Its guide in working out these solutions is the avoidance of pain.[9]

What a task for the black American! How can he achieve a personality with inner balance when confronted by such a harsh outer world? That he so often does so is a tribute to the basic personal strength of blacks in our nation. The burden on the ego is an almost impossible one. The psychic task can be eased in treatment. A ventilation of thoughts and feelings enables the ego to master the debilitating effects of racial experiences and releases energy to deal more actively with the environment.

## Ego Defensive Structure

The handling of aggression is a very difficult aspect of ego functioning for the black person. In a racist country he has a double pressure in developing means to modify the aggressive drive for productive life purposes. There is constant stimulation of his aggression by whites, and, at the same time, he is blocked from making appropriate responses because of survival reasons. In addition, society has offered him limited opportunities to use aggression broadly in personal achievement.

The ego mechanisms available to blacks in handling aggression have often involved a great personal and societal cost. Also, aggression has often been repressed to become a passive-aggressive personality trait; it has been turned inward to become a chronic mild depression; or it has been acted on, usually toward other blacks, to become antisocial behavior. Anger toward whites has had to be suppressed, and accommodation to white expectations has had to be self-imposed.

The civil rights movement, however, has opened new possibilities— although still insufficient ones—for directing aggressive feelings into creative and productive activities. For many black clients the sublimation of aggression can become a new ego response. "As the Negro's self-image increasingly improves, he more realistically directs his anger toward the oppressive social system or channels his aggression toward the acquisition of power." [10] There may be new educational or vocational thrusts or new involvement in civic activity; for some blacks the fresh course will take them into militant social action. Whatever the direction, the psychic health in these endeavors has to be recognized and supported.

## CASE ILLUSTRATION OF EGO DEVELOPMENT

After psychiatric treatment for depression, Mr. N was referred to the social work department for vocational planning. He was twenty-two years old and recently divorced. A high-school graduate, he was working as a drug store clerk and had had numerous unskilled jobs. The psychiatric diagnosis was a personality disorder of a passive-aggressive type. The social work contact lasted two and one-half years, ceased for about a year, and then was resumed for two months. At that point Mr. N was completing his second year of college and planning to become a teacher in his own community.

Mr. N was an articulate, mild-mannered person. When first seen, he was set on becoming an architect. In high school he had done poorly in mathematics and science and was a very slow reader but had won a city-wide prize in creative writing. In treatment his route to educational achievement involved several starts and failures. He began and dropped an evening math class, refused aptitude tests suggested by the social worker, completed an excellent and difficult reading course, started and left college after six weeks as an architectural student, returned to the drug store job for one year, took a precollege creative writing course at another university, and finally was enrolled as a full-time student there because of his excellent work in the course.

The casework interviews centered on the obstacles to Mr. N's achievement. There were the realistic obstacles of racism, finances, and poor academic background; these were the personal obstacles of Mr. N's view of himself as a black man and his unresolved feelings about earlier family experiences. Highlights of the treatment process are given below.

Initiated by the social worker at the start, race was a recurrent topic in early sessions. Mr. N showed little emotion as he mentioned racial tension during his previous schooling and on his job. Anger was voiced for the first time following Martin Luther King's death. When the social worker referred to the tragedy, Mr. N said he had almost not come to the therapy because he knew he would ask about it. With rage he indicted whites for their hypocrisy about Dr. King and for creating a violent nation. Soon after, in another session, Mr. N talked again about racism. With mounting fury he told about blacks having to play the game according to Whitey's rules and the severe difficulty in making it as a black. As he left, he remarked that he never knew he could talk so freely. With this admission, he started plans to enter college for the first time and to wear an Afro-American hair and dress style.

Race became a dominant theme in the reading course. Although tense because of the course demands, Mr. N recounted with pleasure and pride his perusal of black literature. In one session he spoke with dislike about a black co-worker who considered other blacks irresponsible and inferior. Mr. N considered her remarks a reflection of white attitudes toward blacks, but he, too, found himself embarrassed by the behavior of some of his people. Aware of white contempt for blacks, he wanted to dissociate himself from them. Black people have traditionally wanted to be as much like whites as possible, viewing whites as innately superior. Black militants, however, have asserted that a lack of opportunity, not ability, has caused the blacks' lack of progress. For the first time Mr. N saw the truth in this line of thought. He spoke with admiration about specific black activists.

With Mr. N's failure as an architectural student, earlier family experiences involving resentment, guilt, and a nonproductive identification with his father emerged as a dynamic force. Mr. N's distress at his failure led to discussions about demands placed on him as a youngster; this material became a central theme in subsequent interviews. As the oldest of five children, Mr. N had been responsible for his siblings' care because his parents worked. With anger he recounted the hardships of this situation. He gradually revealed his physical abuse of the children, especially the younger brother, in the parents' absence. He recalled his mother's wrath when she learned about it and her frequent comment, "You'll get yours!" He also recalled his trouble in concentrating at school because of his planning explanations of his abuse of the brother to avoid punishment. His father, a hard-working and preoccupied man, punished him with beatings. Mr. N described these episodes in detail, including his hatred of his father and his furious determination not to cry. At the end of one such discussion, Mr. N remarked that perhaps these early responsibilities made it hard for him "to stick to things now."

As Mr. N prepared to enter college the second time, his uneasiness about succeeding was expressed initially in anger at the school. In one tirade about the dean's "racist remarks," Mr. N stopped suddenly to say thoughtfully that blacks always suspected whites of racism. It was so difficult to distinguish between a racist remark and one that would have been said even if the person were not black. With renewed fury, he talked about the demeaning attitudes of whites toward blacks and the feeling among blacks that it was useless to try to succeed. "Look at any family where the father is defeated, and you'll see that the children get no further than the father." With encouragement from the social worker, Mr. N related his own fears about reentering college.

Although tense at the start of college, Mr. N soon relaxed and enjoyed his classes. Despite severe financial hardship, he kept up with his classwork, except in the field of government. Neglecting the assignments, he seemed unconcerned about failure. When this possibility was explored in one session, anger and despair emerged about the irrelevant content of the course. Liking the class at first, Mr. N soon realized that the content described the United States' political-social-economic system as it was structured for white citizens, not black. When he had tried to raise questions, the white instructor and students had not understood. The instructor had insisted that blacks could achieve status and named James Baldwin as an example. Mr. N had replied that without a name tag Mr. Baldwin would be treated by whites with the same harshness as any other black. Mr. N had stopped trying to make his point and had given up on the assignments. Following the interview, Mr. N went to the instructor about his reactions. She was pleased he had come and gave him one make-up assignment, a paper giving his response to the course and recommendations to increase its relevance.

During the second semester Mr. N became the leader of an assertive black student group; its demands on the administration resulted in increased black enrollment, financial aid for black students, and an Afro-American studies program. He was asked by the school to participate on the curriculum committee and to work the next summer in a black recruitment program. In these activities he worked closely with two admired black faculty members, a man and woman, whom he discussed often in interviews.

The casework contact was terminated at the end of Mr. N's freshman year. He did well the second year. His brief return to treatment at its completion was related to uneasiness, quickly dispelled, about being midway through college.

### Reactions of White Social Workers

Like the black client, the white social worker brings his own experiences and feelings about race to the casework situation. If race is a crucial issue for blacks, so it is for whites. White social workers have traditionally handled it by denial and avoidance. In the writers' experience, even when the importance of race in treatment is understood intellectually, the white social worker finds it difficult to introduce or enlarge on this material.

Cultural, personal, and educational factors may be involved. Culturally, white social workers, as part of a racist environment, have incorporated the society's negative stereotypes about blacks, including the underlying psychological components in these stereotypes.

The symbol "Negro" is closely allied with sexuality and aggression. When a society or culture imposes taboos on such forces, as has occurred in Western Europe and the United States, the result is a split image. The dominant culture is seen as good and the instinctual drives (which the society wants to repress) are projected onto a lower caste or outgroup. . . . This suggests that in treating Negro clients, the worker may feel a threat to his own repressions. . . . The Negro as a symbol may arouse acute anxiety in the worker.[11]

Denial and avoidance may be the means used by social work to deal with this anxiety.

On a more personal level, an open discussion about race can evoke a realization of prejudice within the social worker. As part of a profession committed to social justice, the white social worker finds these feelings unacceptable. Every person wants to believe he has no prejudice, and avoidance of racial material may be the way to safeguard that belief. Also, communication brings a true comprehension of the enormity of the racial experience. This may be the first such understanding for many white social workers. Accompanying this realization is an overwhelming sense of responsibility for the racist behavior to which each white person must admit. Unwittingly, the white social worker may feel it is better not to hear it like it is.

Educationally, schools of social work have presented limited content about race until recently. A central aim of social work training has been the development in a student of some understanding about another person's life experiences, needs, and abilities. In contrast, the impact of racism on the particular client or on the responses of the white social worker has received little attention. This educational lack is, perhaps, the institutional representation of the individual white professional's reluctance to face these issues in a forthright way.

## REFERENCES

1.  Thomas Pettigrew, *A Profile of the Negro American* (Princeton, N.J.: D. Van Nostrand, 1964), p. 11.

2.  Melvin Sabshin, Herman Diesenhaus, and Raymond Wilkerson, Dimensions of Institutional Racism in Psychiatry, *American Journal of Psychiatry,* 127:788 (December 1970).

3.  Barbara E. Shannon, Implications of White Racism for Social Work Practice, SOCIAL CASEWORK, 51:275 (May 1970).

4.  Roosevelt Weaver, Slave Trade and Slavery—Part II (Paper read at Black Culture Lecture Series, Boston University Medical Center, Boston, Massachusetts, March 1971).

5.  John Howard Griffin, *Black Like Me* (Boston: Houghton Mifflin Co., 1960), p. 39.

6.  William H. Grier and Price H. Cobb, *Black Rage* (New York: Basic Books, 1968), p. 4.

7.  Charlotte Towle, *The Learner in the Education for the Professions* (Chicago: University of Chicago Press, 1954), p. 56.

8.  Donald E. Meeks, The White Ego Ideal: Implications for the Bi-Racial Treatment Relationship, *Smith College Studies in Social Work,* 37:96–97 (February 1967).

9.  Annette Garrett, Modern Casework: The Contribution of Ego Psychology, in *Ego Psychology and Dynamic Casework,* ed. Howard J. Parad (New York: Family Service Association of America, 1958), p. 43.

10.  Meeks, the White Ego Ideal, p. 97.

11.  Julia Block, The White Worker and the Black Client, *Social Work,* 13:40 (April 1968).

# 15

# Prejudice of Upper-Class Therapists against Lower-Class Patients

## HAROLD GRAFF, LANA KENIG AND GEOFFREY RADOFF

THE CURRENT SWING of the psychiatric pendulum has carried the professional to a greater interest in the mental health of the community. For practical purposes this means increased contact with areas of the general population heretofore avoided by most psychiatrists. Motivated by an increased awareness of the needs of the community for assistance (Srole, et al., 1962), and by the demands of the community at large (especially the groups designated by psychiatrists as lower class) for recognition, rights and services hitherto effectively denied them, psychiatrists are plunging into community psychiatry in an attempt to fulfill this need. As a direct result, the mental health worker, physician or no, is now dealing with a group different from his background and training and even holding different ethical values.

Reprinted, with permission, from the *Psychiatric Quarterly*, 45 (1971), pp. 475–489. HAROLD GRAFF was at the time of writing a senior scientist, Hahnemann Division of Clinical Sciences, Eastern Pennsylvania Psychiatric Institute, Philadelphia, Pennsylvania; LANA KENIG and GEOFFREY RADOFF were senior medical students, Hahnemann Medical College and Hospital, Philadelphia.

Recent studies by Oscar Lewis (1966) have shown that poverty groups have a highly organized culture that is distinct from other groups, with its own patterns, rules, language, ethics and values, differing markedly from the subculture of the middle and upper social classes. In the community mental health center these different, often conflicting cultures meet face to face in the persons of the patient and the psychiatrist. A simple formulation for the initial success of this therapeutic confrontation relies on the ability of each participant to (1) interact meaningfully with the other; and (2) to *believe* that he can interact successfully with his partner in the dyad. Such interaction is essential no matter whether subsequent treatment methods involve hospitalization, drugs, group techniques, or referral to other agencies, because it is this initial contact which both determines how the patient will be handled and whether he will accept any recommendations offered. This manifest responsibility of making the initial encounter successful largely depends upon the therapist; it is he who decides what the agency will offer and how it will do so, and also welcomes the patient to the facility. The fact that this has not been so successful can be illustrated by events in which the community has charged the agency with neglect of the community needs and has literally wrecked the premises, such as at Temple University in the summer of 1970.

The present psychiatric myth is that the task of dealing with lower-class patients is very difficult for the upper-class therapist; of course, this is very often the case (Kaplan, et al., 1968; Carlson, et al., 1965). The typical therapist comes from the middle or upper-middle classes through a long training period during which he absorbs the mores and values of the profession and sees them as meaningful and worthwhile (Hollingshead and Redlich, 1958). These inevitably form his ways and prejudices in dealing with patients; he is usually more comfortable with patients who support his own value system. When a patient who is living under a different system presents himself, the therapist may view his behavior as evidence of pathology, regardless of whether it is really a sign of emotional disorder or simply a manifestation of the sub-culture. At the same time, the lower-class patient can view the therapist in the same fashion and have difficulty in dealing with the upper-class agency therapist.

One aspect of the difficulty is the prevalent myth that the lower-class patient sees all things as involving action rather than internalized processes. Continuing the myth, it is felt that the patient gets into trouble because of deviant behavior and is brought to the psychiatric facility not because he feels something is wrong, but because others in his community finally cannot tolerate his behavior (Zusman, 1966; Smith,

Pumphrey and Hall, 1963; Polak, 1967). He enters the agency against his will accompanied by the police or another authoritarian group who utilize the agency in lieu of arrest and/or threats of punishment. He meets an intake interviewer who comes to the confrontation armed with the incomprehensible view that his behavior has something to do with his head. The therapist then demands he have "insight" (Myers and Roberts, 1959)—i.e., admit he is crazy. If he then goes along with the rules set up by the agency, he will finally be let out (Goffman, 1961).

We have called the above vignette a myth because it is only one view of how the patient sees his meeting with the agency. It is curiously like that of Szasz (1963), even though we do not subscribe to his concepts which perhaps stem from the beliefs of his own patients that mental illness is a myth and that psychiatrists are simply agents of a repressive establishment bent on forcing their demands for conformity on the revolutionary masses. We do believe that many psychiatrists are prejudiced against those who hold different, "lower class" values and that this affects their dealing with outpatients. The question facing us is whether those prejudices can be supported by fact. If so, we can expect conflict to be inevitable, but if they are not, then psychiatrists are creating a conflict because of their attitudes and helping to destroy their own programs.

With the desire to find out whether we had the facts or were indeed prejudiced, we designed a study to test the validity of three widely-held theories:

1.  The lower class patient is brought in by the agents of an authority; thus,
2.  The patient does not believe he has any difficulties attributable to himself and so sees his hospitalization as unwarranted detainment, and
3.  A patient-therapist conflict exists and will reveal itself in a marked difference between the official history of the admission and the patient's own story of his admission, reflecting a conflict of values.

## METHOD

Social group ratings for our study were taken from the classical work of Hollingshead and Redlich (1958). Most of the subjects were rated as belonging to Class V.

We secured our subjects from the psychiatric wards of a large municipal general hospital. Patients are admitted to the service, staffed by a medical school psychiatric unit, from the medical school's community catchment area. This particular catchment area is comprised mostly of slum areas, known colloquially as "The Jungle," interspersed with a few squares of neater, cleaner homes occupied by steadily employed persons. The Jungle is controlled by gangs of youths who divide the area into territories. Older people are in many cases unemployed, officially unmarried, and often alcoholic. The predominant racial group is black. It is an area of struggle, anxiety and desperation, of people trying to survive.

Admission to the inpatient service usually comes after the patient is initially seen by the emergency medical or psychiatric service in the catchment area, or referred by the area psychiatric outpatient services.

We interviewed every available patient on the ward, male and female, until we had a total of 50 subjects. Each was questioned in unstructured interviews separately by a male and female interviewer, so that two histories were taken. The interviewers were members of the so-called upper classes (both at the time were medical students) and so may be considered to be biased. We used two interviews to ascertain whether the stories would hold up regardless of the time of the interview and the sex of the interviewer. Each history was then compared with the official chart history and a judgment was made as to the degree of coincidence among the three, utilizing +1 for high, 0.5 for moderate, and 0.0 for none.

An example of how we made the decisions follows: Patient #1, a 36-year-old, white woman informed the female interviewer that she had a "nervous breakdown" and felt that she needed a cure in the hospital. On a subsequent day she told the male interviewer that she was in the hospital because her husband tried to poison her. The chart stated that her husband brought her to the catchment area mental health facility where she complained of chest pain and said her husband had put a pill in her coffee to poison her. The psychiatric consultant made a tentative diagnosis of schizophrenia, paranoid type, and had her admitted to the inpatient service. In this instance a high correlation with the chart (1.0) was assigned to the interview conducted by the male interviewer, and no correlation (0.0) for the interview conducted by the female interviewer. The story about a "nervous breakdown" given to the female interviewer was considered by the interviewer to be vague and an attempt to avoid stating the details of the hospitalization, especially in view of the acute report to the male interviewer.

Noted for each subject were the following other points: diagnosis, source of referral, the subject's view as to whether his difficulty was of his own creation or forced upon him by others, and length of hospitalization at the time of the interview.

## RESULTS

The number of patients in each general diagnostic category are listed in Table 1. Seventy percent of the subjects interviewed were diagnosed as schizophrenic.

In this group less than one quarter were brought in by police alone, in contrast to our original expectations. In another 14% police were involved at the request of the family. It should be noted that in the areas where these patients lived, the police are often utilized as an ambulance service and as the source of immediate assistance in a difficult situation. The force in this area includes a large number of black officers.

Later in this paper we shall see how the referral method influences the patient's ideas of his hospitalization.

### Patient's Story vs. Official Record

It is necessary at this juncture to put question #2 aside and go directly to question #3, since #2 directly relates to and is dependent upon #3. The basic question we asked ourselves was, "Do the subjects tell the accurate version when asked?" Our most prejudiced position would be that no one would tell the same story as the official one. In that case, any patient-official history agreement could be construed as significant. We decided to treat it, however, as a fifty-fifty possibility or random proposition and to utilize

$$Y = \frac{\sqrt{P \cdot Q}}{N}$$

as a test of significance.

Table 1   DIAGNOSIS

|  | NUMBER | PERCENT |
|---|---|---|
| Schizophrenia | 35 | 70 |
| paranoid | 22 | 44 |
| schizo-affective | 2 | 4 |
| undifferentiated | 10 | 20 |
| catatonic | 1 | 2 |
| Mental Retardation with Psychosis | 2 | 4 |
| Manic Reaction | 2 | 4 |
| Depression (all types) | 6 | 12 |
| Chronic Brain Syndrome | 5 | 10 |
| Totals | 50 | 100 |

Table 3 gives the results, which are significant at the 0.01 level when the negatives for agreement are tested against the combined yesses for agreement and the partial yesses for agreement.

Contrary to our original naïve guesses, people were more likely than not to agree with the official reason for entering the hospital. At the same time, the two interviewers secured the same story 82% of the time, also highly significant; from these data, we assumed that we were getting a "reliable" story which would determine whether the data derived from the interview could be relied upon.

### Insight vs. Denial

Table 4 shows the subjects' attitudes toward the cause of hospitalization. The *Psychiatric Glossary* (1969) defines insight as follows: "Self-understanding, a major goal of psychotherapy. The extent of the individual's understanding of the origin, nature and mechanisms of his attitudes and behavior; more superficially, recognition by a patient that he is mentally ill." Insight for this group refers only to the subject's recognition that the cause of his hospitalization lay within himself.

These figures surprised us, since our bias did not allow us to expect

**Table 2  HOW THE PATIENT IS REFERRED**

| SOURCE | NUMBER | PERCENT |
|---|---|---|
| Family | 16 | 32 ⎤ |
|  |  | ⎬ 46 |
| Family assisted by police | 7 | 14 ⎦ |
| Self | 4 | 8 |
| Social or Medical Agency | 9 | 18 |
| Equivocal Record | 2 | 4 |
| Police Only | 12 | 24 |

**Table 3  NUMBER OF SUBJECTS WHOSE REPORTS TO INTER-VIEWERS AGREED, PARTIALLY AGREED OR DISAGREED WITH OFFICIAL HISTORY OF ADMISSION**

| INTERVIEWER | INTER-VIEWS | YES | PARTIAL YES | NO | TOTAL | SIG-NIFI-CANCE |
|---|---|---|---|---|---|---|
| Male | 50 | 27 | 8 | 15 | 50 | 0.01 |
| Female | 50 | 29 | 6 | 15 | 50 | 0.01 |
| Totals | 100 | 56 | 14 | 30 | 100 | 0.01 |

as high as 72% of the subject population to place their difficulties as caused by something related to them rather than project it onto an outside agency.* Further, while more men than women denied any difficulty, where they did admit one they were more likely to attribute it to an emotional origin.

### Emotion vs. Behavior

A crucial point in the creation of a positive relationship between patient and therapist is the patient's recognition of his illness as due to internal processes, i.e., emotions, rather than due to his disordered behavior. Table 5 lists the pertinent information.

In analysing the data from Table 5 we find that while hospitalization did often occur after some deviant behavior, the patient would mention an emotional background to it.

When the behavioral causes are examined, five were claimed as suicidal attempts, based on depression, further reducing the number of overt actions against others as cause for detainment. Four of them were females. If these four are added to the 11 clearly complaining of emotional difficulty, the percentage of females with emotional causes rises to 75%.

### Source of Referral and Insight

It seemed logical that the more powerful the outside coercive force leading to hospitalization, the more patients would tend to blame their

* The responses of all patients are compared with the official records of admission in the appendix.

**Table 4  ATTITUDES OF PATIENTS REGARDING CAUSES OF THEIR HOSPITALIZATION**

| PATIENTS | NUMBER | INSIGHT | DENIAL |
|----------|--------|---------|--------|
| Male     | 25     | 16      | 9      |
| Female   | 25     | 20      | 5      |

**Table 5  RECOGNITION OF EMOTIONS RATHER THAN BEHAVIOR AS CAUSE OF ILLNESS**

|        | NUMBER | EMOTIONS  | BEHAVIOR |
|--------|--------|-----------|----------|
| Male   | 16     | 11 (69%)  | 9 (56%)  |
| Female | 20     | 11 (55%)  | 10 (50%) |

detainment on the outside force, which could be used as a convenient depository for blame. Table 6 bears this out, but only partially. While one-half of those brought in by the police denied having any disorder, a surprisingly high percentage showed insight when brought in by family with the assistance of police.

## Summary of Results

The impact of the above data upon us indicated that our initial questions came from a prejudiced view of the potential patient from the lower class. We can now answer our initial questions for our population as follows:

1. The lower-class patient is more likely to be brought in by an agent other than the police, although the latter may assist in the process.

2. The patient, once in the hospital, does not tell a story which suggests he views his detainment as a jailing.

3. He has "insight" into his situation, being able to accept his hospitalization as caused by something related to himself. He is likely to identify emotional difficulty as the cause of deviant behavior.

4. He does not dissemble, but tends to tell an accurate story about how he was detained, even when asked to repeat it to a different interviewer.

## DISCUSSION

The general atmosphere surrounding the contact between psychiatrist and lower-class patient has usually been described as one of mutual dislike and distrust. In their study of social class and mental illness, Hollingshead and Redlich (1968) warned the psychiatric profession of

**Table 6  INSIGHT VS. DENIAL BY SOURCE OF REFERRAL**

| SOURCE OF REFERRAL | INSIGHT | PERCENT | DENIAL | PERCENT |
|---|---|---|---|---|
| Family | 11 | 69 | 5 | 31 |
| Family & Police | 5 | 71 | 2 | 19 |
| Social Agency | 8 | 89 | 1 | 11 |
| Self | 4 | 100 | 0 | |
| Police Only | 6 | 50 | 6 | 50 |
| Equivocal | 1 | 50 | 1 | 50 |
| Totals | 35 | 70 | 15 | 30 |

the enormous difficulties therapists, as representatives of an upper class, would face in dealing with the unskilled worker or unemployed person of Class V. The authors noted that Class V people have a deep-seated distrust of authority, including the medical profession. They have difficulties in making use of services available to them (Storrow, 1962). Coleman (1968) found that only in rare instances did emergency room patients identify their problems as psychiatric and rarely showed up for a psychiatric referral.

Even though they may have a sense of uneasiness and distrust (Coleman, 1968) they enter, states Goffman (1961), for cures for social ills rather than internal ones. In this way they in a sense do not wish to participate in the medical model of illness intrinsic to the views of psychiatrists. Such attitudes run counter to the "unconscious" wish of the psychiatrist. The prior training and experience of the psychiatrist is based on the training of the physician, who is taught without recognizing it that he is superior to those who seek his help. This stems not from deliberate fostering of such an attitude, but from the entire selection and educational processes. Because of limited positions available in medical school classes, and because of the choice of the class from the most academically successful, the medical student and his teachers, family and culture, view him as a member of an elite group. His professional education teaches him to make decisions based on knowledge unavailable to his patient and to present it as necessary for the patient to accept or suffer the consequences. In the psychiatric medical profession, the practitioner as well places great emphasis on the patient's willingness to see his illness as the psychiatrist sees it (Meyers and Roberts, 1959), or be labeled as resistant or untreatable and be rejected. For these reasons the upper-class therapist feels more comfortable with the upper-class patient who concurs with him in his views of the world, utilizing the same language structure that expresses the same cultural and moral values (Cole, et al., 1962). He views Class V patients as bad patients, using crude and vulgar language and having either violent or overly passive ways of relating (Hollingshead and Redlich, 1958). In many ways, of course, the therapist is correct.

In a moving book by Grier and Cobbs, entitled "Black Rage" (1968), the dilemma of the black man in dealing with the mental health institutions is eloquently described. Not a research report but an experiential presentation, its message can be applied to all lower-class groups and provide a greater understanding of (1) why the lower class patient waits so long to get help or avoids it until forced into it by his behavior, and (2) why he doesn't show up for appointments.

The book deserves a reading by all psychiatrists as a reminder that the principles of mental function are the same in all people irrespective

of their differing life styles. Grier and Cobbs note that a white therapist
may unconsciously withdraw from intimate knowledge of a black man's
life. At the same time, the black man, because of his life experiences,
is wary and *avoids* the white therapist, as a natural result of prior
experiences with upper-class members. For a black man, survival in
America depends in large measure on the development of a "healthy"
cultural paranoia. He must maintain a huge degree of suspicion toward
the motives of every white man and at the same time never allow this
suspicion to impair his grasp of reality. It is a demanding requirement
and not everyone can manage it with grace. The truth of this is seen
in our data, with its high numbers of schizophrenics, especially paranoid. If the black man finds it "necessary . . . to develop a profound
distrust of his white fellow citizens," then we are deluded if we expect
them to voluntarily enter a dependent therapeutic situation. A true
assessment of the situation must include increased understanding of
the patient's fear of the therapist and the therapy. Moreover, the black
patient may consciously or unconsciously slip into lower-class patois
as a defense, further widening the gap of understanding.

In short, our prejudices cause us to devalue and negate, rather than
to understand and adjust to the problems presented to us by lower-class
patients; so we fail to get them as patients voluntarily and when we
do, fail to treat them correctly. This is a class problem, we believe, as
well as a racial problem. The experience of one of us (H.G.) in instruct-
ing black social workers to deal with adolescent problems of the black
ghetto was that they too could not understand or identify with their
clients. Like the evil son of the old Passover tale, they separated themselves from their racially similar clients; as one asked, "But what can
we do with them?" The problem was not racial, but social. The social
workers were college graduates, many with master's degrees, and as
a correlary, were members of Class III or II.

The information we presented in this paper does not reflect the
level of crudity of the patients or their use of language and cultural
values. What it does suggest is that, more than we expected, lower-class
patients have more awareness of the nature of their problems than
we believed, and that they could view deviant behavior as caused not
by external events, but by internal feelings. We learned that if we
listened to their stories, our patients tended to tell us how they accurately viewed the incident, which reflects, in our view, a measure of
desire to cooperate. Recent reports indicate that these patients' contact
with the police is different than we expected, with the police in this
function being more tolerant of deviant behavior and more supportive
than punitive (Liberman, 1969). This was reflected in the fact that the
patients' contact with the police was often initiated by the family as

an ambulance and semi-medical agency, rather than as a hostile authority. At the same time, most patients brought in by the police are passively compliant (Bittner, 1967).

It may be that this reflects a changing social attitude toward mental illness in both the police and in families. We did not find any change from the oft-stated view that hospitalization is usually precipitated by deviant behavior (Zusman, 1966; Smith, Pumphrey and Hall, 1963; Polak, 1967). What we did find was that police, family and even patients show a greater tendency to accept the relationship between deviant behavior and mental illness. This view was reflected by the report of Lemkau and Crocetti (1962), who found that members of lower classes were able to identify mental illness correctly and not reject it.

Our data, however, must be subjected to criticism. We cannot be sure that our patients have not simply learned what it is that we (the symbols of authority) want, and then comply only as the best means of escape. Prejudice can work two ways: too much against, or too much for. Whether deviant behavior is a sign of mental illness or not, the interests of the patient, his family, his neighborhood and the general society are best served by his learning to handle his behavior. Whether the patient offers himself for aid willingly or not, the therapist, by choosing his profession, has offered his help. It devolves upon him, not the patient, to understand the patient and to initiate effective communication. The lower-class patient's "mental illness" or "disease" is intimately bound to his idiosyncratic mores and values, and the therapist who allows procrustean upper-class expectations to frustrate treatment is only perpetuating an injustice.

Therapeutic maneuvers, described by Oberman et al., (1969), do exist to aid this group. They recommend that the therapist deal first with the presenting social problem before going on to deeper emotional areas. This seemingly simple suggestion, in their experience, tended to overcome their patient's fears and prejudices against the therapist. We believe that our experience in finding that our patients were cooperative and truthful with us will help therapists to overcome some of their prejudices as it did our own.

## *SUMMARY*

Our study of hospitalized lower-class patients failed to confirm the expectation that they would view their hospitalization as jailing by a hostile authority, and that they would illustrate this by refusal to cooperate—i.e., by denying illness or difficulty. In finding our patients both cooperative and willing to see their problems as originating internally, we necessarily rejected the common prejudice of upper-class therapists against lower-class patients, which stems both from the patient's deviant behavior and the therapist's greater comfort with people like himself. We believe that recognition of these prejudicial attitudes will help to break down the barriers which prevent effective therapy of a population who, more and more, is coming for psychiatric assistance.

The success of any mental health program depends on the ability of the therapeutic dyad to interact effectively; to the extent that cultural prejudices interfere, the program will fail.

## REFERENCES

Bittner, E.: Police discretion in emergency apprehension of mentally ill persons. Social Problems, 14: 278–292, 1967.

Carlson, D. A.; Coleman, J. V.; Errera, P., and Harrison, R. W.: Problems in treating the lower class psychotic. Arch. Gen Psychiat., 13: 269–274, 1965.

Cole, N. J.; Hardin, B.; Hand, C., and Allison, R. A.: Some relationships between social class and the practice of dynamic psychotherapy. Am. J. Psychiat., 118: 1004–1012, 1962.

Coleman, J. V.: Research in walk-in psychiatric services in general hospitals. Am. J. Psychiat., 124: 1668–1673, 1968.

Goffman, E.: Asylums. Doubleday. New York. 1961.

Grier, W., and Cobbs, P.: Black Rage. Basic Books. New York. 1968.

Hollingshead, A. B., and Redlich, F. C.: Social Class and Mental Illness. John Wiley. New York. 1958.

Kaplan, M. L.; Kurtz, R. N., and Clements, W. H.: Psychiatric Residents and lower-class patients: Conflict in training. Community Mental Health J., 4: 91–97, 1968.

Lemkau, P. V., and Crocetti, G. M.: An urban population's opinion and knowledge about mental illness. Am. J. Psychiat., 118: 692–700, 1962.

Lewis, O.: The culture of poverty. Scientific American, 215: 19–25, 1966.

Liberman, R.: Police as a community mental health resource. Commun. Ment. Hlth. J., 5: 111–120, 1969.

Myers, J. K., and Roberts, B. H.: Family and Class Dynamics in Mental Illness. John Wiley. London. 1959.

Oberman, E.; Wood, M., and Clifton, A.: Reaching the "Externalizers"—A three phase approach. Am. J. Psychiat., 125: 1404–1411, 1969.

Polak, P. R.: The crisis of admission. Soc. Psychiat., 2: 150–157, 1967.

American Psychiatric Association: Psychiatric Glossary, Third Edition. Washington. D.C. 1969.

Smith, K.; Pumphrey, M. W., and Hall, J. C.: The last straw. Am. J. Psychiat., 120: 228–233, 1963.

Srole, L; Michael, S.; Opler, M., and Rennie, T.: Mental Health and the Metropolis—The Midtown Manhattan Study. McGraw-Hill. New York. 1962.

Storrow, H. A.: Psychiatric treatment and the lower-class neurotic patient. Arch. Gen. Psychiat., 6: 469–473, 1962.

Szasz, T.: Law, Liberty and Psychiatry: An Inquiry into the Social Uses of the Mental Health Practices. Macmillan. New York. 1963.

Zusman, J.: Sociology and mental illness. Arch. Gen. Psychiat., 15: 635–648, 1966.

# APPENDIX

| PATIENT | SEX | INSIGHT | PATIENT'S REASON FOR DIFFICULTIES | | CHART'S REASON FOR HOSPITALIZATION | |
| --- | --- | --- | --- | --- | --- | --- |
| | | | EMOTION | BEHAVIOR | EMOTION | BEHAVIOR |
| 1 | F | Yes | Felt weak | | | Accusatory |
| 2 | F | Yes | Acting funny | Acting funny | | Confused |
| 3 | F | No | | | | Homicidal |
| 4 | M | Yes | Hearing voices | Robbery | | Stealing |
| 5 | F | No | | | Crying, nervous | |
| 6 | M | Yes | Impulses | Set fires | | Set fires |
| 7 | M | Yes | Confused | Mouthed off | | Threatened others |
| 8 | F | Yes | Has delusions | | Upset | |
| 9 | F | Yes | Homicidal wishes | Homicidal tendencies | | Homicidal, undressing |
| 10 | M | No | | | | Acting strangely |
| 11 | M | Yes | Depressed | | Depressed | |
| 12 | M | No | | | | Agitated |
| 13 | M | Yes | Pressure building up | | Pressure building up | |
| 14 | M | Yes | | Arguing with girlfriend | | Threatened wife |
| 15 | M | Yes | Nervous | Fighting | | Threw mother out of house |
| 16 | M | No | | | | Agitation |
| 17 | M | Yes | | Getting on children's nerves | | Bizarre behavior |
| 18 | M | No | | | | Agitated & suicidal |
| 19 | M | No | | | | Hallucinatory |
| 20 | M | Yes | Heard voices | | Heard voices | |
| 21 | M | Yes | Nerves | | | Threatened mother |
| 22 | M | No | | | Paranoid thinking | |
| 23 | F | Yes | | Suicidal | | Suicidal |
| 24 | M | No | | | | Suicidal |
| 25 | F | No | | | | Wandering in street |

# APPENDIX (Concluded)

| PATIENT | SEX | INSIGHT | PATIENT'S REASON FOR DIFFICULTIES | | CHART'S REASON FOR HOSPITALIZATION | |
| --- | --- | --- | --- | --- | --- | --- |
| | | | EMOTION | BEHAVIOR | EMOTION | BEHAVIOR |
| 26 | F | Yes | Nerves | | Upset | |
| 27 | F | Yes | Nerves | | Suicidal thoughts | |
| 28 | F | Yes | Depressed | | Depressed | Agitated |
| 29 | M | No | | | | Violent |
| 30 | F | Yes | | Shoplifting, runaway | | Shoplifting, runaway |
| 31 | M | Yes | Nervous | | | Strange behavior |
| 32 | F | Yes | | Wandering about | | No place to go |
| 33 | F | Yes | | Cursing | | Agitated |
| 34 | F | Yes | Religious fervor | Religious fervor | | Acting funny |
| 35 | F | Yes | | Unconscious | | Reaction to son's death |
| 36 | M | Yes | | Threw plate on floor | | Agitated |
| 37 | M | No | | | | Agitated |
| 38 | F | No | | | | Manic behavior |
| 39 | M | Yes | | Wrote bad check | | Wrote bad check |
| 40 | F | Yes | | Suicidal attempt | | Suicidal attempt |
| 41 | M | Yes | | Suicidal | | Suicidal |
| 42 | M | Yes | Depressed | | Depressed | |
| 43 | F | Yes | Depressed | | Depressed | |
| 44 | F | Yes | | Suicidal | | Suicidal |
| 45 | F | Yes | Depressed | | Depressed | |
| 46 | F | Yes | Epilepsy | | Epilepsy | |
| 47 | F | Yes | Nervous | | | Suicidal |
| 48 | M | No | | | | Wandering in street |
| 49 | M | Yes | Nervous | | | Delirium tremens |
| 50 | F | Yes | Depressed | | | Difficult to handle |

# 16

# An Interracial Analysis: Transference and Countertransference Significance

## NEWELL FISCHER

IN ORDER TO DISCUSS the effects of racial difference between therapist and patient on the unfolding analytic process, I will outline some aspects of the analysis of a negro woman, and focus on the effects of this racial difference on emerging transference and countertransference phenomena.

My thesis is that racial differences between analyst and analysand involve issues of unconscious meaning at many levels. These issues and meanings must be recognized and utilized, for there are serious hazards in either overestimating or in ignoring them. If, on the one hand, the white analyst blinds himself to the racial issue, he may well deny some of the social realities of his black patient's existence. But if, on the other hand, the analyst tends to be overly race conscious and to interpret too much in terms of racial conflicts, the distinct danger

Reprinted, with permission, from the *Journal of the American Psychoanalytic Association*, Vol. 19, No. 4, pp. 736–745. Copyright © 1971 by The American Psychoanalytic Association.

exists of obscuring the latent content of the intrapsychic struggle, thereby depriving the patient of the opportunity to experience and work through his core difficulties. In a more graphic way, I am suggesting that the black-white difference between the analysand and analyst is a significant, contributing, and visible structure upon which the more basic and dynamic infantile fantasies are projected. To ignore or overestimate either the manifest structure or the latent projections leads to an incomplete comprehension and working through.

The literature referring to interracial analyses (specifically where there is a white-black difference, which is the primary interest of this paper) is small, and the number of cases reported is few. The significance and advisability of a racial difference existing between therapist and patient is controversial and shows some polarization. For instance, Oberndorf (1954) stated that interracial therapy could not be effective because of the divergence of psychological biases in such treatment situations. A contrary opinion was voiced by Schacter and Butts (1968): "Racial differences may have a catalytic effect upon the analytic process and lead to a more rapid unfolding of core problems" (p. 792). The few other case reports referring to interracial analyses (Bernard, 1953; Calnek, 1970; Grier, 1967; Kennedy, 1952; Waite, 1968) fall between these two polar positions.

## CASE MATERIAL

Miss R., a 25-year-old, attractive, light-skinned negro woman, came for psychiatric help after experiencing an attack of "panic." While attending a fashion show she began to experience increasing anxiety and a fear that she might scream. She left the room, threw water on her face, and soon felt relieved. Miss R. recalled two similar attacks in the previous eighteen months. One occurred while she was participating in a casual discussion with her co-workers; the second, when having dinner with a friend on a vacation trip. In all three attacks, overwhelmed with fear, she thought she would go insane and yell out obscenities.

Miss R. described, in addition, some chronic symptoms for which she sought help, including periods of depression and the feeling that she was inadequate and inhibited. She also sensed that over the past 10 years she had engaged in a great deal of unrewarding behavior in her relationships with men, and reported having been involved in a number of unsatisfactory affairs.

Miss R. was the third of three sibs. Her two brothers were two and four years her senior. She attained her developmental milestones at the expected times, and her earliest years seemed pleasant and stable. An attractive child, she enjoyed the extra attention she received.

Her childhood and young adult years were spent in a house located in a predominantly middle-class Jewish community. Although she was not aware of any overt racial discrimination, she did sense a boundary beyond which she could not go, and experienced feelings of isolation. When she entered junior high school in which there were other negro children she was often teased because of the lightness of her skin. Both parents were described as affectionate and involved. She felt a particularly strong bond with her father. She resented her father kissing her mother first when he came home from work and felt betrayed by him if he sided with her mother in matters of discipline.

Miss R.'s work was average throughout grade school and college. From early high school on, her very active social life tended to undermine her scholastic achievements. At the time of starting the analysis, Miss R. was a gifted and competent fashion consultant.

From the beginning of the analysis, Miss R. was verbal, introspective, reported three to four dreams each week, and presented a great deal of rich and affect-laden material. For purposes of this presentation, I shall tease out only that thread of material which involved the inter-racial variable of the analysis and how this factor was related to aspects of the transference and countertransference. Clearly, an element of distortion is introduced into this discussion by such selectivity.

## EFFECTS OF THE RACIAL DIFFERENCE ON
## THE DEVELOPING TRANSFERENCE

In the early months of the analysis, when news of racial strife, marches, and murders were covering every paper's headlines and pre-empting all other news on the radio, the fact that a racial difference existed between patient and therapist never arose. References to these daily occurrences or any feelings about talking to a white man did not seem to enter the patient's conscious mind. As the months progressed, however, Miss R.'s dreams began to include more and more references to color. In one dream she was purchasing light pink lipstick, but the saleslady was getting ready to close the shop, so she left without making her purchase. In associating, she said that pink had always been her favorite color in clothing. In another early dream, a tall dark man was walking on a winter night and the ground was covered with white snow. There were many other dreams and associations to color and color differences.

Upon being confronted with this absence of conscious thoughts about the racial difference between patient and therapist, despite the rather frequent references in her dreams to color, the patient began to express the concern she had harbored since the beginning of the analysis about the analyst being Jewish. She assumed he was Jewish from his name and appearance. She expressed with considerable feelings her lifelong envy of Jewish people in her community. This was heavily tinged by a general mistrust and resentment of Jews.

With the unfolding of further materials, this mistrust and dislike of Jews could be understood, and had to be understood, on many levels. At the most superficial layer, the manifest content, she had indeed been subjected to a certain amount of racial discrimination and isolation in her white Jewish community. She recalled often feeling she could only go so far and no further with her school friends, and that she had been subtly excluded by her schoolmates and treated condescendingly. She recalled a number of incidents of traveling in the South and having been barred from restaurants and movies because of her color. Thus, starting treatment with someone who was white and Jewish stirred up many feelings and memories of her past which led to a sense of mistrust and discomfort.

As the analysis proceeded, however, and her feelings about being black and being exposed to a white therapist were further explored and analyzed, the multiple layers of unconscious meaning which found expression through the manifest interracial issue became apparent. For instance, it became clear that unconsciously Miss R.'s blackness came to symbolize for her her instinctual drives and fantasies. One of her earliest memories was playing in kindergarten, knowing that she was the only negro in the room, and feeling that she was different from everyone else. She remembered the image she had of herself, influenced by the book "Little Black Sambo" as being dark black with kinky, oily hair. In actuality she was only a few shades darker than her playmates and had straight brown hair. This memory, which often came into her thoughts, she associated to feeling herself to be different, bad, evil, and to her active masturbatory activity at that time. She reported a dream wherein some boys vandalized and viciously destroyed her beige-colored car, and she chased after them yelling, "You black bastards." She reported another dream in which a black man came through her bedroom window. She felt terrified and helpless. He pulled back her covers and was about to rape her. Her thoughts about this man led her to Stokely Carmichael and how strikingly black he was when she saw him on color television. In addition she associated to another man who had recently made a pass at her and she felt somewhat stimulated. It was in connection with this dream that she associated to the previously mentioned dream about wanting to buy pink lipstick, her favorite color.

Miss R.'s dreams thus included the projection of her sexual and aggressive impulses, with the externalized representation being the blackness of the rapist, the black bastards, and "Little Black Sambo." Her efforts to deny this piece of herself, her "blackness," was seen in her dream about purchasing pink lipstick.

The unconscious association between her skin color and her libidinal and aggressive fantasies set the stage for several aspects of the developing transference. Initially, she denied her "blackness" and its unconscious meanings. Related to this were her efforts to be a "good" patient. She produced rich material with many dreams, and she avoided talking about her negative feelings toward white Jewish people. After the confrontation of this defensive position, Miss R. could begin to talk about her mistrust and dislike of Jews and her concerns about the white analyst. This took root from some of the historical realities of her past experience. Beneath this manifest racial bias, however, it was evident that her attitudes represented in large part an active identification with the aggressor. She first denied and then feared the discovery of her unconscious fantasies. The expected attack on her "blackness" was defensively converted into an attack on the therapist's white Jewishness. She associated this with greediness, miserliness, and exploitativeness. These oral and anal components of her instinctual drives were projected onto the white Jewish therapist. Her oedipal fantasies and conflicts were also first conveyed in terms of racial and ethnic stereotypes. She associated the analyst's white Jewish qualities to the many merchants with whom she came in contact who were polite, friendly, and seductive, but who quickly tossed her aside when she did not buy anything. She felt she was an insignificant and second-rate woman in the analyst's life.

Miss R.'s depreciated concept of herself—part of her presenting symptoms—was also gradually expressed in racial terms. She compared her-

self negatively and resentfully with the analyst's white patients. This
again was a manifestation of the underlying equation of her blackness
and her unconscious instinctual fantasies. In addition, the projection
of her punitive and harsh superego onto the white therapist augmented
these feelings of worthlessness.

Interwoven with her struggle with her "blackness," Miss R. utilized
the therapist's whiteness and the conventional black-white racial barriers as the backdrop for her reawakened incestuous transference wishes
and conflicts. The tabooed, illicit, and stimulating qualities of breaching
this interracial barrier soon became equated with an oedipal victory
and with the attainment of the cherished penis.

At first there was an admiration of the white men, and especially
white doctors. She told countless stories about black-white couples and
evidenced considerable envy of the girls who dated white men. A white
friend was living with a militant black man. Miss R. could not understand how her friend could be attracted to this man, whom she felt
to be gross and ugly because of his exaggerated negroid features. Once
Miss R. went socially to a white psychiatrist's home and felt in awe
of him. In association to this incident, she spoke of a black psychiatrist
she knew whom she felt was second-rate. She would not consider seeing
a black doctor for medical care.

From these fragments, one can see that the instinctual and defensive
components of her oedipal struggles, reawakened in the transference,
were first expressed in racial terms.

As noted above, the black-white barrier came to be highly instinctu-
alized. The white man became the stimulating and forbidden object of
her incestuous wishes. This whiteness was also used defensively in her
conflicted state and symbolized the transference object's control and
asexual qualities. In one dream, a white man who was scribbling on
a pad began to make sexual advances toward her. She fended him
off by saying "You're too young for me." In her associations, the whiteness of the transference object symbolized his sexual impotence which
was a safeguard against her own incestuous wishes.

The analyst's color also became a vehicle for the expression of her
intense penis envy. Miss R.'s desire for a white man, a white baby and
to be white (or pink) expressed at an unconscious level her wish for
a penis. Her castrated and narcissistically wounded self-representation
was closely tied to, and unconsciously associated with, her black skin.
The denial of her blackness, the wishes in her dreams, and the efforts

in her daily life to be white, were all aimed at possessing the lost phallus. Miss R.'s father was the product of a black-white union and was brought up by his black grandparents. He was much lighter than his cousins. This whiteness was a very cherished, valuable, and almost worshiped characteristic to Miss R. and her family. It was extremely important that she marry someone who was light-skinned and that her offspring be fair-complexioned. The family's prestige, power, and self-esteem were intimately connected with the possession of this whiteness, thereby laying the ground-work for the patient's unconscious equation between having the powerful penis and being white.

## EFFECTS OF THE RACIAL DIFFERENCE ON THE COUNTERTRANSFERENCE

Just as the patient's developing transference often found expression through the color difference between herself and the analyst, so too did the racial factor disguise and serve as a vehicle for a countertransference phenomenon. That a countertransference response was present became evident on at least two occasions. Once, early in the analysis while presenting a clinical vignette of this case to a senior colleague, the analyst noted that he had repeated several times how light-skinned this woman was and how easily she could pass for being white. He had emphasized that she was almost the same color as himself. On a later occasion, after writing up a brief report of the case, which included a rather detailed clinical picture of Miss R., the therapist noted that he had neglected to mention that the patient was negro.

It became obvious that, just as the patient denied the interracial factor in the therapy setting for the reasons outlined above, so, too, was the analyst trying to deny the existence of this racial difference and, more specifically, attempting to deny the patient's blackness. At a conscious level he rationalized this on the basis of his nonbiased stance, that color differences were insignificant, and the work of analysis had no relation to black-white issues—all valid enough at the manifest level. Underlying this view, however, the racial difference took on far greater meaning. In an effort to understand the meaning of his inappropriate behavior, the analyst tried to re-examine his own feelings and biases about race and color. Associating to his patient's blackness, his thoughts and memories took him back to when, at age 4 or 5, he moved from an all-white neighborhood in New York City to a predominantly black area of Philadelphia. In kindergarten, for instance, he was one of four white children in an all-black class, and a similar situation had existed throughout elementary school. This early exposure was experienced with a great deal of fear, terror, and pain. This period of life was associated with black militant girls, who were seen as violent and uncontrollable. He had a vivid memory of having been kicked in the face, sustaining a fractured nose, and of his first exposure to obscene words written on walls which at the time were incomprehensible but sensed as bad and forbidden. Also associated to this time was a white policeman cleaning his revolver and saying he would kill those "niggers." Further reflection on this period convinced the therapist that though the external reality warranted fear and discomfort, the blackness of his schoolmates soon became an external symbol of his own sexual and aggressive fantasies about which he was in considerable conflict.

As a result, just as the patient unconsciously equated her blackness and her unconscious instinctual life, so too the therapist made this unconscious association, and by denying the patient's blackness was in fact denying his own blackness, that is, his unconscious sexual and aggressive fantasies stimulated by the developing transference ("she was as white as I was"). It was only after this countertransference was understood that the patient's intense sexual and aggressive fantasies stimulated within the analytic situation could be fully appreciated.

## SUMMARY

Fragments of the analysis of a negro woman by a white therapist have been presented. The focus has been on the influence of racial difference on the analytic process, with emphasis on certain transference and countertransference phenomena. The thesis of this presentation is that the racial difference between analyst and analysand, involves issues of unconscious meaning at many levels, and there are serious hazards in either overestimating or in ignoring the interracial factor.

In the analysis reported on, interracial differences and sterotypes were often used to convey deeper transference and countertransference projections. To ignore the manifest black-white issues is to avoid a piece of the patient's and the therapist's everyday reality. To become overly invested in this apparent interracial content, however, represents an effort to deny and negate the deeper intrapsychic conflicts.

## REFERENCES

Bernard, V. W. (1953), Psychoanalysis and members of minority groups. *This Journal,* 1:256–267.

Calnek, M. (1970), Racial factors in the countertransference: the black therapist and the black client. *Amer. J. Orthopsychiat.,* 40:39–46.

Grier, W. H. (1967), When the therapist is negro: some effects on treatment process. *Amer. J. Psychiat.,* 123:1587–1592.

Kennedy, J. A. (1952), Problems posed in the analysis of negro patients. *Psychiat.,* 15:313–327.

Oberndorf, C. P. (1954), Selectivity and option for psychiatry. *Amer. J. Psychiat.,* 110:754–758.

Schachter, J. S., & Butts, H. F. (1968), Transference and countertransference in interracial analyses. *This Journal,* 16:792–808.

Waite, R. R. (1968), The negro patient and clinical theory. *J. Consulting and Clinical Psychol.,* 32:427–433.

# 17

# Transference Variations Evoked by Racial Differences in Co-Therapists

## THOMAS BRAYBOY AND MALCOLM J. MARKS

THE DISTURBING IMPACT upon any group of the introduction of a co-therapist has often been described in the literature.[1] The focus in this paper, however, will be upon the manner in which the real differences between co-therapists influenced the transference reactions within the group, brought unconscious ideas of various group members to awareness, and how these reactions were modified during the course of a year. The real differences between the co-therapists included race, religion, professional discipline, and personality type.

## DESCRIPTION OF GROUP

The group was one which was dynamic in its orientation with focus upon unconscious factors, especially multiple transference reactions within the group. Derivatives of unconscious ideation expressed through dreams, associations to other patients' dreams, and projection of ideas or feelings on other patients were all utilized as part of the analytic

Reprinted, with permission, from *American Journal of Psychotherapy*, 22 (July 1968), pp. 474–480.

process within the group.[1] It was an open, mixed group which had been initiated four years prior to the introduction of the co-therapist. At the time of the entry of the co-therapist, the group consisted of four members who had been in the group from one to two years and three members who had entered during the preceding four to six months. One new member entered the group at the same time as the co-therapist which rounded out the membership to four male and four female patients. There were no psychotic patients in the group. The membership included several professionals seeking both therapy and help in their felt difficulties in interpersonal relations. Several of the women were housewives with fears of aggressive impulses. Impulse control was a manifest problem for several male members related consciously to stealing, sexual perversions, and related outer-directed destructive impulses.

The type of group interaction that predominated prior to the entry of the co-therapist was reflective of dependency needs expressed through deceptive, positive, transference modalities. These were often expressed as open flattery which could turn to snide criticism if not accepted at face value. There were open expressions of the fantasy of the group as a good family making up for the original family experience which was felt and perceived as depriving, although some of the memories were obviously distorted. One patient described the group as a nest of baby fledglings squawking for bits of food, impatiently waiting their turn and fearful of being pushed out of the nest.

Except for one member who was himself a beginning therapist, group members avoided dynamic interpretations and dwelt on external problems related to marriage, work life, and situations outside of therapy. Despite members' rejections of interpretations of dependency in relation to the therapist, the introduction of a co-therapist brought out evidence that something had gotten past the resistances and surface denial. Members responded with the suggestion that the therapist was tired, drained by his work and, therefore, needed someone to help him since the group was too demanding. Others felt apprehensive and had fantasies of being abandoned by the therapist. Several members who had allied themselves with the therapist felt rejected at the prospect of a co-therapist who would supplant them in their unconscious desire to be joined to the therapist.

## REASONS FOR A CO-THERAPIST

The unconscious motivation of the therapist for the introduction of a co-therapist was related to the induced reaction (countertransference) in the therapist that he really was unable solely to cope with the psychic needs of so many demanding patients. The therapist's personal history of being a twin also influenced him to join with a friend and colleague of long standing. The known differences in professional discipline, theoretical orientation, and personality tended to recapitulate the original twinship and an unconscious wish for a repetition of an alliance in which both members could supplement one another in mutual support and protection.

The surface and reality motivation for bringing in a co-therapist was not the usual one occurring in clinic settings of one therapist being prepared to take over another therapist's group. It was closer to the reasons therapists in private practice admit, of mutual learning and an opportunity to discuss cases. Also, from a practical point of view, it would enable patients with insurance policies to be reimbursed, since the original therapist was a psychologist and, therefore, not covered by many of the policies. In addition, since the psychiatrist was new to the area he appreciated an opportunity for professional exposure in the community. The therapists were old friends and colleagues, having worked together in an institutional setting for several years.

Theoretical orientations were basically similar, being conceptualized in variations of neo-Freudian theory. The original therapist, however, was Jewish and quite supportive in manner while the psychiatrist was Negro and more assertive in personality. Both were aware of their personality differences and the resulting differences in therapeutic approach which they hoped to use in dealing with multiple transference phenomena in group. The impact upon the group made by differences in race and professional discipline had not been anticipated and this development became the primary focus of this paper.

## INITIAL IMPACT OF CO-THERAPIST

The basic response of group members was not atypical as regards the introduction of a new therapist to an ongoing therapy group. Underneath questions as to why a second therapist was needed and opposite expressions to the effect that several patients felt they would get twice as much, there were feelings of rejection and fears of abandonment by the original therapist. When this was interpreted, several members readily accepted it and openly voiced their feelings that the original therapist was going to leave them. Other members expressed unconcern while several reacted negatively to the second therapist. (While co-therapist and therapist will be used to designate the new therapist and the original therapist, this usage does not imply any hierarchy of competence or position regarding the two therapists in this group.)

When the co-therapist entered the group, a new white female patient was introduced at the same time. The group had been told only that a co-therapist would be joining the group but no further details of personal identification were offered. Several group members automatically assumed that the female patient was the co-therapist.[2] One group member, Bob, the sole Negro patient in the group, openly refused to accept this new Negro male as the co-therapist, insisting that the new female patient must be the co-therapist.

Bob had been in this group for more than a year and a half. Following some superficial references to Bob's color on his entry into the group, with claims of full acceptance by the intellectual "liberals" in the group, there had been more soul searching on the part of other members as to their unconscious prejudices. Primitive images of the Negro emerged. In turn, Bob revealed through dreams and fantasies his image of the original therapist as a white devil with supernatural powers. He had dreams in color which revealed his own unconscious feelings of inadequacy and helplessness and his fears of the primitive violence of the white male. When a male member of the group had sexual dreams about Bob, he reacted with anger and felt demeaned. As a patient, Bob showed persecutory ideation and fear of his attraction to and dependence on the therapist. Following the co-therapist's entry into the group, Bob dreamed of being consumed by a wolf like the piggy in the nursery tale whose house was made of straw. He was overtly threatened by the co-therapist, claiming he did not know that Negroes could be psychiatrists or psychoanalysts.

This apparent naïveté was clearly a blind spot in view of his academic training and his work as a professional in a metropolitan area. He saw the co-therapist as a rival who had destroyed his unique position as the only Negro in the group and one who might refute some of his rationalizations concerning race. It is of interest to note that Bob had been able to talk of his own bias regarding shadings of color and of admiring the therapist's bronze color during the summer. When this was picked up as some identification with the therapist, he smilingly agreed. However, when the co-therapist was introduced in the spring of the following year, Bob withdrew steadily and finally wrote a "flight into health" note saying that he had decided not to return to the group in the fall because he was doing so well.

Two other male members reacted with extreme anxiety to the co-therapist's entry into the group and one of them expressed the fantasy that the co-therapist would overpower the therapist and gain control of the group. In one session, when the co-therapist was silent, one patient was certain that the therapist had ordered him to be passive and, thereby, had regained his power. The unconscious idea that all inter-personal transactions are power struggles seemed to be the latent matrix for this fantasy. In addition, one patient who was also a psychotherapist, openly expressed the wish to become a partner to the therapist and, therefore, felt threatened by the intrusion of the co-therapist.

The reaction of the male patients was associated with their concern about how to handle their own aggression. They perceived a battle of two males locked in a power struggle. The difference in color enhanced the fantasy of a fight for survival. In subsequent sessions, the projection by white males of primitive, instinctual, animal drives onto male Negroes was a frequent theme.[3] That the white male expects the Negro male to be as cruel and predatory in a position of power as the white male has been in his treatment of the Negro was overtly brought out. It is of relevance that Bob, the Negro patient, projected onto the white therapist primitive magical powers aligned with evil and the devil.

The female patients responded to the co-therapist quite differently. They freely accepted him without apparent anxiety and their only complaint was that he did not say more to them or offer more overt support and protection. This positive attitude and type of transference to the co-therapist was maintained quite consistently during the entire year.

## SUBSEQUENT PATTERN OF INTERACTION

During the summer, the therapist was away for six weeks on vacation while the group continued to meet with the co-therapist. The resistance which was expressed through superficial talk by some and nonparticipa-tion by others magically disappeared during this interim. The hostility to the "intrusion" of the new therapist was now directed at the original therapist. Members expressed feelings of greater closeness and more intimacy during his absence.

When the therapist returned in the fall these feelings were openly expressed as well as fears of having been abandoned by him. This reaction also fitted into a pre-existing pattern of criticism of either therapist when one or the other happened to be absent. This operation is not unfamiliar to parents whose children attempt to exert a divisive influence on them. It also took the form of criticizing the therapeutic techniques of the absent therapist. The group then taxied back and forth between a kind of tea party attitude and that of a department store complaint counter as an expression of their frustration that the therapists were not taken in by these devices of separation. Nevertheless, changes and movement on the part of various members were evident. One female patient with excessive dependency needs took a more assertive position at home and re-entered the work world as well. Another was no longer troubled by suicidal and homicidal impulses and also was able to evaluate her marital situation more realistically. A male patient who had been troubled by his passivity took a more assertive position in the group and carried over his gains into a fuller personal and sexual adjustment.

For some time the struggle for dominance which most members constantly projected onto the therapists was not placed on a racial basis. This occurred later, however, when a new white male who was overtly bigoted entered the group. He was of working class background and was openly insulting to the Negro co-therapist. The group members refused to respond to his antics. In the meantime another woman, a Negro, also entered the group and reacted to the co-therapist in much the same manner as had the other women. She angrily challenged the bigotry of the white male but got no support from the group on this issue. Some members, however, did condemn him on other grounds, such as ignorance and stupidity.

The issue of professional rivalry recurred frequently since several members were professionals and had a vested interest in it. All group members remained loyal to the original therapist although during the course of the year most became tolerant of the co-therapist and often spoke of the desirability of double protection. The fact that the therapists did not act out this power struggle helped to diminish the issue. Recently, one member called the old therapist a benevolent father and the new one a stern demanding father but conceded that both were necessary. On another level, patients seemed to see co-therapists as complementary parental figures rather than as competing males.

Religious differences proved to be of least significance. Although Jews, Catholics, and Protestants were represented, the only time that religion became a significant issue was when it was race connected.[4] The bigoted white male mentioned above started a tirade against the Black Muslims but was quickly subdued by the group.

Cultural differences came up but seemed to be unrelated to the therapists who come from similar backgrounds. Several group members were second generation Americans and still strongly influenced by the culture of their parents. Italian, West Indian, Lithuanian, and Greek customs and philosophy caused some difficulty in understanding but overt chauvinism was not present.

## SUMMARY

In group therapy interaction is of the essence. This requires that the therapist be able to become a real person. However, the reality of his personality, no matter how forceful, does not prevent the projection of massive transference distortions upon him. The process of separating the distortions from the apparently real is therapeutic. The more co-therapists vary from the conventional stereotypes, the greater the potential area of investigation. In time, however, as the process deepens, the superficial differences become obscured and the transference overwhelms all in an illusion of a reconstituted family situation.

In this group such a pattern emerged. However, there seemed to be some sex-linked differences. The males were challenging and competitive while the females were passive. Racial differences between co-therapists was the major factor affecting the attitudes of the men. The distortions of prejudice were obvious with both white and Negro but the group as a whole would not take a stand in either case. In this regard, the evasion by the group reflects the attitude of current American society. Indifference and denial seem to be stronger forces determining this collective attitude than either overt prejudice or a definite commitment to a rational position in terms of race relationships. However, the connection between sex and race was well demonstrated in this group as well as the sexual basis of prejudice.

The gross distortion afflicting some Negroes concerning the white authority figure also was obvious. That stereotyped attitudes strongly affect both groups in their relationships with each other can hardly be denied. Even in a group setting designed to promote communication, racial conflicts are avoided in exactly the same manner as is characteristic of the culture. The inability to discuss such emotion laden areas as sex, race, and aggression limits the effectiveness of group therapy just as it prevents understanding in general between the races.

## REFERENCES

1. Powdermaker, F. B. and Frank, J. D. *Group Psychotherapy*. Harvard University Press, Cambridge, Mass., 1953.

2. Fibush, E. The White Worker and the Negro Client. *Soc. Casework*, 46:5, 1965.

3. Herndon, C. *Sex and Racism in America*. Doubleday, New York, 1965.

4. Curry, A. E. The Negro Worker and the White Client: A Commentary on the Treatment Relationship. *Soc. Casework*, 45:5, 1964.

# 18

# Interracial Conflicts as Resistance in Group Psychotherapy

## HOWARD D. KIBEL

RELATIVELY LITTLE ATTENTION has been paid in the literature to interracial psychotherapy, both individual and group. The articles that have appeared to date have dealt mainly with the question of whether interracial treatment is a limitation. Some articles [1-3] have contended that racial attitudes impose some degree of handicap to treatment. Others,[4] have contended that it is an advantage. Still others [5-7] contend that it makes no difference at all. This author basically agrees with the latter point of view, namely, that interracial attitudes simply become a focal point for basic dynamic components of emotional pathology, reflecting conflicts over sex and aggression. In interracial group psychotherapy, racial feelings become the focal point for multiple transference phenomena. The therapist should deal with these as he would any other

Reprinted, with permission, from *American Journal of Psychotherapy*, 26 (October 1972), pp. 556–562. HOWARD D. KIBEL was at the time of writing an instructor in psychiatry at Mount Sinai Medical School, New York, New York.

221

transference phenomena, keeping in mind that if they are neglected, they may serve as resistance.

While it is important to analyze transference and dreams, they may also serve as resistance against the emergence of other significant material.[8-10] This can be the case with interracial conflicts in group psychotherapy. In this paper, an example of interracial conflict which serves as resistance will be presented. In this instance, the entire group participated, forming a group resistance. It was a displacement from a more immediate emotional conflict that had greater significance.

## THE LITERATURE OF INTERRACIAL TREATMENT

Psychotherapists are definitely reluctant to have interracial groups.[11] This reluctance has historical, cultural, and emotional roots and has resulted in limited experience with interracial group therapy.

Most of the available literature [1, 2, 12] stresses the limitations imposed by interracial group psychotherapy. For many authors these limitations are moderate. However, one recent article [3] warns of the possibility that racial conflict within the group can lead to total disintegration. Some recent work [4, 13] has indicated that interracial group treatment is workable, even with an interracial co-therapist team.

One would have to conclude that racial feelings in a mixed group create certain tensions. But so do transference feelings, and rigid attitudes toward sex and anger. Freud showed us that sexual attitudes can be discussed in treatment, despite the victorian attitudes of his time. This author feels that the same is applicable to racial feelings of our time. We, as therapists, must be aware that our own discomfort with racial feelings may prejudice us against mixed group therapy.

Whenever whites and blacks get together, a certain amount of fear and distrust is usually evident. This is readily seen in group psychotherapy where patients have such feelings anyway, based upon fear of closeness. Moreover, Negroes have experienced considerable direct and indirect mistreatment from whites. Thus, in groups they may feel resentment and anxiety based upon past experience. A Negro patient's basic distrust of others may become focused around his fear of revealing weaknesses to whites. Feelings of self-hatred may be manifested by a dislike of one's blackness, and attempts to adopt the mannerisms, attitudes, and appearance of whites. Sometimes, attempts to deny this self-hatred result in overemphasis on blackness. Childhood fears of aggression from parents may later produce fear of aggression from others. This may cause some to act as "Uncle Toms." These attitudes will eventually be manifested in the transference.

White patients who are themselves members of minority groups may overidentify with the Negro, and thus lean over backwards to please. Reactive guilt about treatment of Negroes may produce similar reactions. In their review of the literature, Schachter and Butts [5] note that the fear of the Negro unconsciously represents the fear of the hated father, particularly the father at night. This fear of the dark man has many cultural counterparts. Our culture has always used white to signify good things, and black to signify the bad. In addition, the fear of the Negro's supposed supersexuality is evident. Patients may use such attitudes as a focal point for heterosexual and homosexual conflicts. Thus, Brayboy and Marks [13] conclude that among whites there is a projection of primitive, instinctual, and animal drives onto male Negroes.

## GROUP RESISTANCE

In order to deal with racial material that arises during any session, the therapist must understand the relationship of the discussion to the over-all therapeutic process. For example, in a young racially mixed group, expression of the early manifestations of racial feelings among members should be encouraged by the therapist. Such feelings may well reflect deeper conflicts of self-identification and transference. However, the conflicts are too far removed from awareness for interpretation at this point. On the other hand, later on in treatment a similar discussion by the same patients may signal that the deeper conflicts are ready for conscious recognition. At this point, the racial feelings in the group serve as a resistance against recognition of the transference among patients.

Group psychotherapy works well when patients have learned to point their resistance out to each other. However, sometimes they band together to form a common or group resistance.[14, 15] The prerequisites for this phenomenon must be twofold. First, there must be a cohesiveness among members that allows their egos to partially blend together, forming a common defensive pattern. Secondly, they must be faced with a common threat. If this threat is strong enough, members may reinforce each other's defenses yielding resistance—which now becomes quite difficult for the therapist to penetrate. After all, every one of the patients has a vital stake in maintaining it. The final group response may seem quite real to all the patients, just as characterologic resistances seem quite real to patients on an individual basis.

Occasionally there can be an added complication. Not only may the group response appear nonresistant to the members, it may also appear so to the therapist. This happens when the patients resist immediately significant material by substituting other less emotionally charged material under the guise of serious therapeutic work. This is exactly what happened in the example to be presented.

This concept has its precedent in the psychoanalytic literature. Eder [8] demonstrated how dreams, instead of being used as the "via regia" to the unconscious, could be used as resistance. Natterson [16] showed how feelings of Jewishness could serve a similar function. Waite [17] dealt with the same issue involving individual therapy of a Negro adolescent girl.

The kind of recognition of deceptive ways in which racial feelings can be used in therapy is not to be found in the group psychotherapy literature. Articles to date [4, 7, 13] have described how uncovering racial feelings is an important step in the therapeutic process and how the resistances to the uncovering process must be dealt with. These authors have seen the racial issues themselves as the via regia to unconscious conflicts. But like any via regia, it too can become a resistance. Unlike other resistances used by groups, the use of racial issues can be particularly deceptive for several reasons. The patients will have previously recognized such feelings themselves and withheld them from discussion. The therapist will have felt that this issue has been suppressed for too long. In addition, since race is laden with much emotion, the resistant discussion of the issue may appear to all to be genuine therapeutic work.


## CLINICAL ILLUSTRATION

The setting is an outpatient clinic of a large teaching institution located on the edge of a Negro ghetto in a large city. At this particular time, the group consisted of eight patients, six white women and two Negro men. The therapist, a psychiatrist with previous experience as a group therapist, had been with the group for one year.

For many months the group had only one Negro member who was rather light-skinned and appeared to consciously identify with "white society," thus perhaps avoiding conflict within the group. The other members did not react to him in any apparent way to indicate that they saw him as "different."

When the second Negro man joined the group, about six months prior to the following incident, the reaction of the group changed. He was a very dark-skinned, robust, good-looking man, who dressed in a manner that was more in keeping with the style of the young Negroes today. Initially, the group seemed afraid of him and spoke as if he might be someone with a potentially violent temper. Interestingly, the therapist recognized a similar countertransference reaction in himself. However, this quickly changed for all, at least on a conscious level, as it became clear that this man considered himself to lack assertiveness, to be timid and unmanly.

Although he was consciously accepted by all, the therapist noted that on a few occasions when both Negro men were absent, the women would discuss their prejudices toward Negroes in their neighborhoods. However, when the therapist asked how they felt about the mixed racial nature of the group, he met with either denial, defensiveness, or avoidance. Thus, the therapist felt, for some time, that there were significant feelings about racial matters that were being withheld or suppressed.

The present incident centers around Miss M., a single woman in her mid-thirties with a long history of psychiatric difficulties. She entered the group about four months prior to the session involved. At first she participated little, and soon the therapist began to suspect that she might be decompensating. She rapidly developed a delusional system and the therapist recommended hospitalization. The patient refused. Instead she left and returned to the group unannounced five weeks later.

When she entered the room she stared blankly, seemed expressionless, and appeared quite frightened. The therapist was convinced she had returned to seek hospitalization. She sat in silence as the group proceeded as though it were business as usual. They were obviously uncomfortable with her presence as they totally ignored her, not asking about her absence or sudden return.

Scarcely ten minutes of the session had elapsed when she suddenly blurted out, in a tense, raised voice that crescendoed as she spoke, as she tensed her hands, slowly raising them, in open fashion, to tightly grasp the side of her face: "I can't stand this, I can't stand the talking in the group, I'm losing control of myself. I'm going out of my mind." Then, shouting: "Stop talking!" Finally, much more subdued and sounding desperate: "Doctor, can I talk to you?"

The therapist told her that they would talk privately. He asked the other patients to continue while he spoke to her, and then took her to the emergency room to arrange for her immediate hospitalization. He returned to the group 45 minutes later. The rest of the patients had not discussed the preceding incident and at this point were talking about one patient's husband who had a history of frequent violent disturbances. The therapist interrupted by pointing out that what they had seen today and what they should be talking about was someone who had appeared to them to be on the verge of a nervous breakdown. This reference to Miss M. was, by and large, ignored. Only direct focusing on the above incident enabled the group to ask the therapist what had happened to Miss M. He briefly told them that he had arranged for her admission to the hospital. The group immediately returned to its former discussion of one patient's husband.

Little time was left in the session and so the therapist again interrupted, reviewed what they had seen happen to Miss M., and asked them how they felt about it. Some said they were shocked. One patient felt that Miss M. might have felt under great pressure talking to so many people in a group. Another claimed that he saw it coming weeks ago. Another patient expressed relief that Miss M. was able to control herself, come back, and seek the proper help. Another spoke of how the incident reminded her of her own mother's nervous breakdown. With this discussion the session ended.

It was in the next session that the feelings generated by the incident were displaced onto a discussion of interracial feelings. The session began with one woman asking how Miss M. was getting along. The therapist responded by saying that she was adjusting well to the hospital routine and invited the group to discuss their feelings about the events of the previous session. A long pause followed and then another female patient said vehemently that she was tense and angry. She was upset that there were disruptive elements in her daughter's school. She spoke of the Negro and Puerto Rican children as acting like "little monsters." She felt that she was being driven out of her neighborhood by their parents who were "drunkards, had ten wives or ten husbands." She felt that it was difficult to control her own anger over this situation. The other women joined in to support her argument. They spoke of Negro boys in high school attempting to molest white girls, of drug addiction, of "reverse discrimination" that made it harder for white students to enter college, and of Negro families creating a dirty neighborhood.

The two Negro men were silent. Turning toward the men, the therapist asked the group how they all felt about this discussion. As the men started to defend blacks, the women cut them off, claiming they felt that the Negroes were entitled to a decent life, but that they objected to the anger that Negroes showed and to recent violent protests. This made them afraid of being harmed. The men tried to explain that less dramatic demands for equal rights had been ignored in the past. As one man put it: "We need to get your attention. Look, it's part of the Negro's emotional problem. It can't be done in any better way."

After the men had described their own personal experiences with discrimination and persecution there was a shift to several other topics. Finally one patient asked the group what "paranoid schizophrenia" meant. She and two other patients wished to know their own diagnoses at the clinic. They felt that the psychiatrists knew which patients were the sickest and which ones might some day steal or kill. The therapist's questioning of whether their concerns were related to the incident of the previous week was ignored. The subject was changed and the therapist was ignored in his attempt to help them see that the switch in topics might be an avoidance maneuver.

The subsequent conversation, which centered around the theme of rejection, caused them to focus on their resulting feelings of anger. In discussing their concern about controlling anger, there were several spontaneous denials, without any comment from the therapist that this had nothing to do with the incident of the previous week. The session ended in that way.

In the following session, the therapist felt much more successful with his interventions. The group began discussing relatives who demonstrated poor impulse control. It was sufficient for the therapist to simply clarify the theme that people with emotional problems might lose control of themselves and become violent. The group members were then able to focus on their fears of their own potential violence and revealed some significant historical material. The therapist, asked how they felt, in light of such concerns, seeing

Miss M. having a breakdown. They were now able to express their fears that the same thing could happen to them.

During the rest of this session and in subsequent sessions, the group explored some of the effects of the incident. They feared that confronting other group members might have unpredictable, possibly devastating results. Moreover, they could see how the recent incident had aggravated their fears. They tended to identify with the desperate nature of Miss M.'s pleas for help. Lastly, they felt some comfort that during such a crisis, the doctor could act promptly.

## DISCUSSION

This group had always been uncomfortable in discussing racial feelings. The light-skinned Negro was able to avoid his own inner conflicts over race, as well as possible clashes within the group by expressing attitudes that identified him with "white society." When the second man, whom they saw as more typically black, entered the group, the racial issue was more difficult to avoid. The countertransference reaction of the therapist can be seen partly as the product of the therapist's unconscious fears of the black man, but also as a response to the other members' attitudes. Concern about racial matters began to appear in the sessions, but only if the black men were absent. Thus, one may conclude that exploration of interracial feelings within the group was needed, but avoided.

When the group was faced with a more immediate threat, namely Miss M.'s acute disturbance, they were able to discuss their racial feelings. At this point, these racial feelings were less disturbing to discuss, could metaphorically express their concerns, and were charged with enough affect to make them seem to be of immediate emotional significance. In this way the discussion of racial issues served as an intense resistance for the entire group. Consequently, it was very difficult to interpret.

It was soon evident that the group was quite disturbed by Miss M.'s symptoms. When she returned to the group after a five-week absence and appeared very upset, the group inappropriately proceeded as though it were business as usual. After the therapist arranged her hospitalization, they avoided the subject despite the therapist's efforts to encourage discussion. Even when the therapist insisted that they focus upon it, they were only able to discuss their feelings on a superficial level.

At the next session, the description of Negroes as initiators of violence and as violating the usual standards of social behavior can be seen as a projection of their own fears of loss of control. The racial theme included feelings of anger as a result of environmental stress, frustration leading to violent outbursts, the fear of violence from others, and a need to demonstrate in somewhat extreme ways when one feels that the cry for help has not been heeded; all of which can be seen as metaphorically expressing their reactions to the provoking incident. This is made glaringly apparent by one patient who pointed out that this need to demonstrate in a dramatic fashion to get the white man's attention is "part of the Negro's emotional problem." Despite this and their expressed concerns about paranoid schizophrenia, they were unable to accept the therapeutic interpretation.

In subsequent sessions, their reactions to the provoking incident were discussed in great detail. These later sessions proved fruitful therapeutically. In contrast, the discussion of interracial conflict was a resistance. As such, at this point, it did not represent a true therapeutic exploration of the racial issue. This would have to come later on in treatment when the material would no longer serve as resistance.

## SUMMARY

This paper presents a clinical illustration in which members of an interracial psychotheray group were confronted with a disturbing experience, namely, they saw one of their members become acutely disturbed, requiring immediate hospitalization. This incident aggravated previous latent fears within group members. Afraid to discuss their feelings and faced with this common threat, they banded together and displaced the feelings onto a less threatening but significant issue—the racial feelings within the group. This discussion revealed, metaphorically, some of their reactions to the provoking incident, thus serving as resistance. This paper explores the phenomenon of group resistance and concludes that such an intense resistance is particularly difficult for the therapist to handle. In previous papers on interracial group psychotherapy racial feelings were regarded as serving as a "via regia" to basic conflicts, rather than as resistance.

## REFERENCES

1. Frank, J. D. and Powdermaker, F. B. Group Psychotherapy. In *American Handbook of Psychiatry*, Vol. II, Arieti, S., Ed. Basic Books, New York, 1959, pp. 1362–1374.

2. Heckel, R. V. Effects of Northern and Southern Therapists on Racially Mixed Psychotherapy Groups. *Ment. Hyg.*, 50: 304, 1966.

3. Brayboy, T. L. The Black Patient in Group Therapy. *Int. J. Group Psychother.*, 21: 288, 1971.

4. Mintz, E. E. and Maliver, B. L. Inter-racial Co-Therapist Teams: Transference and Resistance. *J. Long Island Consultation Center,* 4: 52, 1966.

5. Schachter, J. S. and Butts, H. F. Transference and Countertransference in Interracial Analysis. *J. Am. Psychoanal. Ass.,* 16: 792, 1968.

6. Snell, J. E. Psychiatric Evaluation in Open Biracial Groups. *Am. J. Psychiat.,* 122: 880, 1966.

7. Sommers, V. S. An Experiment in Group Psychotherapy with Members of Mixed Minority Groups. *Int. J. Group Psychother.,* 3: 254, 1953.

8. Eder, M. D. Dreams—As Resistance. *Int. J. Psychoanal.,* 11: 40, 1930.

9. Freud, S. The Dynamics of Transference. In *Standard Edition,* 12: 97, 1912. Hogarth Press, London, 1958.

10. Wolstein, B. *Freedom to Experience.* Grune & Stratton, New York, 1962.

11. Rosenbaum, M., Snadowsky, A., and Hartley, E. Group Psychotherapy and the Integration of the Negro. *Int. J. Group Psychother.,* 16: 86, 1966.

12. Rosen, H. and Frank, J. D. Negroes in Psychotherapy. *Am. J. Psychiat.,* 119: 456, 1962.

13. Brayboy, T. L. and Marks, M. J. Transference Variations Evoked by Racial Differences in Co-Therapists. *Am. J. Psychother.,* 22: 474, 1968.

14. Redl, F. Resistance in Therapy Groups. *Human Relations,* 1: 307, 1948.

15. Spotnitz, H. A Psychoanalytic View of Resistance in Groups. *Int. J. Group Psychother.,* 2: 3, 1952.

16. Natterson, J. M. Jewishness as Resistance. *Psychoanal., Rev.,* 53: 418, 1966.

17. Waite, R. R. The Negro Patient and Clinical Theory. *J. Consult. Clin. Psychol.,* 32: 427, 1968.

# Part Three

# COMMUNITY ORGANIZATION

# 19

# Community Organization and the Oppressed

## ANATOLE SHAFFER

## *INTRODUCTION*

TRADITIONALLY, the core of professional social work education has been the teaching of method in preparation for practice. In general, method has been focused on learning a specified set of skills with the greatest emphasis placed on case work activities. Until the past few years secondary emphasis was on group work. More recently these two methods have become submerged under the general category of therapeutic or "clinical" intervention, predicated on theoretical perspectives which emphasize psychological malfunction, maladaptation, or distress. Further, both the problem and the cure are seen as located in the "client population." Any distinction between the two methods that remains seems to be related to the practice setting rather than method, "client need," or the knowledge base underpinning practice.

Reprinted, with permission, from *Education for Social Work*, 8 (Fall 1972), pp. 65–75. ANATOLE SHAFFER was before his death in 1971 an associate professor at California State University, San José, California.

The submersion of group work into clinical practice tended to close off the primary social action involvement of social work since, in addition to a focus on socialization, group work had also been seen as a prime tool for social change. What little community organization (CO) was being taught tended to be limited to an introductory course focused on community chest activity, interagency relationships, public relations, and fund raising. The career line in community organization was one in which workers who were trained as case workers and group workers became agency executives and ultimately became community chest personnel, or staff for a national federation of local agencies. With the advent of the Economic Opportunity Act (EOA), and the emphasis on community action and "grassroots" efforts, there as a mushrooming of demand for CO practitioners and a concommitant growth in CO courses and curricula in schools of social work.[1] One result of this growth was development of a new outlet for social action interests and the attraction of students with social action commitments.

Despite this growth and new interest, CO trails the "clinical" method in both the number of students and its general influence on schools and the field. In fact, given the trends in government funding, social programs and the character of the job market, it is reasonable to expect that at best CO method development will stabilize at the present level. It is perhaps more probable that CO method instruction will shift increasingly in the direction of social planning as a technocratic enterprise in an effort to supply the demand in government programs for increasing numbers of *technocrats and bureaucratic managers.*

Contrasted with this restrictive picture is the fact that student demands and pressure from newly emergent groups of the oppressed has caused both new and old schools to make adjustments in curriculum. Methods courses have undergone strain and debate. In large measure the changes that have resulted have been less contentual and more formalist. The concept of a generic social worker and that of conceptualizing practice in terms of micromethod (clinical) and macromethod (social) have had some popularity and been experimented with. The changing character of the job market and the effect of growing utilization of paraprofessional personnel to perform traditional social work tasks has resulted in efforts to upgrade and identify professional responsibility. Methods curricula have reflected these changes by giving greater attention to administration and supervision and increased emphasis on new approaches in psychotherapeutic practice.

Faced with these inadequate alternatives to CO as a social change method, the new School of Social Work at San José State College is in the process of developing a new approach to method instruction.

## THE ROOTS OF METHOD DEVELOPMENT

Although method instruction has been generally inadequate to meet the changing needs and conditions of the last decade, it has not lessened the importance of method, only its effectiveness. In our judgment, one of the problems has been the emphasis on methods as the skills and techniques of practice—the technocratic approach. However, method/practice cannot stand alone. It has been said, "Practice without theory is blind and theory without practice is impotent." We would propose that method in its technocratic form be viewed as the externalized form of consciousness. Thus, certain techniques will emerge as predominant depending upon the relationship of practice to the consciousness of the worker, the client, the employer. The problem of consciousness will be discussed more fully below.

In regard to the theory base of social work practice, this has been largely limited to a psychological view of men and women and their work, and, even dominated by the psychoanalytic perspective.[2] Attention to the dynamics of social change has either been non-existent or has been limited to formalist discussion in which social change is seen as disruptive of system functioning. What little social theory has found its way into the curricula has been rooted in corporate liberal ideology with its primary concern for social control and system maintenance.[3] This limited view has emphasized a concern for rationalizing controlling such change as to minimize it effectively. Given the class origins of social work, its commitment to industrial society and its monocular view of social problems as reflecting individual deficit rather than social imperative, the limited development of theory and practice is not surprising.

The difficulty involved in effecting change in the social work approach seems to result from several forces acting independently and in combination on the field. As mentioned above, perhaps the primary impediment has been social work philosophy which derives from the ascension of corporate liberal ideology in the early 1900s. This ideology legitimized controlled social reform through governmental action of a 'welfare state' type. It also sanctified corporate capitalism and established it as the apex of man's political-economic development.[4] Social work, like corporate capitalism was a product of the Industrial Revolution and, in large measure, a primary institutional structure through which social reform and welfare statism was generated *and* mediated. It is therefore not surprising that the field should develop a philosophic commitment to corporate liberal ideology. (Thus, for example, the era of "do-goodism" and the humanitarian "ladies bountiful" did not disappear so much as they shifted from individual to agency action. Behavior and understanding didn't change—only the structure. The right of individuals to self-determination has only recently been extended to oppressed communities. This extension in analysis however has been made by the oppressed and has yet to be fully understood or accepted by social work. As a result we have dicta in the form of "professional articles" warning against the use of certain strategies and tactics by social workers in realizing client goals or sanctioning client behaviors which are "activist" and liberating. These warnings do not necessarily reflect the failure of such strategies and tactics but rather their success and the subsequent threat to the *status quo* which they represent. The commitment to the *status quo,* the assumption that this is a good society requiring only a "motor tune-up," is most distressing because it serves to block the effort to seek new and more equitable forms of social organization.) [5]

Social work has so long been the adjuster, it has difficulty comprehending, let alone functioning for, social change.

History and tradition are not the sole factors responsible for social work's present irrelevant position re: oppressed people and communities. Unlike other professions which are largely entrepreneurial and somewhat economically independent, social work is almost totally dependent on the good will and philanthropy of government and the wealthy. It is unreasonable to expect a profession as dependent on the existing ruling class and its governmental machinery to act contrary to their interests which include maintaining their position of socio-economic hegemony, with oppression and oppressive humanitarianism as prime tools to this end.[6] If the social welfare enterprise is a multi-billion dollar business, and functions to maintain the status quo adequately, it is inconceivable that the wealthy and the political state would consider dismantling such a business with the catastrophic economic and political risks this might entail. However, as will be discussed below, it may not be as inconceivable as it appears. The monolithic character of state machinery (despite its bureaucratic image of decentralization); the contradictions in the society; the very character and inevitability of the social change process; and the development of class and ethnic forces with radical proposals for change acting as a counter-vailing force to those who uphold the *status quo,* may all combine to make independent action by social work and social workers both necessary and possible.

Still another major factor operative in social work development is the character and structure of the profession itself. Professions, while socially sanctioned and often legally recognized, are largely self-governing. This is less so for social work than other professions. Despite the development of a single professional organization and moves to license and restrict practice, it has not succeeded in establishing its independence either in law or in fact. It seems apparent that to achieve such status the profession must move even further into a defense of the society and itself rather than vigorous action for change. It seems clear that the greater the commitment to professionalism the lesser the commitment to serving the interests of the oppressed and meeting the needs of people. (The more positive alternative would be to seek sanctioning of practice and support for service from the "client population" of the oppressed.)

## THE OPPRESSOR AND THE OPPRESSED

The significance of these interrelated factors of origins and history, capitalist development and welfare statism, and the growth of professionalism is not limited to the question of whether social work is (or is capable of being) either a social change or an adjustmental force in society. More importantly it speaks directly to the challenge of the last decade, *relevance,* and more particularly, the relationship (or lack of relationship) to the needs and goals of the oppressed in our society. The use of the word oppressed is not accidental. The dominant forces in this society have been able to absorb, distort, misconstrue or modify most efforts at developing language that points to the essential inequities which exist. For example, racism has been diverted from the institutional analysis pointed to in the Kerner report to a conceptual category that includes such oppressive notions as "cultural deprivation," as well as more moderate concerns of prejudice and disadvantage.[7]

Such conversion is difficult, if not impossible with the category of "oppressed." To speak of the oppressed immediately requires recognition and consideration of the oppressor. The two categories are essentially linked in a dialectic which forces an analysis of the causes and effect of the relationship. To be oppressed requires an oppressor. To end oppression is to end oppressing and oppressors. Further, acts designed to end this relationship can be fairly well measured and evaluated by the degree to which oppression is in fact lessened.

For social work this dialectic, oppressor-oppressed, is problematic. As an intermediary force, social work has been caught in dual behavior: towards the oppressed as "helpers" and toward the oppressor as social control agents. This contradiction has been resolved through the humanitarian attitudes of social work which serve to lessen the pain of oppression while effectively controlling the resistance of the oppressed. If we are to break this bind of "help" as an oppressive instrument we must abandon humanitarianism in favor of humanism, in which the necessity of self-determination of the oppressed is recognized as necessary and right, control is abandoned in favor of liberating consciousness and the oppressing class is eliminated.[8]

This stance of social work as oppressor, or instrument of oppression (if such a dichotomy is possible) is observable in social work education. Although schools are theoretically training independent professionals, the reality is that the overwhelming number of graduates are employed by agencies. Their professional function is at least comprised if not completely inhibited, by their performing as agents of agencies. At best these agencies are humanitarian. More typically the agency, bound by its source of income, the class composition, and interests of its board or legislative policy-making body, uses service as an instrument of oppression.[9]

## TRAINING AND THE JOB MARKET

While the school may attempt to dichotomize training the professional from his ultimate employment, in fact the curriculum and training is essentially responsive to the job market. It is not by error that a large part of training occurs in agencies and significant attention is given to socializing the worker to bureaucracy. Nor was it accidental that community organization method was virtually non-existent in social work education until the EOA and other federal programs created a demand for community organizers. The need for community organization service was not created by these programs. However, they did create jobs. In rapid order, sequences were developed, faculty recruited, and students enrolled. In the last half of the decade the number of CO students has grown significantly (with a large percentage of these being "social activists") and the demand for faculty experienced and/or trained in community organization, could not be met.[10] If the dominant relationship of the traditional or readily available job market to training needs further data, one need only look at the effect on training of the cutbacks and switches in federal programming. In California the number of students being accepted for CO sequences is either being frozen or cut back. In addition, the content of the sequences seems to be shifting heavily away from grassroots organizing and toward bureaucratic management and toward "Social Planning" as a technocratic process. This shift seems less reflective of changes in "social need' and more reflective of "market realities."

The effect of job market on training is a critical variable in curriculum. Even though federal programming expanded the field, the school focus in curriculum and method still seemed related to agency setting. While the agency may have been minus the traditional settlement and community chest setting, the potential new directions offered by the poverty program seemed less influential than the character of the new agencies and the organizational features of the agency.[11] The "community" was seen as an environment for clients. Major attention continued to be given to a "community of agencies." Agency sanction for practice continued to dominate. Rarely was the student trained to relate to a community as an interactive network of people and institutions. Even less often was the student trained to relate to a community of oppressed peoples as a partisan in their struggles. Never was attention given to how organizers with oppressed people must derive their sanction and support from the oppressed and not the oppressor. At all times training was modified by the factor of federal funding, official agencies, and institutions. These were the reality boundaries. Program goals emphasized the induction of the oppressed into existing institutional frameworks. The possibility of developing, extending, and expanding indigenous communal institutions of the oppressed was honored more in rhetoric than in practice. Attention to the issue of developing consciousness among the oppressed relative to the oppressed condition and as a step to liberation, or even developing consciousness among professionals about their role with the oppressed, was non-existent.

## CONSCIOUSNESS AND A NEW APPROACH

Given this brief overview, what are the implications for a new school of social work? How can these traditions, which have operated contrary to the interests of the oppressed, be overcome? More particularly, at San José State we have placed our emphasis on developing practitioners capable of serving the oppressed. Further, we have decided to place our emphasis upon community organization method including community development, social planning, and social action. Clearly, little of social work tradition or existent knowledge and theory base, will be helpful to us in our task. If method is essentially the observable behavior of developing consciousness and the goal is one of extending consciousness, then a primary interest is developing skill in the worker and the community in problem-solving analysis. The necessity of such an approach is that it requires both reflection and action, both critical variables in praxis. In turn the importance of praxis is the implication the concept holds of "man making his world," a necessary step in developing consciousness.

The model of the problem-solving process is not a new one. It has been used not only by those who seek change but by corporate liberal ideologues as well. The essential difference in the model as it is used here is the sanctioning source, the oppressed, and the social goals, the end of oppression. In the traditional form, the process has seen the oppressed as the group to be acted upon, and the goal, either minor modification in the system or more typically, the maintenance of the *status quo*.

In the following schematic of the process it should be understood that the stages or steps are not discreet but are interactive. Further, the process does not always continue from start to finish but may, at various times depending on conditions, follow a variable course of forward and back movements.

1.   Defining the problem from the perspective of and with relevance to the oppressed.

2.   Gathering relevant data and information in conjunction with the oppressed or sanctioning group(s).

3.   Developing initial understanding and analysis of the etiology of the problem and initiating the consciousness process.

4.   Setting of goals for modification, reform and/or change which appear relevant to the problem analysis and which are considered realistic given objective social conditions. This last includes, but is not limited to, the level of consciousness of the oppressed.

5.   Devising a set of action strategies and tactics which, again, are related to objective social conditions.

6.   Organizing necessary and appropriate resources.

7.   Undertaking the action.

8.   Assessing the results in conjunction with the actors.

9.   Repeating the cycle if the problem remains unsolved; in relation to newly identified problems; or most importantly, in relation to a new level of consciousness on the part of the oppressed.

(It should be noted that there are action components at each step of the process. The critical feature is the ability to control action and reflection co-incidentally.)

While the process outlined is a simple one, it is in practice quite complex. For example, at the level of problem definition the question arises, "Who defines the problem?" Traditionally, agencies, by determining the nature of their practice and adopting specific theoretical premises, have in fact played a major role in problem definition through a process of selective recruitment of clients.[12] It guarantees the potential for 'client' control of the process. However, one of the characteristics of the oppressor-oppressed dialectic is that the oppressed, given their limited resources and living in a reality defined by the oppressors, begin to view their existence and themselves as does the oppressor.[13] Given this, for the worker to simply accept the community definition is to make little or no contribution. While recognizing and valuing the condition of oppression as containing the seeds of liberation, he must also recognize that oppression is both self-negating and communally negating. He must therefore make his own analysis and plans and bring his knowledge and experience to bear in an effort to raise the level of community consciousness and deepen the definition of the problem. All the while his benchmark is the ultimate right of the community to decide. To insist on defining the problem at worker level of understanding is not only in violation of the democratic principle, it also runs the great risk of action failure; or exposing the community and its members to risks which are beyond their capacity to withstand or accept; and creates conditions of risk and danger which the worker rarely shares or which he has the capacity to withstand. Perhaps of equal importance is the fact that the lack of communal definition of problems guarantees minimal growth or understanding (consciousness) in the community as a result of action.

The importance of problem definition is critical since it largely determines step two and each succeeding step in the process. If we take step two and three as an example of the gathering and analysis of relevant data and information, we can begin to see the way the process effects worker role relative to consciousness. The importance of growing community consciousness requires that the worker function as much like a teacher as like a technician. The worker functions to assist the community to gather its own data, acting only in consort with community members, or on his own only at the knowledgeable direction of the community and when his acting alone is in some ways advantageous. In regard to the latter, there may be occasions when acting as a professional, the worker can get information from agencies and other workers which are not normally available to citizens. At every step of the process, the worker needs to assist the community in understanding the process and the implications of various analyses and actions. Further, the worker must be cognizant of the complex interaction between himself, the community, and the oppressing group.

The ultimate goal of this process is the end of oppression. Clearly this means ending the monopoly control over resources, power, and politics by the oppressor. More, it means an end to the oppressor qua oppressor. This obviously cannot be done by action of the oppressors since it is clearly counter to their class interests. The best one may hope to expect from the oppressor class are some minimal humanitarian efforts designed to maintain their hegemony. Humanitarianism has historically shifted to repression as the consciousness of the oppressed develops towards liberation. This however is a stage of development in the dialectic which goes beyond our immediate concern. In any event, meaningful social change in the context of the oppressor-oppressed dialectic must emanate from the oppressed. Here lies the paradox. The effect of oppression on the oppressed is deep and lasting. In general, given the educational and other socializing institutions to which they are subjected by the oppressor, the oppressed view their confreres (and themselves) as does the oppressor. The reality of being oppressed saps the oppressed of physical and political strength. They doubt their capacity to effect change and set their goals within boundaries determined by the oppressors. They cannot and are not allowed to look beyond the confines of the present socio-economic relationships. It is only in the context of major contradictions in the larger society that conditions develop which shift the framework of control sufficiently to permit the oppressed to move in their own behalf. Unfortunately they have, in the past, lacked sufficient technical, educational, and political support to maintain these efforts. The poverty program is an example of this. The poverty program never questioned the essential relationships in the society. Rather it effectively set its goals at permitting a few of the poor to gain entry to those levels of society which provided them with additional resources to move toward middleclass status and identity and to become "trustworthy." In large measure this was the fate of most new career programs and the new careerists employed. Allegedly designed to employ community representatives to make programs more relevant, these representatives were soon alienated from their communities, became oriented to protection of their own job and improvement of their own job and improvement of their own conditions. They were used to legitimate programs and services rather than to change them.[14]

Given these conditions, what is the appropriate starting point for work with oppressed communities to induce change in the oppressed-oppressor relationship? Freire, building on his experience with urban and rural oppressed in Latin America, argues for the development of a "liberating consciousness" among the oppressed.[15] He accepts the limiting conditions of oppression as the starting point for working toward change but allows for the input of professionals committed to the struggle for liberation. In his formulation the professional role is not limited to technician, leader, follower, or any other single set of behaviors. Rather, the professional is all of these and more with a primary function of raising with the oppressed the societal contradictions their condition represents so that the community can begin to identify problems, propose solutions and initiate action. Continued growth and increasing consciousness results from the dialectic that is initiated by such self-action.

Extending Freire's notions then, method, the techniques and actions of the professional, are the visible features, the actual reflection of the level of consciousness of the actors (the community and the worker). In this context, the technological character of method is secondary to and determined by the consciousness of the people. Further it becomes necessary for the worker to develop the skill of controlled praxis, the simultaneous process of action and reflection. In this way the worker and community can come together and move toward liberation together. Finally, community organization practice is rooted in the community with the goal of ending oppression through broad social change.

## LEARNING CONTENT AND APPROACH

With this perspective as the framework for method development, we are still faced with the problem of specifying course content. It must be emphasized that the content will be developed within the above framework. Thus, while it is not unusual for CO method courses to present a history of the field, we believe that historical perspective projected against a theoretical perspective of the oppressor-oppressed dialectic will produce significantly different understanding. It is expected that at least the following content areas will be emphasized in a two-year program.

1. *Historical analyses of the growth and development of the present socioeconomic relationship between the oppressor and oppressed.*
   a. The historical development of CO practice against the backdrop of this relationship.
2. *Theoretical explanations and implications of this development.*
   a. The colonial analogy.
   b. Corporate liberalism and the welfare state.
   c. Theories of individual deficit.
   d. Cultural deprivation theories and paradigms.
   e. Social deficit (structural) theories.
   f. Oppression, class struggle, and consciousness.
3. *Models for effecting social change in regard to the oppressor-oppressed dialectic.*
   a. Reform models. The modification and reform of the existing system; the quantitative approach to change.
   b. Revolutionary models. Basic system change. The qualitative approach.
   c. Reform, consciousness, revolution, and social change. A continuing process or discrete entities?
4. *Organizational patterns*
   a. Organizational theory of bureaucracy.
   b. Agency as bureaucratic/matrix phenomenon.
   c. Agency as community institution.
   d. Community organizations as communal institutions distinct from agencies.
   e. Multi-faceted organizational structures, i.e., churches, fraternal groups, business enterprises.

5. *Organizational arrangements and decision making*
    a. Centralized planning and action on local, state, regional, and federal levels.
    b. Decentralized planning and action on local, state, regional, and federal levels.
    c. The balance and interaction of centralized-decentralized arrangements.
6. *Traditional and varying CO models and approaches*
    a. Community organization. ⎫
    b. Community development. ⎬ Methods and implications in
    c. Social planning. ⎪ relation to the oppressed.
    d. Social action. ⎭
7. *Traditional and varying worker roles*
    a. Enabler ⎫
    b. Advocate ⎬ Relation to levels of
    c. Activist ⎬ consciousness and
    d. Partisan ⎭ oppression.
8. *Worker/community skills*
    a. Developing and designing strategy and tactics.
    b. Development and coordination of resources.
    c. Knowledge and application of group theory.
    d. Program planning and project proposal writing.
    e. Administration.
9. *Analysis and use of power*
    a. Pluralistic model. ⎫
    b. Power Structure model. ⎬ Relevance and applicability
    c. Community power research. ⎭ to condition of oppression.
10. *The relationship of community-sanctioned CO practice to traditional professional social work practice.*
    a. Is it social work?
    b. Nature of possible relationships.
        i. funds.
        ii. information.
        iii. political support.
        iv. converting humanitarianism to humanism.

The list of potential content areas to be covered could be almost unending. The logic of their organization into some sequential model is also not limited to a single approach. The content could be organized in terms of some internal logic inherent in the material. On the other hand, the content could be organized flexibly enough to be almost immediately responsive to community need as revealed in field experiences.

It is our opinion that an *a priori* sequencing is less significant than ultimate integration of the material.

No matter the ultimate organization of the course content. It still remains to provide a structure for learning and experiencing the content.


## CONCLUSION

The simplest answer to this problem would be to adopt the traditional model of four courses over two years, taught in a classroom setting, with content divided relatively equally and hopefully in response to some logic. This approach raises the question of developing joint consciousness in worker and community.

Does the classroom have a contribution to make to the community? Is the class experience appropriately limited to students or can the community both contribute to and benefit from the experience? How will the community, the sanctioning authority, make its input?

We don't have the answers to these question. However, in keeping with our commitment to conjoint consciousness, community participation, and conjoint learning, we propose to develop classes in a manner that is open to members of the community as well as regularly enrolled students. Classes should be located in the community and every effort should be made to recruit community participants as well as class members.

It is recognized that there is a danger of romanticizing community participation in education. We also recognize that responsibility to students includes assisting them in being able to abstract and generalize their experiences so that they will possess generalized principles and theoretical foundations when they complete their studies. Such abstracting and generalizing, while ultimately useful to the community, is generally viewed as (and in fact is) irrelevant to the day to day struggle the community experiences. Further, in the specific case of San José State, we have a commitment to research and knowledge building relevant to the experiences of the Spanish speaking in the U.S. Such research is often seen as irrelevant to the immediate needs of the community and devalued, no matter the long range benefits of such research.

However, despite problems and contradictions, we believe avoidance of artificial barriers between workers and community to be beneficial and we will therefore experiment with community/student classes. To fulfill our obligations to the student and academic community, we will develop individual studies and small group seminars aimed at assisting the student in abstracting and generalizing his experience as well as conducting research and experimentation.

## NOTES AND REFERENCES

1. See for example the discussion of CO growth in Arnold Gurin, *Community Organization Curriculum in Graduate Social Work Education* (New York: Council on Social Work Education, 1970).

2. The development and effect of the psychoanalytic perspective is excellently discussed by Herman Borenzweig, "Social Work and Psychoanalytic Theory: An Historical Analysis," *Social Work*, Vol. 16, No. 1 (January, 1971).

3. For a discussion of Corporate Liberalism, see James Weinstein, *Corporate Ideal in the Liberal State* (Boston: Beacon Press, 1968).

4. Herman Schwendinger and Julia Schwendinger, *Sociologists of the Chair* (New York: Basic Books, in press).

5. See for example Daniel Thursz, "The Arsenal of Social Action Strategies: Options for Social Workers," *Social Work*, Vol. 16, No. 1 (January, 1971) and Harry Specht, "Disruptive Tactics," *Social Work*, Vol. 14, No. 2 (April, 1969).

6. For a discussion of the relationship between government behavior and ruling class interests, see Ralph Milliband, *The State in Advanced Capitalist Society* (New York: Basic Books, 1970).

7. U.S. Riot Commission, *Report of the National Advisory Commission on Civil Disorders*.

8. Paulo Freire, *Pedagogy of the Oppressed* (New York: Herder & Herder, 1971), pp. 39, 47.

9. See as an example of this functioning Anatole Shaffer, "Welfare Rights Organization: Friend or Foe?" in *Social Work Practice* (New York: Columbia University Press, 1967); Betty Mandell, "Welfare and Totalitarianism," *Social Work*, Vol. 16, No. 1 (January, 1971).

10. Gurin, *op. cit.*

11. Ralph M. Kramer, *Participation of the Poor* (Englewood Cliffs, N.J.: Prentice-Hall, 1968); Peter Marris and Martin Rein, *Dilemmas of Social Reform* (Chicago: Aldine-Atherton, 1967).

12. Richard Cloward and Irwin Epstein, "Private Social Welfare's Disengagement from the Poor," Mayer Zald (ed.) *Social Welfare Institutions* (New York: John Wiley, 1965).

13. Freire, *op. cit.*

14. Robert Blauner and Anatole Shaffer, *New Careers and the Person*, Council of Community Services Technical Monograph Series, #116, 1967.

15. Freire, *op. cit.*

# 20

# The Black Community's Challenge to Social Work

## BILLY J. TIDWELL

THERE ARE MANY REASONS to conclude that the tumultuous decade of the sixties represented a period of unique significance for the black community and its relations with American society. Indeed, when analyzed as part of a continuous historical process, the developments during this period symbolize a dramatic turning point. In making this observation I do not suggest that other critical historical junctures cannot be identified, for to do so would reveal either a glaring ignorance of the facts of history or a dogmatism which borders on the maniacal—neither of which shortcoming I am prepared to concede. I am convinced, however, that one may justifiably and with appreciable utility isolate the developments of the past decade and evaluate their peculiar impact upon the body politic.

Reprinted, with permission, from *Education for Social Work*, 7 (Fall 1971), pp. 59–65. BILLY J. TIDWELL was at the time of writing a doctoral student at the University of Wisconsin School of Social Work, Madison, Wisconsin. This paper was originally presented at the Eighteenth Annual Program Meeting of the Council on Social Work Education, Seattle, Washington, January 1971.

It is virtually undeniable that the black community has undergone profound social and ideological changes in recent years, and that these changes and their ramifications have direct and weighty bearing upon the institution of social work. In effect, the black community has confronted social work with a demonstrably new and important set of issues which, in my opinion, constitute one of the most formidable challenges ever to face the field. At base, the challenge questions the utility of the social work enterprise relative to the fundamental problems and needs of the black community, as these have undergone reassessment and redefinition by black people.

I have not yet resolved that the challenge is an insurmountable one. It seems clear, however, that in order for social work to meet it with competence and efficacy a serious reexamination and reorganization of some of the profession's most basic operating assumptions, principles, and technologies is imperative.

What precisely is the nature of the challenge to which we refer? I will treat this question by: enumerating several of the significant developments which, in my opinion, helped to distinguish the 1960s; by elucidating the implications of these developments and their collective meaning in terms of the status and disposition of the black community; and by suggesting some of the vital ways in which these implications bear upon the institution of social work.

## BLACK HAPPENINGS IN THE 1960s

Any single catalogue of salient aspects of black community movement during the past decade is bound to be both incomplete and arbitrary. Incomplete because this period was so extraordinarily eventful; arbitrary because of the inevitable biases and predilections of the analyst. With these cautionary stipulations in mind, I propose that the following items should be included in any adequate accounting:

1.  *The urban revolts*   The series of violent upheavals which beset virtually every major urban area clearly stand out as the most momentous and conspicuous development. These massive violent episodes denote the appearance of a new social phenomenon. In contrasting them with the typical race riot of the past, one analyst has observed that contemporary mass violence has been initiated by blacks instead of whites and has sought to eradicate the more blatant physical symbols of white oppression.[1] In a similar vein, another investigator has posited this cogent analogy:

The ghetto riots, in one sense, are antiimperialist, guerrilla movements, like those appearing throughout the Third World. That is, our ghetto riots are being waged against a kind of despotism inside our own culture that is similar to the imperialist despotism carried out by the rich nations against the poor.[2]

2. *The transformation of black students* The widespread and radical insurgency on the part of black students within the previously tranquil context of higher education is organically related to the revolt in the streets and represents a development with which social work educators should be most intimately familiar. The black student movement has imposed upon academia issues identical in substance to those which have generally galvanized and directed the black resurgency. The significance of this development is reinforced by the fact that it indicates a drastic readjustment of the traditionally apolitical *modus vivendi* that more fortunate blacks have cultivated and maintained while isolated on college campuses. The crux of this change, as postulated by Harry Edwards in his provocative analysis of the black student movement, is that the characteristically middle-class black student has reordered his priorities. In Edwards' words,

. . . the middle-class negro [sic] has traditionally regarded a degree as a status symbol and union card, and has not had a primary interest in the intellectual skills to be gained through the educational experiences accrued while earning that degree. Second, he has not infrequently enrolled in courses of study which have had only a marginal and indirect relevance and applicability to the problems of the black community.[3]

3. *The emergence of radically-minded organizations* The 1960s saw the ascendancy of a veritable plethora of autonomous and semi-autonomous grassroots organizations. Needless to say, organizations of sundry types have existed in the black community for decades. However, never have there been so many espousing radical political objectives, nor has grassroots participation in such organizations been so extensive. The Black Panther Party is an instructive example in this regard.[4] Even the most learned critics of the Panthers are forced to concede that the organization has effectively mobilized and politicized a sizeable and heretofore reticent segment of the black community.[5]

It is also noteworthy that many organizations which were established as of and prior to 1960 have since undergone profound ideological and programmatic reorientation. The Student Nonviolent Coordinating Committee and the Congress of Racial Equality are two exemplary cases.[6]

4. *The demand for community control*  The issue of community control is not entirely new to American political tradition.[7] However, the expansive popularity which it has come to enjoy among blacks is unprecedented. Many, if not most, of the organizations alluded to above share the conviction that community control is a necessary precondition for the welfare of black people. The following statement by Roy Innis, national CORE director, is representative of prevailing sentiment:

Blacks must manage and control the institutions that service their areas, as has always been the case for other interest groups. There is an immediate need in the institutions of education, health, social service, sanitation, housing, protection, etc. Black people must be able to control basic societal instruments in the social, political, and economic areas.[8]

We might also mention here the highly explosive demand for reparations, originally ignited by James Foreman and embodied in the controversial Black Manifesto.[9] The spirit of this demand alone reflects a decisive departure in the black community's perennial quest for justice and redress of grievances.

5. *The new set of verbal symbols*  The sudden popularity of a new parlance in the black community may well be the most reliable indicator of the depth and direction of the ideological change that has occurred. Heretofore, such terms as imperialism, oppression, exploitation, liberation, and revolution have become increasingly standard vocabulary for even the most unlettered blacks. One need not look very far for the sources of this new affinity for revolutionary rhetoric. Among other things, the writings of Frantz Fanon and Ché Guevara and the mesmerizing speeches of Malcolm X have exerted powerful influence. The new rhetoric, and the imagery to which it gives rise, has not been without its behavioral concomitants. To the contrary, it has motivated and justified actions which but a short time ago would have been deemed unthinkable. It is largely responsible for producing what one writer has aptly termed "the urban guerrilla," a breed almost unique to the contemporary black community.[10]

The development listed above are obviously not exhaustive, nor was it my purpose to examine them in depth. I merely suggest that they represent facets of a broad configuration of developments which reflect pronounced changes in the status quo of the black community. To reiterate, I am chiefly concerned with the interpretation of these changes and their implications for the relationship between the black community and the institution of social work.

## *INTERPRETING BLACK COMMUNITY MOVEMENT*

One of the most prominent impressions generated by our abbreviated review of the sixties is that a significant segment of blacks have fundamentally shifted their perspective vis-à-vis American society and the status of the black man in it. To state the point in overly simplistic terms, blacks view themselves as occupying the status of colonial subjects —a status, moreover, which vested politico-economic interests systematically maintain for power and profit.[11] Although the colonial analogy is far from perfect,[12] any hasty attempt to dismiss it categorically is remiss. For one thing it must be acknowledged that the historical experience of the black man in America resembles in some crucial respects that of groups in a typical colonized territory. In addition, and perhaps more importantly, the analogy has produced a vastly different set of objectives and strategies for achieving them from those which have characterized the traditional civil rights movement.

The civil rights movement has been guided by the relentless conviction that blacks are bonafide American citizens whose constitutional rights are violated by irrational acts of discrimination and racism. Its overriding objective has been the achievement of equal rights and opportunities. Its basic strategies have involved persuasion, cooperation, and mild forms of civil disobedience. Conversely, the more recent black resurgency, guided largely by the colonial analogy, espouses the objectives of "liberation" which, operationally, requires the consolidation and application of group power by blacks so as to effect basic social changes beneficial to the masses of black people.

This new thrust constitutes a more sophisticated and realistic assessment of the problems and needs confronting the black community. Revolutionary rhetoric aside, blacks are now cognizant of the fact that their fundamental problems are systematic and structural in substance, emanating from the oppressive nature and operation of this nation's major political and economic institutions. These institutions, and their deleterious practices, relative to blacks, have been undergirded and sustained by a pervasive racism, as is so forcefully documented in the timely book, *Institutional Racism in America*.[13]

Thus those analyses, recently so popular among liberal social scientists, holding that the problems of blacks are primarily attributable to dysfunctional family patterns [14] and individual social maladjustment have been called into serious question.[15] Moreover, blacks have adopted justifiably a very cynical stance toward programs to ameliorate their conditions whose emphasis is on individual rehabilitation. In view of the structural constraints which are operative, such remedial efforts are at best palliatives and at worst consciously designed pacification devices.

The structural constraints are maintained through the exercise of power, and because power is not relinquished voluntarily, efforts to eliminate these structural constraints which eschew power considerations are hopelessly ineffectual. It is for this reason that the need for black group power is so essential.[16] Similarly, the foremost criterion by which blacks evaluate the utility of contemporary social programs is the degree of power-producing potential exhibited by them.

I should underscore another point here, which is inextricably related to the interpretations above. It concerns the fact that the black community has endorsed a new set of strategies and tactics as being integral to the achievement of power and the realization of institutional change. This movement toward the employment of abrasive conflict strategies and violent tactics should come as no surprise. For one thing, as I have intimated, attempts to uproot powerful vested interests through appeal and persuasion are little more than pathetic exercises in futility. Furthermore, it must be recognized that blacks as yet do not enjoy the control over wealth and resources, mass media, solidarity groups, values, and prestigeful interaction which, according to Rossi, are the mainstays of power.[17] The most effective source of power for black people accrues from the ability to disrupt through violence and conflict. As social workers, imbued with humanitarian motives, we might lament this condition, but its existence cannot be rationally denied. Its reality is poignantly confirmed by the recent proliferation of paramilitary organizations in the black community.[18]

In summary, it is apparent that the black community has determined to define its own needs, assume the offensive, and employ means that though contrary to American cultural sensibilities, are most germane to the problems facing the black masses. American society and her institutions may no longer rely upon the black community to behave as a passive, uncritical recipient of paternalistic dispensations.

Many of the above observations are admittedly vulnerable to the charge of overstatement. On the other hand, they do reflect important trends which have progressively altered the context within which social work must function. In concluding I will deal with some of the more serious implications of these trends for social work practice in the black community.

## A CONFLICT OF PREMISES

The institutionalized enterprise of social work is in some ways a unique one. For one thing, it is most prevalent in highly industrialized societies.[19] That this should be the case is readily understandable. History has demonstrated that industrialization processes are not completely beneficent in their consequences. Almost inevitably these processes engender artifactual changes which would undermine human welfare. Put another way, technological advancement is often messy and highly inconsiderate of the human costs involved. It is not entirely anomalous, therefore, that within our own society, unparalleled in modernization and affluence, there exist widespread pockets of human misery, degradation, and functional incapacity. (Needless to say, black people have been inordinately victimized by these social afflictions.)

Despite the profession's (vaguely) expressed commitment to social action, social work's societally prescribed obligation has been to alleviate the suffering of what I call the "systemic casualties," but without reorganizing the social order which caused them. In this sense, social work's institutional function is a conciliatory one. In large it derives from—or is at least consistent with—a conception of society diametrically opposite to that which the black resurgency subscribes.

In *Class and Class Conflict in Industrial Society,* Dahrendorf proposes two pivotal conceptions of society.[20] One of these relates to what the author calls the "integration theory." According to this view, society is comprised of "voluntary associations of people who share certain values and set up institutions in order to ensure the smooth functioning of cooperation." Interdependency and cooperation are the salient features of the system. The second conception represents "the coercion theory." This view recognizes the existence of opposing interests and a differential distribution of power and resources by which interests can be protected and enhanced. Such differential distribution acts as the ultimate determinant of "systematic social conflicts." The structural origin of such group conflicts inheres in the arrangement of social roles endowed with expectations of domination or subjection.

It is safe to say that social work has embraced the integration theory. Conversely, as indicated earlier, the black community has begun to think and act on the basis of the coercion theory. This divergency implies that the two parties adhere to different sets of premises, different ways of viewing and relating to the social world, if you will.

A practical manifestation of social work's societal perspective is the exclusion of conflict strategy from the profession's self-legitimized repertory of technologies. Practitioners who engage in or actively encourage the use of conflict are denounced as performing illegitimate professional roles. Even in the community organization specialty, which perhaps possesses the greatest relevance to the collective problems of black people, conflict utilization is defined as off limits. Perusal of most basic community organization literature, for example, would illuminate the primacy accorded to the conflict-free "enabling" and "cooperative" modes of intervention.[21]

Fortunately, there is an incipient movement of community organization scholars and practitioners toward reorienting the profession's position on this issue. A small but expanding number of writers are beginning to argue in terms of the inevitability and necessity of conflict in
efforts to effect significant social change.[22] From the practice standpoint,
some community organizers have attempted to relate realistically to
problems of the poor and black but have found themselves ill-prepared.
And, as Kramer and Specht point out, they have not been able to look
to the profession for direction. The authors state that:

> As social problems such as racial segregation and poverty came to the fore,
> community organization practitioners found themselves on the side of the
> disadvantaged groups and in situations where change occurs only through
> the mobilization of power in various forms of social action. Finding little
> support for their professional judgments in the more traditional forms of
> practice, change agents sought guidelines from the experience of the civil
> rights, labor, peace, and other social movements.[23]

While there is a faction appearing among social workers who recognize
and appreciate the relevance of conflict and power phenomena to their
professional roles, there is no reason to consider their opinions prevalent
within the profession. In fact, the findings of at least one researcher
suggest an overwhelming deprecation of the use of conflict strategies by
professional practitioners.[24]

The basic challenge that the new thrust by black people presents to
social work, then, is to reconstitute its assumptions and modify its
technology so as to be more realistic about the dynamics of power and
their relationship to the problems and needs of the black community.
Unless the challenge is taken seriously the profession's utility relative
to these problems and needs will remain marginal at best.

The primary responsibility for realizing these changes, it seems to
me, must lie with social work education. We must become more critical
of the kinds of attitudes and skills being imparted to our students.
We must counteract the growing tendency toward preoccupation with
a function orientation to the severe neglect of a cause orientation.[25] We
must emphasize that the problems of some client groups do not stem
from social maladjustment and are not amenable to rehabilitative or
cooperative solutions. Most importantly, our students must be taught
that a vital part of the societal function of social work must be to
remove the structural and attitudinal constraints that make our democratic system an abusive and oppressive one to large segments of the
population. The extent to which we succeed in these endeavors will
be a measure of our relevance to the problems and needs of the black
community.

## REFERENCES

1. Joseph Boskin, "The Revolt of the Urban Ghettos, 1964–1967," in Richard P. Young (ed.), *Roots of Rebellion: The Evolution of Black Politics and Protest Since World War II* (New York: Harper and Row, 1970), pp. 309–327.

2. Harvey Wheeler, "A Moral Equivalent for Riots," in Larry Ng (ed.), *Alternatives to Violence* (New York: Time-Life Books, 1968).

3. Harry Edwards, *Black Students* (New York: Free Press, 1970).

4. Gene Marine, *The Black Panthers* (New York: Signet Books, 1969).

5. Tom Milstein, "A Perspective on the Panthers" in *Commentary* (September, 1970), pp. 35–43.

6. Edwards, *op. cit.;* Alex Poinsett, "Roy Innis; Nation Builder," *Ebony* (October, 1969): and Alex Poinsett, "The Economics of Liberation," *Ebony* (August, 1969).

7. Alan A. Altshuler, *Community Control* (New York: Pegasus, 1970).

8. Roy Innis, "Separatist Economics: A New Social Contract" in William F. Haddad and G. Douglas Pugh, *Black Economic Development* (Englewood Cliffs, New Jersey: Prentice-Hall, Inc., 1969), pp. 50–59.

9. Arnold Schuchter, *Reparations* (Philadelphia and New York: J. B. Lippincott and Co., 1970).

10. Martin Oppenheimer, *The Urban Guerrilla* (Chicago: Quadrangle Books, 1969).

11. Robert L. Allen, *Black Awakening in Capitalist America* (Garden City, New York: Doubleday and Co., 1970).

12. Poinsett, "Economics of Liberation," *op. cit.*

13. Louis L. Knowles and Kenneth Prewit (eds.), *Institutional Racism in America* (Englewood Cliffs, New Jersey: Prentice Hall, 1969).

14. Daniel P. Moynihan, *The Negro Family: The Case for National Action* (Washington, D. C.: U. S. Department of Labor, Office of Planning and Research, March, 1965).

15. Andrew Billingsley, *Black Families in White America* (Englewood Cliffs, New Jersey: Prentice-Hall, Inc., 1968); and Elliot Liebow, *Tally's Corner* (Boston: Little, Brown & Co., 1967).

16. Stokely Carmichael and Charles V. Hamilton, *Black Power* (New York: Random House, 1967); and Nathan Wright, Jr., *Black Power and Urban Unrest* (New York: Hawthorn Books, Inc., 1967).

17. Peter H. Rossi, "Theory, Research, and Practice in Community Organization" in Ralph M. Kramer and Harry Specht (eds.), *Readings in Community Organization Practice* (Englewood Cliffs, N. J.: Prentice Hall, Inc., 1969), pp. 49–61.

18. Oppenheimer, *op. cit.*

19. Harold L. Wilensky and Charles N. Lebeaux, *Industrial Society and Social Welfare* (New York: Free Press, 1965).

20. Ralf Dahrendorf, *Class and Class Conflict in Industrial Society* (Stanford, California: Stanford University Press, 1959).

21. Arthur Dunham, *Community Welfare Organization: Principles and Practice* (New York: Thomas Y. Crowell Company, 1958); and Ernest B. Harper and Arthur Dunham, *Community Organization in Action* (New York: Association Press, 1959).

22. Kramer and Specht, *op. cit.;* and Lyle E. Schaller, *Community Organization: Conflict and Reconciliation* (Nashville: Abingdon Press, 1966).

23. Kramer and Specht, *op. cit.,* p. 324.

24. Irwin Epstein, "Social Workers and Social Action: Attitudes toward Social Action Strategies," *Social Work* (April, 1968), pp. 101–109.

25. Donald S. Howard, "Social Work and Social Reform," in Cora Kasius (ed.), *New Directions in Social Work* (New York: Harper and Brothers, 1954).

# 21

# Black Power Through Community Control

## DOUGLAS GLASGOW

DOES SOCIAL WORK as a profession have the vitality to be an effective
force in abetting the development of ethnic communities? This question
has been seriously raised again and again.[1] The argument gravitates
around the basic issue of whether social work's focuses and methodology
are an advantage or an impediment in furthering minority concerns.

The social work profession is charged with focusing too long on patch-
ing up the afflicted and ignoring the primary causes of their troubles.
The conditions, many say, that generate the major trauma experienced
by minority people are growing out of society's basic structures. Social
workers, therefore, should concentrate on intervention strategies that
seek to change these structures. For ethnic minorities and specifically
for blacks, current social work interventions provide only the temporary
relief of palliatives, rather than the sustained effort needed to ameliorate
living conditions through sociostructural changes.

Reprinted from *Social Work*, 17 (May 1972), pp. 59–64. DOUGLAS GLASGOW was at the
time of writing dean of the School of Social Work, Howard University, Washington, D.C.

The profession has been reticent about analyzing the uniqueness of ethnicity as a major factor contributing to extraordinary oppression. Some social workers seem to have an unarticulated fear that if they admit the criticism is deserved they may find it necessary to depart significantly from traditional social work focuses and adopt models and ideological orientations alien to them. On the other hand, many forward-looking members of the profession have acknowledged today's imperatives for broad social action and radical societal changes.

The author contends that one of the sharp conflicts about the profession's orientation has been produced by black Americans' contemporary thrust toward self-determination and independent efforts to attain increased power and control. Ideological beliefs supported by misconceptions stand in the way of a major change in the profession's focus.

## SEPARATISM AND INTEGRATION

The movement of black people toward self-determination and management of their own destiny has been grossly misunderstood. Many professionals consider this accelerated movement as the black community's decision to reject white involvement. Others characterize it as moving along a "separatist" path, implying that blacks seek solutions to their problems outside accepted, traditional American channels. These critics forget that the use of traditional channels has permitted whites to define problems, formulate solutions, and implement programs ostensibly for blacks' interests. It has permitted whites to carry out these efforts from an "all national" viewpoint, acting from what is often called an "integrationist" perspective. Further, it has sanctioned the right of social scientists, activists, and researchers unobstructedly to devise plans and intervene in projects affecting black people's lives.

It is clear that blacks and whites hold sharply different views about separatism. When whites apply the concept to race relations, they usually impute a negative connotation to it. They view separatism as excluding whites and imply that rejection and antagonistic positions are involved. In contrast, most blacks give little attention to separatism as such. They perceive their concerns to be expanding self-determination, promoting self-reliance, and participating in programs that encourage independent development. To appreciate the essence of the black perspective, one must realize that the liberation movement of black Americans is not primarily antiwhite but problack. What is said and done about separatism varies according to the perspective from which it is viewed.

Understanding the black position and evaluating black people's needs have been hindered by the practice of comparing blacks and whites, then conjecturing about when the black viewpoint departed from the white viewpoint. Studying the requirements of black or white people involves a sound and comprehensive analysis of the specific group's actual living conditions. Once fundamental needs are determined, then intervention strategies can be developed and priorities established.

Any sound analysis of the conditions of poor whites or general poverty populations as against ethnic minorities—in particular black Americans —shows that unique differences exist among the groups.[2] There are not only the quantitative status or ranked differences generally expected; there are also qualitative distinctions. Correcting them demands intervention strategies that take divergent paths. Many social workers fail to understand this dialectic and thus negate the legitimacy of various change strategies.

In oversimplified and inaccurate terms, black people's liberation is generally said to involve alternative directional choices: integration or separatism. They are considered as antithetical positions rather than different strategies directed toward a common goal. Lack of clarity about these concepts is not surprising. The precise meaning of integration has become so distorted by racism when applied to black-white relationships that some authorities suggest its utility as a term is doubtful. One writer has proposed that "transformation" be used instead.[3]

Integration formerly denoted a projected social goal that the early multinational nonblack immigrants could attain. It was seen as an ultimate state of union for Americans, in which the people's cultural traits would be blurred. This state of union would represent the American culture. The American dream that the melting-pot or some other amalgamative process would eventually produce unique Americans without any obvious old-country earmarks did not become a reality. More typically, the various national and religious groups maintained, sometimes even reinforced, early identifiable features. Many undergirded group aspirations by creating an institutional network to strengthen their group's efforts. Nationally, their adaptation to the American scene tended to be more pluralistic than amalgamative, and continues to be so. Significantly, the melting-pot ideal was never viewed as encompassing black Americans or any other nonwhites—e.g., American Indians or Mexican-Americans.

## RACISM

Racism and the emergence of blacks as a migratory population brought dramatic shifts in the interpretation of integration. Applied to black concerns, what was initially a goal for whites became centered around a process for blacks—a process of adaptation, not amalgamation or cultural pluralism. Since blacks were not deemed to have a culture or an ethnic heritage, their task was defined as attaining white cultural standards. In essence, the black American was to work toward the liquidation of his own people. Thus those blacks who engaged in the process with great energy for over two decades, seeking to obtain social mobility, in many respects became entrapped in a process of voluntary cultural and ethnic genocide.[4]

At different times during their quest for freedom black Americans have adopted various strategies to resist annihilation. During slavery, they were confronted by a closed society in which they were clearly classed as chattel. They found then that in large measure specific actions and strategies geared to survival were expedient.[5] During Reconstruction, a short-lived period of growing democracy in America, blacks united with poor whites, trying to build a degree of equality through such organizations as the Freedmen's Bureau. This period ended when southern landed power was resurrected.[6] The post-Reconstruction period introduced a harrowing era in black people's lives, when the parameters for mobility were purposefully made obscure. The potential for change was unhesitatingly acclaimed, but opportunity systems were denied development.

## BLACK PERSPECTIVE

Decades of frustration and unfulfilled expectations have contributed to the direction of the black thrust today. Blacks began to realize that the task set for them—achievement through ethnic negation—was neither attainable nor desirable. Furthermore, society was holding out to them the ideal of individual mobility, but limiting its fulfillment by perpetuating racist obstructions. Therefore large groups of black Americans shifted to action planned and directed from a black perspective.

Blacks have had a long and invidious experience with racism in America and thus have a specific and unique perception of this phenomenon. Whites have had a contrary experience. Blacks are primarily objects of racism. In the main, racism has served as an expedient doctrine for whites, despite some negative residual effects. Social scientists continue to posit increased similarity in behavior and aspirations of blacks and whites.[7] However, they are overlooking fundamental differences that become apparent when the two groups' perceptions, feelings, and responses are examined in regard to racism. Racism has been the major stimulant affecting black people's functioning.

A black perspective is basic for mobilizing black people. It indicates direction, embodies a philosophical view of life, provides a framework for interpreting events, and speaks to the issue of black people's continuity. In essence, it is an ethnocentric view that points the way for blacks to analyze conditions and determine the action most appropriate from their own unique vantage point. This view may well be colored, but this does not lessen its validity. It represents a positive ethnocentric emphasis that guides black people's striving for mobility.[8]

## COMMUNITY CONTROL

One of the main avenues for black mobility is through ethnic group advancement anchored in community development. Assessment of black experiences in white America has led increasing numbers of blacks, from professionals to street brothers, to focus on attaining community control.

This objective grew out of the realization that American society functions through various power blocs and that many interest groups— e.g., businesses, unions, voluntary and professional associations, and religious organizations—negotiate a viable existence through organizing their own forces and forming alliances. Thus blacks, in working for increased community control, are not departing from traditional American modes of action; rather, they are initiating a potentially aggressive thrust into American sociopolitical life.

Essentially this thrust is an astute adaptation of the power bloc–interest group interaction in American society. It acknowledges that power is needed to negotiate an acceptable existence in this country. It recognizes that in the American social pattern power is not manifested by individuals but through the organizations and systems to which individuals belong. Community control leads to management of instruments of black survival and growth and ultimately the institutions through which black power can be manifested.[9]

Achievement of community control goes to the heart of a major issue: blacks becoming a viable force, as a people and as a constituent element of American sociopolitical life. Being part of a community, determining their own direction, and having community institutions administered to meet their special needs can provide blacks with invaluable assets for counteracting the destructive effects of institutional racism.

Community control—notwithstanding its contemporary vitality or the importance of working to attain it—does not truly represent a radical or revolutionary social change. Rather, it reflects a developmental stage in black action to attain equity within the current arena of American power politics. Within this context, the issue is neither separatism nor integration, but self-determined action to achieve group viability, directed from a black perspective.

When a thrust to put black community control into actual operation is initiated, certain ambiguous terms must be clearly understood and several pertinent questions require attention. For example, one must distinguish between black communities and the ghettos where great masses of blacks reside. On the one hand there is voluntary residence with community control of institutions and on the other, a living area in which people are confined, alienated, and powerless. The question often arises as to whether to revitalize a decayed, bankrupt central-city municipality or seek ways to relocate in other areas. What are the practical strategies involved? What types of service systems can and should be developed to meet black people's needs either in revitalized areas or new locations? Another formidable question: Must the community develop new business and industry to sustain the area adequately as a whole and ultimately enrich it? Obviously there are no simple answers to these and the myriad other questions that will arise. Solutions may demand extensive sociopolitical analysis or require long-term cooperative effort and sustained financial support.

The federal government's position is important. Will the federal bureaucracy continue to remain essentially passive in regard to black activities for community revitalization? Will its main contribution be to encourage programs of black capitalism? Federal passivity connotes nonsupport. Those who helped create ghettos or who help maintain them through various institutional devices will no doubt continue to resist community redevelopment. They will be encouraged by a passive governmental position.

## WHITE OPPOSITION

A situation that is more immediately explosive—and one hazardous for the country's future race relations—is the emergence of blue-collar and other marginal middle-class whites who oppose black achievement of community control and at times even resist black residence in their neighborhoods. The blacks' struggle to gain structural command of their communities is a critical issue in today's urban politics.

It is important to reassess interracial relations in the middle socioeconomic range of the population. Many blacks and whites who were allies in the civil rights efforts of the 1960s find themselves at opposite poles in the 1970s. This is likely to occur increasingly as more whites of an earlier generation, formerly oppressed and poverty stricken, achieve this marginal middle-class status. These struggling whites blame their binds and pressures on the blacks' rise, failing to see that the power-wielders have permitted them to have only a circumscribed and precarious existence.

Already broad coalitions of middle-class and marginal whites have begun to form, primarily focused on efforts to maintain their special interests. This is a direct result of the dynamics of the black perspective. As long as blacks did not mobilize for structural and environmental control, they were not considered as a fundamentally threatening force. What may have begun as attitudinal polarization between blacks and whites is now being transformed into active opposition, with the recently emerged middle-class and marginal whites assuming an active buffer role between the black population and the power establishment. If this trend continues, a time-consuming and unproductive clash between striving blacks and striving whites will probably occur as the whites try to hold on to their tenuous positions and assume the status and function of a new overseer class.

## SUMMARY AND CONCLUSIONS

The author has explored issues involved in the contemporary liberation struggles of black people, examined components of the black agenda for action, and identified some areas of potential conflict. The choice between separatism and integration, as traditionally viewed by whites, is not a principal issue at hand since these concepts represent strategies rather than ends in themselves. An analysis of the black thrust for community control has pointed up the decisive issues. An understanding of these issues can help social workers, community planners, and other environmental interventionists come to grips with primary problems affecting any potential work in areas populated by blacks and other ethnic minorities. The discussion also pointed out that the black movement toward self-determination and community control has unleashed strong countervailing forces among the upward-climbing poor whites who have emerged into the marginal middle class.

Professional social work practice is influenced by the community's ideological and ethnocentric currents as well as by the clients' economic, national, and religious background. Social workers need to reorient their work and retool their practice to conform to the needs, aspirations, and directions of black people and the other ethnic minorities they serve. This can make practice relevant to the community, and enable social workers to realize their potential as valuable resources to the community.

With an appreciation of the black perspective, black social workers should increasingly find ways to utilize their professional skills in line with black people's thrust toward community development. White social workers may find a profoundly important role within communities of striving marginal middle-class whites, perhaps helping them to define more precisely the sources of their restrictions. These differential roles may ultimately serve to decrease the conflict between the two groups, thus allowing community energies and people's movements to focus on appropriate targets and helping to bring about fundamental change. Many social workers are ready to work more constructively in the urban political arena, and the profession must support their efforts so there can be dynamic movement ahead.

## NOTES AND REFERENCES

1. Billy J. Tidwell, "The Black Community's Challenge to Social Work," *Journal of Education for Social Work*, Vol. 7, No. 3 (Fall 1971), pp. 59–65.

2. See Michael Harrington, *The Other America* (New York: Penguin Books, 1966); and H. Hanna Meisner, *Poverty in the Affluent Society* (New York: Harper & Row, 1966).

3. For an excellent discussion of these concepts, *see* Lerone Bennett, Jr., "Liberation, Integration or Separatism," *Ebony*, Vol. 25, No. 10 (August 1970), pp. 36–45.

4. *See* E. Franklin Frazier, *Black Bourgeoisie* (New York: Free Press, 1957); and Nathan Hare, *The Black Anglo-Saxons* (New York: Marzani and Munsell, Publishers, 1965).

5. *See* John Hope Franklin, *From Slavery to Freedom: A History of Negro Americans* (3d ed. New York: Random House, 1967), pp. 70–88; and Herbert Aptheker, *Negro Slave Revolts in the United States, 1526–1860* (New York: International Publishers, 1939).

6. *See* W. E. B. DuBois, *Black Reconstruction* (Philadelphia: Albert Seifer, Publisher, 1935), pp. 346–347.

7. Eli Ginzberg et al., *The Middle-Class Negro in the White Man's World* (New York: Columbia University Press, 1967).

8. For a discussion of positive, effective use of ethnocentrism by the Japanese, *see* Harry L. Kitano, *Japanese Americans* (Englewood Cliffs, N.J.: Prentice-Hall, 1969), pp. 85–115.

9. *See* Stokely S. Carmichael and Charles V. Hamilton, *Black Power: The Politics of Liberation in America* (New York: Random House, 1968), pp. 78–84.

# 22

# The Ghetto: Some Perceptions of a Black Social Worker

MARIE SIMMONS SAUNDERS

THE BLACK GHETTO will at best speedily become an obsolete phenomenon and at worst, a national catastrophe. In any case, it will no longer lurk as a vampire to rob the black man of his freedom and the white man of his soul.

Perhaps the optimistic revolutionary aspect of my own personality begins to show here. But let me explain my optimism, lest there be any misunderstanding that it rests with the Establishment. How could I, as a black woman, have faith in the existing hostile society that has locked arms against me and my black sisters and brothers? An Establishment that incorporates with such ease contempt and hatred of black people, that prides itself on this hypocrisy, makes it difficult to be black and live in America. Malcolm X once said:

Reprinted from *Social Work*, 14 (October 1969), pp. 84–88. MARIE SIMMONS SAUNDERS was at the time of writing supervising psychiatric social worker, Division of Community Services, Department of Social Welfare, Fresno, California. The essence of this paper was delivered as a lecture to students at the Division of Social Work, Fresno State College, November 1968.

> How can I love the man who raped my mother, killed my father, and
> enslaved my ancestors, dropped atom bombs on Japan, killed off the Indians,
> and keeps me cooped up in the slums? [1]

I am black; I am also an American. These two facts, unfortunately,
create a dilemma. If I sound angry, *I am*. And most black people are
angry. Anger, dammed up for years and years, now flows freely. But
there is some hope. Cleaver, impressed by the youth of America, black
and white, says:

> I am proud of them because they have reaffirmed my faith in humanity. I
> have come to feel what must be love for the young people of America and
> I want to be part of the good and greatness that they want for all people. [2]

The future, he adds, rests with those whites and blacks who have
liberated themselves from the master/slave syndrome, who are found
mainly among the youth. [3] Youth serves as a catalyst of the protest
phenomenon that cuts across the lines of age, sex, religion, social class,
and political affiliation. And youth is always a symbol of hope.

White Americans have developed the art of misunderstanding black
people into a high skill. You look and see not, listen and hear not. For
instance, on one occasion when I was looking for a house to buy, one
of my more knowledgeable and less prejudiced white friends suggested
that I buy a house in his neighborhood and offered to help me locate
one. Later the same day he came to me, rather bewildered, with this
comment: "You know, it just occurred to me: you are black. You can't
buy a house anywhere you like, even though you may have the money."

Americans characteristically are unwilling to think about the past. We
are a future-oriented nation and looking backward is an impediment
to progress. Although our press toward the future may be what has
propelled us to the moon, we have been deficient when human conflicts
need resolution.

The revolutionary aspect of my personality I believe to be self-explana-
tory. Current law and order are the conservators of the status quo,
aiding and abetting the preservation of the Establishment at great cost
to the disenfranchised blacks and other minority groups. It should not
be difficult to understand why those who have not benefited from the
system are ready to overthrow it and to abridge the freedom of those
who have benefited for so long. Should blacks continue to allow white
Americans the freedom to exploit blacks and treat them as subhumans?
Should we happily remain in the ghetto? Why should I respect and abide
by laws that were made to repress rather than protect me? The question
here seems not what has caused the eruption of anger and aggression,
but what has kept it in check so long.

The hatred of blacks is so deeply bound up with being American that it has developed as part of a national life-style. Such feelings have been engrained in the national character, so that many individuals no longer feel personal guilt or responsibility for the oppression of black people. The nation has incorporated this oppression into itself. Grier and Cobbs point out:

> For black and white alike, the air of this nation is perfused with the idea of white supremacy and everyone grows to manhood under this influence. No man who breathes the air can avoid it, and the black man is no exception.[4]

Blacks are taught to hate themselves.

Although the wounds of the black man are deep, along with their scars there is strength and pride. Their genius is that they have survived.

## SURVIVAL

With recognition that society has long been hostile to black people, consideration is focused on some of the characteristics that are essential to an understanding of the black man's survival in the ghetto.

The black family, first of all, is an extended family. Relatives readily share responsibility for child-rearing. The family usually comes to the aid of a troubled member; for example, it is unusual for a young black unwed mother to give up her child for adoption. More likely the baby will be accepted into the larger family and be reared by the maternal grandmother, behavior that, although frequently the target of criticism by whites, reflects a human quality. The young white unwed mother, on the other hand, is likely to consider abortion first and, failing that, to go the adoption route. Contrary to popular statistics, the young black female is not more promiscuous than her white counterpart.[5] Nor do black families condone illegitimate pregnancy; they simply have more compassion for the child once it has been conceived.

It has long been common practice for the oldest male in a black family to migrate from the South, establish himself in a northern city, and make arrangements to import his entire family. As many as three or four generations may live in a single dwelling in the black ghetto. It is sometimes argued by white America and well-meaning middle-class social workers that such overcrowded conditions are primary factors in property deterioration. The reason for the overcrowding is that most black families are close-knit and tend to maintain family relationships even though physically separated.

Black men have been conditioned to expect exploitation, ridicule, and pain from white men. Such forces have tended to make black men accept others with black skin without much question. An easy salutation, "Hey, Bro," usually links some meaningful personal network. Such linkage helped the black man travel and survive.

The usual laws do not have much meaning for people in ghettos or in other unnatural environments for that matter.[6] While specific mores and ethics may develop in a ghetto, there is little internalization of certain laws that are deterrents to survival. In recalling my own experiences as a young ghetto-dweller, it seemed that every black male over the age of 18 had a "nickel job"—a low-paying legitimate job used as a front—and a side "hustle." The hustles ranged anywhere from petty theft to that of a high-class pimp with several prostitutes and shoplifters in his "stable." In the ghetto, a man's status was determined not by his moral character as defined by white America, but by the size of his hustle, its monetary yields, and how successful he was at avoiding apprehension. The same black man would be viewed with scorn and contempt, however, if he stole from his relatives or another "soul brother." On the other hand, a clever black domestic worker will speak with pride of how she outwits and exploits "Miss Anne."

Black men removed from the protection of the social code can hardly be expected to honor the responsibilities imposed by that code. Excluded from all benefits of the social order, indeed preyed upon by that social order, they wear lightly the injunction that a white man's property is sacred. What more efficient way is there to produce a thief than to steal a man's substance and command that he hold his peace?

Black men have stood so long in such peculiar jeopardy in America that a black norm has developed—a suspiciousness of one's environment that is necessary to survival. The black man must be on guard to protect himself against physical hurt. He must cushion himself against cheating, slander, humiliation, and outright mistreatment by official representatives. If he does not protect himself, he will live a life of such pain and shock as to be unbearable. For his own survival, then, he must develop a form of cultural paranoia in which every white man is a potential enemy (unless proved otherwise) and every social system is set against him (unless he *personally* finds out differently). Protective paranoia, or self-protection, as Cleaver terms it, is the least a man can do for himself.

Many of the characteristics and traits cited are adaptive devices developed in response to a stressful environment. The majority of the blacks who survived (and many do not) did so because they could accurately read the environment and use cunning, prudence, and imagination in adapting to it.

In their adaptation, blacks have developed a vigorous style of life that includes religion, music, and the broad canvas of creativity. It is of major importance that the black man has developed a unique sense of humor and learned to laugh at himself. The psyche of black men has been distorted, but out of that deformity has come a majesty. It began in the chants of the first religious sons—"Father, I stretch my hand to Thee, no other help I know"—and it continues in the timelessness of the blues. The genius of it all is that we have survived.

### ENTRY

Having completed our rather brief journey into the ghetto, let us look at how one gains entrée through these black iron gates. For those of you who choose to make the journey, appreciate the fact that you are trying to make an entry rather than an exit.

Remember this as you enter: (1) This is an angry black sea. The white man has crushed all but life from blacks from the time they came to these shores to this very day. The black man's grief has been realistic and appropriate. What other people have so earned a period of mourning? If the depth of this sorrow is felt, we can then consider what can be made of the emotion. As the grief lifts and the sufferer moves toward health, the hatred he has turned on himself is redirected toward his tormentors, and the fury of his attack on those who caused him pain is in direct proportion to the depth of his grief. (2) It has been said that hating blacks is as American as apple pie. Do you like apple pie? The ingredients of prejudice are cancerous and can destroy this nation. (3) From practiced survival experiences, black people have developed perceptiveness to a science.

If you can put these three concepts together, you will get the picture. Again recall that the black man's very life has depended on his accurate perception of your feelings toward him. He may be more aware of them than you are yourself. He is highly skilled in nonverbal communication. Let me share with you a few examples of what I mean by this.

A receptionist in a public office was discussing the high cost of rent with a co-worker. She said: "I would rather live on the West Side [where the black ghetto is located] than pay that kind of rent." To her, living in a black ghetto was next to living in hell. I am sure she had absolutely no awareness of her preconceived ideas and negative attitudes toward the black ghetto. On another occasion, I asked a receptionist at one of the California state hospitals for a key to a professional building on a Saturday afternoon. She telephoned the building and informed the janitor: "This little colored gal over here wants the key and you have the only one we have." When confronted with her words, she claimed that she was totally unaware that she had referred to me as "this little colored gal." Hating blacks is probably such an integral part of her personality that all condescending feelings and ideas are ego-syntonic for her.

## SUMMARY

For those of you who believe you have successfully extricated yourself from the slave/master syndrome and have decided to enter the black sea, remember that you are in unfamiliar surroundings. Roll a bit with the wailing tide; *ask,* do not *tell.*

To paraphrase, can you honestly expect to be the master in another man's home? Leave your middle-class standards, values, and moral judgments at your own place of abode. They are not welcome here. To be liberal implies high tolerance of differences, some permissiveness, and even overindulgence at times. Out of necessity, the ghetto-dweller has developed his own values and moral structure. He can no more live by yours than you can by his. *Can you think black?* This, I believe, is the key to the locked iron gates of the ghetto. Once inside, your primary function is not to change the man but to help him effectively change his environment. The appropriate changes in his behavior will come when he recognizes the need to acquire new adaptive techniques because those he previously used are no longer needed or effective. An analogy can be made here to a basic social work principle: Help the client modify his behavior in accordance with reality as he perceives it, and internal changes in feelings and attitudes will naturally follow with his new-found success and personal gratification.

To paraphrase James Baldwin, white people cannot be taken as models of how to live. Rather, the white man himself is in sore need of new values that can release him from his confusion and place him once again in fruitful communion with the depths of his own being. We have now come to a fork in the road; a divided house cannot stand. Since both of our present life-styles leave much to be desired, can we not sit down and reason together and combine our forces in the quest of viable brotherhood? Or will it be, as Baldwin reminds us of the biblical prediction: "God gave Noah the rainbow sign, no more water, the fire next time!" [7]

## NOTES AND REFERENCES

1. As quoted in Eldridge Cleaver, *Soul on Ice* (New York: McGraw-Hill Book Co., 1968), p. 38.

2. *Ibid.,* p. 15.

3. *Ibid.,* p. 67.

4. William H. Grier and Price M. Cobbs, *Black Rage* (New York: Basic Books, 1968), p. 198.

5. Variance (statistically) about unmarried motherhood appears partially related to differences of values—to keep the child or not. A number of other factors could play a role in the statistical picture, such as the large proportion of blacks who have limited formal education, are financially poor, and are pressed to work at an early age. These factors contribute toward a somewhat fatalistic attitude with respect to an unmarried woman who has a child. The fact that mortality rates are higher for blacks than whites probably plays an implicit role in the values expressed. Collectively these factors seem contributory to compassion, expressed in acceptance of the mother and the child.

6. Among such environments are mental institutions and prisons (*see* Erving Goffman, *Asylums: Essays on the Social Situation of Mental Patients and Other Inmates* [Chicago: Aldine Publishing Co., 1961]) and concentration camps (*see* Elie A. Cohen, *Human Behavior in the Concentraion Camps,* trans. by M. H. Braaksma [New York: Universal Library, 1953]).

7. James Baldwin, *The Fire Next Time* (New York: Dell Publishing Co., 1962), p. 141.

# 23

# Social Work in the Black Ghetto: The New Colonialism

## HENRY MILLER

IT HAS BECOME quite fashionable to use the analogy of colonialism when discussing the black man and his relation to the rest of American society. It is not only Black Nationalists who discourse in the dialectic of Fanon; white intellectuals also invoke the image of Algerian peasants grappling with French paratroopers—a struggle leading to existential and political liberation.[1] The purveyors of the analogue see a people constrained by a network of forces to live within the confines of an American Casbah; a people exploited economically; a people forced to live with laws conceived by aliens, administered by aliens, and, indeed, enforced by aliens.

But colonialism takes many forms and is fed by diverse motivations. The colonial metaphor frequently gets out of hand when applied in the current context. Harlem is not the Casbah, South Chicago is not

Reprinted from *Social Work*, 14 (July 1969), pp. 65–76. HENRY MILLER was at the time of writing associate professor, School of Social Welfare, University of California at Berkeley, Berkeley, California. This paper was presented at the National Conference on Social Welfare, San Francisco, California, May 1968.

Lagos, and Mississippi is not Vietnam. The differences have to do with the events of the past 350 years, which serve to make the American racial dilemma quite unique. The colonial rhetoric ought to be applied with selectivity and with care.

It is, for example, a serious error to see colonialism—at least in its nineteenth- and twentieth-century versions—as being based primarily on Machiavellian premises or to view it through the lens of a Marxian analysis. It may well be true that the edifice of empire is rooted in a web of markets, cotton, rum, and economic inputs and outputs. Surely if the textile mills of Manchester were to operate, Egyptian cotton was needed, and Ceylon supplied the tea for the four o'clock break. It is conceivable, then, that the gunboats were originally powered by such considerations. And it is equally conceivable that the sight of the Union Jack or the Tricolor was in itself sufficient rationale for the spread of empire. But whatever the original impetus of the colonizer, a new motivation emerged to be added to the complexity of the phenomenon —the humanitarian ideology of "uplift." Kipling provided the linguistic flag for this new philanthropy—"the white man's burden." [2] We might refer to it as philanthropic colonialism.

## PHILANTHROPIC COLONIALISM

We must be careful not to misconstrue the precise nature of such a colonialism. It was real, powerful, and motivated by that most relentless of all propellants—good intention. If the notion of the white man's burden is seen only as a mask for the atrocity of economic spoilage or political machination, an important point is missed. It is necessary to see the idea for what it was and still is, for it is the ideology of the white man's burden that characterizes the posture of social welfare programs and policies in regard to the black man.

Nor should we be deceived by crass and primitive formulations of the white man's burden. Only stupid theoreticians built the doctrine on a base of race and racism. Surely there were those who argued that it was the heaven-sent duty of the white man to care for the lives and souls of God's colored children because they could not care for them-selves. And they could not care for themselves because they were not quite men; left to their own devices they would live as they had lived for ages, with cannibalism, sacrifices, incest, infanticide, and the other abominations made necessary by a savage nature. Such was the heart of the system of thought developed by the racist philanthropist: for the sake of civilization and the souls of brown and black children, he would spread his benign umbrella of colonial uplift. The colonized were inferior, and just as the biblical patriarchs rested their oxen, so did the colonizer—in the tradition of humanity—care for his charges.[3]

But this was a crass and crude position. Although it has always been an important strand in the fabric of the doctrine, it offended the enlightened, those committed to an ideology of equality and steeped in biological theory. The white man's burden was a much more subtle ideology; it was built not on a base of racial inferiority, but rather on the firmer bedrock of cultural inferiority. The colonized needed the colonizer, not because of genetic accident, but because of historical accident; not because of a stunted cerebral cortex, but because of a stunted social structure; not because of intellectual insufficiency, but because of technological insufficiency. The distinction is crucial. To put down a rebellion of Sepoys in the name of white superiority is criminal, to put it down in the name of law and order is just, but to put it down in the name of eventual self-determination is downright charitable.

The stance of the philanthropic colonialist might be paraphrased as follows: The modern world is complex; nation-states, in order to survive in any meaningful way, require a minimum level of economic maturity. This implies much more than bustling steel mills, communications networks, and national airlines. It implies a skilled labor force. Moreover, it requires a constitution, a legislature, an executive, a judiciary, and all the other elements of a society governed by the rule of calculated law. The contemporary nation-state demands a complex administrative machinery to moderate its economy and its polity. It requires stability and the blessing of tranquil transition, for it must live not only with itself but with its neighbor states, which, in this shrunken world, comprise all nation-states.

The precondition for a viable nation-state, then, is an educated, enlightened, and self-controlled population. Now, the philanthropic colonialist will add, it was only through the caprice of historical fortune that Western man developed the attributes requisite to the task of bearing the white man's burden. He might even continue, modestly, that European man, in and of himself, had little to do with such requisites; rather, it is the fortuitous combination of random variables— climate, topography, Caesars, mercantilism, and an apple falling from a tree—that accounts for the efficiency of Western man. If he is contrite he might even add that Europe initially had no business in Africa, Asia, or America; he will wince at the chronicle of the conquistadores or the pillage of Africans. But it happened, and now, he goes on, we have no choice but to be responsible and take on the burden of bringing wrongly subjugated people into the twentieth century.

Note the sweet reason of the philanthropist. He is much too decent a fellow to allow a racist taint to color his good deeds. He is a realist governed by a soft heart. His analysis is predicated on scholarship and empiricism. It was not superiority but randomness that allowed for the dominance of Western civilization. It is a relentless technology that has created the plight of the colonized. The modern colonialist ministers to the underdeveloped rather than to the primitive—to the deprived rather than to the despised. Most pernicious of all, he looks to the future with hope; through charity and patient instruction his charges will be brought into today with strength and vigor and the real equality that comes from competitive viability.[4]

The writer has not invented this portrait of the philanthropic colonialist. Queen Victoria, in many missives to her ministers, anguished over the sufferings of her Indian subjects. She cared more for hospitals and schools than she did for commerce.[5] Moreover, the doctrine of philanthropic colonialism is explicitly articulated in the collective policies of Western states. The white man's burden was mandated by the League of Nations, in its Covenant, to the philanthropic powers who happened to win the Great War.[6] More recently, the Charter of the United Nations allows for the trusteeship of underdeveloped peoples.[7] The charge to the Trusteeship Council is to work toward the self-determination of peoples, but only when, in the wisdom of the council, the colony is ready—that is, when it has become equal to the task.

The impact of this colonialist stance or the serious generosity with which it was promulgated cannot be overemphasized. And it is not a dead or even dying position. Take, for example, the sad shaking of heads when, in 1956, President Nasser of Egypt expropriated the Suez Canal. Certainly a substantial part of the negative Western reaction to this event was premised on economic and political considerations. But there were some who said that the Egyptians simply would not be able to run the canal. They did not have the pilots whose skill was needed to navigate the ships; they did not have the engineers to keep the ditch from filling with sand.[8] When it soon became apparent that the canal was being run quite efficiently, there was a note of puzzlement among the philanthropists; somehow it just did not seem right that a backward nation could operate such a marvel of engineering.

A second example is, however, much more tragic. When the Belgians left the Congo (it is more accurate to say when they were forced to leave), they left with every expectation of coming back. It was as though they said, "Foolish children, do you think you can run this vast country without our help?" And with a smiling indulgence they said, "Well, try it and see what happens." The Western world felt a smug satisfaction as it surveyed the turbulence that followed Independence Day in Leopoldville. It seemed to be as they said it would be—the Congo was not yet ready to govern itself. It still needed a period of instruction and guidance.[9]

## SOCIAL WELFARE'S ATTITUDE

Social welfare as an institution and many social workers as individuals adopt a posture toward the black man and the ghetto that is nearly identical to the one just detailed. The ideology that characterizes our perception of Black America can best be described as philanthropic colonialism. Again, it must be emphasized that this is *not* a racist position. Indeed, it is counterracist. It is motivated by dogmas of equality, opportunity, and true integration. And these dogmas are held sincerely. It is in this respect that the advocates of Black Power—both white and black—make their most serious error. They fail to see that there may be an evil more terrible than racism, an enemy more powerful than ignorant prejudice, a doctrine more insidious than exploitation. That iniquitous and pernicious doctrine is, of course, the kind of philanthropy just discussed.

Let us look at it more carefully, this time within the context of the United States. The diagnosis made by white America for the black ghetto is, apart from historical detail, very much like that made for the Congo. It would run as follows: The Negro was brought to this country some 350 years ago, in chains, after having been torn from his African culture. He was dispersed among the plantations, exploited in the most barbarous of fashions; his status was that of private property; his women were not his own, nor were his children; he was, in sum, brutalized, emasculated, looked upon as a nonperson, and robbed of his heritage. The seeds of matriarchy were sown during these two and a half centuries of slavery—unparalleled in its ferocity. Emancipation brought nothing but a fictitious freedom. For one hundred additional years the black man, although nominally free, was exploited and victimized. Without dignity, without integrity, without that essence of identity that goes by the name of manhood, without education, without skills—he has become more and more marginal to the mainstream of American life.

These things have happened, so the colonialist argues, through no fault of the black man. But 350 years have left their mark and it shows itself in a life-style that is essentially maladaptive to the wider society. This culture, if you will, was forced on the black man. In order to survive he had to develop structured mechanisms of an ingenious order. His culture, then, is marvelously adaptive to the realities of his unhappy life situation, but serves to work against him now that the democratic processes are beginning to operate in his favor.

The solution, then, is one of uplift. The black man must first have opportunity, but in order to avail himself of opportunity he must "get with it." And so social welfare has constructed a network of institutions that have as their aim the uplift of the Negro; services that include job training and retraining, education, housing, and, of course, a wide variety of rehabilitative and therapeutic services.

## PATERNALISM

There are two aspects to the kind of colonialism being discussed that need further elaboration. The first is more fundamental: it is *paternalism,* a paternalism predicated on the assumption of cultural underdevelopment. The idea is that the black man living in a ghetto must endure a period of preparation before he can participate effectively in the world of middle-class America. This does not mean that he is to be deprived of his civil rights; he is, of course, equal, but his equality is that of a child to an adult. He can be indulged with all the trappings of adulthood—voting rights, open housing, and the rest—but in those matters that really count—commitment to a system of values, aspiration, competence, political sophistication—he needs instruction. This paternalistic stance is not exclusive to social welfare; it characterizes the point of view of white America generally, and social work has probably been more uncomfortable with the position than most other segments of society. Yet it exists and it is pervasive.

For example, in a paper describing casework techniques with low-income families, a professional social worker wrote:

> With many families I appear weekly with the notebook, see the paycheck stub (if I am lucky) and plan with the wife on how the money is to be spent. In a few instances, at their request, I have served as banker, holding money for rent or other necessities until it is due. In crisis periods, and if there is a good reason, I run innumerable errands, get prescriptions filled, take the family to pick up surplus foods. I have gone with clients to see creditors and discuss refinancing of debts.[10]

There may be some commendable elements to this kind of activity, but surely an underlying dimension of parenthood can be detected—of doing things warmly and kindly for childlike people.

Hollis, describing a special project in Boston, wrote:

> The workers in this program found that they could visit these clients without an invitation and that if they returned regularly, chatted in a neighborly fashion, and offered help with practical problems when they could, they

would be allowed to stay. They might then have the chance to demonstrate that a baby stops crying more quickly if someone feeds him, changes his diaper, turns him over, or picks him up than if he is yelled at or hit. Gradually the workers learned that even these little-girl mothers wanted to do better by their children than they themselves had been done by; that the mother yelled at the baby and hit him partly because she actually did not know why he was crying or what else to do and partly because the crying made her feel so bad—so inadequate in the care she was giving her child.[11]

An extremely influential work that triggered a wave of concern for the multiproblem family—the *Casework Notebook*—articulates the paternalistic nature of the white man's burden as a credo:

> We believe in social work's responsibility for the most deprived families, who are failing their central function of child care. These families are a basic and proper charge upon the community; therefore the citizens who support social work have a right to expect us to give them top priority in service.
>
>                     .   .   .   .   .
>
> You don't wear a uniform or carry a gun, nor need you, because that isn't your job. . . . Yet in a sense, you too have a badge, but it is a symbol of authority rather than something you wear on your coat. . . . You as a social worker are an instrument of social control. You represent the community's intent to influence people to accept social control, rather than force them to submit.[12]

In answer to the question of what the social worker is to do if his child-man client wants no part of him, this document states:

> What will you do if you are ordered out? This is one of the reasons for careful advance preparation to give yourself a stronger initial position. If you have this, you will feel so concerned about this family that you can't back away. You will be able to stand up to hostility by a full statement of your concern. . . . The fact that we have returned in the face of initial rebuff has been one of the strongest points in our favor with the families.[13]

What is interesting about these citations is that their referent is not exclusively the Negro family—rather it is a class of families of which Negroes comprise a substantial segment. It is exquisitely nonracial; paternalism knows no skin color.


## CLINICALISM

Social work's unique contribution to the ideology of the white man's burden could be called *clinicalism*. It is founded on a presumption of damage—that is, as a result of the sad and brutal history of the Negro people the individual member of that race is likely to have been psychologically injured. The nature of the damage is seen as multifaceted.

One instance of such damage concerns the vital matter of sexual identity; the villain is the infamous matriarchy. The argument holds that as a result of the dominance of the maternal figure and a lack of consistent and esteemed male objects in the early developmental years, the Negro male reaches adulthood with a confused and deprecated masculine identification. After all, the males he had to emulate were held in contempt not only by the larger society but also by Negro women; they were transitory, drifting, and aloof men who held no status except in the harsh and cruel environment of the "cool world." So, the clinician tells us, the Negro male is damaged in that most decisive of all arenas —that of manhood and sexual identity.[14]

The philanthropic solution to this damage is directed at the very soul of black culture. The family must be molded into a different kind of structure. As the controversial Moynihan report states:

> . . . Three centuries of sometimes unimaginable mistreatment have taken their toll on the Negro people. The harsh fact is that as a group, at the present time, in terms of ability to win out in the competition of American life, they are not equal to most of those groups with which they will be competing. Individually, Negro Americans reach the highest peaks of achievement. But collectively, in the spectrum of American ethnic and religious and regional groups, where some get plenty and some get none, where some send eighty percent of their children to college and others pull them out of school at the 8th grade, Negroes are among the weakest. . . .
> . . . these events, in combination, confront the nation with a new kind of problem. Measures that have worked in the past or would work for most groups in the present, will not work here. A national effort is required that will give a unity of purpose to the many activities of the Federal Government in this area, directed to a new kind of national goal: the establishment of a stable Negro family structure.[15]

Moynihan has been much misunderstood; he was not arguing for a crash program in family therapy (much to the chagrin of many clinicians), and he was not for the abandonment of a push toward a massive program of employment and income redistribution. He was saying, however, that if the Negro is ever to become economically self-sufficient the damage must be repaired; he must acquire both the cultural and individual attributes necessary to make him a competitive member of the labor force. It is because of such considerations that the alleged matriarchal character of the Negro family is seen as most obnoxious. It is essential within the context of the larger American society that manhood be defined in terms of wage-earning, vocational competence, and employment security. The homily of "bringing home the bacon" is the summarization of the American concept of manhood. If there is no home there is no need for the bacon, hence the inextricable matrix of family, manhood, and employment.

But as if such damage were not enough, the clinicians see other wounds in the most important structure of the mind—the ego. It is well known, clinicalism argues, that an important function of the ego is to delay gratification and otherwise control the instinctual impulses. The Negro has suffered serious damage in this instance. Immediacy is the rule: nowness, instant gratification, the essential irrelevance of a future orientation are seen as the hallmarks of Negro character. To further confound the damage, the clinician adds a predilection for aggressive expression rather than the more cultivated verbal expression. Action rather than deliberation, wanting rather than working, today rather than tomorrow—these are seen as signs of ego damage. Indeed, they are signs of the human being in the process of development—the signs of the child.[16]

Hollis argues along Moynihanian lines:

> Both experience and study show that long-time poverty results not only in actual deprivation of food, inadequate and shabby clothing, crowded and run-down housing but also in illness or at least depleted energy, a strong sense of inferiority or lack of self-esteem, and often a great sensitivity to criticism, even though this sensitivity may be overlaid by defensive hostility, denial, and projection. The client who is the victim of persistent poverty is often discouraged to the point of being chronically depressed. He almost surely has underlying resentment, anger, and disbelief that the caseworker—a well-dressed, healthy, well-educated member of the middle class—can respect him or be relied upon to help him. Motivation and aspiration are often not absent; but disappointment after disappointment and frustration after frustration may have forced him to bury his hopes for himself—if not for his children—so that he will no longer be vulnerable to so much pain.[17]

In all fairness it should be noted that Hollis, like Moynihan, is all for the elimination of poverty through the implementation of massive programs of public welfare; she is definitely *not* a proponent of psychotherapy as a means of lifting people out of poverty. But she does note that poverty has left its mark on them.

Such is also the thesis of the authors of *The Mark of Oppression*, who, in a careful analysis could claim:

> The result of the continuous frustrations in childhood is to create a personality devoid of confidence in human relations, of an eternal vigilance

and distrust of others. This is purely a defensive maneuver which purports to protect the individual against the repeatedly traumatic effects of disappointment and frustration. He must operate on the assumption that the world is hostile. The self-referential aspect of this is contained in the formula "I am not a lovable creature." This, together with the same idea drawn from the caste situation, leads to a reinforcement of the basic destruction of self-esteem.[18]

The profound subtlety of clinicalism must be recognized. It is based on high-level and sophisticated theory and it appeals to impartial empiricism. There are case histories. There are articles in learned journals. It is not racism, it is not ideology, it is not bias—it is objective reality. The conclusions of psychological damage are based on disciplined observations and these data can be explained by an elaborate theory of cause and effect. And they are made by men of goodwill, men pained by the findings a relentless objectivity yields, men righteously angry at the evil system that led to such far-reaching damage. But these men are also hopeful and they allow for change; individuals can be healed, the damage can be undone, but more important, the system can be changed to preclude further damage in future generations. Prophylaxis is the clinicians' contribution to the ideology of civil rights.

What is found, then, in the welfare stance toward the black man in this country is the philanthropy of the healing father: a welfare system designed to bring damaged and bewildered children to health and clear vision so that at last the American dream can be fulfilled. Whereas Queen Victoria's burden was that of bringing a culturally retarded people into the adult community of nations, social welfare added an element of clinical uplift and we are now charged with bringing a people both culturally deprived *and* psychologically damaged into the adult community of middle-class America.

## WHAT IS WRONG WITH SOCIAL WELFARE?

What is this axe-grinding all about? Where lies the evil in philanthropy and what is wrong with a social welfare that helps people make it? The point has to do with a scheme of values and is this: Nations cannot be backward, men are not children, and ethnic diversity is necessary to the good life.

First, within the context of nation-states, the issue is not that the Congo lacks a well-trained bureaucracy, not that there is a high infant mortality rate in Guinea, not that there is tribal vengeance in Nigeria. The issue is that of self-determination. It is the only issue. People have the right to determine their own destiny, for good or ill, with or without strife, wisely or foolishly—it is their business. This is not an empirical matter; it is a matter of right. In the face of such a right the white man's burden becomes a moral atrocity. Kindness and benevolence become anathema when they transcend the supreme value of a people's choice of life-style and destiny. It is not for Victoria or Gladstone to pass judgment on a culture. In a hierarchy of values that places self-determination at the top, it does no good to argue mortality rates, economic viability, tribalism, or political chaos.

But how do these considerations apply to the ghetto? In this respect the philanthropy of social work errs on two counts. First, the diagnosis of psychological damage, when applied to a people, is an absurdity.[19] Individuals may be sick, but ethnic or social entities cannot be. They may be Apollonian or Dionysian, sacred or secular, autocratic or democratic, matriarchal or patriarchal, but they can hardly be sick in any absolute sense.[20] They can be evaluated, but the evaluation must take place along dimensions exterior to the system itself. Herein lies the error of clinicalism. The standard of health is embodied in the ethos of the wider society. When collectivities are characterized as sick, the metric is found in a quantum of disparity from the standard. Clinicalism, when applied to ethnic entities, flounders on the rock of an arbitrary standard.

But even if this were not so, the ethic of philanthropic colonialism in regard to the ghetto would be wrong. And this is a central point: The value of ethnic self-determination in America takes its operational form in an ideology of cultural pluralism. To the extent that social welfare's allegiance to a colonialist model subverts that ideology it becomes an evil enterprise.

## A SUCCESSFUL MELTING POT

This country has had a long and tortured history of attempting to accommodate to diverse ethnic groups. The attempt has been governed by a principle that, although it has faltered at times, has been surprisingly successful. This is the principle of the melting pot. Irishmen, Czechs, Poles, Germans, Greeks, Jews, Italians, Slavs, and many more have been admitted to this country (not always warmly), housed in this country (not always comfortably), employed in this country (not always fairly), educated in this country (not always diligently), and melted down into what many thought would be a new breed—an American. Although there is controversy about this, the writer claims that this melting process has been successful.[21] In spite of reluctance, resistance, and recalcitrance, in spite of hostility and down-right prejudice, in spite of the conscious attempt by some groups to avoid it, within the course of two, three, or at most four generations the melting pot notion has prevailed.

It has prevailed—or more accurately, it is prevailing—because of calculated public policy and the homogenizing nature of our institutional life. The ethnic entities that once made up the patchwork quilt of this country have either died or are in the process of dying. Remnants remain and they will continue to be with us for some time. Certain groups were denied entry into the crucible; the black man is the striking example of that denial. But the ideology of the melting pot—or, speaking pejoratively, America as homogenizer—runs deep in this country and has powerful machinery. Television is only the latest in a series of devices used to propagate a mass culture.

The Sons of Italy, the Franco-Americans, the Pulaskis, even the tongs, are rapidly becoming anachronisms. The Italo-American Club can hardly compete with Kiwanis and Lions; when a Jew can become a Mason and join the Westchester Country Club he hardly has use for the B'nai B'rith. When the melting pot is well fired, the process of homogenization can take place with amazing rapidity. The great wave of Jewish immigration into this country took place during the first quarter of this century. The grandparents of contemporary young Jews were greenhorn immigrants; the old ones died in New York knowing but a handful of English words. Their children made it to Westchester County and the country clubs. And their children, in turn, are now making it in Haight-Ashbury. These semitic hippies have little in common with their grandparents; a spastic nostalgia or the improvisation of Hassidic mandala may be groovy, but it is hardly Jewish. The swinger knowns no ethnicity; the American dream is realized when the Sons of Italy make it with the daughters of Erin.

## CULTURAL PLURALISM

The ideology of the melting pot, however, is not the only one that could have governed public policy. A less influential ideology, that of cultural pluralism—equally compatible with the spirit of democracy—could have set the tone for this country.[22] And it is even remotely possible that it could still prevail, which, of course, is the rationale for this paper. The difference in ideologies can best be illustrated by their spokesmen. First, the notion of the melting pot by its great protagonist, Israel Zangwill:

> America is God's crucible, the great Melting Pot where all the races of Europe are melting and re-forming! Here you stand, good folk, think I,

when I see them at Ellis Island, here you stand in your fifty groups, with your fifty languages and histories, and your fifty blood hatreds and rivalries. But you won't be long like that, brothers, for these are the fires of God you've come to—these are the fires of God. A fig for your feuds and vendettas! Germans and Frenchmen, Irishmen and Englishmen, Jews and Russians—into the Crucible with you all! God is making the American.[23]

It is a noble idea, it governs our policies, and if it has not worked perfectly, our stance is to make it work more perfectly. But here is an alternative:

[With cultural pluralism] the outlines of a possible great and truly demo-cratic commonwealth become discernible. Its form would be that of the federal republic; its substance a democracy of nationalities, cooperating vol-untarily and autonomously through common institutions in the enterprise of self-realization through the perfection of men according to their kind. The common language of the commonwealth, the language of its great tradition, would be English, but each nationality would have for its emo-tional and involuntary life its own peculiar dialect or speech, its own indi-vidual and inevitable esthetic and intellectual forms. The political and economic life of the commonwealth is a single unit and serves as the foundation and background for the realization of the distinctive individuality of each nation that composes it and of the pooling of these in a harmony above them all. Thus "American civilization" may come to mean . . . a multiplicity in a unity, an orchestration of mankind.[24]

Lest it be feared that the nurturance of ethnic differences must inevi-tably lead to an inequality of privilege and power, Kallen continues:

Female and male, Indian, Negro and White, Irishman, Scotchman and Englishman, German and Spaniard and Frenchman, Italian and Swede and Pole, Hindu and Chinaman, butcher, baker and candlestick maker, working-man and gentleman, rich man and poor man, Jew and Quaker and Unitarian and Congregationalist and Presbyterian and Catholic—they are all different from each other, and different as they are, all equal to each other.[25]

It is to this dream of difference that the writer appeals. And it is to such an ideology that social welfare should attend. Probably the most passionate and eloquent advocate of this point of view was a former social worker who later became Commissioner of Indian Affairs. His concern was with humanity and he agonized over the irreparable loss to the world that comes from the homogenization of peoples. The forces of the melting pot, he contends, imply

that through polite "engineerings of consent," or if need be through brute force, there shall come about a dead manipulable flatness of human life in the United States and in the rest of the world; that the individual isolate, "freed" from grouphood, culture and home, an atomized "go-getter," shall become—each individual—one among three billion interchangeable grains of sand in an unstructured sandheap of the world.[26]

Social welfare, historically, has taken an ambivalent position between the melting pot and the pluralistic society; the settlement house movement was a striking example of that ambivalence.[27] But no matter—the settlement house movement is dying; sectarian agencies are dying. Perhaps with some reluctance, we seem to be stoking the fires of the melting pot.

This is really what is being done. What would be the outcome of a truly successful Economic Opportunity Act? What is the intent of Head Start programs? To what is urban renewal going to lead? The writer is not against equal opportunity, income redistribution, education, open housing, or the elimination of slums—these programs ought to be implemented immediately and heavy taxation imposed to achieve them. But the country and people in need are done a hideous disservice if these programs are designed along the lines of their prototypes—if job training, Head Start, and urban renewal lead to the homogenization of people into a vast ocean of white-collar suburbia.

### ETHNICITY IS DESIRABLE

Let there be no misunderstanding. The pluralistic utopia of Collier or of Kallen has nothing in common with *apartheid*. Nor is it a reversion to the farce of the old separate-but-equal doctrine. The difference is fundamental: it revolves around the issue of individual choice. Whereas *apartheid* grows out of an enforced ethnicity, cultural pluralism depends on a voluntary ethnicity. *Apartheid* is terror-stricken in the face of differences; it builds walls around its enclaves and requires armed men to police its barriers. A vision of cultural pluralism thrives on differences; the membranes of Collier's enclaves are permeable.

But if individuals are to opt for the choice of maintaining their ethnic identity, the choice must be a viable one. And it is precisely that lack of choice to which attention is being called here. In some perverse way, the choice exists but the price is dear. In order to keep out of the melting pot, the price is either poverty and stigma or antagonistic militance. It is indecent to say to an individual: "You must either homogenize yourself or you must remain poor or you must become an angry man."

This vision of cultural pluralism has its problems. The most tormenting one is trying to maximize what some think are two negatively correlated goods, the goods of individual autonomy and of ethnic integrity. But these are not necessarily contentious values. Martin Luther King was immersed in black culture and yet he was not narrow; Freud was a thorough Jew and yet his perspective was rather large. U Thant is Burmese as well as Secretary-General of the United Nations. Culture is not the enemy of personality; indeed, it is the ally of selfhood. It is likely a prerequisite of the full personality.

But if we, as social workers and as citizens, buy this idea of cultural pluralism, it means that we must radically revise our programs and policies. We would, for example, think much differently about the nature of public education. We would entertain the possibility of parochial schools and neighborhood schools with curricula and teachers selected by local parents rather than by state boards and financed by public funds. Surely this rankles, but perhaps we are ingenious enough to construct an educational system that accommodates to both parochial interest and the interest of the general public. We could hardly do worse than what has been done.

Further, we would—as cultural pluralists—react quite differently to the Panther cry for black policing of black neighborhoods. We would have to rewrite as well as refinance the Economic Opportunity Act of 1964. Job training would be not only for General Motors or Metropolitan Life or IBM: it would also be for indigenously owned and operated industry and craft. White America stole the black man's music; it ought, at least, to return the record companies to him.

And so we think of black schools and black police and black commerce —and we steer a difficult course between *apartheid* and Black Nationalism. But in a very real sense the programmatic aspects of cultural pluralism are self-evident—they are built into the ideology. For social workers it means, at long last, that we work in behalf of clients (the advocacy role), we visit them only when we are invited, we let them use us to get things that *they* want, whether money, housing, jobs, or treatment. Above all, it means that we interact as equals—different perhaps, but still equal. And it means that we do not see them as culturally deprived (what a demeaning term!), educationally disadvantaged (education for what?), matriarchal (with a snicker of superior manhood), or injured, damaged, or helpless.

## THE GREAT EXPERIMENT

Let social workers begin to think of these things—of philanthropy and paternalism and clinicalism and the melting pot and cultural pluralism. If we opt for the desirability of ethnicity, we are then obligated to con-

struct institutions and mechanisms that would allow for the flourishing of ethnic groups while at the same time allowing for a decent standard of living and the opportunity to enter the mainstream. It may be impossible; it may be that the seductions of Levittown and television and instant dinners are too great to withstand; it may be that pluralism is unworkable. But we do not know, we have never seriously tried it, and before it is too late, before we all become as "three billion interchangeable grains of sand," perhaps we ought to undertake the great experiment.

## NOTES AND REFERENCES

1. Frantz Fanon, especially in his *The Wretched of the Earth* (New York: Grove Press, 1963), provided the ideological base for the colonial model of race relations. Negro spokesmen quickly took it up. *See,* for example, Kenneth B. Clark, *Dark Ghetto: Dilemmas of Social Power* (New York: Harper & Row, 1965); Stokely Carmichael and Charles Hamilton, *Black Power* (New York: Vintage Books, 1967); and the spate of press interviews, television panel shows, and so on with Carmichael, H. Rap Brown, Eldridge Cleaver, and other Black Nationalists. The white use of the colonial model is best illustrated by Charles Silberman, *Crisis in Black and White* (New York: Random House, 1964). *See also* Robert Blauner, "Whitewash Over Watts," *Transaction*, Vol. 3, No. 3 (March–April 1966), pp. 3–9, 54.

2. From his poem, "The White Man's Burden."

3. Indeed, such was the rationale provided by some southern apologists for the institution of slavery. *See,* for example, Ulrich B. Phillips, *American Negro Slavery* (Magnolia, Miss.: Peter Smith, 1918).

4. The stance here described has been called by some neo-racism. *See* Robert Blauner, "Internal Colonialism and Ghetto Revolt." Paper presented at the University of California Centennial Program, "Studies in Violence," Los Angeles, June 1968.

5. In writing to the Earl of Derby in August 1858, she urged that the forthcoming India proclamation ". . . should breathe feelings of generosity, benevolence, and religious feeling, pointing out the privileges which the Indians will receive in being placed on an equality with the subjects of the British Crown, and the prosperity following in the train of civilization." John Raymond, ed., *Queen Victoria's Early Letters* (New York: Macmillan Co., 1907).

6. *See* Article 22 of the Covenant of the League of Nations, which established the mandate system.

7. *See* Chaps. XI, XII, and XIII.

8. *See,* for example, the following: "In addition a steady flow of large scale revenue from the canal must involve the question of technical operation and maintenance. It is extremely doubtful if President Nasser has the required skills at his command. He cannot keep non-Egyptians as virtual prisoners indefinitely and it will take time, pains and skill to train replacements. This has nothing to do with nationality. It is simply a matter of training and experience." Editorial, *New York Times,* July 30, 1956.

9. Thomas Hamilton, for example, wrote: "In the Congo, however, the problem arises from the fact that a new government in a primitive backward country—no

doubt because of past Belgian policies—is unable to govern itself." *New York Times,* July 17, 1960.

10. Janet E. Weinandy, "The Techniques of Service," in Frank Reissman, Jerome Cohen, and Arthur Pearl, eds., *Mental Health of the Poor* (New York: Free Press of Glencoe, 1964), p. 372.

11. Florence Hollis, "Casework and Social Class," *Social Casework,* Vol. 46, No. 8 (October 1965), p. 466.

12. Alice Overton, Katherine Tinker, and Associates, *A Casework Notebook* (St. Paul: Greater St. Paul Community Chest and Council, 1959), pp. 160, 137.

13. *Ibid.,* p. 66.

14. The impact of slavery and postslavery racism on the Negro male has been described by many observers. As a start, the reader may refer to E. Franklin Frazier, *The Negro Family in the United States* (Chicago: University of Chicago Press, 1939); and Elliot Liebow, *Tally's Corner* (Boston: Little, Brown & Co., 1967).

15. Daniel P. Moynihan, *The Negro Family: The Case for National Action* (Washington, D.C.: U.S. Department of Labor, March 1967), Preface.

16. The most persuasive case for this point of view can be found in Abram Kardiner and Lionel Ovesey, *The Mark of Oppression* (Cleveland: Meridian Books, 1962). The counterargument is graphically articulated in Liebow, *op. cit.,* p. 308.

17. *Op. cit.,* p. 466.

18. Kardiner and Ovesey, *op. cit.,* p. 308.

19. The different conclusions one can arrive at in this regard, by adopting another perspective can be found in Robert Coles, *Children of Crisis: A Study of Courage and Fear* (Boston: Little, Brown & Co., 1967).

20. This is the most important lesson of contemporary anthropology: Mankind is equisitely versatile in the kinds of institutionally sanctioned behaviors he can invent: cultures may be different from each other but, unless one makes the chauvinistic error of claiming a unique vision of right, one culture cannot be seen as superior to another.

21. For a counterargument *see* Nathan Glazer and Daniel P. Moynihan, *Beyond the Melting Pot* (Cambridge, Mass.: MIT Press, 1963). A more thorough discussion of the success or failure of the melting pot can be found in Milton Gordon, *Assimilation in American Life* (New York: Oxford University Press, 1964).

22. Again, a full discussion of this alternative is found in Gordon, *op. cit.*

23. Israel Zangwill, from his drama *The Melting Pot* (1908), as quoted in *ibid.,* p. 120.

24. Horace M. Kallen, "Democracy vs. the Melting Pot," *The Nation* (1915), as quoted in *ibid.,* pp. 142–143.

25. *Ibid.,* p. 146.

26. John Collier, "Divergent Views on Pluralism and the American Indian," in Roger Owen, James Deetz, and Anthony Fisher, eds., *The North American Indians* (New York: Macmillan Co., 1967), p. 685.

27. This ambiguity as to the ultimate mission of the settlement house movement can be found in Jane Addams, *Twenty Years at Hull House* (New York: Macmillan Co., 1910).

# Part Four

# EDUCATION

# 24

# The Impact of Racism on Social Work Education

## JOHN LONGRES

IN THE RHETORIC of today's social philosophy, racism is an ugly word. We are aware that racism reflects itself in prejudice, discrimination, separation and even genocide, and we feel that these are against the values which we would like to perpetuate as a nation. We condemn racism, yet many of us do not fully understand what it is and how it operates within our society and especially within our own social work educational settings.

Popularly racism is associated with racist individuals: individuals whose attitudes and behaviors indicate hostility toward groups which differ in color from theirs.

The notion of a psychologically abnormal racist individual was given empirical support through the famous studies of *The Authoritarian*

Reprinted, with permission, from *Education for Social Work*, 8 (Winter 1972), pp. 31–41. JOHN LONGRES was at the time of writing assistant professor of social work and sociology at Portland State University, Portland, Oregon. This paper was originally presented at the Eighteenth Annual Program Meeting of the Council on Social Work Education, Seattle, Washington, January 1971.

*Personality*.[1] Using clinical and survey methods, this study suggested that prejudiced individuals demonstrated weak, insecure egos and were positively oriented toward authoritarianism. In spite of the fact that this study has been severely criticized, many have accepted its findings as definitive. Only recently has the adequacy of the formulations evident in *The Authoritarian Personality* been severely questioned.

No pragmatic value is found in equating racism with individual problems for then only two possibilities for dealing with the problems of our society would be open; clinical treatment and education. With regard to clinical treatment, so far as I know, social agencies are not filling up with individual racists seeking cures. With regard to education, there is little to suggest that education has made major inroads in this area. Despite popular beliefs, there is no evidence that educated people are more liberal in their beliefs.[2] Likewise, a recent study of fifteen metropolitan areas seems to indicate that education has not helped in breaking down racist beliefs. After a quarter of a century of mass education on the subject of prejudice, white Americans no longer believe that Afro-Americans are innately inferior. Now white Americans merely believe that Afro-Americans are lazy and won't try to better themselves.[3] Obviously, the United States has come a long way.

There is also a certain comfort in viewing racism as a problem of particular individuals, for the buck can then be passed to those "few" who are "causing the trouble." In so doing, attention is taken away from the majority of white Americans who contribute to the perpetuation of racism through their own subtle and rationalized behaviors.

To see racism as the problem of certain neurotic individuals is too simple, since the history of the United States is permeated with racist laws and doctrines. Racism in the United States has enjoyed official sanctioning in the past and unofficial sanctioning in many sectors today. Moreover, the behavior of most white Americans indicates an acquiescence to the racial inequities evident in our society. Quite normal children are taught racial prejudices in quite ordinary ways in many families across our nation.[4]

Racism in the United States needs to be understood in larger, societal terms. Only by assuming such a view can the complexity of the racial problems be fully realized and can we begin to grasp the contributions social work education makes to the maintenance of a racist society.


## A VIEW OF SOCIETY

Societies may be understood as composed of social groupings in various kinds of association with one another.[5] Perhaps the most basic association involves encounters concerned with the elaboration of authority. Authority differs from power in the fact that authority derives from the nature of the social structure whereas power accrues to individuals or groups due to their own potential and abilities. Power may, and frequently does, lead to authority with the acceptance of particular legal and normative arrangements, in which case one group is said to have authority over another.

Authority relationships are necessary in that they give order and stability to societal interaction. However, they also set the stage for conflict and change. Authority relationships—on any one issue—necessarily break down into two and only two positions: those in authority whom we may call dominant, and those not in authority whom we may call submissive. Although the payoff to the dominant and submissive elements may be sufficient to maintain an existing authority arrangement intact, the perception of inequities coupled with the perception of more rewarding alternatives leads to attempts at structural change.

Thus, authority relationships are typified by a constant state of conflict in which the structure of the relationship is always undergoing change. The nature of the change may differ in radicalism and suddenness, and the nature of the conflict may differ in intensity and violence. Nevertheless, the interaction always involves the dominant seeking to solidify their domination and the submissive seeking to become less subjugated.

It is within this framework that race relations in the United States can be understood. Two social groupings may be distinguished. White Americans, who form the majority, are in a position of dominance because of their control of important social institutions and, more importantly, because of a history of legal and normative sanctioning. Specifically, white Americans enjoy rights and privileges to better education, employment, housing, respect, trust, empathy—among other things—which are not enjoyed by non-whites. The non-white Americans, who form the minority, are in a position of submission. The nature and degree of submission may differ among the various non-white groups, but they all share the same lot: when all is said and done they are submissive to whites.

Thus, racism in the United States is the reflection of authority patterns between whites and non-whites or, rather, it is the means by which whites seek to maintain their dominance over non-whites. Prejudice, discrimination, and segregation are the more obvious means used, but racism may even be built into the value system of a nation.

We must emphasize that the dominance of whites over non-whites is built around authority or legitimated power rather than mere power. It is that fact which frequently makes working "outside the system" so necessary because in authority relationships the rules (i.e., social norms and laws) work in favor of the dominant element. If power were the only source of control, the racial tensions could be altered by changing the power structure. In the case of authority, however, not only must the power structure be altered but the rules themselves changed. For instance, many whites are concerned that educational scholarships are going to "non-deserving" non-whites. The value system of the United States is built around achievement and somehow such a state seems unfair. In order to maintain domination, white people do not have to admit that they don't want educational advancement for non-whites; they merely have to point to the rules in order to neutralize non-whites. Unfortunately, many whites do not go beyond the value statement to realize that since the educational system already works in favor of whites there will rarely be deserving non-whites unless the rule is suspended, changed or destroyed, depending upon the particular rule under consideration. Every rule in the United States needs to be examined for its effects on maintaining the existing dominance of whites over non-whites. This is exactly what the racial turmoil in the United States today is all about; it is a questioning and restructuring of the rules. The intensity of that turmoil testifies to the desperation of whites who are seeking to maintain their privileged position and of non-whites seeking to do away with their submissive status.

Although we have been discussing authority arrangements among social groupings, i.e., whites and non-whites, we are not necessarily discussing social groups. The former implies merely aggregates or classes while the latter implies organization and goals. This is an important point since it enables us to realize that much of the conflict within authority relationships takes place latently without either side actually becoming manifestly involved or even without either side becoming particularly aware of the nature of the conflict. Both sides assume and accept the existing authority structure and act accordingly. Usually this is the case, because socialization patterns have led to the internalization of the authority pattern such that it becomes the normal state of affairs.

It is only as conflict becomes more apparent and open that interest groups are formed and whites and non-whites are confronted with the need for manifest behavior. For example, the polarization taking place in the United States today would indicate that the conflict is becoming less latent and more manifest. Americans are being forced to decide on which side they will align themselves. This, of course, makes our present situation particularly dangerous and threatening and makes it crucial that we make choices which will alleviate conflict rather than intensify it.

Through the remainder of this paper we hope to accomplish two things:

1.   To demonstrate how social work education has contributed to and been affected by racism in the past and what it must do to rid itself of racism in the future. Throughout the discussion we will assume that social work educators are collectively desirous of putting an end to racial strife in the United States by putting an end to racism. That is, we assume that social workers would want to change existing authority relationships so that more equitable arrangements come about.

2.   To explain why social work education has contributed to racism and why it may be difficult for social work education to commit itself to a course of action which will eradicate racism. By realizing this we can begin to grasp what we are up against as a profession.

## SOCIAL WORK EDUCATION

If we were to take a poll of social work faculty, we would undoubtedly find attitudes and individual behavior indicating a relatively high degree of racial liberalism. Most social workers come from minority groups— albeit not necessarily minority racial groups—and are generally sympathetic to the cause of racial equality. This is undoubtedly true for NASW and CSWE members as well. Does this mean that social work education is free of the racism which permeates and threatens our society? The answer must be negative.

Social work education contributes to racism in a number of ways. We can subsume many of these by focusing on: 1) the selection procedure by which non-white students and faculty enter social work education, 2) the educational process within schools of social work, and 3) the socialization process within schools of social work.

## SELECTING STUDENTS AND FACULTY

In the past one of the most apparent areas where social work education has seemed to maintain and foster racism has been in the exclusion of non-white students and faculty from schools of social work.

Historically, educational institutions have treated whites and non-whites differently (this is less true for Japanese-Americans than for most other non-white groups.[6]) Not only have schools and universities been segregated according to race, but far more importantly schools have afforded differential opportunities along racial lines. Most schools attended by non-whites employ less qualified teachers, have less facilities and have less financial backing than most schools for whites. By the same token, subtle extinction of educational and career aspirations takes place, such that non-whites are not motivated toward educational and occupational achievement.

Schools of social work have not alleviated this problem. Until recently there have been few non-whites in social work education. Even today, with the exception of such universities as the University of Puerto Rico and Howard University, the number of non-whites in social work education is exceedingly low.[7]

To some extent the lack of non-white students and faculty can be explained. Graduate education—and undergraduate education as well—hinges on completion of lower levels of education. In effect, many social work faculty argue, the damage already has been done by the time social work education comes into the picture.

Although the low number of non-whites in social work education is to some extent explainable, to a large extent it is not. The low number of non-whites indicates a basic failure of social work educators to seek out and attract non-whites. It is interesting that while schools of social work bemoan the lack of non-white students, physical education departments have systematically recruited non-whites for over a generation. These departments have found ways of attracting non-whites—especially Afro-Americans—and maintaining them in schools at least until their athletic eligibility expired. Unfortunately, physical education departments have frequently not been interested in the education and advancement of non-whites so that it is not surprising that athletic programs have recently come under assault. However, given that physical education departments have been capable of attracting non-whites, there is no reason why schools of social work could not have done likewise. Certainly schools of social work have not demonstrated to non-whites that the social work profession is an area in which they can succeed and make a contribution to their society. Quite the contrary, the poor reputation of social work among non-whites would discourage entry into the social work profession.

Today social work education has realized its mistake and it is becoming fashionable to recruit non-white students and faculty. This, by the way, has not come about through the realization that non-whites can make valuable contributions to social work, but has largely come about through external pressures. The mere fact that there has to be recruitment programs is in itself evidence of the contributions social work makes to racism since it is an admission that the formal and informal mechanisms are not operating to channel non-whites into social work. Be this as it may, social work faculties are recruiting non-whites, but the recruitment is done hesitatingly and reluctantly. The recruitment program is frequently a search for the good "nigger," the non-white who will be grateful for the hand-out and who will not make waves. There is a cautious analysis of numbers so that too many will not come about too soon. There is enormous consideration given to grade point averages and a reluctance to accept "non-qualified" students in spite of the fact that in the past schools of social work have circumvented grade point averages to insure increases in male enrollment.

Educational institutions, although manifestly concerned with instilling knowledge about the world, are gateways to positions of responsibility, of power and influence, in society. To the extent that social work education continues to make entrance into the social work profession difficult and unappealing, it is effectively limiting the upward mobility of non-whites. No more obvious contribution to the maintenance of racism within the United States could be made.

## THE EDUCATION OF NON-WHITES

The educational process is another area in which social work education contributes to racism.

Although it is becoming increasingly fashionable to recruit non-white students, it has not become fashionable to alter the social work curriculum to meet the expectations of many non-whites. Too frequently, social work education, emphasizes subject areas and theoretical viewpoints which are not particularly helpful to non-whites—and whites—who are interested in working with the poor and non-white groups. A case in point is the prevalence of psychoanalytic and psychological thinking in schools of social work. Because of the prevalence of an over-psychological view of man it has not been uncommon for social workers to view poverty and a whole host of other social problems as a function of individual ego-structure. That this contributes to racism is obvious: by over-psychologizing man, social work has been steered away from examining deficiencies in social structure; moreover, an over psychological view of man tends to blame the individual or the subculture and exonerate the society; finally, an over-psychological view of man focuses on the need for individual change and adaptation rather than on social change and social adaptation.

The necessity for more than lip service acknowledgement of culture and social structure in the thinking of social workers is being increasingly demanded by those interested in eradicating racism. Courses which focus on social structure, the culture of minority groups, race relations, and especially on social change and social change tactics cannot be incidental to social work curriculum, but must in fact be central.

Racism is also evident in the "knowledge" we teach. At the 1968 National Conference on Social Welfare, Afro-American social workers expressed concern about the misconceptions, misinterpretations, and myths prevalent among white social workers.[8] In spite of the fact that few schools of social work have any major curriculum content on non-whites, it is still not uncommon for myths about non-whites to be advanced. Unfortunately these myths are advanced as empirical truths and therefore not subject to the critical appraisal they deserve. Particular myths which exist concern the values non-whites hold toward education, the degree to which some non-white groups are unable to delay gratification, and the non-verbal ability of particular non-white groups.

It is not uncommon to hear that Afro-Americans, Puerto Ricans, Chicanos, and American Indians do not value education and educational achievement. Such a "truth" has been substantiated through census statistics and through interviews with school teachers and officials. However, it has not been substantiated in the non-white communities. Non-whites may not behave according to white middle class school-room standards, nor are non-whites likely to receive appropriate intellectual stimulation from family members, but it is not true that they do not want education.[9] The failure of non-whites in schools cannot be attributed to their value system, but to the schools themselves and the racist society at large.

Similarly, the notion that many non-white groups do not persevere in school because they are unable to delay gratification can also be questioned. How can a materialistic and hedonistic society like the United States point to sub-cultures within its sector which are unable to delay gratification. Is the white college student delaying gratification as he vacations in Fort Lauderdale or Laguna? Is white America delaying gratification as it uses up natural resources and litters the environment in the name of productivity and economic advancement? The concept of delayed gratification is too simple and converts a societal problem into a deficiency of an individual or sub-culture.

Another myth about non-whites—especially Afro-Americans—which is quite prevalent among social workers is the "non-verbal" myth. Because many social workers believe that non-whites are non-verbal, it is generally assumed that traditional casework methods will not be useful. Although some social workers have advocated the development of non-verbal casework approaches, most social workers have used the non-verbal myth as an authoritative excuse for abandoning work with non-white communities.

Recently, evidence has been presented which demonstrates clearly that Afro-Americans are every bit as verbal as whites.[10] It is also reasonable to assume that these findings are applicable to other non-white groups as well. The problem of doing casework with non-whites is not that non-whites are non-verbal, the problem is that white social workers have never learned to communicate with non-whites.

In spite of attempts at objectivity, the search for knowledge does not take place in an environmental vacuum. The phrasing of thought, theory and research are in themselves bounded by social events and social positions. It is not surprising, therefore, that what is called "knowledge" should be called "white knowledge" or knowledge from the perspective of white Americans. This is not to imply that theoreticians and researchers deliberately behave as white supremacists, but rather that given the fact that most theoreticians and researchers are white, their ability to take the role of others is limited. The sad part of this is that educational training has the effect of maintaining myths, under the guise of fact. Such a situation can only contribute to racism. In effect, we are giving white students doctrinal armament solidifying their position within society and we are "white-washing" non-whites.

## THE SOCIALIZATION OF NON-WHITES

For many students the experience of professional education may be profound, leading to lasting changes in values, attitudes and behaviors. This may especially be true for students from non-white groups whose forebearers have had limited educational experiences. For these students, "making it in the system" is a crucial test of their worth and self-esteem. They are sensitive and vulnerable in competitive situations which pit them against whites and many non-whites come to schools of social work believing in their own intellectual inferiority. Experiences in schools of social work frequently intensify these difficulties and leave the non-white with a sense of incompetence.

A case in point is the not uncommon paternalistic behavior of white faculty toward non-whites. The attitudinally liberal white faculty member is confronted with non-white students whom he frequently perceives as "disadvantaged" or in some other way inferior. When problems arise in classroom assignments, he becomes intimidated and fearful of treating the problem directly. Not wanting to appear like a "bad guy," paternalistic behavior follows. Thus, it is common for non-white students to complain of the straight B syndrome; regardless of the amount of work performed or regardless of the quality of the work an automatic "B" grade is given.

The contributions paternalism makes to racism are devastating. Faculty come to disbelieve in the cause of non-white groups and whatever latent prejudices they have may become apparent. On the part of non-white students the effect can be more devastating. The paternalistic faculty is judging the student not as an individual but as a race. The student, if he has done badly, never gets the attention he needs for improvement. Likewise, if the student has done well, he never gets the social reinforcement he deserves. Besides the suspicion and distrust which is generated through such a situation, the self-esteem and sense of competency of the student is undermined.

The answer to paternalism is not found in a "get tough" honesty. For the student who is not performing well, punishment will not be of great help. Punishment may be just as deleterious as giving non-deserved rewards, since punishment may lead to hostility and eventually to dropping out of school. Given the present urgency for non-white social workers, the social work profession cannot afford a "get tough" approach.

The faculty member must treat non-white students as individuals. When academic problems are encountered they must be dealt with directly and steps taken to foster improvement. When good academic performances are encountered, the student should be rewarded accordingly. Non-white students cannot afford the luxury of failure and we must make it possible for them to succeed and to experience a sense of achievement and competence in their success.

Social work education does not only affect the self-esteem of students, it also influences their professional tastes, desires and goals. In short, social work education influences professional identity.

At present, the models available for emulation on social work faculties and in social work practice are not generating a social work professional identity which is conducive to the eradication of racism. The social work profession is more committed to helping the white middle class American rather than the non-white and poor. Moreover, social work appears more committed to following in the footsteps of pyschiatry than in carving out a unique professional identity committed to the poor and to social reform.

Most professional social workers practice in mental health settings which do not have particularly large non-white clientele. An increasing number of practitioners are going into private practice where attention is given not only to middle class whites but not unusually, to upper class whites. It is also not unusual for social work faculty to consult on the problems of large business organizations, either to give service to executive personnel or to teach organizational personnel how to handle line workers. This is where the status and the money lies in social work and social workers who do these things, gain our admiration and are emulated by our students, non-white and white. There is no status in social work with the poor and non-white as is evidenced in the deplorable low number of professional social workers working in public assistance agencies. Likewise, in spite of the recent enrollment gains in community organization programs, most social work students still enroll in casework courses, hoping to be the next best thing to a psychiatrist. That this contributes to racism is obvious. Many bright, young students who could influence changes in the racial inequities of our society, are diverted into other areas.

If these things are to change then it is up to the schools of social work to revamp their images and to bring in students and faculty who are committed to the poor and non-white. This does not necessarily mean that we must disband casework programs or that we must stop dealing with the middle classes. What it does mean is that we must realize that casework is limited in its ability to influence changes in social structure and that the real emphasis in social work should be with racism and poverty and ultimately with social reform.

## RACISM AND SOCIAL WORK EDUCATION

In the preceding discussion we have attempted to describe various ways in which social work education contributes to racism. Within this discussion we have alluded to or implied reasons for the racism evidenced in social work education. At this point we will make these reasons more explicit.

As pointed out in our initial comments, much of the racism evident in the United States takes place on a latent level. This is the case because to a great extent the authority relationship between whites and non-whites has been accepted—at least until recently—by both sides. Social work education is no different. For instance, it would be untenable to argue that social work faculty hold racist attitudes, that they represent authoritarian personalities or that they consciously strive to maintain the inequities of a racist society. This is not to say that some social work faculty could not be described in these terms, but that most could not be.

To understand racism in social work education we would have to delineate social, psychological, and sociological characteristicss of social workers and the social work profession—in particular the individual identification of social workers and the involvement of the social work profession in various institutional sectors.

For the most part, social workers are white, affluent, and uninvolved with non-white communities. To some extent even non-white social workers may be described as affluent and uninvolved in non-white communities. Most social workers do not live among non-whites, do not have many non-professional friendships with non-whites, and do not deal with many non-whites in their professional work. However, attitudinally liberal, behaviorally and experientially white social workers have effectively separated themselves from non-whites.

Many of the contributions social work education makes to maintaining racism, can be traced in part to this social distance which exists between social work faculty and non-whites. Because few friendship ties cross racial lines the informal mechanisms which normally bring students and faculty to schools of social work do not operate as a means of bringing non-whites to schools of social work. The frequently voiced problem that there are no available non-whites to man faculty positions is often the result of just this phenomena. It is not that there are no non-whites available—although it is true that there are few—it is rather that the normal course of social interaction and friendship alliances do not make obvious the non-whites that are available. Formal recruitment and many of the problems which it entails becomes unavoidable.

By the same token paternalism in student-faculty relations may also be attributable in part to social distance. Social work faculty are not accustomed to relating to non-whites and become awkward and self-conscious when doing so. Likewise, the abandonment of the poor, the identification with psychiatry, and the involvement of social work with the problems of the middle classes, all may be understood as consequences of social distance. Being white and affluent it is simply less dissonant to create a social environment which is homogeneous rather than heterogeneous.

The enormity of the social distance between social workers and non-whites has other ramifications as well which are even more basic to the maintenance of racism. Given that most social workers are white, it is frequently impossible for them to do more than understand, empathize and commiserate about the plight of non-whites. In times of conflict, the white social worker must contend with both his own involvement and identification with the white community and his sympathy for non-whites. Generally this conflict leads to "seeing both sides" of a problem and although objectivity is to be admired, such a stance is more helpful to maintaining white domination than generating racial equality and justice. Being identified with the white community, the total individual commitment necessary to accomplishing social change is very difficult. The immediate danger of this limited commitment is stalling and hestitancy in making decisions on racial matters. The ultimate danger of this limited commitment is that as polarization between non-whites and whites occurs, white social workers may find themselves choosing to side with whites and become overt in their suppression of non-whites.

The individual identification of social workers is not the only reason for the racism evident in schools of social work. Social work is also involved in a number of authority relationships with other national institutions, the effect of which fosters the continuance of racism. In all of these relationships, social work finds itself in a submissive status, attempting to make changes in that status. Unfortunately, in seeking solutions for its own inequity problems, social work has frequently taken a course which encourages racism.

Social work has been described as an ancillary profession. Ancillary because it often operates in agencies with the "primary" professions of psychiatry and psychology. In spite of the fact that teamwork is a popular method of service delivery, teamwork generally means that the psychiatrist is leader and the social worker is follower. Because authority relationships between social worker and psychiatrist have been established, it is not uncommon to find social workers fulfilling the role of "nigger." We delight in the small attentions paid us by doctors, we vie for acceptance among doctors, we ridicule social work, and worst of all, we set up the psychiatric profession as our model of emulation. There is little feeling among social workers that social work is beautiful. More importantly, by identifying with the psychiatric aggressor we have turned our backs on the very people we were intending to serve. The rewards which could have been earned by maintaining our individuality have become secondary to the rewards obtained from recognition in psychiatric circles.

Social work has also had problems in distinguishing itself as a university discipline and department. On many campuses, schools of social work are considered academically weak and it is not unusual to hear negative comments about social work students and faculty. Although this has changed to a certain extent, schools of social work have not been able to attract the academically excellent student frequently found in other graduate programs. By the same token, the D.S.W. does not carry the prestige of the Ph.D. so that even our doctoral faculty have lower status in academic circles.

Since without some form of educational organization the social work profession would find it difficult to survive, we are frequently in a position of dependence. The approval or disapproval of school administrations and other academic departments becomes an important factor in policy and curriculum planning. We become nervous about accepting non-whites who have low grade point averages, we become nervous about social activists, we teach a psychology and sociology which exonerates society or at least puts it beyond the reach of change, and we do little to alter the university curriculum so that it reflects the espoused ideals of social work.

Finally social work schools are intimately related with the functioning of city, county, state, and federal governments. This is particularly a problem with regard to funding student scholarships and faculty salaries not to mention research and program grants. In all cases, social work schools are subject to the authority of various governmental agencies. This, of course, makes the profession vulnerable to attacks by political figures and makes it likely that we will choose to follow governmental dictates rather than professional ideals. Given the temper of the times, this can only lead to a lessening of efforts to eradicate racism.

The involvements with psychiatry, universities, and governmental agencies have led directly and indirectly to the incorporation of racism within social work education. In a very real sense social work has been co-opted by its relative success in dealing with these institutions. By not rocking the boat, benefits accrue to the profession. These are not to be scoffed at since they involve issues of survival but we should be aware of the unintended and invidious consequences of those benefits.

## SUMMARY AND CONCLUDING COMMENTS

Racism *is* an ugly word and it cannot be thought of as a product of a few neurotic individuals. Racism should be understood in societal terms as a reflection of authority relations between whites and non-whites. As such the maintenance of racism involves the entire society including the social work profession and social work educational programs.

Schools of social work contribute to racism through the selection of students and faculty, and through their educational and socialization processes. However, it would be untenable to argue that the contributions social work makes to racism are manifest, overt, or in other ways deliberate attempts at suppressing non-whites. Racism in social work education is a function of the individual involvement and identification of most social workers with the white sectors. Likewise, racism is a function of authority relationships with other professions, universities and governmental agencies.

Early in its history social work was concerned with social change and social reform. Unfortunately, as social work went from social movement to established institution, the problems of maintaining the profession have become more important than the problems of changing the nation. It is this situation which must be remedied. Although social work education has made strides—and this cannot be overlooked—social work as a profession and social work education have not gone far enough. We must recommit ourselves to social reform and we must think of the profession as a social movement bent on making major changes in our society. Specifically, we must integrate ourselves in the sense of increased contact so that we might learn to communicate and be one with the non-white community. We must abandon psychiatry as a professional ideal and forge an independent identity around social rather than individual change. We must not be intimidated by university and governmental alliances and be willing to risk disenfranchisement. By doing these things, social work may make a valuable contribution not only to the non-white community but to the people of the United States as a whole.

## NOTES AND REFERENCES

1. T. W. Adorno, et. al., *The Authoritarian Personality* (New York: Harper & Row, 1950).

2. W. Gamson, and A. Modigliani, "Knowledge and Foreign Policy Opinions: Some Models for Consideration" *POQ*, Vol. 30 (Summer 1966), pp. 187–199.

3. H. Schuman, "Sociological Racism," *Transaction*, Vol. 6 (December 1969), pp. 44–49.

4. For an interesting study which demonstrates the normal socialization of prejudice, see: H. Kitano, "Passive Discrimination: The Normal Person," *Journal of Social Psychology*, Vol. 70 (1966), pp. 23–31.

5. The sociological analysis of racism used in this paper has been greatly influenced by the writings of Ralf Dahrendorf. See: R. Dahrendorf, *Class and Class Conflict in Industrial Society* (Stanford, Calif., Stanford University Press, 1959).

6. For an analysis of the Japanese American see, R. Daniels, and H. Kitano, *American Racism* (Englewood Cliffs: Prentice Hall, 1970).

7. Kurt Reichert, "Survey of Non-Discriminatory Practices in Accredited Graduate Schools of Social Work" in Carl Scott ed., *Ethnic Minorities in Social Work Education* (New York: Council on Social Work Education, 1970), pp. 39–51.

8. See L., Gary, "Social Work Education and the Black Community: A Proposal for Curriculum Revisions" in Carl Scott, ed., *Ethnic Minorities in Social Work Education* (New York: Council on Social Work Education, 1970), pp. 80–81.

9. F. L. Strodtbeck, "The Hidden Curriculum in the Middle-Class Home" in J. D. Krumboltz, ed., *Learning and The Educational Process* (Chicago: Rand-McNally, 1965), pp. 91–112.

10. W. Labov, *The Study of Non-Standard English*, E.R.I.C., Center For Applied Linguistics, January 1969.

# 25

# Education for Practice with Minorities

## JOHN B. TURNER

DURING THE PAST FEW YEARS social welfare and social work have been increasingly faced with overt expressions of the racial and ethnic consciousness that presently grips America.[1] Therefore, two issues confront social work education: (1) how to equip social workers with the knowledge, skills, and attitudes that will enable them to improve the status of minorities and (2) how to attract more minority-group students into social work education. Schools of social work must bear the major responsibility for recruiting minority students and faculty and preparing all students to work competently in this area.

Given the sensitivity of many social workers to ethnic issues and the special activities of the Council on Social Work Education, especially with regard to accreditation standards, most schools of social work probably are already engaged in efforts to make their schools more responsive

Reprinted from *Social Work*, 17 (May 1972), pp. 112–118. JOHN B. TURNER was at the time of writing dean, School of Applied Social Sciences, Case Western Reserve University, Cleveland, Ohio.

to ethnic concerns.² The range of responses is wide, however. Some schools limit their efforts to "handling" a local campus or community situation rather than adopting a broader educational approach to minority-majority power relations. Other schools limit their approach to a more abstract view of ethnic status and relations, ignoring the existence of pressing ethnic concerns within the agencies and communities in which their students are being educated.

## TOOLING UP FOR CHANGE

To be responsive to the difficulties faced by racial and ethnic groups, an educational institution's efforts must be comprehensive, systematic, and sustained over time. Such a response should involve the school's mission, its curriculum, students, faculty and staff, and cooperating institutions. For some it may be a difficult and even painful step, but all schools must make the commitment to educate all students. They must be concerned, relevant, and more effective with regard to the differential socioeconomic status of minority groups. The importance of consistency in response throughout the educational enterprise cannot be overstated.

The policy implications of education for ethnic practice with regard to all aspects of the school's mission and educational programs should be examined and acted on by the faculty. If the school has an advisory committee or board or other related policy-setting groups within the school or university, they too should be involved in developing and sanctioning such policies. The composition and deliberations of these groups should reflect appropriate representation of minority concerns.

At a minimum the schools' policies should seek to (1) clarify educational goals and programs, (2) make explicit professional and staff personnel and employment policies, and (3) specify student recruitment, admission, and support objectives.

Appropriate guidelines should be developed for use by faculty, staff, students, and cooperating agencies, and administrative procedures should be established to facilitate compliance and developmental feedback. The implications of policies for resource allocations should be made explicit.

It is difficult to single out any one component of a school as being more important than another. But the faculty's centrality in developing and operationalizing the school's mission is indisputable. By its composition, promotion patterns, choice of activities, and formal and informal behaviors, the faculty conveys to all the extent of the school's concern.

Employing minority faculty is an obvious first step. Both the Council on Social Work Education, in its accreditation standards, and government regulations, when federal funds are involved, require such action. A realistic problem has been the shortage of minority persons who are interested and have the formal educational qualifications to teach. Thus the following specific responses by the schools are necessary: (1) developmental recruitment, (2) willingness to pay a significant portion of the cost of teacher preparation, (3) willingness to employ minority group members at senior as well as junior levels, with appropriate supports for upgrading, (4) employment of more than token numbers of minority faculty, (5) reeducation of existing faculty about their roles in supporting employment of minority faculty, and (6) developing university administration support for employment of minority persons. These responses are not meant to define conditions that must be satisfied before employing minority faculty; they are responses that are necessary if the schools' efforts are to be sustained and reasonably successful.

## RECRUITMENT PLANS

Developmental recruitment suggests that a school must have a recruitment plan that not only is aggressive and competitive with other recruitment efforts, but offers the recruit realistic opportunities to continue his preparation through advanced study, short-term seminars, participation in research projects, tutorial arrangements, and the like. Such a plan should allocate money to support faculty participation in such activities. It means recruiting people who have the potential for growth and upward career mobility through university hierarchies. Schools must also avoid concentrating their efforts on employing minority faculty at junior levels, especially if they clearly will remain frozen at these levels.

How many minority faculty should be employed? Using what criteria? Which minorities should be employed? It is difficult to find universally accepted formula for answering these questions. One thing seems clear, however: the number of minority faculty employed must be above that defined as tokenism by interested parties. In most situations, except perhaps when the faculty in extremely small, one minority faculty member is simply insufficient.

For the time being, at least, two guides appear to be relevant in determining which minorities should be hired: the composition and backgrounds of the student body and the composition of the population within the training community. The important thing for schools to remember is that the presence of able and promising minority educators at all levels is better than a thousand statements of intent.

## WHO HAS THE RESPONSIBILITY?

The burden of operationalizing the school's commitment cannot be the exclusive responsibility of minority faculty. It must be shared by the entire faculty and the administration. To this end there must be agreed-on plans to pursue the definition, understanding, and instruction of relevant and useful solutions and remedies to problems created by America's treatment of minority groups. Experience indicates that most faculty members, even the more enlightened, need to reeducate themselves about their attitudes and behaviors. This is concomitant to tooling up the school to be more responsive. Administrative and faculty sanction is often necessary to provide adequate opportunities for this type of re-education.

Few will dispute the desirability of having students from all minority groups. However, once again there are no universally accepted guidelines for establishing minimum enrollments. Frequently the goal is stated in terms of numbers that reflect the size of social service target populations in the geographic areas served by the school through its graduates, as well as the percentages of socioeconomically disadvantaged members of ethnic groups. Practically speaking, it appears that for most schools the number and makeup of minority students who apply for admission will be partly based on the ethnic makeup of the proximate geographic areas, since costs of education will be an important factor for many ethnic students in their choice of a school.

Among the several factors that must be taken into account in acquiring and maintaining adequate ethnic representation among students are (1) developmental recruitment, (2) adequate tuition and stipend support, (3) a climate of acceptance, and (4) educational programs perceived as relevant to ethnic concerns. In this context, developmental recruitment suggests a stronger reaching out, not merely to college seniors but to young adults who may be working in human service programs, college freshmen, and high school students. The latter group is particularly important with regard to ethnic groups whose college populations are still small.

For minority students who are ready for admission, the strongest attraction will be the school's ability to provide scholarships. A closely related factor will be the school's ability to help out-of-town students find decent housing in a nonhostile environment. In addition, students may need group and individual counseling or tutoring with regard to academic programs as well as cultural and class relations. The importance of the quality of relationships between students and faculty cannot be overstressed. Faculty must learn to be sensitive and responsive without being patronizing, to identify without losing their own identity, and to communicate in terms other than those that they alone have set.

It is quite likely that for a considerable time to come minority students will want to organize themselves. The school can view the existence of such groups or caucuses as a threat or as a potentially positive influence in the learning and teaching transaction. It is also of utmost importance that the school be prepared to assist students who have no ethnic and racial identification to function comfortably in a multiethnic and racial context. A major part of this objective will be met in student-to-student interaction.

Minority students will be intensely interested in whether the curriculum is relevant to their concerns. They will want the opportunity to discuss and judge for themselves and have an input. The nature of their input may well change from year to year, from subgroup to subgroup, and from ethnic group to ethnic group. However, it is essential that the faculty accept its responsibility and initiative in designing and implementing curricular responses to ethnic concerns.


## CURRICULUM

If the faculty is central to implementing the school's mission of educating students for work with racial and ethnic groups, the educational program—the curriculum and its format—is the medium through which that mission is accomplished. What content should be required for all students? What should students learn about all racial and ethnic groups? What special content should be taught to those students who are especially interested in working for racial and ethnic justice? Do learning objectives differ between students with and without ethnic and racial group identities? One way of identifying curriculum content is to specify worker performance—i.e., what should a worker be able to do in behavioral terms? It would be useful if practitioners, educators, and consumers as well could develop ongoing collaboration to devise such a statement on worker performance. The author suggests that in addition to the core expectations of social worker performance, all workers should be able to do the following:

1. Recognize racist policies and acts, individual or institutional, whenever they occur and know the facts about racial and ethnic injustice, its causes and consequences for human status, dignity, and society.
2. Bring racist practices to the attention of those who have the professional responsibility and the potential for stopping such practices.

3. Commit whatever resources they have at their administrative disposal to change or redesign policies, procedures, and services that are racist in orientation or consequences, intentionally or not.

4. Respond constructively and instrumentally to minority- or majority-group efforts that are intended to eliminate racism.

Social workers who specialize in minority-majority problems should be able to do the following:

1. Interpret and work constructively with norms, family patterns, leadership patterns, communal organization, and other cultural patterns of minority groups receiving major professional service. These factors include patterns of self-help among members of a specific minority group and how they respond to authority, stressful situations, and dependency.

2. Distinguish between behavior that is distinctly culture based and behavior that tends to be a function of class status.

3. Design and implement organizational activities that will help minority persons improve their status and help majority groups eliminate racist policies and practices. Workers should also be able to help both groups achieve racial, ethnic, and social justice.

4. Provide technical assistance in relevant areas such as economics, justice, education, health, family, and child development.

5. Provide technical assistance to bring about appropriate coalitions among minority groups and between minority and majority groups to achieve common objectives that neither can achieve effectively alone.

6. Translate minority groups' needs and problems into appropriate political and economic objectives.

7. Assist minority and majority groups to engage political structures and processes appropriately and effectively to achieve needed resources and policies.

8. Assist minority and majority groups to engage economic structures (public and voluntary) appropriately and effectively to achieve needed resources for economic development and employment.

9. Provide technical assistance to minority groups to help them develop the political solidarity and discipline required to select and carry out political strategies and tactics.

10. Help political leaders use their policitial power to meet the legitimate social needs of their minority constituency.

11. Utilize administrative and legislative procedures to help minority group members obtain their rights and needed services.

Educators and students of various racial and ethnic groups generally agree that curriculum modifications are indeed necessary. However, they do not agree on the extent and nature of such modifications.

Van Til suggests that society's responses to complex social problems are characterized by five stages; missionary zeal, simple answers, practices that are promising, research, and the quest for desegregation and integration.[3] It may be that social work education is emerging from the simple-answer stage with regard to curriculum and is struggling to find some promising practices. The following is a brief discussion of some areas of curriculum content, issues, and questions that are related to worker performance.

## SOCIAL JUSTICE

Tradition and history have made problems of ethnic and racial justice an inextricable part of the more general problem of social justice. The curriculum must make this connection clear to the student, for he who fights for one must be committed to fight for both.

The curriculum must also help students understand that the way various life-chance sytems work in this country leads systematically and repeatedly to unjust consequences for the poor, uneducated or undereducated, and racial and ethnic minorities. For example, the curriculum must help students understand how institutions behave with regard to (1) hiring, upgrading, and firing practices, union apprentice procedures, lending and investment practices, and merchandising, franchising, and pricing practices, (2) pretrial and court practices in determining guilt and innocence, establishing punishment for violation of laws, and administering the laws differently, (3) determining the distribution, costs, and administration of health care resources, facilities, and services, (4) educational practices with regard to selection, assignment, and performance expectations of teachers, curriculum content selection and administration, class and school size, and student performance expectations, and (5) determining who is eligible for social agency help and under what conditions, what help is to be given, how, for how long, and for what purpose.

Today there is much talk about an *open* society— a society of plural cultures. The struggle for satisfactory ethnic and racial minority-majority arrangements has caused some people to question or reject the concept of ethnic and racial integration at a time when many have just begun to support the idea. Others have become proponents of organized ethnic and racial solidarity as a necessary requisite for achieving and maintaining social justice. Still others seek a more complete separation of ethnic and racial groups into relatively independent socioeconomic-political units.

Forced segregation and voluntary separatism appear to have much in common and thus may be rejected by many. On the other hand, the concept of integration has proved so impotent in its impact on racism that doubts are raised in the minds of the most ardent believers.

Given the multiethnic and racial composition of American society, what would ethnic and racial relations be like if racism could be eliminated? Perhaps an even more meaningful question is: What must such relations be like if we are to move more decisively toward eliminating racism? What must be learned about the impact of social class and other patterns of inclusion-exclusion and exploitation? Perhaps more important, what is to be taught about how to eliminate such practices?

Curriculum designers must decide what is to be taught about separate, integrated, and pluralistic structures, what conditions must be satisfied if an open society is to be created, what subgroup requisites, norms, and political and economic requirements must be satisfied, and how these conditions are to be brought about. Social work education must deal with the related functions of social work and the concomitant roles that social workers should be educated to perform.

Students should have an opportunity to become knowledgeable about the cultural symbols and patterns, community norms and organization, traditions, family patterns, decision-making behavior, and sex and age roles of their own as well as other ethnic or racial groups. Courses should deal with the days in which minority groups have been politically and economically exploited and the consequences of this exploitation. In addition, they should cover individual and group coping behavior. Material should also be included about minority leaders and their social and intellectual ideas.

An important issue related to content concerns language and communication skills. As bilingualism increasingly becomes the norm, students should be encouraged to develop proficiency in a second language if it is relevant to their career goals. For some students, the goal may be to communicate across educational and class lines—rather than to speak a foreign language.

Thus the curriculum must deal with three distinct educational needs: (1) the need of the minority student to have a systematic and in-depth knowledge of his own group, (2) the need for all students to have basic information about the major ethnic and racial groups in America today, and (3) the need of the minority-majority problem specialist for more in-depth knowledge about any minority group he expects to work with.

Hopefully, students will increasingly have the opportunity to learn about their racial and ethnic heritage at the undergraduate level, if not earlier. At the present time, however, graduate schools must assume some responsibility in this area.

## STRATEGIES FOR CHANGE

Whose responsibility is it to end ethnic and racial injustice? Who has a stake in bringing about racial and ethnic egalitarianism? The immense changes that have occurred in racial and ethnic relations over the past ten years seem attributable largely to the self-interested activities of minority groups. Nevertheless, it is unlikely that the more fundamental goals of ethnic and racial justice can be achieved without the white majority's collaboration and initiative.

This fact should not obscure the need for minorities to take action within and on behalf of their respective groups and work with each other and white majority groups. The curriculum must not ignore or downgrade the importance of working with white majority groups. All four arenas of action are required; thus the curriculum must include the social psychology of white persons' responses to racial and ethnic minorities' struggles as well as the social psychology of various minority groups. Not only is there a role for social work with minority groups, there is an equally important function and role with white majority groups.

Social work interventions must be incisive and sustained with respect to strategic objectives that improve the life chances of racial and ethnic group members in significant ways. Some of these goals are provision of stable and sufficient income over time; random distribution of minority persons throughout the social institutions that control and confer status, opportunity, and responsibility; and development of the capacity for instrumental action by minority groups in their own behalf.

What is suggested here is that social work interventions must deal not only with methods of working with people, but must exercise equal competence in substantive issues of economics, politics, education, justice, housing, health, and mobilization of group capacity. The approach cannot be a "welfare" orientation. Its objectives must be developmental systems change and social rehabilitation.

If curriculum reform is to occur, schools will need to prepare class and field teachers. First, faculties must learn new subject matter with regard to substantive as well as methodological areas. In addition, white middle-class interpretations of individual and group behavior must be revised. Schools must also help teachers to change their attitudes and behavior. For example, how can a teacher learn to think of ethnic and racial groups other than as problems? How can he learn to handle the transactional problems with students that will develop in a multiethnic and multiracial student population?

## CONCLUSION

Graduate schools of social work must face squarely the need for major curricula, faculty, and student changes, rather than merely tinker with the educational enterprise. Those who are responsible for making these changes must be more flexible, encourage greater creativity, look for alternative ways of meeting standards, and discard requirements that are no longer relevant and only block access to learning by racial and ethnic minority students.

Preparation for practice that supports and reinforces in its totality a concept of a multiracial and ethnic society will initially be threatening to some faculty and students and perhaps the institution. Therefore, the school must be prepared to back up its intentions consciously by steadfast and aggressive policy implementation and resource allocation. The task is too large for any school to tackle alone. Thus it will be necessary for schools and agencies to share their successes and failures and their brainpower and other resources if they are quickly and successfully to prepare professionals who are committed and able to help bring about social justice.

## NOTES AND REFERENCES

1. John B. Turner, "Racial and Other Minority Groups," *Encyclopedia of Social Work*, Vol. II (New York: National Association of Social Workers, 1971), pp. 1068–1077.

2. Among the Council on Social Work Education's activities are the Commission on Minority Groups, which sponsors several special task forces on the American Indian and Asian, Black, Chicano, and Puerto Rican Americans; publication of five bibliographies on minority groups; and the publication of a casebook for group relations practitioners (Jack Rothman, ed., *Promoting Social Justice in the Multigroup Society*, 1971).

3. William Van Til, as described in Maxine Dunsee, *Ethnic Modification of the Curriculum* (Washington, D.C.: Association for Supervision and Curriculum Development and National Education Association, 1970), pp. 38–39.

# 26

# Social Work Education and the Black Community: A Proposal for Curriculum Revisions

## LAWRENCE E. GARY

THERE IS considerable unrest on university campuses across the nation, and this restlessness has had its impact on schools of social work. At several universities social work students, especially black students, are demanding changes in the content, structure, and philosophy of social work education. Typically, these students are demanding (1) the incorporation of more materials on the black community into existing courses, (2) the addition of new courses on the black community to the curriculum, (3) the appointment of more black and minority-group faculty members and field instructors, (4) a review of the criteria for admission and scholarship or fellowship aid in schools of social work, and (5) the issuance of position papers by these schools to set forth standards for field agencies relating to non-discriminatory practices and overall commitment

Reprinted, with permission, from *Social Work Education Reporter,* 16 (December 1968), pp. 47–50 and 68–69. LAWRENCE E. GARY was at the time of writing a lecturer at the School of Social Work, University of Michigan, Ann Arbor, Michigan.

to social work ideals and principles.[1] As one can see, the concerns of these students have many implications for social work education.

The objectives of this paper are to elucidate some of the problems of social work education as it relates to the black community and black professional social workers, and to propose new courses on the black community so that social work education can become more meaningful to students, especially black students. One of the basic concerns of black students and of the author is to make professional education more pertinent to the needs of blacks, both as practitioners and as clients. In relating social work education to the black community, one would be concerned with some of the demands which have been mentioned above. This paper is concerned primarily with the content of social work education rather than its structure or philosophy. We will not discuss the type of field placement situation for black students, the criteria for admission or fellowship, or even how to recruit more black students or faculty members. Some consideration will be given to faculty needs and competence. One of the basic assumptions of this report is that, besides incorporating more materials pertaining to the peculiar needs of black people into the existing courses at schools of social work, it is absolutely essential to have *separate* courses. And it is for this reason that the major discussion will focus on new courses on the black community. For the proposed courses, it is assumed that there is ample relevant literature on many aspects of the black community.[2]

## THE BLACK COMMUNITY AND
## SOCIAL WORK EDUCATION

### A.  Social Work Education and the Black
### Community: The Past

In trying to provide proposals for curriculum revisions, some discussion of the relationship between social work education and the black community is necessary.[3] The black community is demanding self-determination—black power, or participation on the part of black people in decisions that affect their lives. Their leaders are even more committed to this ideology, to which, for the most part, social work has paid only lip service. In general, not enough consideration has been given to the culture, values, aspirations, and needs of the black community. In the past, what was relevant to social work education has been defined by people (generally speaking, white professionals and educators) who have had little appreciation or understanding of the black community.

In the past, moreover, the content of social work education has been primarily psychotherapeutically oriented casework.[4] This approach places emphasis on helping the client to develop mechanisms or abilities for coping with stress or for reducing the stress with which the client had to cope. By focusing on modifying individual behavior rather than on restructuring society or elements of the social system, social work education has been tied both ideologically and conceptually to the white community. Therefore, before we can make social work education meaningful to the black community, we must acknowledge the fundamental fact that in the past the social work profession had no intention of dealing with the structural constraints that prevent black people from realizing their potential.

In the black community there is considerable disenchantment with the psychotherapeutic approach in social work. There are signs that other sectors of the profession are disenchanted with this approach also.[5] Black professionals and many white professionals are well aware that many of the problems that black people face—poor housing, discrimination, inadequate education, police brutality, limited marketable skills, under-employment, unemployment, inadequate income, etc.—cannot be attributed to individual pathologies. Social work education must now focus on a way in which institutional and organizational change can be brought about; this re-focusing is just beginning,[6] but techniques and tools for effecting social and organizational change are not yet well-developed. Until now, social work education and research have been too concerned with the individual to develop techniques to deal with changing structures in society.

A casual review of the literature suggests that culture was an important factor in social work education and practice during the early fifties.[7] In the late fifties, the emphasis on integration (the Supreme Court decision of 1954 and subsequent decisions on civil rights) and on the Americanization of minority groups created a corresponding de-emphasis in social work education on cultural differences among people. Moreover, it was assumed that the black man had no culture or that his culture had only an American origin.[8] Of course, this assumption is being questioned.[9] With the exclusion of blacks from the social and cultural history of our society, there has been a tendency in our profession to point out only the weaknesses of the black community and to assume that social problems have their roots in the nature of the black community. These tendencies and assumptions must stop and re-introduction of the concept of culture into social work education must be accelerated.[10]

Social work education has not been geared particularly for the black man. In the process of getting a social work education, the black student has not been prepared for work in his community. The student learns concepts, mannerisms, language, etc., which, more often than not, create barriers to the understanding of the majority of his own people. This results from the exclusion of meaningful knowledge about his own culture and life in the curriculum of both undergraduate and professional schools. In the few cases in which they do receive some knowledge about their culture and life, it is presented essentially from a negative perspective, with emphasis on pathology, deviancy, and social disorganization. Of course, since students receive inadequate or negative knowledge about the culture and feelings of the black community, they, as well as professionals, have difficulties in relating to black people. Given the above perspective, social work education in the past has failed to speak to the needs of the black community.

### B.  The Role of the Black Social Worker and Professional Education: The Challenge

In discussing and analyzing the urban crisis, many people have criticized the social work profession. This year, the theme of the National Conference on Social Welfare was "An Action Platform for Human Welfare." At this conference, many speeches and papers, including the presidential address, made references to "the welfare crisis" and "telling it like it is." [11] If these statements about the dilemma of social welfare are true, then some adjustments must be made in the kind of education which social workers have been receiving. Black professionals were concerned about the misconceptions, misplaced emphases, misinterpretations, and myths prevalent at this conference.[12] In many cases, these participants had social work degrees or were intimately involved in the social work field. Again, if we are to correct these misconceptions about black people and are to understand the power relationships between blacks and whites, we must make major innovations in social work education and research.

Today, the black social worker, like his white counterpart, is challenged on every front to be productive. His relative position as a leader is slipping in the black community; leaders other than those with a social work education are moving into political roles of crucial importance. It is my position that these new leaders have much more to offer their community because they have a realistic conception of the present-day and emergent needs and aspirations of their sisters and brothers. Unfortunately, black social workers have not been educated to give the leadership necessary to the black community today.

The challenge suggests that we must continue to deemphasize the psychotherapeutic approach in social work education and place more emphasis on the "environmental" approach—that is, emphasizing structural changes in our society.[13] Regardless of method, social work education must develop its content so that it can help all students, and especially black students, to develop the knowledge, skills, and attitudes that will enable them to effect structural changes in the social system.

## C. Some Policy Decisions

Social work education must become relevant to the black community, and, in doing so, schools of social work will have to make some crucial policy decisions.[14] One such decision is whether the schools intend to help develop black leadership by offering a program of study which relates to the peculiar needs of the black community. Social work should not be relevant to the black community alone, but it should be recognized that, in the past, social work education has been tied both ideologically and conceptually to the white community. Therefore, it must deal with this basic issue and offer a program of study for black students which is tied to the black community.

The policy questions (criteria for admission and scholarships, the hiring of black faculty members, courses on the black community, etc.) are all interrelated. These issues must be decided and the decisions implemented in a systematic way. If training is to be significant, the profession *must* participate in the struggle for human justice and understanding. Often the rigidity of organizations or institutions prevents them from dealing effectively with their clientele or environment. Student unrest is a manifestation of this issue. Emphases on cognitive knowledge, professionalization, and non-innovative curricula are examples of this rigidity at many schools of social work. Therefore, we should be open to new approaches and structures so that our training will remain relevant.

Many black workers and others are beginning to recognize the conflict of priorities which exists between the needs and goals of social work education and those of the black community. This conflict of priorities can be seen from several perspectives: (1) the use of resources, i.e. hiring for teaching positions scholars who have doctoral degrees vs. hiring practitioners who have master's degrees plus experience; (2) the content of the knowledge base, i.e. socio-behavioral or psychoanalytic models vs. social action or more radical models of change. The conflict becomes very vivid when we try to relate social work education to the black community. Most schools of social work are much more concerned about the content of the knowledge base, which places more emphasis on socio-behavioral or psycho-dynamic theory than on social action or more radical models of social and organizational change, and the recruitment of scholars with doctoral degrees for teaching positions, than they are about the needs of the black community.[15] Black professionals and students are demanding that the content of social work education be related more to the needs, aspirations, and goals of the black community. Therefore, this conflict of priorities must be recognized and dealt with. It seems to me that some type of compromise must be made. The way in which we define the problem influences the solution. It is obvious that, at most universities or schools of social work, black people are not in a position to help define the problem. If schools do not see the issue or problem as one of policy, then solutions might be irrelevant.

## A MODEST PROPOSAL FOR CURRICULUM REVISIONS

### A. Proposed New Courses

Let us assume that the schools of social work plan to help develop black leadership. If so, then new courses on the black community are absolutely necessary, because it is very difficult for teachers to add to existing courses sufficient content on blacks in American society. In addition to new courses, however, attempts should be made to incorporate meaningful materials in other courses so that the curriculum for all students includes content about black America.

In order to make social work education more relevant to the black community, the following courses should be added to the social work curriculum: [16] (1) Afro-American Culture and Life, (2) Politics and Economy of the Black Community, (3) Racism in American Society and Culture, (4) Developing New Institutions and Services in the Black Community, and (5) Selected Topics on Socio-ethnic Systems and Social Work Practice.

As stated earlier, the curriculum at most American universities has blanked out the Afro-American contribution to the nation's history. The black students have been taught an alien culture, and the white students have received inadequate information about the black community. Therefore, many students have come into the schools of social work with a deficient background on the black experience in the New World. It seems quite appropriate to supplement their professional education with a course on Afro-American culture and life, a general introduction to the social and cultural life of the black community. It should draw upon theories and research which have examined the experiences and responses of black people to basic American institutions. Major consideration should be given to misconceptions, misplaced emphases, and myths about the black community and the dynamic shifts and changes within this community. Consideration should also be given, moreover, to some of the basic problems in studying sub-cultural communities. Some of the subject matter areas which should be covered in this course are: (1) a cultural perspective on the black community: problems and issues; (2) aspects and roots of Afro-American culture, including such concepts as cultural stripping, cultural relativity, etc.; (3) black family patterns, with some consideration of the effects of history, kinship patterns, role systems, communication networks, and "the fatherless family;" (4) the identification process in the black community; (5) attitudinal and belief systems, with respect to different institutions; (6) behavior and life styles, with emphasis on language, mannerisms, recreation, etc.; (7) cultural contributions in areas such as art, music, and science; and (8) some applications for social work practice. The basic objectives of this course would be to provide the student with a basic understanding and appreciation of the cultural and behavioral patterns of the black community and with a framework for appraising and relating this knowledge to social work practice and problems.

The course on the politics and economy of the black community should draw upon current theory and research relevant to examining the political, social, and economic processes in the black community. Major consideration should be given to the power relationships between black and white institutions. The course should also focus on formal and informal organizational development, especially the role of the church in the black community. The following topics should also be included in the course: (1) economic, political, and social models for analyzing the power relationships between the black and the white communities; (2) formal and informal organizational development; (3) political behavior, political socialization, voting behavior, political participation, status, and action; (4) political leadership and occupational and social characteristics; (5) employment and manpower; (6) consumer behavior, price systems, buying habits, spending-saving ratios, etc.; (7) capital development and formation in the black community; and (8) the problem of change in the black community. The objectives of this course are to provide the student with a basic understanding of some of the key political and economic problems facing the black community and with basic knowledge of the societal variables that condition the behavior of black organizations, and to acquaint the student with the forces and variables with which he must deal in designing meaningful strategies for change at the personal, group, organization, or community level.

It is very surprising that in the human growth and social environment component of the curriculum we do not have courses on racism in American society and culture. Perhaps this again reflects the extent to which American universities are tied to the white community, but this is a necessary course in light of the Kerner Report on the extent of racism in American culture. This course should focus on the nature and determinants of racism in American culture. It should draw upon current theories and relevant research to examine the evolution of racism in America and, to some extent, in the world at large. Institutional racism should be examined from several conceptual perspectives. As a starting point, some consideration must be given to personal attitudes of students involved in a course of this nature. It is important that students learn about institutional policies and practical decisions which limit their effectiveness in solving the problems of all people, both black and white. In general, this course will detail the extent of racism in all aspects of American culture: language, institutions, beliefs, values, social systems, etc. The following topics might be included in a course of this nature: (1) the nature and determinants of discrimination and prejudice; (2) the evolution of racism in American culture and life (ideological factors, socio-cultural factors, economic power and status factors, personality factors, and language and mass communication factors); (3) institutional racism (schools, government, business, churches, etc.); (4) minority reaction to racism (acceptance, aggresion, avoidance, assimiltaion, conflict); and (5) social work practice and racism. This course would provide the student with a basic understanding of the extent of racism in American culture and society and supply him with analytical tools for assessing the impact of racist policies which inhibit his effectiveness in a given setting. As a final objective, it would offer the student some frame of reference for understanding his own attitudes and feelings about racism.

Most schools of social work lack adequate information on black organizations which are providing services to the black community. In a given black agency, a worker must be prepared to develop a variety of community development services. The experiences of these black organizations should be incorporated in a new course. This course, besides acquainting the student with basic knowledge about these services and programs, should also provide him with some experience in designing them. The course should cover the following topics: (1) the community development ideology and black organizations, (2) the social and political contexts of black organizations, (3) structural arrangements (indigenous leadership, citizen participation, etc.), (4) economic programs and services (development corporations, non-profit corporations, etc.), (5) cooperative developments (groceries, housing, credit unions, etc.), (6) socio-cultural programs and services (Afro-American culture societies, drama and theater groups, etc.), (7) political programs and services, (8) sources of funds, including linkages to existing resources and development of new ones, and (9) program writing.

Selected Topics on Socio-Ethnic Systems and Social Work Practice should center on research and theories of socio-ethnic systems and social work practice. It should be concerned with integrating knowledge about these systems and this practice. The course would acquaint the student with some of the basic problems in designing treatment strategies for clients from different socio-ethnic groups, and provide him with appropriate opportunities to apply his knowledge in designing treatment strategies and with analytical tools for assessing and testing these strategies and instruments.

It should be pointed out that this is primarily a methods course with a generic orientation. As stated earlier, the specific topics covered in this course would vary from semester to semester. For example, the theme for semester X might be "Social Treatment in the Inner City." The theme for Semester Y might be "Models for Analyzing the Black Community: Implications for Social Action." The theme for semester Z might be "Principles and Practices of Mass Demonstration and Political Action." Under the last theme, the seminar would consider principles and techniques of picket lines, sit-ins, petitions for legitimate rights, and political lobbying for practical political action. Moreover, under this theme, one could use the experiences of labor unions, political action groups, and the civil rights movement. After determining the theme, different topics could be developed. For example, under the theme "Social Treatment in the Inner City," the following topics could be utilized: [17] (1) the appropriate determination of goals for black clients; (2) new means of forming treatment contracts with inner-city clients; (3) the effects of culture and race of the client upon treatment planning and methods; (4) issues presented by assigning either a white worker or a black worker to a black client; (5) new models for professional behavior when working with black clients; (6) the impact of communication patterns of these clients upon diagnosis and treatment; (7) critique of theoretical formulations and practice currently employed with such clients; and (8) new treatment strategies for work in the inner city.

### B.   The Social Work Curriculum and the Proposed Courses

One might ask this question: What has been the response of schools of social work to the racial and poverty crisis in our society? More specifically, how has the social work curriculum responded to these problems? In 1967 the Council on Social Work Education conducted a survey on the involvement of member schools in the inner city, racial, and poverty concerns.[18] This survey indicated that these schools are slowly responding to recent developments and demands of our society. Although these schools reported many activities, such as term paper topics on race, poverty, etc., research projects, and new content areas in existing courses, only a few indicated that they were developing new courses to respond to the changing conditions and knowledge base.

The curriculum at schools of social work is usually organized around three major areas: (1) practice methods, i.e. casework, groupwork, administration, etc.; (2) human behavior and social environment, i.e., developmental psychology, group dynamics, the family, theories of personality, etc.; and (3) social welfare policy and services, i.e. school social work, income maintenance programs, corrections, etc. The courses which have been recommended can be related to the three major components of the social work curriculum. Of the five, only one—Socio-Ethnic Systems—is directly related to practice methods, but assumes a generic orientation with respect to such methods. Since the content will vary, however, the course might be more meaningful or useful to a particular method in a given semester. For example, in surveying the literature on disadvantaged children, the professor and his students might want to develop treatment strategies. Since the target of change is the individual or the group, casework, groupwork, and social treatment students might be more interested in this course during semester X. On the other hand, a group of students and professors might want to combine their knowledge of culture and discrimination or prejudice into a treatment plan, with the target of change at the community level, so that the course might appeal more to students in the social treatment or community practices sequences. For this course, necessary prerequisites are a course on Afro-American culture and life and one methods course. Since in most schools a student has to take at least one methods course outside of his sequence, this course should be made an alternative to satisfy the second methods requirement.

Each student is required to take a specified number of courses in the social welfare policy and services area of the curriculum. Since the course, Developing New Services and Institutions, falls into this area, a student taking it could fulfill a part of his social welfare policy requirement. Since this course assumes considerable knowledge about the black community, prerequisites are necessary. The course on Afro-American culture and life or on the politics and economy of the black community should be sufficient. Moreover, this course would be primarily for students who plan to work in the black community.

The courses, Afro-American Culture and Life, Politics and Economy of the Black Community, and Racism in American Society and Culture, are directly related to the human behavior and social environment component of the curriculum. The general orientation of these courses should be from a theoretical and conceptual perspective. There should be no prerequisite for these courses. However, it would be desirable for a student to take Afro-American Culture and Life before taking the course on the politics and economy of the black community.

In each sequence a student is required to take a minimum number of hours in the human behavior and social environment area. One can note that, in professional social work, a large percentage of students and practitioners play roles which affect the lives of the black people. One can also assume that a significant number of graduates from schools of social work, especially prestigious schools, will rise in the social welfare hierarchy to establish policies and administer programs which affect the lives ot many black and minority-group people. Consequently, it is necessary for all potential social workers to be knowledgeable about the black community and to understand the processes and dynamics of racism. Therefore, in fulfilling their human behavior and social environment requirements, all students should be required to take at least one of the courses which I have proposed in this area.

## C.  Faculty Qualifications

In discussing curriculum revisions and proposing new courses, some consideration must be given to teaching qualifications and competence. A basic requirement to teach any of these courses is some experience with the black community. This experience must, of course, be supplemented by knowledge about the black community in the particular areas considered. This may require that assigned teachers be given time in advance to work out course materials, since the subject matter is not well established or organized.

Two courses, Afro-American Culture and Life, and Developing New Institutions and Services, should be taught by a black man who is knowledgeable about black history and minority-group relations, either formally or informally. In both courses the teacher should try to utilize outside resources and keep in close contact with scholars, teachers, leaders, and professionals from the black community. Ideally, the course on the politics and economy of the black community should be taught by a black man; this is not essential, though the teacher should have some experience with black political organizations, civil rights groups, and black nationalist and militant groups. Moreover, he should have considerable knowledge about the American political system and the international significance of the black struggle in America. Some knowledge of economics is also a desirable qualification to teach this course. The teaching responsibility for the course on racism should be shared between a white and a black man.[19] Both should have some knowledge of minority-group relations and black history. Some experience with inter-group relations programs would be helpful. For this course to be useful and meaningful, dialogue must exist among the students, between the students and the teachers, and between the teachers. Thus, a particular kind of non-white person is needed to assist in teaching this course, in order to assure the desired outcome. This individual must feel comfortable in terms of his own identity, ability, potential, and uniqueness. Of course, this also applies to the white teacher, but he should be involved in the process of looking at himself as a product of a racist society. It should be clear that the competence for this course places more emphasis on self-awareness and interpersonal skills than on cognitive knowledge. This is essential if the course is to deal with the racist aspect of our culture. Personal awareness of the extent of racism is crucial in understanding it impact on the total system. Because the course, Selected Topics on Socio-Ethnic Systems and Social Work Practice, would depend mainly on the interests of the faculty members and students, course content would vary from semester to semester. Thus the qualifications would depend on the theme of the course.

In discussing teaching competence and needs, I have placed more than the usual emphasis on practical experience. This is necessary at this point in time, for, to keep social work education relevant, it must have a closer relationship with the black community so that information and knowledge can be communicated from the community (where practice takes place) to the classroom (where knowledge is systematized and criticized) and vice versa. This two-way communication must be institutionalized in schools of social work. For example, we might have more people from the field on curriculum committees, or we might have an extensive lectureship program where people from the field could either be part-time instructors or guest lecturers. In some cases, a black person is needed to teach specific courses. This is in keeping with my assumption and assertion that social work education cannot be relevant to the black students and community unless black instructors are a part of the educational process. Therefore, the appointment of regular full-time black faculty members is crucial if these courses are to be meaningful for both the white and the black students. It is to be noted that by a "black" teacher I mean someone who has developed a power perspective on the racial crisis in America. This does not necessitate a particular political ideology, but rather a close identity with the aspirations, goals, and needs of the black community.

## CONCLUSIONS

This paper assumes that the outlook of most white social work students is different from that of most black students because of their different backgrounds and the area in which they must work. It is primarily concerned with developing a program of study that will offer the black students a type of education that will be relevant to the black community and useful in the struggle for human justice and understanding. This program of study will also be useful to the black student in that it will provide him with a framework for understanding his community. Moreover, white students need these courses so that they can get a more meaningful perspective on the black community. I stated that, in the past, social work education, because of the focus of its knowledge base, did not speak to the needs of the black community or of poor people in general. Therefore, these courses and others should help to correct the imbalance in the content of social work knowledge by focusing social work education and research on developing principles and techniques for restructuring some of the basic institutions in America. If social work is to become relevant and remain significant to the black community, it *must* develop technologies to deal with structures in our society.

## NOTES AND REFERENCES

1.  *Agreement among Students, Faculty, and Staff Council and Administration,* Columbia University School of Social Work, May 13, 1968; C. M. Hall, *A Proposal for a Course on Racism,* School of Social Welfare, University of California, Berkeley, May 16, 1968; *Martin L. King, Jr., Symposium Workbook,* Graduate School of Social Work, New York University, April 29, 1968; *Report of Black Social Work Student Group to the Dean,* University of Michigan School of Social Work, Winter, 1968; and Student Curriculum Committee, *Race Relations Course,* Washington University School of Social Work, Spring, 1968.

2.  For information on source materials for each proposed course, see Lawrence E. Gary, *Relating Social Work Education to the Black Community,* Part I, University of Michigan School of Social Work, July 9, 1968, pp. 20–31.

3.  Gary, *ibid.,* pp. 2–6.

4.  Alfred Kadushin, "Two Problems of Graduate Programs: Level and Content," *Journal of Education for Social Work,* Vol. 1, no. 1 (Spring, 1965), p. 41.

5.  *Ibid.,* pp. 41–42.

6.  *Ibid.,* p. 43.

7.  Council on Social Work Education, *Socio-Cultural Elements in Casework: A Casebook of Seven Ethnic Case Studies* (1955); Anne F. Fenlason, "Anthropology and the Concepts of Culture," *Social Work Journal,* Vol. 31, no. 4 (Oct., 1950), pp. 178–82; Sol Werner Ginsburg, "The Impact of the Social Worker's Cultural Structure on Social Therapy," *Social Casework* (Oct. 1951), pp. 319–25; William Gioseffi, "The Relationship of Culture to the Principles of Casework," *Social Casework,* Vol. 32 (May, 1951); Florence R. Kluckhohn, "Cultural Factors in Social Work Practice and Education," *Social Service Review,* Vol. 25, no. 1 (March, 1951) pp. 38–47; Henry Maas, *et al.,*

*Smith College Studies in Social Work,* Vol. 25 (Feb. 1951); John M. Martin, "Socio-Cultural Differences: Barriers in Casework with Delinquents," *Social Work,* Vol. 2, no. 3 (July, 1957), pp. 22–25; Otto Pollak, "Cultural Dynamics in Casework," *Social Casework,* Vol. 34, no. 7 (July 1953), pp. 279–84; and Mark F. Zbrowski, "Cultural Components in Response to Pain," *Journal of Social Issues,* Vol. 3, no. 4 (1952), pp. 6–30.

8. Seaton W. Manning, "Cultural and Value Patterns Affecting the Negro's Use of Agency Services," *Social Work,* Vol. 5, no. 4 (Oct., 1960), pp. 3–13; Lois Pettit, "Some Observations on the Negro Culture in the U.S.," *Social Work,* Vol. 5, no. 3 (July, 1960); and F. J. Woods and A. C. Lancaster, "Cultural Factors in Negro Adoptive Parenthood," *Social Work,* Vol. 7, no. 4 (Oct., 1962).

9. Ralph Ellison, *Shadow and Act* (New York, 1964); Romeo Garrett, "African Survival in American Culture," *Journal of Negro History* (Oct., 1966); William Kelley, "On Africans in the U.S.: Roots of 'Soul'," *Negro Digest* (May, 1968), pp. 10–15; Charles Keil, *Urban Blues* (Chicago, 1967), pp. 1–29; and L. Lipton, "Negrification of American Culture," *Negro Digest* (Nov., 1965), pp. 63–69.

10. This process is slowly taking place. See: Mary Huff Diggs, "The Significance of Cultural Patterns in Family Life," *Public Welfare* (Oct., 1961), pp. 145–48; Ann Fischer, "Culture, Communication and Child Welfare," *Child Welfare* (April, 1964), pp. 161–69; Sol W. Ginsburg, *A Psychiatrist's Views on Social Issues* (New York: Columbia University Press, 1963), pp. 105–45; Florence Hollis, "Casework and Social Class," *Social Casework,* Vol. 46, no. 8 (Oct. 1965), pp. 463–71; Morton Levitt and Ben Rubenstein, "Some Observations on Relationships between Cultural Variants and Emotional Disorder," *American Journal of Orthopsychiatry,* Vol. 34, no. 3 (April, 1964), pp. 423–35; Inabel B. Lindsay, *Influence of Socio-Cultural Factors on the American Family Today* (1963); E. G. Meier, "Social and Cultural Factors in Casework Diagnosis," *Social Work,* Vol. 4, no. 3 (July, 1959), and W. B. Miller, "Implications of Urban Low-Class Culture," *Social Service Review* (Sept., 1959), pp. 219–36.

11. *An Action Platform for Human Welfare,* National Conference on Social Welfare, May 26–31, 1968, San Francisco, California.

12. *Position Statement,* National Association of Black Social Workers, May 29, 1968, San Francisco, California.

13. Kadushin, *op. cit.,* pp. 42–46.

14. Gary, *op. cit.,* pp. 5–6.

15. Kadushin, *op. cit.,* pp. 41–46, and Herman Stein, "Cross-Currents in Practice and Education," *Journal of Education for Social Work,* Vol. 1, no. 1 (Spring, 1965), pp. 59–60.

16. Gary, *op. cit.,* pp. 7–9.

17. These topics were suggested by Professors Richard English and Charles Garvin at the University of Michigan.

18. Kurt Reichert, *The Relationship of Schools of Social Work to Inner-City Concerns, Racial Problems and Anti-Poverty Activities,* Jan. 23, 1968, pp. 5–12.

19. Hall, *op. cit.,* pp. 1–2.

# 27

# Inclusion of Content on Ethnic and Racial Minorities in the Social Work Curriculum

## MARY ELLA ROBERTSON

TODAY, we are educating people to live and work in a society in a state of constant change, such that, in the words of Margaret Mead, "no one will live all his life in the world into which he was born, and no one will die in the world in which he worked in his maturity." Under conditions of change, it is no longer appropriate to assume that the knowledge and practices that served us adequately in the past are sufficient for the present or the future. We are living in a daring and exciting era of extraordinary scientific and technological change, a time of almost unprecedented social revolution marked by assertiveness for human dignity. Basic assumptions

Reprinted, with permission, from *Social Work Education Reporter*, 18 (March 1970), pp. 45–47 and 66. MARY ELLA ROBERTSON was at the time of writing professor of social work at the Boston College Graduate School of Social Work, Boston, Massachusetts. This paper was originally presented at the Seventeenth Annual Program Meeting of the Council on Social Work Education, January 21–24, 1969, at Cleveland, Ohio, and appeared in the Council on Social Work Education's publication *Ethnic Minorities in Social Work Education*.

about the nature of man and his relationships to social institutions are being confronted, and alienated out groups are no longer willing to accept their subjugation. Colonialism, in all forms, is dead, as evidenced by the break-up of empires, student uprisings, and the black revolt in our cities.[1] This latter is fundamentally one of identity, of personhood. Freedom is the choice to perceive and define a situation on one's own terms, and then to act on the basis of that definition. The determination of blacks to define the circumstances of their identification, their own models and heroes, and their intent to define what is relevant for themselves, has aroused the kinds of fears and distortions among the white community which encourage attempts at more brutal repression, however, they are attempts which will no longer work.

Among the pivotal considerations affecting what to teach and how to teach it, is the current emphasis upon human dignity and radical social change. While the quest for human dignity is not new in the long story of human existence, it has now reached a level of conscious concern which may be the hallmark of our times. While we fumble ineptly, make compromises and temporize, and are weak willed in critical situations, the future will surely note the deliberate attempts made to struggle against inequalities, against loneliness and separateness, and against the waste of mind and spirit. The struggle for human dignity is a struggle for the right to stand with other men as an equal, and to have confidence that one has worth as a man. Education has the responsibility to assure such dignity for all persons.

This can be done because, deeply embedded in the rhetoric of American life, there is the belief in a pluralism which allows for differences, and indeed the American ideal provides for diverse patterns of expression. Such diversity of opinion revitalizes norms by forcing society to consider problems that might be overlooked and to seek solutions to them.

The cultural traditions of America's past give evidence of this diversity and pluralism. In early New England, people of agrarian villages built their homes around a central commons at the end of which they erected the meeting house that served the religious and civic functions of the community. Many of these New Englanders were deeply committed to communal equalitarianism, preparation for which required a minimum level of literacy. The New England pattern of farm subsistence has long been abandoned, but its idealistic qualities have been woven into the fabric of our national life.

The hills and mountains that we now call Appalachia were settled by people of a Celtic tradition, who had a strong loyalty to kinship groups and were deeply equalitarian, even to the extent of rejecting education because it fostered inequalities among men. Since the middle of the nineteenth century Appalachia has been outside the main stream of American development, and only recently has its plight become a matter of national concern.

In the Delta areas of the South, production for a world market required large acreages and a plentiful supply of field labor. The need both for capital, and for managerial skills contributed to the development of a clearly defined upper class, which excluded blacks into servitude, designating them inferior.

The changes in modern America have included the majority of people, but the continued existence of large groups in marginal roles represents a serious defect in the fabric of American society. For, despite the ideals of pluralism, there is a basic strain towards conformity, toward standard life styles and values. We have underestimated heterogeneity, variability, and change. The terms "culture" and "sub-culture" are used to describe life styles and behavior under contemporary urban conditions, and often summary statistics alone are employed to explain the social characteristics of an area. Although they are not so intended, these concepts and statistics are frequently interpreted as indicating a kind of homogeneity and a degree of regularity that does not exist.

For social work practice, this attempt to draw a broad, though undetailed picture of complex, multi-dimensional behavior is premature and dangerous, and the loose use of concepts and statistics tends to obscure the issues, and, what is worse, to dehumanize them. It is mandatory that we examine the differences in all of their ramifications—ethnic, racial, social class, etc.—avoiding the inclination to condemn or condone, to denigrate or to romanticize, as they interfere with accurate description and interpretation. Underscored here is the necessity for correct answers about: the significance of differences, the bases of the differences, and of their persistence, if they persist, and the organization of these differences and the collective life around them.

As social work educators, we are constantly reappraising curriculum, policies, and educational practices, for the curriculum is a major key to organized exchange between faculty and students as they strive to master an understanding of some aspect of man and his changing environment. In reassessing curriculum, the educator is guided by the need to:

1. Help the student develop intellectual and moral integrity, an ability to think independently and critically about problems of society, and to recognize and accept personal responsibility for value judgments.

2. Provide grounds for the student to understand and express the fundamental values and philosophies that underlie our social institutions, policies, and practices.

3. Prepare the student, through understanding, to act *among all*

*people,* an ability which often includes a major change in outlook and attitude.

4. Guide young people to cultivate the character and intellectual resourcefulness which will enable them to live with uncertainty and to effect change.

Because of the nature of our times, and the need to serve ethnic minorities in their quest for human dignity, social work educators have to review the various curriculum areas and determine whether they are as responsive and pertinent as is desirable to the requirements of professional functions. There is an urgent need to analyze current practice patterns, identifying those which are dysfunctional, and those which continue to be effective. Appropriate means should then be devised for changing those practice patterns which appear to be dysfunctional.

Social work educators have developed two points of view regarding the development of content on ethnic minorities in the curriculum. One point of view asserts that the curriculum, in all of its components, should be enlightened with content about differences and diversity among people, that these differences and variations, cast in a positive framework, are the appropriate and necessary content for every course or sequence of study, and should be reflected in the curriculum.

## ORGANIZATION OF THE CURRICULUM

The practice sequence, which is being given a great deal of attention in most schools of social work, should focus more directly upon innovative tools and techniques of social change in rendering individual, group, and community services.

Mary Richmond's significant effort in the professionalization of social work and her development of techniques of data collection and its utilization to individualize the client did much to set the stage for the monumental impact of Freud's theories on social case work. Although we have been concerned for some time with expanding the theoretical base of social casework to include other concepts, Freudian thought and ego psychology still have a great impact upon casework practice. As casework has become more clinical, developed more assumptions about client readiness and treatability, it has become less effective with blacks and other ethnic minorities who, as a prerequisite for service, had to be socialized to work as the agency wanted. For example, it was necessary for him to keep appointments punctually, and to be articulate. To the extent that he learned to be a client, he could expect to receive service, otherwise, he was designated as untreatable or unmotivated. The focus of practice, as seen by ethnic minorities, has been upon getting them to accommodate themselves to societal expectations and to their low status, while they remained abused, exploited, and self-blaming for their condition, ashamed of their person and their past. The repression, dependency, and pseudo-helplessness that ethnic minorities have felt has not been alleviated by professional social work. It is for this reason that the community organization worker is more popular with ethnic groups. He is perceived as a professional who is interested in changing social structure and social conditions. There is an urgent need for educators to determine how to make the casework method more effective in developing the personhood of ethnic minorities.

Rejection by others is about as devastating an experience as a human being can encounter, and it is especially destructive when such rejection becomes chronic or categorical because of his ethnic origin, or the color of his skin. Such distortions cannot be contained within the private life of an individual person. We have seen how they release tensions that soon spread beyond the psychological boundaries of interpersonal relations to the larger dimensions of the nation.[2] If we value individuals, it is in order that the practice sequence direct the student to re-examine basic assumptions and principles in respect to social work's responsibility in making human fulfillment possible for all. Many ethnic and racial minority-group members envision their freedom and the development of their personhood in societal change. Regardless of the method learned, present-day practice requires that the social work student attain knowledge, skills, and attitudes that will enable him to affect structural changes in the social system. It has been suggested that the practice sequence be expanded to include new ways of forming helping contracts with inner-city clients, to take into consideration the effects of culture and race upon treatment planning and methods, to utilize new strategies for working with clients in poverty, and to account for the impact of communication patterns upon diagnosis and treatment.

The other alternative is that social welfare policy sequences might be reorganized to include in their philosophical content the values and philosophical postures of black power advocates, the strain of oriental communities in the welfare system towards self sufficiency, the development of community services in the ghettos, the relationship of ethnically oriented welfare organizations to the total welfare system, the contribution of ethnic and racially oriented organizations to the groups they serve, and historical perspectives on welfare which include those primarily concerned with minorities. For example, analysis of national social policy with respect to the American Indian helps the student to understand the latter's current isolated and alienated condition. And although an astute analysis of its structure and function would afford many insights into the antecedents of the current war on poverty, the Freedman's Bureau, America's first war on poverty is almost never mentioned in the social work curriculum. The enlargement of content in this sequence to include the aforementioned areas would provide the student with a wholeness in his knowledge base.

Similarly the student's knowledge of the current welfare system and of the need for income maintenance programs can be broadened by an in depth analysis of the economic condition of racial and ethnic minorities.

The research sequence should be expanded to include inquiry into selected topics on socio-ethnic systems and social work practice. It should serve to integrate knowledge about these systems with practice, affording the student the opportunity to become familiar with the basic design of research and its outcomes in areas of inter-group and intra-group relations.

Field instruction should be expanded to include broader learning in ethnic communities, and in newly developed interventive modalities which are useful to the people being served.

The Human Growth and Social Environment sequence in most schools needs considerable revision to include more content on ethnic minorities, particularly such subject matter as cultural perspectives on ethnic communities, black family patterns, poverty, and race. Major emphasis should be placed upon becoming aware of, and analyzing misconceptions, stereotypes, and myths about minorities. Inadvertently, social work has managed to join with other social scientists in promoting stereotypes such as those made about fatherless families.[3] Intimate, comprehensive, and detailed information about the members of any group is absolutely necessary if the student is to be prepared to combat myths and stereotypes.

Because racism in America has not been squarely dealt with, because we avoided acknowledging it, we have rarely included any content on the subject in the social work curriculum. The Kerner Report is clear and unequivocal about the extent of racism in our society, and if we are preparing students to participate in the struggle for human justice and understanding, they must examine racism in our society and in themselves.[4] The social work curriculum cannot afford to ignore racism. Course content dealing with this subject area should include an examination of theories and principles of action regarding the nature of prejudice, institutionalized racism, and minority reaction to racism. The knowledge gained from this content would afford the student a more realistic understanding of the nature of our society and the nature of man, and should provide a framework for an understanding of his own attitudes and feelings about race.

Because most students come to a school of social work knowing nothing about black history in the U.S., a few schools are giving elective credits for Afro-American history, which is taught in the Humanities department. This provides a necessary perspective for all students, although the content of these particular courses is sometimes difficult for the students. For the first time they become aware of the fact that even a great American like Thomas Jefferson was a slaveholder all of his life, and that, despite repeated requests from the black writer Bannecker that Jefferson serve as an example to his countrymen and renounce the institution of slavery, he never did. As students become immersed in Afro-American history, they find it an unsettling psychological hazard, for many of their models are called into question. As a result, they denounce "the establishment" further. Once they grow beyond this initial reaction, they move with confidence and appreciation into Afro-American History, and find it useful in re-evaluating their attitudes and interpersonal relations. The addition into the curriculum of electives about the history of other ethnic groups would have the same effect. The way to learn to know and appreciate a person is through a study of his history, literature, art, folkways, and traditions.

There is another position regarding the inclusion of content about ethnic minorities in the social work curriculum. Many black professionals and students feel that the content of social work education is not related to the needs of the black community, and that our profession has not prepared professionals to deal with the social constraints that prevent black people from realizing their potential. They feel that separate courses about blacks and other ethnic minorities are essential, in addition to incorporating such material into the already existing courses at schools of social work. It is thought that incorporation of this content only into other courses will not be sufficient, that it will not receive the in-depth study that it requires, and that it will easily slip into a non-significant spot, as the overall orientation is to the majority. This point is well taken. There is no reason why specific courses devoted to ethnic and racial content, courses perhaps following the suggestions made earlier in this paper, cannot be incorporated into the curriculum.

If the social work curriculum is to be effective, however, it must in no way continue to present minority-group content in terms of the multi-problem family, the delinquent, the non-contributing, non-productive members of society. How can anyone, whether he be of the minority or the majority, respect a people who are systematically presented as a problem and inherently worthless?

In conclusion, I have briefly commented upon the nature of our changing times, and on the social revolution which bears promise of bringing all of us into a higher level of living if we can solve our human relations problems. If we ask how the greatest social change of our age is being brought about, in terms of the decolonization of American poor and the civil rights movement in the U.S., it is hard to attribute much of it to whites whose leaders, despite one hundred years of superior education, failed to initiate any kind of solution. We all have a stake in bringing about these changes. They are as vital to the well-being of the majority as to the minority. The problem of racism in America has been exposed and must be resolved. A profession such as ours must clearly reorient itself in its goals and practice. We have developed sophistication in therapeutic procedures, and we must now develop the same degree of expertise and commitment in social action geared to structural changes in our society. As a necessary prerequisite, the social work curriculum must prepare students to understand and appreciate racial and ethnic differences, to understand how these factors have influenced social institutions and their policies, and develop knowledge, attitudes, and skills in social change.

Content about ethnic minorities should permeate all sequences in the curriculum. This can be accomplished both by incorporating it into established courses and by offering very specific courses that deal with minority-group concerns. Such an approach broadens the basis of social work education and prepares professionals to participate in the most compelling social roles of our times.

We believe in our country, in its capacity to create the kind of society in which men can be free and equal, and we believe that our professional education can be designed to prepare students to diminish ethnic and racial prejudice, to reorder the socio-political structure of society so that it provides for human realization.

## NOTES AND REFERENCES

1. Colonialism, as used here, means the exercise of powerful authority and control of one group over another.

2. Charles Hendry, *Social Workers: Catalysts in a Changing Society* (Buffalo, New York: University of Buffalo, 1962), pp. 2–3.

3. Elizabeth Herzog and Cecilia Sudia, "Family Structure and Composition Considerations for Research Toward Improving Race Relations," unpublished paper delivered at Institute on Research Toward Improving Race Relations of the National Association of Social Workers, August 13–16, 1967, Airlie House, Warrenton, Virginia, p. 1.

4. *Report of the National Advisory Commission on Civil Disorders* (New York: E. P. Dutton Press, 1968).

# Part Five

# RESEARCH

# 28

# Staff-Patient Interaction, Race, and Patient Behavior on a Psychiatric Ward

## CAMILLE ORSO TURNER AND GEORGE SPIVACK

DURING THE PAST TWO DECADES considerable evidence has accumulated supporting the contention that hospitalized psychiatric patients are extremely responsive to their milieu.[1, 2, 6, 12] As a consequence, an increasing number of mental hospitals are abandoning the custodial approach to patient care and are modeling their psychiatric wards on the concept of the "therapeutic community." Following this change have come discussion and research concerning both the impact of specific aspects of the ward milieu on patient behavior,[8, 10, 13] and the role of non-professional

Reprinted, with permission, from *Mental Health*, 55 (October 1971), pp. 499–503. CAMILLE ORSO TURNER was at the time of writing research anthropologist at Hahnemann Medical College and Hospital, Division of Research and Evaluation, Philadelphia, Pennsylvania; GEORGE SPIVACK was director of the Division of Research and Evaluation and a research associate professor in the Department of Mental Health Sciences, Hahnemann Medical College and Hospital. This paper was adapted from one presented at the Forty-first Annual Meeting of the Eastern Psychological Association, Atlantic City, New Jersey, April 2, 1970.

personnel in mental health programs on the ward.[5, 11, 14, 15] The effects of staff-patient interaction have ben examined in different contexts by Kaldeck,[9] Collarelli and Siegel,[3] and Ellsworth,[4] and each has reported some positive impact on patient behavior resulting from interpersonal contact between patients and non-professional staff.

This paper presents the results of a program designed to modify the traditional functions of the attendants and practical nurses on a psychiatric ward in a general hospital. The goal of this program was to increase the frequency of social interaction between these staff and the patients. It was hypothesized that an increase in interaction would result in a positive change in the ward behavior of the patients. The program was introduced six months prior to the present study. In a series of meetings, the new service chief informed the attendants and practical nurses that he wanted them to substantially increase the frequency of their interaction with the patients. Formerly, the attendants' function had been largely custodial, and the practical nurses had taken care of routine medical treatments under the supervision of the registered nurses. The service chief requested that these staff get to know individual patients, and become familiar with their problems. He explained to them the therapeutic value he believed would result from their interaction with the patients. In addition to such verbal encouragement, the attendants and practical nurses were assigned active roles in the group and milieu therapy sessions for the patients, and were included in case conferences and team meetings. To further facilitate their involvement with patients, the case history charts were made available to them.

Although both patient and staff groups were racially mixed, the possible effect of this demographic fact upon patterns of interaction was not considered when the program was introduced. As will be shown later, failure to incorporate this phenomenon in the program design resulted in the restriction of the program to one racial group of patients.


## METHOD

*Subjects* Another psychiatric ward in the same hospital was used as a control. The two wards were similar in physical layout, number and types of personnel, admission criteria and characteristics of the patient population. The 112 patients on the experimental and control wards resided in two low-income inner city areas of Philadelphia which were similar in socio-economic and cultural characteristics. There were no significant differences in length of stay, medications and therapies received, age, sex or racial composition of the two wards. The average length of stay was six weeks, and the average age 35. Although patients with all types of mental illness were accepted on both wards, during this study only the control ward had patients diagnosed as psychoneurotic. These patients' data were not included in the analyses reported below. On both wards all practical nurses and attendants were Negroes, and the vast majority of other staff was Caucasian.

Considering the above facts, it seemed reasonably safe to assume that the only major difference between the two wards was the new program on the experimental ward, which stressed the involvement and increased interpersonal contact of the attendants and practical nurses with patients.

*Measurement Technique* Patient and staff ward behaviors were evaluated using an objective, time-sampling observation technique. Thirty-one behavior units were derived from preliminary observations of patient ward behavior and from the Location Activity Index devised by Hunter, Schooler and Spohn.[7] The ward behavior units were tested and refined during a pilot study. These units were used to categorize readily observable, overt behavior, and included such items as: speaking; playing social games; awake but inactive; sleeping; and walking.

*Procedure* Ward behavior was evaluated during 78 observation periods over three consecutive weeks. No observations were made during structured situations such as meals and ward meetings. The observer always started in the same location, and walked through the ward checking off the behavior categories of each person as she encountered him.

## RESULTS

### Staff Behavior

1. In order to determine whether the program was operating (i.e., the attendants and practical nurses had actually increased their interaction with patients), the number of contacts between these staff and patients on the experimental and control wards were compared. A chi-square test revealed that the difference between the two wards in attendant-patient and practical nurse-patient contacts was significant at the .05 and .01 levels, respectively. The experimental ward staff interacted more often with patients than their control ward counterparts.

2. Further examination revealed that the experimental ward staff interacted five times more frequently with Negro patients than with Caucasian patients. Even taking into consideration the slightly greater number of Negro patients, a chi-square test indicated that this difference

was significant at the .01 level. No such selective interaction pattern was found on the control ward.

### Ward Behavior Measurement Technique

1. A test of rater reliability revealed that the two observers agreed in their category assignments of behavior in 85 percent of 280 randomly selected instances.

2. Statistical tests of interrelationship were carried out between the behavior items. Rank order correlations and chi-square tests clearly indicated that speaking, listening, social games/dancing, listening to the radio, and ward service each related positively to one another (at the .05 level or better), and each related negatively to being awake but inactive, and sleeping.

3. A measure was devised combining the scores for these seven inter-related behavior items. This measure was judged as reflecting the degree to which each patient was actively and positively involved in interactions with the ward social environment. The measure was called the positive environmental interaction, or PEI, score, and attention was focused upon it in the subsequent analyses.

### Patient Behavior

1. No significant relationships were found between PEI scores and age, sex, length of stay on the ward or medications received. Most patients diagnosed as psychoneurotic or personality disorder were found to have scores above the median PEI scores (i.e., more positive inter-action). Since only one ward had neurotic patients, they were eliminated from subsequent comparison between the two wards.

2. Although the behavior scores of the experimental ward patients tended to be higher than those of the control ward patients, a median chi-square test revealed no statistically significant difference.

3. Despite the absence of a significant difference between the patient behavior scores on the two wards, an examination of the relationship between the race of the patient and the PEI score revealed that on the experimental ward most Negro patients, but very few Caucasian patients, had scores above the median PEI score. A chi-square test revealed this difference to be significant at the .01 level. On the control ward however, race was not related to scores.

4. Within the group of Negro patients on the experimental ward, all of those who had many staff contacts also had PEI scores above the median, while five out of six with few contacts had PEI scores below the median. A chi-square test revealed that this relationship was sig-

nificant at the .01 level. This relationship was not found among the experimental ward Caucasian patients nor among either group on the control ward.

5. Experimental ward Negro patients interacted among themselves three times more often than they did with Caucasian patients, and four times more frequently than Caucasian patients interacted with one another. Using a chi-square test this difference reached the .01 level of significance. It was also found that the experimental ward Negro patients interacted among themselves twice as often as either group did on the control ward, and on the control ward there was no difference between the frequency of Negro-Negro, Negro-Caucasian and Caucasian-Caucasian patient interaction.

## DISCUSSION

The data suggest that the increase in contact between the staff and the Negro patients caused the positive environmental interaction which is reflected in the higher PEI scores of the Negro patients, and the greater occurrence of social interactions among the Negro patients than among the Caucasian patients, or among those on the control ward.

It appears that when the practical nurses, who were all Negro, were asked to become personally involved with patients and their problems, race became a critical factor in their choice of patients with whom they became involved. They chose patients of the same race—that is, Negro patients.

Selective interaction on the basis of race was absent on the control ward, probably as a result of the different function of the attendants and practical nurses on this ward. Their relationships with the patients were largely impersonal, as presumably would have been the case on the experimental ward, had no change in program been instituted. The control ward practical nurses' contacts with the patients were generally restricted to the delivery of medications and medical treatments. The attendants carried out a variety of tasks at the request of the clinical staff. These included taking patients off the ward to the medical clinics, helping patients who had difficulty performing basic tasks such as dressing or eating, restraining agitated patients, and some aspects of ward maintenance. Both the practical nurses and attendants on the control ward had some free time during the day when there was no work for them to do. At these times they usually sat in the hall or the nurses' station and chatted among themselves. Only occasionally did they engage in a conversation or a card game with a patient. Since their contacts with patients were task oriented, impersonal, and often at the request of a clinical staff member, it is not surprising that race was not a determinant of interaction patterns on the control ward.

The results of this study support those of earlier research which have suggested that social interaction between patients and staff can have a positive effect on patient ward behavior. In addition, it has revealed that race, an infrequently considered variable, can play a definitive role in determining which patients the staff will choose to interact with on a personal level. It is not a big leap to suggest that the quality of interactions between staff and patient may also be affected by such a variable. Considering its importance in regulating patterns of interaction on a psychiatric ward, this variable must be considered when any program requiring interaction is being planned.

The results also have a somewhat broader implication for ward clinical administrators interested in improving the quality of the treatment milieu. It is not enough to state a new social policy; and even creating program circumstances abetting the new policy (although necessary) may not be sufficient. Staff interaction with patients is not only influenced by professional role, but also by personal likes and dislikes, shared values and culture. These factors must be considered in hiring, inservice training, and in the social supports staff may at times need to carry out their professional roles effectively.

## REFERENCES

1.  Artiss, K. L. Milieu Therapy in Schizophrenia, New York: Grune and Stratton, 1962.

2.  Caudill, W. The Psychiatric Hospital as a Small Society, Cambridge, Mass.: Harvard University Press, 1958.

3.  Collarelli, N. J., and Siegel, S. M. Ward H: An Adventure in Innovation, Princeton, N. J.: D. Van Nostrand Co., Inc., 1966.

4.  Ellsworth, R. B. Non-professionals in Psychiatric Rehabilitation: The Pyschiatric Aide and the Schizophrenic Patient, New York: Appleton-Century-Crofts, 1968.

5.  Goldman, A. E., and Lawton, M. P. The Role of the Psychiatric Aide, Mental Hygiene, 46: (April) 288–298, 1962.

6.  Greenblatt, M., York, S. H., and Brown, E. L. From Custodial to Therapeutic Patient Care in Mental Hospitals, New York: Russell Sage Foundation, 1955.

7.  Hunter, M., Schooler, C., and Spohn, H. E. The Measurement of Characteristic Patterns of Ward Behavior in Chronic Schizophrenics, Journal of Consulting Psychology, 26:(February) 69–73, 1962.

8.  Jungman, L., and Bucher, R. Ward Structure, Therapeutic Ideology, and Patterns of Patient Interaction, Archives of General Psychiatry, 17:(October) 407–415, 1967.

9.  Kaldeck, R. Group Psychotherapy by Nurses and Attendants, Diseases of the Nervous System, 12:(May) 138–142, 1951.

10. Kellam, S. J., and Chassan, J. B. Social Context and Symptom Fluctuation, Psychiatry, 25:(November) 370–381, 1962.

11.   Sobey, F.   The Non-professional Revolution in Mental Health, New York: Columbia University Press, 1970.

12.   Stanton, A. H., and Schwartz, M. S. The Mental Hospital: A Study of Institutional Participation in Psychiatric Illness and Treatment, New York: Basic Books, Inc., 1954.

13.   Thrasher, J. H., and Smith, H. L. Interactional Contexts of Psychiatric Patients: Social Roles and Organizational Implications, Psychiatry, 27: (November) 389–398, 1964.

14.   U. S. Department of Health, Education and Welfare, Public Health Service. The Psychiatric Aide in State Mental Hospitals, Publication No. 1286, March 1965.

15.   U. S. Department of Health, Education and Welfare, Public Health Service. Non-professional Personnel in Mental Health Programs: A Survey, Publication No. 5028, November 1969.

# 29

# Some Effects of a White Institution on Black Psychiatric Outpatients

## RICHARD L. KREBS

MANY RESEARCHERS [1, 3, 5, 7, 10–13, 16] have pointed to the deleterious impact that white people have on black people, in regard to such factors as performance on psychological tests and the black person's image of himself. Partly as a result of such findings it has been suggested by one black mental health professional [17] that black patients only be treated by black therapists. However, it is often the case that black people who want help with psychological problems have to go to white people for help because many mental health facilities are staffed by white professionals. This study reports on some of the effects that the white staff of one institution, Sinai Hospital of Baltimore's Adult Outpatient Psychiatric Service, has had on one group of black people. The first part of the study attempts to find out whether or not a white mental health

Copyright, the American Orthopsychiatric Association, Inc. Reproduced by permission from the *American Journal of Orthopsychiatry*, 41 (July 1971), pp. 589–596. RICHARD L. KREBS was at the time of writing affiliated with the Department of Psychiatry, Sinai Hospital of Baltimore, Baltimore, Maryland.

staff does have a deleterious effect on black psychiatric patients. The second part of the study focuses on the black female patients, who appeared to be particularly affected by exposure to a white psychiatric staff.

## PATIENT POPULATION AND TREATMENT PROGRAM

The sample for the present study consisted of all cases opened between January 1, 1969 and September 30, 1969 in the Adult Outpatient Service. During the nine months of the study, 273 people contacted the Outpatient Service, asking for help. What happened to those people is presented in Table 1. The people asking for psychiatric help are classified by sex and race. Since no accurate figures were available for the population of the area surrounding Sinai no comparisons were made between the frequencies of people asking for help and the population at large.

To determine if there were any differences for the two variables of race and sex in the proportions of people asking for help and people entering treatment, two analyses were done. The first analysis compared the people in the four groups who were discharged (A) with those who were scheduled for treatment (B). In this analysis it was found that the proportions of black females, black males, white females and white males were significantly different. This difference was accounted for

Table 1  **PEOPLE EVALUATED FOR PSYCHIATRIC HELP BETWEEN JANUARY 1, 1969 AND SEPTEMBER 30, 1969 (N=273)**

| PEOPLE EVALUATED | BLACK FEMALE | BLACK MALE | WHITE FEMALE | WHITE MALE | TOTAL |
|---|---|---|---|---|---|
| Total (N=273) | 32% | 10% | 41% | 17% | 100% |
| A. People Discharged (N = 37) | 27% | 22% | 19% | 32% | 100% |
| B. People Scheduled [a] for Treatment (N=236) | 33% | 8% | 44% | 15% | 100% |
| C. People Refusing Treatment (N=23) | 30% | 9% | 39% | 22% | 100% |
| D. People Entering [b] Treatment (N=213) | 33% | 8% | 45% | 14% | 100% |

[a] Proportion of 4 groups of people in A & B is significantly different ($X^2=16.42$ p.<.025).
[b] Proportion of 4 groups of people in C & D is not significantly different ($X^2=.88$ p. N.S.).

by three of the groups. An inordinate number of white and black males were being discharged, while an inordinate proportion of white females were being assigned to therapy.

There was no difference in the proportion of people refusing treatment (C) as compared to those actually entering treatment (D). The group that ended up in treatment had a somewhat higher proportion of white females than the group that initially requested help and a somewhat lower proportion of black and white males. This situation was caused by a higher discharge rate for black and white males. This result will be discussed more fully later.

People were not assigned to diagnostic categories on the basis of race or sex. The numbers of black females, black males, white females and white males in each of the four broad diagnostic categories (Psychotic, Neurotic, Situation Disturbances and Others) were not significantly different from chance ($X^2 = 10.73$—N.S.).

However, the same did not hold true for assignment to therapy. The

Table 2  **THERAPY ASSIGNMENT FOR EACH OF THE FOUR GROUPS (N=213)**

| | THERAPY TYPE | | |
| | INDIVIDUAL | | FAMILY AND GROUP THERAPY |
| Group | Crisis | Long Term | |
|---|---|---|---|
| Black Female (N=70) | 54% | 39% | 7% |
| Black Male (N=17) | 23% | 71% | 6% |
| White Female (N=95) | 35% | 47% | 18% |
| White Male (N=31) | 32% | 52% | 16% |

Table 3  **PERCENTAGE OF FIRST 10 APPOINTMENTS KEPT BY EACH GROUP OF PATIENTS (N=213)**

| GROUP | APPOINTMENTS MADE | APPOINTMENTS KEPT | PERCENTAGE KEPT |
|---|---|---|---|
| Black Female (N=70) | 362 | 256 | 71% |
| Black Male (N=17) | 119 | 104 | 87% |
| White Female (N=95) | 694 | 609 | 87% |
| White Male (N=31) | 198 | 162 | 82% |

therapy offered was either individual, family, or group. The individual therapy was either crisis-oriented, ten-session therapy or long-term therapy. The family and group therapy programs were not time limited programs. The assignment to therapy was related to the race or sex of the patient ($X^2=13.49$ p$<$.05). It appeared that a major contribution to the difference in therapy assignment was that a disproportionate number of black females had been assigned to crisis intervention therapy ($X^2=8.12$ p$<$.005). This result will also be discussed later.

The next step was to try to discover what happened to people who entered therapy.

It is notoriously difficult to assess the efficacy of psychotherapy. The present study, however, was concerned with the potential deleterious effect of a white staff on black patients. It was an attempt to assess failure rather than success. The variable chosen was attendance.

While the fact that a person does not show up for treatment is not a completely accurate measure of failure, attendance can reasonably be used as a baseline measure of the effectiveness of a therapeutic approach. Frequent absences generally mean that therapy is not going well.

The percentage of appointments kept during the first ten scheduled sessions was used as the measure of "failure" or "non-failure" therapy. "Non-failure" therapy was defined as attendance by the patient at more than 50% of the scheduled sessions; "failure" therapy was defined as 50% attendance or less. Fifty per cent was chosen as the cut-off point because it seemed unreasonable that a person who missed half of his sessions could be considered to be involved in therapy that was going well.

The proportion of missed appointments for the four groups varies from chance to a highly significant degree ($X^2=49.89$ p$<$.001). The major contribution to this significant difference was made by the black women ($X^2=44.92$, p$<$.001). For some reason or series of reasons, black women were attending at a significantly lower rate than the other three groups. The remainder of the paper focuses on this group of black women, trying to assess two things: 1) In what way might the black women be different from the other groups, particularly the white female group, and 2) How do "failure" and "non-failure" black women differ from each other.

The first variable to consider was that black women had been assigned to crisis-oriented, time-limited therapy at a significantly higher rate than any of the other three groups. An analysis of the attendance rates indicated that patients were attending the different treatment modalities at significantly different rates. ($X^2=4.93$ p$<$.05). However, this difference was not accounted for by the black females, who attended the crisis intervention therapy and the other therapies at almost identical rates

(71% crisis therapy attendance, 70% at non-time limited therapies). It was therefore necessary to look for other factors that might account for the lower attendance rates of the black women.

One such factor might be a conflicting commitment, such as a job. To control for sex related differences, only women were considered in the next analysis. The difference between the two groups was significant ($X^2=17.55$ p<.01). Fewer black women than white women were unemployed. The black woman was therefore somewhat more likely than the white woman to be faced with the choice, "Should I go to work or to my therapy appointment." Furthermore, the black woman may have been less likely than her white counterpart to be able to get away from work even if she decided to give therapy priority over her job. More white women than black women in the sample (13% vs. 3%), were employed in professional jobs, jobs in which a woman is her own boss or in which her supervisor is likely to be sympathetic to a request to keep a therapy appointment. Moreover, for the professional person, time away from work probably does not mean a loss of wages. The black woman, on the other hand, was likely to be employed in a job that paid hourly wages and to have an employer less sympathetic to a request to leave work to keep a therapeutic appointment (64% vs. 40%).

To discover more about the factors influencing the black woman's attendance rate, it seemed reasonable to take a closer look at the black female group for other clues about their higher failure rate. A considerable proportion of the women in the black female group were not "failures." Fifty of the seventy black women attended more than 50% of their sessions. How did those fifty women differ from the twenty who are defined as failures?

The failure and non-failure groups did not differ significantly from one another on the variables of employment ($X^2=1.20$ N.S.), diagnosis ($X^2=2.70$ N.S.) or type of therapy ($X^2=.45$ N.S.). While none of these variables proved fruitful in distinguishing between the two groups of black females, there was a fourth variable that did—being on medical assistance. In the failure group, 44% of the women were on medical assistance, while in the non-failure group 20% were receiving medical assistance ($X^2=4.23$ p<.05). This result will be discussed fully later.

To better understand the situation of the black female patient, the next series of factors to be investigated involved the other side of the therapeutic dyad, the therapist. The first factor to be investigated in the failure cases was the race of the therapist. Only two black women were seen by black therapists. One of these women was seen by a black female social worker; her case was not a failure. The other black woman was seen by a black male graduate student; she was a failure. Since the numbers of black females seen by black therapists were too small to permit analysis, the next step was to look at the results obtained by white therapists. It seemed possible that among the white therapists, some would be more successful than others in getting a therapeutic relationship started with a black female patient.

None of the three therapist variables was significantly different for the failure and non-failure groups: neither Sex ($X^2 = .04$ N.S.), Profession ($X^2 = 1.20$ N.S.), nor Therapists' Experience ($X^2 = .76$ N.S.). The failure patients were equally distributed among different therapists.

## SUMMARY AND DISCUSSION

The preceding investigation attempted to find out if the observation that blacks are negatively affected by whites would also obtain in a mental health clinic setting. The investigation proceeded by looking at a series of easily observable variables in a large number of patients. There were several findings:

1. Decisions about diagnosis were apparently not made on the basis of the race of the patient. However, the sex of the patient affected the likelihood of his entering treatment.

2. Black females were assigned to crisis intervention therapy at a significantly higher rate than were any of the other three groups.

3. When the attendance records of the patients' first ten sessions were compared it was found that black females were attending at significantly lower rates than were white patients of either sex or black males.

4. It seemed likely that one reason that black women attended therapy at a lower frequency than white women was that they were more likely to have difficulty keeping appointments because of employment commitments.

5. Within the black female group, only the fact of being on medical assistance helped to distinguish between a failure and a non-failure group.

6. No therapist variables distinguished between the failure and non-failure group of black females.

It was clear that mental health professionals who were doing evaluations were partially basing their decision about whether or not someone needed therapy on the sex of the patient. As a consequence of this practice a number of black males were discharged and never entered the treatment program. It is therefore impossible to determine if the black female's lower attendance rates would also have obtained for black males had not 47% of the black males (10 out of 27) been discharged or decided not to accept an appointment for therapy. In other words, it is possible that therapy with a white therapist would have had a deleterious impact on black males if a proportion equal to that of the black females had entered therapy. However those black males who did enter treatment did attend therapy at a rate comparable to the white patient group.

In any case, it was clear that the black females as a group were attending therapy at a significantly lower rate than any of the other three groups. While this result is not in agreement with Adler et al,[1] who found no racial differences for therapy attendance, Adler does not give numbers so it is difficult to know how to interpret his results.

The two patient factors that did seem to be related to lower attendance rate (the black woman's greater likelihood than the white of being employed, and of being employed in a job paying hourly wages; and the black woman on medical assistance being much less likely to attend therapy than the black woman who was not) made possible some administrative interventions.

The fact that being employed at an hourly job made it difficult for a woman to attend therapy was fairly easily remedied. The adult out-patient clinic added evening hours. In the near future results will be available that will show whether or not black women are attending with greater frequency at this evening clinic.

The second significant variable, however, is more difficult to interpret. It is possible to interpret the medical assistance finding to mean that black women on medical assistance attend at a lower rate because they are poor. Being poor might mean that it would be difficult for them to find transportation to the clinic. However funds are available to pay for carfare, and medical assistance pays for the psychiatric treatment. Money alone does not seem to be the issue.

To find out if being poor was the crucial variable (rather than being poor and a woman and black), the attendance rates of the white women who were on medical assistance were compared with those who were not on medical assistance. For white women there was no relationship between being on medical assistance and attendance ($X^2 = .36$ N.S.).

The finding of no relationship between being poor and having poor attendance rates is generally supported by the study of Meyer et al [14] but not supported by the work of Hollingshead and Redlich,[8] Imber et al,[9] Gibby et al,[6] Rubenstein and Lorr,[15] or Cole.[4] Since none of these studies reported their data in the same manner as the present study, it is difficult to know if different trends might be canceling one another out. For example, in the present study, black males were attending at the same rate as the white population. If the proportion of black males and females had been reversed no significant relationship between race and attendance would have appeared. Or if all lower-class patients had been compared with all upper-class patients the poorer attendance rates of the black females would have been masked by the lack of relationships between social class and attendance in the other groups.

Further, the above studies usually use drop-out rates rather than attendance as the measure for comparison. Whether or not a patient "drops out" is open to a number of interpretations. How many appointments must a patient miss before he is considered a drop-out? What constitutes "dropping out" as opposed to being discharged? Attendance rates were used to measure failure in the present study because a person is either present or absent.

In summary, it is difficult to compare previous studies of the therapy behavior of black patients because these studies have either used different measures of therapeutic failure or the data have been reported in such a way as to make direct comparison impossible.

Another way to look at the medical assistance variable is from a phenomenological stance: What is it like to be a black woman who is on medical assistance? Grier and Cobbs [7] have noted that a black woman —any black woman, they feel—is likely to have a negative self-image. (They use the term narcissism). If this is true, if a black woman already feels somewhat worthless, how is she likely to respond to being on medical assistance? A woman who is poor is caught in an intricate web of circumstances that tend to give her a negative view of herself. If she is a mother she will find it difficult to take good care of her children. If she works, she probably works at a job that pays her low wages and gives her little sense of satisfaction. If Grier and Cobbs are right, if even a non-poor black woman has doubts about her self-worth, it seems reasonable that a poor black woman would be constantly faced with circumstances and feelings that would push her toward feelings of hopelessness and despair.

From the therapists' side, it would be understandable unconsciously to reject a black woman who was poor. If the therapist did not reject her on the basis of racial prejudice, he might well reject her to protect himself from the despair and anger of the patient. There is some limited data to suggest that the therapist might have been involved in an unconscious rejection of the black woman who is poor—a rejection that would not only protect the therapist from being engulfed by the black woman's despair and her anger at white authority but also protect him from experiencing failure. The problems of a black psychiatric patient who is poor are often so great that unless the therapist can set limited goals for himself and his patient, he is likely to fail. One way to avoid failure is unconsciously to encourage the patient to disappear.

The evidence that suggests that the therapist might be involved in a subtle rejection of the patient comes from a limited study of several patient-therapist pairs. When it became obvious that there were no clear patterns of therapists' variables that seemed to contribute to failure, I decided to look at the four therapists on our staff who had both a failure and non-failure black female case. The four therapists were all white: an experienced female mental health counselor, an inexperienced female mental health trainee, a female psychiatric nurse and an experienced male psychologist. The only common factor that turned up was that in the failure cases the racial difference between the therapist and patient had not been discussed. In the non-failure cases race had been discussed in the first few sessions. While this result can only be taken as suggestive it does receive support from the work of Richard Waite [18] and Maynard Calneck,[3] who feel strongly that race must be dealt with when the patient is black.

The current study has not demonstrated that white therapists can work successfully with black patients. The present study does suggest, however, that some of the factors involved in failure of therapy with black female patients can be identified and perhaps alleviated.

It remains for future studies to demonstrate whether or not black patients can be successfully treated by *white* therapists.

## REFERENCES

1.  Adler, L., Goin, M. and Yamamato, J. 1963. Failed psychiatric clinic appointment: Relationship to social class. Calif. Med. 99:388–392.

2.  Baratz, S. 1967. Effect of race of experimenter, instructions and comparison population upon level of reported anxiety in Negro subjects. J. Pers. Soc. Psychol. 7:194–196.

3.  Calnek, M. 1970. Racial factors in the counter-transference: The black therapist and the black client. Amer. J. Orthopsychiat. 40(1):39–46.

4.  Cole, N., Branch, C. and Allison, R. 1962. Some relationships between social class and the practice of dynamic psychotherapy. Amer. J. Psychiat. 118:1004ff.

5.  Frazier, E. 1957. Black Bourgeoisie. Free Press, New York.

6.  Gibby, et al. 1954. Validation of Rorschach criteria for predicting duration of therapy. J. Cons. Psychol. 18(3):185–191.

7.  Grier, W., and Cobbs, P. 1968. Black Rage. Basic Books. New York.

8.  Hollingshead, A., and Redlich, F. 1958. Social Class and Mental Illness. John Wiley, New York.

9.  Imber, S. et al. 1956. Suggestibility, social class and the acceptance of psychotherapy. J. Clin. Psychol. 12:341–344.

10.  Katz, I. and Greenbaum, C. 1963. Effects of anxiety, threat and racial environ-

ment on task performance of Negro college students. J. Abnorm. Soc. Psychol. 63: 562–567.

11. Katz, I. et al. 1965. Effects of task difficulty, race of administrator and instructions on digit symbol performance of Negroes, J. Pers. Soc. Psychol. 5:53–59.

12. Katz, I. et al. 1968. Effects of race of tester, approval-disapproval and need in Negro children's learning. J. Pers. Soc. Psychol. 8:38–42.

13. Lindsey, I. 1947. Race as a factor in the counselor's role. Social Casework 38: 101–107.

14. Meyer, E. et al. 1967. Contractually time-limited psychotherapy in an outpatient psychosomatic clinic. Amer. J. Psychiat. 124:57–67 (Oct. Supp.).

15. Rubenstein, E. and Lorr, M. 1956. A comparison of terminations and remainers in outpatient psychotherapy. J. Clin. Psychol. 12:345–349.

16. Silberman, C. 1964. Crisis in Black and White. Random House. New York.

17. Thomas, C. 1970. Different strokes for different folks. Interviewed in Psychol. Today. Sept.:49–58.

18. Waite, S. The Negro patient and clinical theory. J. Couns. Clin. Psychol. 32(4): 427–433.

# 30

## Attitudes and Emotions of the Psychiatrist in the Initial Interview

### PAUL L. LOWINGER AND
### SHIRLEY DOBIE

A THERAPEUTIC RELATIONSHIP between the patient and the doctor is fundamental to all medical treatment as well as to psychotherapy. All psychotherapists accept this view even though their theoretical frameworks may differ widely. The historical development of psychotherapy leads us to consider the contributions of psychoanalysis to an understanding of the role of the doctor-patient relationship. The discovery and description of transference by Freud in 1905 was crucial for the evolution of psychotherapy from the early hypnotic technique of Breuer into classic psychoanalysis. All psychotherapies are dependent on the utilization of the patient-therapist relationship for the therapeutic goal.

Psychotherapy always involves the patient with symptoms and a dis-

Reprinted, with permission, from *American Journal of Psychotherapy*, 20 (January 1966), pp. 17–32. PAUL L. LOWINGER was at the time of writing associate professor of psychiatry and SHIRLEY DOBIE was assistant professor of psychology, the Lafayette Clinic and the Department of Psychiatry of Wayne State University School of Medicine, Detroit, Michigan. The paper was originally presented at the Annual National Meeting of the Association for the Advancement of Psychotherapy, St. Louis, Missouri, May 5, 1963.

turbed pattern of behavior, a therapist with a healing or helping role, and a medical-therapeutic situation which defines their roles according to current theory and practice. The most frequent object of study has been the patient. The technique or process of psychotherapy has received a moderate amount of study. The doctor is the variable that has received the least attention.

Research in psychotherapy and even clinical reports of treatment with only a few exceptions omit detailed attention to the doctor. An explanation for this omission must be sought in the realm of the irrational; that is, through psychodynamics, and receives this type of attention from Tower,[1] Searles,[2] and Alexander.[3]

The psychotherapeutic process may also be conceptualized on a conscious-unconscious continuum. Some aspects of each previously mentioned variable, the patient's illness, the doctor's role, and the therapy situation are conscious, while other aspects are completely or partially unconscious. This view of various levels of consciousness in the doctor's function is similar to that of Berman [4] who refers to the difference between the "attitudes" of the analyst which are largely conscious and the countertransference which is an unconscious phenomena.

Countertransference is a crucial factor in the understanding of the doctor-patient interaction. Nonetheless, it is the subject of "widespread disagreement" according to Orr [5] who made a comprehensive review of this topic in 1954. The term originates in the concept of transference which Freud [6] first described in 1905 as, "new editions or facsimiles of the *tendencies* and fantasies which are aroused and made conscious during the process of the analysis . . . which . . . replace some earlier person by the person of the physician. . . ." Countertransference received relatively little attention in Freud's works except for an admonition that neurotic problems in the analyst had to be resolved before he could carry out psychoanalytic treatment. Psychoanalysts differ widely in current opinions on the territory covered by countertransference, varying from the relatively broad view of Balint [7] and Alexander [8] to the more restricted definition offered by Annie Reich.[9]

The significance of the doctor's emotions during the first psychotherapeutic interview is generally acknowledged [10–14] and is discussed by Leon Saul [15] who states that in the initial interview ". . . the analyst may sense within himself feelings which he regards to be inappropriately strong, and this reaction is a clue to the motivation in the patient that evoked them."

There have been a number of papers [16–18] which have encouraged research into the doctor variable in the therapeutic relationship. A need for the measurement of transference and countertransference was stated by Glover [19] in 1952, while the research value of clinical reports of therapy had been criticized by Alexander.[20] Psychologists have contributed some noteworthy objective studies of the personality and behavior of the therapist in psychotherapy through the work of Fiedler,[21-24] Strupp,[25] and Bandura.[26, 27]

In 1959, the Lafayette Clinic began to examine the doctor-patient interaction in order to better understand its relationship to psychiatric diagnosis, recommendations, and the treatment process with the eventual goal of specifying its role in psychotherapy. The initial interview was selected because it allows a clarity and precision of research methodology and also because it is the point of crucial psychiatric decisions and the beginning of psychiatric treatment. The theoretical framework of this study avoids the varying conflictual definitions of countertransference and its proper area, as well as the controversies about its origin and usefulness in therapy. *We are examining the therapist variable in the patient-therapist relationship at the time of the initial interview.*

## METHOD

A questionnaire (reproduced as an appendix to the study in *American Journal of Psychotherapy*) with 39 items and utilizing a Likert-type scale was developed. The questions asked for an evaluation of various characteristics of the patient, such as ego strength, appearance, motivation, and extent of impulsivity. The personal reactions of the therapist were elicited by questions on how uncomfortable, tense, or anxious he felt during the interview. In addition, there were questions dealing with patient-therapist interaction, recommendations, and prognosis. A typical question is the second one in the questionnaire: What was the general appearance of the patient? The answer calls for a choice between (1) Unsatisfactory, (2) Poor, (3) Satisfactory, (4) Good, and (5) Excellent.

The questionnaire was completed immediately following an initial psychiatric interview with a new patient by 16 resident psychiatrists. Each resident completed the questionnaire on 19 consecutively and randomly assigned patients. The eight residents assigned to the inpatient service completed these questionnaires following the first interview with a newly assigned inpatient while the eight residents on the outpatient service completed their questionnaire after the first diagnostic interview with a new outpatient.

The plan and goal of the research as illustrated in Figure 1 gave rise to a number of questions. Can the psychiatrist's attitudes be meaningfully defined and reported by questionnaire? Do these attitudes form categories that go beyond "positive" and "negative"? Do physicians' attitudes differ according to patient characteristics such as age, sex, race,

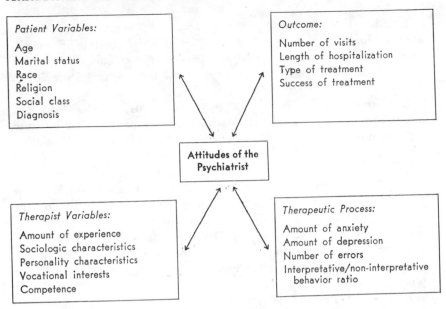

**Patient Variables:**

Age
Marital status
Race
Religion
Social class
Diagnosis

**Outcome:**

Number of visits
Length of hospitalization
Type of treatment
Success of treatment

**Attitudes of the Psychiatrist**

**Therapist Variables:**

Amount of experience
Sociologic characteristics
Personality characteristics
Vocational interests
Competence

**Therapeutic Process:**

Amount of anxiety
Amount of depression
Number of errors
Interpretative/non-interpretative
  behavior ratio

**FIGURE 1    Research Design for Study of the Attitudes of the Psychiatrist**

and diagnosis? What is the effect of these patient characteristics on the decision to treat the patient and the quality and quantity of treatment? What is the effect of the therapist attitudes on the decision to treat the patient and the amount and kind of treatment offered? The aspects of the research plan shown in Figure 1 which are not discussed in this paper are reported elsewhere by Lowinger and Dobie.[28]

## RESULTS

A factor analysis was performed by an IBM 650 computer to reduce the 39-item questionnaire on 300 patients for 16 doctors to useful dimensions. Factor analysis is a mathematical technique which permits us to discover which of the 39 items cluster together. Eight factors emerged:

1. *Communication-Ego Strength.* This factor contains high loadings for five questions,[3, 10, 13, 23, 27] dealing with the effectiveness of communication, reality testing, ego strength, and acceptability for psychotherapy.
2. *Therapist Discomfort.* This is clearly defined by three questions,[17, 25, 32] dealing with the therapist's reactions during the interview.

3. *Patient Dependency and Acceptance of Therapist.* This is defined by four questions,[4, 19, 29, 38] dealing with the amount of compliance and dependency shown by the patient, the extent to which the patient appeared to like the therapist, and the degree to which the interview ended satisfactorily.

4. *Patient Aggression and Acting Out.* This is defined by five questions [8, 18, 22, 24, 31] which deal with the amount of acting out and aggression expected during treatment and the amount of hostility and impulsiveness evident in the initial interview.

5. *Physical Attractiveness.* This is clearly defined by three questions,[2, 11, 26] on how attractive and how masculine or feminine the patient appears and a question on the general appearance of the patient.

6. *Acceptability for Treatment.* Four questions,[12, 27, 36, 37] have high factor loadings: They deal with acceptability and desirability of the patient for psychotherapy; the psychiatric treatment of choice; and prognosis without treatment.

7. *Patient-Therapist Similarity.* This is identified as a factor of patient-therapist similarity by the high factor loadings on four questions,[6, 14, 20, 30] dealing with the degree of similarity between the patient and therapist in socioeconomic status, childhood and adolescent experiences, personality, and present problems.

8. *Therapist's Like for Patient.* The therapist's feelings of liking or disliking the patient and the degree of change in these feelings during the interview appear on three questions,[7, 21, 35] which have significant factor loadings.

In order to evaluate the functional interpretation of these factors, comparisons between the diagnostic groups of the patients were made with respect to each factor. Eight factor scores for each patient were obtained. Each factor score was composed of a sum of the items with high factor loadings. No question was scored on more than one factor, although there were only two instances where questions had high loadings on more than one factor.

Factor scores for patients in five diagnostic groups were obtained. These diagnostic groups include 56 psychoneurotic patients, 20 patients with involutional or manic-depressive depressions, 94 patients with personality disorders, 78 schizophrenic patients, and 16 patients with organic brain syndromes. Figure 2 shows the results of the analysis of variance of the factor scores for the five diagnostic groups which offer support for the validity of the factor scores. Five of the eight factors significantly differentiated the diagnostic groups at the 5 per cent level as shown in Figure 3. Neurotics were high on physical attractiveness and patient-

| Factor Scores | Schizo-phrenia N–78 | Depression N–20 | Neurosis N–56 | Brain Syndrome N–16 | Character Disorder N–94 | Analysis of Variance F | Analysis of Variance Level of Significance |
|---|---|---|---|---|---|---|---|
| Communication and ego strength | 11.19 | 13.30 | 16.52 | 13.69 | 14.88 | 22.00 | .01 |
| Therapist discomfort | 6.36 | 6.65 | 6.02 | 5.12 | 5.84 | 2.12 | NS |
| Patient dependency and acceptance of therapist | 11.46 | 11.60 | 12.32 | 12.94 | 12.12 | 1.73 | NS |
| Patient aggression and acting out | 13.44 | 12.65 | 12.98 | 12.00 | 14.54 | 2.53 | .05 |
| Physical attractiveness | 11.29 | 10.60 | 12.62 | 11.12 | 11.87 | 5.03 | .01 |
| Acceptability for treatment | 12.69 | 14.25 | 14.05 | 11.87 | 12.23 | 4.96 | .01 |
| Patient-therapist similarity | 5.77 | 6.90 | 7.77 | 5.44 | 6.13 | 7.31 | .01 |
| Therapist liking for patient | 9.91 | 10.15 | 10.66 | 11.31 | 10.12 | 2.00 | NS |

FIGURE 2  Analysis of Variance of Factor Scores for Five Diagnostic Groups

| | Schizo-phrenia | Depres-sion | Neurosis | Brain Syn-drome | Char-acter Disorder |
|---|---|---|---|---|---|
| Communication and ego strength | — | 0 | + | 0 | + |
| Therapist discomfort | 0 | 0 | 0 | 0 | 0 |
| Patient dependency and acceptance of therapist | 0 | 0 | 0 | 0 | 0 |
| Patient aggression and acting out | 0 | 0 | — | — | + |
| Physical attractiveness | 0 | — | + | — | 0 |
| Acceptability for treatment | — | + | + | — | 0 |
| Patient-therapist similarity | — | 0 | + | — | 0 |
| Therapist liking for patient | 0 | 0 | 0 | 0 | 0 |

FIGURE 3   Summary of the Analysis of Variance of Factor Scores for Five
Diagnostic Groups which Shows Relationships Significant
at the Five Percent Level

therapist similarity, as well as on acceptability for treatment. They were
also high on the factor which dealt with communication and ego strength.
They were low on the aggressiveness factor. Depressives were low on
physical attractiveness; but, like neurotics, were high on acceptability
for treatment. Patients with character disorders were high on the communication-ego strength factor, patient-therapist similarity, and acceptability for treatment. Those with organic brain syndromes were low on
aggressiveness, acceptability for treatment, and patient-therapist similarity.

One of the issues raised by these results is whether the attitude scores
reflect factors in the patient or in the therapist, or some combination
of the two sets of behavior and personalities. While a group of 16
psychiatrists has many common responses to a large group of patients
with the same diagnosis, it is of interest to compare two different

| WHITE | NON-WHITE |
|-------|-----------|
| Less Physically Attractive<br>Less Dependent | More Physically Attractive<br>More Dependent |

FIGURE 4  Summary of the Analysis of Variance of Factor Scores for White and Non-White Patients Significant at the Five Per Cent Level

therapists' responses to the same patient. The possibility of doing this was present because 14 patients were admitted to the hospital a few days after their outpatient examination and initial interview questionnaire was completed. After their admission to the hospital, an examination was conducted by an inpatient psychiatrist who completed another initial interview questionnaire.

A correlation comparing the two initial interview questionnaires failed to reveal any significant relationship between these evaluations of the same patient. The highest correlations were physical attractiveness (.39) and communication-ego strength (.33); however, they were both insignificant.

The attitude scores showed no significant relationships to age, sex, and marital status of the patients. There were significant relationships to race, religion, social class, referral source, and the extent of treatment.

A significant difference in therapist attitudes between white and Negro patients was obtained. As seen in Figure 4, the white patient was given a lower score for dependency and acceptance of the therapist, while the Negro patient received a higher score on this factor. The Negro received a higher score on physical attractiveness than the white patient. With regard to diagnosis, the 276 white patients were essentially identical to the 35 Negro patients.

Social class measured by the Hollingshead [29] occupational and educational criteria correlates positively with the communication-ego strength factor, and the patient-therapist similarity factor as seen in Figure 5; that is, the higher the class, the higher these two factors.

| HIGHER SOCIAL CLASS | LOWER SOCIAL CLASS |
|---------------------|--------------------|
| More Communication<br>More Patient-Therapist Similarity | Less Communication<br>Less Patient-Therapist Similarity |

FIGURE 5  Summary of the Analysis of Variance of Factor Scores for the Hollingshead Social Class Criteria

An attitude factor that was related to the religion of the patients showed significance at the 5 per cent level. There was positive correlation between the physical appearance factor and Catholic patients and a negative correlation between this factor and Jewish patients. Protestant patients were in between.

It will be of interest to relate the religion, race, sex, age, and other characteristics of the resident physicians themselves to the attitude factors. The social class of the parents of the resident doctor will be used as a variable. It may be that the religion, race, or social class background of the resident physician influences the attitudes toward patients on these same variables. In other words, it may be that a resident physician whose parents were in a lower social class will not show a positive correlation between social class and the two significant factors: communication-ego strength and patient-therapist similarity.

The source which referred the patient to the clinic correlated positively with two attitude factors: Therapist discomfort and acceptability for therapy. Patients referred by themselves or their relatives caused most therapist discomfort; while patients referred by a religious or legal source caused least therapist discomfort. It was the patient referred by a religious source or a private psychiatrist who was highest on the factor associated with acceptability for treatment. Lowest on the factor of acceptability for treatment were the patients referred by a legal source.

The ultimate test for validity of therapist attitude factors must rest in the effect on therapy. Many variables enter into the decision to treat or not treat the patient, as well as the effectiveness of treatment. According to psychiatric research,[30-41] aspects of the doctor-patient interaction are responsible for the number of psychotherapeutic appointments, the duration of hospital stay, the choice of treatment, as well as variations in diagnosis.

In order to learn something about the effects of psychiatrists' attitudes on patient fate or outcome, the intensity of treatment of 278 patients was studied. The number of visits of 117 outpatients who did not receive hospital care were related to the attitude scores. These patients were divided into those who visited the clinic only once for a diagnostic visit; two, three and four appointments; five to 19 visits; 20 to 29 visits; and those who made over 30 visits. In this group of patients, the analysis of variance showed the attitude factors mentioned in Figure 6 of physical attractiveness, acceptability for treatment, and patient-therapist similarity to be correlated positively with the greatest number of clinic visits. These same factors, as well as the one for communication-ego strength, were significantly correlated (.05, .001, .05, .01, respectively) with the doctor's recommendation of out-patient psychotherapy. The

| MORE OUTPATIENT VISITS | LESS OUTPATIENT VISITS |
|---|---|
| High Physical Attractiveness | Low Physical Attractiveness |
| High Acceptability for Treatment | Low Patient-Therapist Similarity |
| High Patient-Therapist Similarity | Low Acceptability for Treatment |

**FIGURE 6** Summary of the Analysis of Variance of Factor Scores for the Number of Outpatient Visits

recommendation for no psychiatric treatment and for treatment elsewhere were negatively correlated with these same factors.

A separate group of 59 patients who were evaluated on the attitude scores at their initial interview had only hospital care. These patients were divided according to the length of hospitalization: less than two weeks, two weeks to three months, and over three months. The duration of hospitalization was not related to the attitude factors. Age and marital status were related to the duration of hospital stay as seen in Figure 7. Those hospitalized for two weeks to three months were significantly older than those hospitalized for over three months, while patients who had never married were more likely to be hospitalized longer than three months when compared to those hospitalized from two weeks to three months. It appears that acceptance for outpatient care is clearly related to subjective attitudes in the doctor, while duration of hospital care is determined *in part* by more definite social characteristics of the patient—as interpreted by the doctor.

The analysis of the data for 101 patients who had both inpatient and outpatient care is not complete, but shows relationships to attitude factors as well as to age and marital status.

We have already reported that social class played a role in determining attitudes by correlating positively with the communication-ego strength factor and the patient-therapist similarity factor; however, social class variables in our patient group had no effect on the number of outpatient appointments or the duration of inpatient care.

| LONGER HOSPITAL STAY | SHORTER HOSPITAL STAY |
|---|---|
| Unmarried | Married |
| Younger Age | Older Age |

**FIGURE 7** Summary of the Analysis of Variance of Factor Scores for the Length of Hospital Stay

This is contrary to the studies of Myers and Schaffer at Yale,[42] Frank at Hopkins,[32] and Lief at Tulane [43] on the experiences of residents in psychiatry with outpatients. There is a considerable range in the social class of the patients coming to the outpatient service at the Lafayette Clinic, as in these other departments of psychiatry. It is possible that the social class backgrounds of our residents may differ from these three departments. A larger number of outpatient appointments and the greater duration of inpatient stay are often understood as indicative of more psychotherapy; however, this is being reviewed in our records. Another psychosocial variable that may play a role is that Lafayette Clinic is a program in which the patients seen by the senior staff in psychiatry are the same in social class as those seen by the residents, which differs from most departments of psychiatry. The New Haven, Baltimore, and New Orleans programs are, to some extent, supported with fees paid by patients treated by staff and residents; this is not true in our department. Thus, a department which is not dependent on the higher socioeconomic groups out of realistic economic needs or status concerns, or both, may not be biased in the utilization of treatment.

## DISCUSSION

These findings lead us to attempt to answer the several questions that were posed when the goals of the research were defined.

The psychiatrist's attitudes toward patients can be defined by the use of a questionnaire. This approach is not a comprehensive picture of all aspects and levels of the therapeutic relationship; nonetheless, it provides a technique to measure the reactions of the doctor in their natural setting. The interpretation of the attitude questionnaire in the light of other information about the patients and doctors make this a study of emotions in the initial interview rather than in a laboratory situation. On the other hand, a formulation of the psychiatrist's attitudes about the patient using a questionnaire is not an attempt to introduce a new therapeutic tool or a substitute for the free associations of the psychiatrist so useful to his understanding of the patient-therapist transaction.

This approach to an understanding of psychotherapy is part of a trend toward operational and controlled studies which allow a dissection of the therapeutic process into its categories with an evaluation of the components. It is akin to the recent research by clinicians who are applying statistics, electronic computers, sound movies, observation, rating scales, and physiologic recording to psychoanalysis and psychotherapy.

Research on the attitudes and characteristics of the therapist is related to the theory of psychoanalytically oriented psychotherapy. This receives emphasis in the recent report of Alexander on his studies in Los Angeles, according to which "the detailed observation of the therapeutic process reveals a highly complex emotional and cognitive interaction between therapist and patient, which cannot be accounted for exhaustively by the current conceptualizations: transference and countertransference . . . much of the therapist values . . . are transmitted to the patient. In other words, the incognito of the psychoanalysis is a fiction. The emotional interpersonal experiences, which the patient undergoes during his treatment, have a great influence in bringing about changes in his emotional patterns." [20] The distinction between the reality of the therapist's personality and behavior in the interview situation, his empathic responses, and finally his countertransference should be emphasized. Our study makes its primary contribution in the first two of these areas which are closer to consciousness and thus more readily exposed to objective examination.

What can be said of "negative" and "positive" attitudes toward the patient? It should be pointed out that eight empirically derived attitude factors play roles in varying combinations, thus expanding our ability to define therapist reactions toward patients. These factors are meaningfully related to diagnosis in a descending hierarchy: neurosis, psychotic depression, character disorder, schizophrenia, and organic brain syndrome. However, the attitudes of the doctor show significant variation as a function of his personality, a variation which is independent of diagnosis. Attitude factors in combination with patient variables such as age and marital status play a significant role in the duration of treatment. The role of the doctor is a great deal more complex than is implied in studies which speak of "the touch" or "liking your patient" [35] or of "the interest of the therapist" [44] as a key to successful treatment.

The role of patient characteristics in determining acceptance for treatment is of considerable interest as long as the demand for psychotherapy exceeds the supply of therapists. The patient who has the highest acceptability for treatment (Factor 6) is more likely to have a neurosis or a depressive psychosis. The patient who has a high acceptability for treatment factor score is significantly more desirable for outpatient psychotherapy. The patient who remains in outpatient therapy longer is the one who was highly acceptable for treatment. Acceptability for treatment also appears related to the profile of the competent therapist on the supervisors' ratings and the Strong Inventory as discussed in another report on this project.[28] The data on patients remaining in outpatient psychotherapy for longer intervals suggest that in addition to the therapist's perception of acceptability for treatment (Factor 6), the perception of physical attractiveness (Factor 5) and the perception of patient-therapist similarity (Factor 7) play a significant role. The psychologic meaning of the physical attractiveness of the female patient for the male psychiatrist has been the subject of a discussion on countertransference by Lehrman.[45] It is of interest that liking for the patient (Factor 8) is unrelated to acceptability for treatment, patient-therapist similarity, or physical appearance. In another report of these studies,[28] liking for the patient (Factor 8) does relate positively to the doctor with a shorter period of experience in psychiatry and to personality characteristics of the doctor on the Strong Inventory, Edwards Personal Preference Scale, and supervisors' ratings associated with the less effective therapist. Perhaps we should change the question we ask in order to elicit the therapist's feelings about the patient from "Do you like the patient?" to "How physically attractive is the patient?" and "How similar is the patient to you?"

The role of patient characteristics such as race, sex, diagnosis, religion, and social class in attitudes of the doctor receives clarification in our study. While significant differences in attitudes and preferences for male or female patients do not appear in our data, a separate analysis of attitudes for male and female doctors is planned.

The findings on religion must be considered in the light of several viewpoints. Do religious groups differ in "attractiveness" when judged in nonpsychiatric situations? Is beauty in the eye of the beholder? Are Catholics represented by their more "attractive" members while Jews are represented by their less "attractive" adherents? Do our doctors have cultural stereotypes with respect to the perceived attractiveness of these three religious groups? Do our doctors differ with respect to judgments of attractiveness of religious groups according to their own religion?

The difference between white and Negro patients on attitude factors raises a number of possibilities. This difference is not related to social class, age, sex, or diagnosis, since the white and Negro patients closely resemble each other with respect to these characteristics.

An explanation of the aggressivity-passivity difference may lie in the fact that the white patient approaches the physician in a more aggressive or demanding fashion than the Negro patient, who is more dependent and passive.

The higher rating for physical attractiveness of the Negro patient is intriguing. It must be noted that the proportion of Negro patients who come to the Lafayette Clinic for psychiatric examinations (about

10 per cent) is less than the proportion of Negroes (about 17 per cent) in the Detroit Metropolitan area, which furnishes about 90 per cent of the Lafayette Clinic population. Studies [46] indicate that the incidence and type of emotional disturbance and mental illness does not differ with respect to race in Detroit. The Negro patients who come to the Lafayette Clinic may represent a group which is more "attractive" than an average of the Negro population. The white patients, on the other hand, are an average example of their social class. This selectivity may be determined by the fact that the average Negro with an emotional disturbance thinks in terms of his family physician or the public city general hospital, while the average white patient may more than often request Lafayette Clinic care. Another factor which may play a role is the attraction for the exotic in both the white doctor and the Negro patient which may cause these patients to receive a higher rating for physical attractiveness. Negro attractiveness as well as the racial attraction between Negro and white people are discussed by James Baldwin [47] and also by Podhoretz.[48]

A more complete analysis of the data should cast more light on these questions since two of the 16 resident physicians were Negroes and it would be of interest to see if their attitude factors show deviations with respect to Negro and white patients which were similar to the white doctors.

Attitudes of psychiatrists toward patients who are members of white, Negro, Protestant, Catholic, and Jewish groups may also be understood in terms of sociology of these groups in Detroit. A recent study of the major socio-religious groups in Detroit by Lenski [49] divided them into white Protestant, Jewish, Negro Protestant, and Catholic. His main thesis is of interest to psychiatry, "socio-religious group membership is a variable comparable in importance to class, both with respect to its potency and with respect to the range or extent of its influence." It is of interest that white Protestants and Jews had many attitudes in common, including a positive attitude toward work, a belief in intellectual autonomy, small families, and self-employment. Negro Protestants and Catholics had similar characteristics and tended to value the kin group above other relationships and obedience above intellectual autonomy. These differences in the study by Lenski remained, regardless of social class and educational levels and in fact appeared exaggerated at the middle class level. Although Lenski does not discuss medical or psychiatric care, this dichotomy in social attitudes and behavior tends to reinforce the possibility that because of group cultural influence white Protestants and Jews may more often seek private psychiatric care than Negro Protestants and Catholics. This may provide a situation in which the less "attractive" white Protestant or Jew is seen in a public clinic while the selection of Catholic and Negro Protestant patients involves some members of these groups who are more "attractive."

A preliminary conclusion is that there is some bias in the doctor whenever he confronts patients of different races and religions in the initial psychiatric interview. These stereotypes should be looked for in both the patient and doctor, especially in perceptions of dependency, aggressivity, and physical attractiveness.

The significance of findings with respect to differences in social class of patients should receive some additional comment. Social class rated by the Hollingshead criteria correlated positively with the communication-ego strength and patient-therapist similarity factors. The same factors were among those significantly correlated with the doctor's recommendation for outpatient psychotherapy. The doctor sees upper class patients as having more ability to communicate, greater ego strength, and more similarity to himself and then is more likely to recommend outpatient psychotherapy. Bias due to social class is present, but it is not expressed by more psychotherapy or longer hospitalization.

The speculations about the milieu of our clinic and the investigation of social class backgrounds of our doctors could only be a part of the answer. The ability of the social class of patients to influence attitude factors and recommendations for treatment, but not the length of stay in the hospital or the number of outpatient appointments, suggests the need to go beyond these events in determining the relationship between social class and psychiatric treatment. The kind and effectiveness of treatment in producing symptomatic improvement and personality change must be examined in relationship to social class before these relationships can be understood.

It is planned to repeat this project with a larger group of patients and doctors. Some of these same studies have been performed at a large state hospital with a different group of doctors and patients. The variables studied, including attitude scores, patient outcome, supervisors' ratings, and personality characteristics will also be related to a content study of psychotherapy.

## SUMMARY

Psychiatrists' attitudes with respect to the initial interview can be reported in a meaningful fashion. Attitude factors and scores can be derived. The psychiatrists' attitudes in the initial interview are related to patient diagnostic groups in a coherent fashion. Attitudes of the therapist in the initial interview are significantly related to patient variables including social class, race, religion, and source of referral. Social class affects psychiatrists' attitudes and recommendations for psychotherapy, but does not play a direct role in determining the extent of treatment for psychiatric patients. Psychiatrists' attitudes in the initial interview significantly determine the number of return visits for treatment of psychiatric outpatients. The doctor's feelings and response to patient variables, such as marital status and age, play a role in the duration of psychiatric hospitalization.

# REFERENCES

1. Tower, L. Counter-transference. *J. Am. Psychoanal. Ass.*, 4: 224, 1956.

2. Searles, H. Oedipal Love in the Counter-transference. *Int. J. Psycho-Anal.*, 40: 180, 1959.

3. Alexander, F. Psychoanalysis and Psychotherapy. In *Psychoanalysis and Human Values*. Masserman, J., Ed. Grune & Stratton, New York, 1960, pp. 250–259.

4. Berman, L. Counter-transferences and Attitudes of the Analyst in the Therapeutic Process. *Psychiatry*, 12: 159, 1949.

5. Orr, D. Transference and Countertransference: A Historical Survey. *J. Am. Psychoanal. Ass.*, 2: 621, 1954.

6. Freud, S. Fragments of an Analysis of a Case of Hysteria. In *Collected Papers*, vol. 3. Hogarth Press, London, 1924, p. 39.

7. Balint, A. and Balint, M. On Transference and Counter-transference. *Int. J. Psycho-Anal.*, 20: 223, 1939.

8. Alexander, F. Current Views on Psychotherapy. *Psychiatry*, 16: 113, 1953.

9. Reich, A. Further Remarks on Counter-transference. *Int. J. Psycho-Anal.*, 41: 389, 1960.

10. Gill, M., Newman, R., and Redlich, F. *The Initial Interview in Psychiatric Practice*. International Universities Press, New York, 1954, pp. 65–74.

11. Group for the Advancement of Psychiatry, *Reports in Psychotherapy: Initial Interviews*, Report No. 49, 1961.

12. Sullivan, H. *The Psychiatric Interview*. Norton, New York, 1954, pp. 113–137.

13. Menninger, K. *A Manual for Psychiatric Case Study*. Grune & Stratton, New York, 1952, pp. 3–17.

14. Stevenson, I. *Medical History-Taking*. Hoeber, New York, 1960, pp. 13–21.

15. Saul, L. The Psychoanalytic Diagnostic Interview. *Psychoanal. Quart.*, 26: 76, 1957.

16. Jackson, D. Countertransference and Psychotherapy. In *Progress in Psychotherapy*, Vol. 1. Fromm-Reichmann, F. and Moreno, J., Ed. Grune & Stratton, New York, 1956, pp. 234–238.

17. Frank, J. Problems of Controls in Psychotherapy as Exemplified by the Psychotherapy Research Project of the Phipps Psychiatric Clinic. In *Research in Psychotherapy*. Rubenstein, E. and Parloff, M., Ed. Grune & Stratton, New York, 1958, pp. 10–26.

18. Balint, M. and Tarachow, S. General Concepts and Theory of Psychoanalytic Therapy. In *The Annual Survey of Psychoanalysis*, Vol. 1. Frosch, J. Ed. International Universities Press, New York, 1950, pp. 227–240.

19. Glover, E. Research Methods in Psychoanalysis. *Int. J. Psycho-Anal.*, 33: 403, 1952.

20. Alexander, F. An Approach to Research in Psychotherapy. Paper presented at the Annual Meeting of the American Psychiatric Association, May 9, 1962, Toronto, Canada.

21. Fiedler, F. The Concept of the Ideal Therapeutic Relationship. *J. Consult. Psychol,* 14: 239, 1958.

22. ———. A Comparison of Psychoanalytic, Nondirective, and Adlerian Therapeutic Relationships. *J. Consult. Psychol.,* 14: 436, 1950.

23. ———. A Method of Objective Quantifications of Certain Countertransference Attitudes. *J. Clin. Psychol.,* 7: 101, 1951.

24. ———. Quantitative Studies on the Role of Therapists' Feelings toward Their Patients. In *Psychotherapy Theory and Research.* Mowrer, O., Ed. Ronald Press, New York, 1953, pp. 296–315.

25. Strupp, H. *Psychotherapists in Action.* Grune & Stratton, New York, 1960.

26. Bandura, A. Psychotherapist's Anxiety Level, Self-insight, and Psychotherapeutic Competence. *J. Abnorm. Soc. Psychol.,* 52: 333, 1956.

27. Bandura, A., Lipsher, D., and Miller, P. Psychotherapist's Approach-Avoidance Reactions to Patients' Expressions of Hostility. *J. Consult Psychol.,* 24: 1, 1960.

28. Lowinger, P. and Dobie, S. An Evaluation of the Role of the Psychiatrist's Personality in the Interview. In *Science and Psychoanalysis,* Vol. 7, Masserman, J., Ed. Grune & Stratton, New York, 1964.

29. Hollingshead, A. and Redlich, F. *Social Class and Mental Illness.* John Wiley & Sons, New York, 1958, pp. 66–136.

30. Frank, J., Gliedman, L., Imber, S., Nash, E., and Stone, A. Why Patients Leave Psychotherapy. *Arch. Neurol. Psychiat.* 77: 283, 1957.

31. Hollingshead, A. and Redlich, F. *Social Class and Mental Illness.* John Wiley & Sons, New York, 1958, pp. 273–274, 292–293, 296–302.

32. Rosenthal, D. and Frank J. The Fate of Psychiatric Clinic Outpatients Assigned to Psychotherapy. *J. Nerv. Ment. Dis.,* 127: 337, 1958.

33. Imber, S., Nash, E. and Stone, A. Social Class and Duration of Psychotherapy. *J. Clin. Psychol.,* 10: 281, 1955.

34. Brill, N. and Storrow, H. Social Class and Psychiatric Treatment. *Arch. Gen. Psychiat.,* 4: 340, 1960.

35. Cole, N., Branch, C., and Allison, R. Some Relationships between Social Class and Practice of Dynamic Psychotherapy. *Am. J. Psychiat.,* 118: 1004, 1962.

36. Srole, L., Langner, T., Michael, S., Opler, N., and Rennie, T. *Mental Health in the Metropolis.* McGraw-Hill, New York, 1962, pp. 240–252.

37. Kahn, R., Pollack, M., and Fink, M. Social Factors in the Selection of Therapy in a Voluntary Mental Hospital. *J. Hillside Hosp.,* 6: 216, 1957.

38. Kahn, R., Pollack, M., and Fink, M. Sociopsychologic Aspects of Psychiatric Treatment in a Voluntary Mental Hospital. *Arch. Gen. Psychiat.,* 1: 656, 1959.

39. Raines, G. and Rohrer, J. The Operational Matrix of Psychiatric Practice. I. Consistency and Variability in Interview Impressions of the Different Psychiatrists. *Am. J. Psychiat.,* 111: 721, 1955.

40. Pasamanick, B., Dinnitz, S., and Lefton, M. Psychiatric Orientation and its Relation to Diagnosis and Treatment in a Mental Hospital. *Am. J. Psychiat.,* 116: 127, 1959.

41. Wallach, M. and Strupp, H. Psychotherapists' Clinical Judgments and Attitudes toward Patients. *J. Consult. Psychol.,* 24: 316, 1960.

42. Myers, J. and Schaffer, L. Social Stratification and Psychiatric Practice: A Study of an Out-Patient Clinic. *Am. Social Rev.,* 19: 307, 1954.

43.  Lief, H., Lief., V., Warren, C., and Heath, R. Low Dropout Rate in a Psychiatric Clinic. *Arch. Gen. Psychiat.*, 5: 200, 1961.

44.  Board, F. A. Patients' and Physicians' Judgments of Outcome of Psychotherapy in an Outpatient Clinic. *Arch. Gen. Psychiat.*, 1: 185, 1959.

45.  Lehrman, N. The Analyst's Sexual Feelings. *Am. J. Psychother.*, 14: 545, 1960.

46.  Dunham, H. *Community and Schizophrenia, An Epidemiological Analysis.* Wayne State University Press, Detroit, 1965, pp. 226–227.

47.  Baldwin, J. *The Fire Next Time.* Dial Press, New York, 1963, pp. 67, 91, 110, 119.

48.  Podhoretz, N. My Negro Problem—And Ours. *Commentary*, 35: 93, 1963.

49.  Lenski, G. *The Religious Factor.* Doubleday & Co., Garden City, N.Y., 1961.

3M—P&K—12/73
2M—P&K— 1/75